Promoting Change Through Paradoxical Therapy

Revised Edition

Promoting Change Through Paradoxical Therapy

Revised Edition

Edited by
Gerald R. Weeks, PH. D.

BRUNNER/MAZEL, *Publishers* • NEW YORK

Library of Congress Cataloging-in-Publication Data
Promoting change through paradoxical therapy / edited by Gerald R.
Weeks.—Rev. ed.
   p. cm.
   Includes bibliographical references and index.
   ISBN 0-87630-645-8
   1. Paradoxical psychotherapy. I. Weeks, Gerald R.,
   [DNLM: 1. Psychological Theory. 2. Psychotherapy—methods. WM
420 P9655]
RC489.P37P76   1991
616.89'14—dc20
DLC
for Library of Congress   91-10961
                                                CIP

Published by
BRUNNER/MAZEL, INC.
19 Union Square West
New York, New York 10003

Manufactured in the United States of America

10 9 8 7 6 5 4 3 2 1

Contents

Contributors

L. Michael Ascher, Ph.D.   Professor and Director of the Behavior Therapy Unit, Department of Psychiatry, Temple University Medical School, Philadelphia, Pennsylvania.

Michael J. Bopp, Ph.D.   Private practitioner in Philadelphia, Pennsylvania.

Brian W. Cade, C.S.W.   Family Therapist and Course Organizer at the Family Institute, Cardiff, Wales.

Steve de Shazer   Associate Professor at the School of Social Welfare, University of Wisconsin-Milwaukee, and Director of the Brief Family Therapy Center. Steve de Shazer is the author of *Patterns of Brief Family Therapy* (Guilford Press, 1982).

Klaus G. Deissler, Diplompsychologe.   Co-founder and Director of the Institut für Familientherapie Marburg. Dr. Deissler was founding member of the German Association of Family Therapy, editor of *Kontext*, and an editorial board member of *Familiendynamik*.

Joseph B. Eron, Psy.D.   Director of the Catskill Family Institute in Kingston, New York, and a family therapist in private practice. He received his doctorate in psychology at the University of Illinois at Champaign-Urbana. Dr. Eron is a clinical faculty member at Albany Medical College, Mt. Sinai Medical Center, and Beth Israel Medical Center.

Viktor E. Frankl, M.D., Ph.D.   Professor of neurology and psychiatry at the University of Vienna Medical School and distinguished professor of logotherapy at the United States International University (San Diego). Dr. Frankl is the author of 26 books that have been translated into numerous languages, including Japanese and Chinese.

Ray S. Kim, M.A.,   Ph.D. candidate, Department of Psychology, Division of Clinical Psychiatry, Temple University, Philadelphia, Pennsylvania.

Luciano L'Abate, Ph.D.   Former Professor and Director of the Family

Psychology Program at Georgia State University. Dr. L'Abate has authored numerous books and articles, including *Paradoxical Psychotherapy* with Gerald Weeks.

Carol H. Lankton, M.A.   Private practitioner in Florida. She conducts workshops on Ericksonian Therapy throughout the world. She is the co-author of several books and articles that describe the use of Ericksonian psychotherapy with families, children, and adults.

Stephen R. Lankton, M.S.W.   Private practitioner in Florida. He conducts workshops on Ericksonian therapy throughout the world. He is founding editor of *The Ericksonian Monographs* and author or co-author of several books and articles that describe the use of Ericksonian psychotherapy with families, children, and adults.

Elam Nunnally   Staff member at the Brief Family Therapy Center in Milwaukee, Wisconsin.

James Poling, M.A.,   Ph.D. candidate, Department of Psychology, Division of Clinical Psychology, Temple University, Philadelphia, Pennsylvania.

Michael Rohrbaugh, Ph.D.   Associate professor of psychology, College of William and Mary, and Director of Family Therapy Training for the Virginia Consortium for Professional Psychology.

Howard Tennen, Ph.D.   Associate Professor of Psychiatry at the University of Connecticut School of Medicine, where he is director of psychology training. He received his graduate training at the University of Massachusetts. His research interests include responses to uncontrollable stress, coping with serious illness, and the role of paradox in strategic therapy.

Christine Watson, Ph.D.   Private practitioner in Houston, Texas.

Gerald R. Weeks, Ph.D.   Director of Training, Marriage Council of Philadelphia; and Clinical Associate Professor of Psychology and Psychiatry, University of Pennsylvania School of Medicine.

Preface

A few years ago paradox in psychotherapy was used by only a few practitioners. Many perceived it as strange, noncommonsensical, and too directive. Yet it was powerfully attractive because of its sometimes rapid and dramatic effects. When paradox is used adeptly, the results have been so startling that early practitioners—and some of the more recent ones—have been called "therapeutic magicians."

Following the publication of the book *Paradoxical Psychotherapy: Theory and Practice with Individuals, Couples, and Families* (Weeks & L'Abate, 1982, Brunner/Mazel, New York), a keen interest in this approach developed. In *Paradoxical Psychotherapy* we attempted to demystify the approach by explicating the different methods of working paradoxically. Shortly after the book's publication, several others appeared, which focused directly or indirectly on this approach.

The psychotherapeutic field was and is rich with excitement, controversy, and new ideas about the application of paradoxical methods. Many of those writing about this approach did so in the context of other therapies such as logotherapy and behavior therapy.

The purpose of this volume is to bring together the writings of a number of well-known therapists who are pioneers of this approach. Although this book was originally published in 1985, and the editor acknowledges that the subsequent writings of the authors show further reprimand, elaboration, and development, the basic theories and conceptual frameworks are timeless in their capacities to teach.

The book is divided into four parts. Part One asks the question, What is paradoxical therapy? It examines the issue of what we claim to do—how we define a therapeutic paradox.

Part Two is the theoretical section of the volume. Contributors describe their own theories of paradoxical therapy, which is a unique focus considering that most of the literature in this field goes over technique. In the third section of the book Michael Ascher and his colleagues have completely revised and updated their chapter to present the latest research findings.

The last part of the text, Part Four, is designed to help synthesize and integrate the different perspectives offered in this volume. Of particular interest is the final chapter, which develops a metatheory of paradox to help to unify thinking about paradox and to tie together what appear to be divergent theories.

Since the publication of this book in 1985, articles on paradox have proliferated at an astounding rate, especially in behavior therapy. This volume is an important marker for all those interested in this approach. It contains much of the seminal theory that has lead to the use of paradoxical techniques in different systems of therapy.

Gerald R. Weeks, Ph.D.

Part One

Introduction

1

A Delphi Study of Paradox in Therapy*

by Christine Watson, Ph.D.

The purpose of this study was to provide an operational definition for the concept of therapeutic paradox. Much of what has been written about paradox in psychotherapy has been in books explaining theory and ways to use paradox and in articles giving case study examples. In these publications, paradox as a technique for strategic communication is described in many varying ways. Further, clinicians appear to differ about which persons can benefit from its therapeutic use. Part of the difficulty in talking about the concept in sharing creative solutions with each other has been the several different languages being spoken with respect to paradox. Thus, this study attempted to develop operational definitions of therapeutic paradoxes and to formulate them hierarchically.

*A few participants of this study did not wish to be identified. The author gratefully acknowledges the cooperation of all the participants, including: Philippe Caille, Gina Ables, Y. L'amontagne, David Keith, Jeffery Brandsma, Susan McDonald, Lynn Hoffman, Rachel Hare-Mustin, Seymour Radin, Joseph Lisiecki, Bradford Keeney, Clint Phillips, L. Michael Ascher, Phoebe Prosky, Paul Dell, Richard Rabin, Donald S. Williamson, Steve de Shazer, Arthur M. Bodin, Carlos E. Sluzki, Brian Ackerman, Luciano L'Abate, and Gerald R. Weeks.

Since the concept of paradox is still in the formative stages, a most suitable design was the Delphi process, a method originated by the Rand Corporation for exploring group opinion and decision formation. In using this process, participants, who are usually experts, are asked to give their opinions on an unresolvable or currently evolving topic or theory. Statements are collected and a composite is formed, without acknowledgment of individual authorship. The composite is returned to each participant for consideration. Participants are asked to rewrite their opinions based on the new knowledge contributed by other experts. This process is repeated until some consensus is reached.

The process of gathering written anonymous statements and providing controlled feedback derives from psychological principles that reduce or eliminate many distortions that may occur in open communication where high status group members, dominant personalities, majority opinion, and prior public sentiment are likely to affect the formation and expression of individual judgment and thus influence group consensus. The idea of controlled feedback is related to information theory and cybernetics and is a technological development of World War II (Weiner, 1967).

In this study, the Delphi method was used to explore three questions. Participants (panel experts) were persons who had either published on paradox in therapy or who were known to use paradox as a major therapeutic approach. The 26 panel members (who had responeded to an invitation to participate in the study) were asked to give their opinions on three questions. Their responses were collected and analyzed, and composites were formed for each of the three questions; individual authorship was kept anonymous. The composites were returned to each participant for reconsideration. Panel members were asked to reformulate their opinions based on the new knowledge they had gained as a result of contributions by other experts and their knowledge of the "whole." This process was repeated for three rounds, with a final, fourth step consisting of the completed research and a request for further comments.

The three questions asked dealt with (a) operational definitions of paradoxical intervention, (b) options for paradoxical intervention involving a hypothetical family, and (c) what criteria, if any, the therapist used when choosing paradoxical language in therapy.

This chapter contains the responses to and comments on the first question—the experts' operational definitions of paradoxical intervention.

An interesting sidelight on the Delphi is found in the meanings associated with the naming of the technique. Originally, the Delphi experiments were created to aid in predicting the future via informed consensus of a group of experts. The name *Delphi* was used for the process; it is associated with the historical Greek oracle at Delphi, a place where the divinities gave answers to those who consulted them about the future. The findings from the original Delphi experiments did not predict the future; rather, the process took an unexpected twist. The Delphi was instrumental in creating future directions by stimulating informed consensus among anonymous experts. The name *Delphi* seems apropos for the results of the original experiments, as the priestess of the oracle at Delphi was known for her ambiguous, paradoxical, multilevel utterances.

Instrumentation

The research instrument used in this study was the questionnaire, which was sent to a panel of experts considered knowledgeable about paradox in therapy.

Data Collection

The data collection followed these procedures:

1. Fifty-five persons who had published on paradox in therapy or who were known to use paradox as a meaningful therapeutic approach were sent a letter describing the study and its purpose and inviting them to participate. A stamped postcard was included which those interested in being on the panel were asked to return to the researcher. Thirty-seven persons responded to the invitation. Of these, 26 said yes to participation, 7 said no, and 4 dropped out after the first round. All 26 respondents who returned the card saying yes were sent each round of the questionnaire. Participation was not consistent over the length of the study period. Some members responded to Round One and not to Round Two; some did not respond until Round Two; some answered certain portions of the questionnaire and not others; and some wrote letters sharing their views in depth.

Panel members were given a choice in Rounds Two and Three of responding either by mail or telephone. Six experts who were contacted by phone shared their views orally, an alternative that proved viable for persons with time constraints.

2. The process of sending the first round of questionnaires, re-

ceiving the responses, and analyzing and formulating the composites from the first set of answers is referred to as Round One.

[Round One]

Each panel member was asked to provide a brief definition (no more than five or six sentences) in his/her own words of what constitutes a paradoxical intervention. Ten days after the first questionnaires were sent to the panel members, follow-up reminders were mailed.

3. Representative definitions of paradoxical intervention were formulated by the researcher based on the definitions found in the existing literature.

Definitions obtained from this round were read by the researcher and composite definitions were created based on those received from the panel members and on the representatives from the literature. The composites were formulated by conducting a conceptual analysis of the data.

[Round Two]

4. A second questionnaire, containing the composites drawn from the first round, was sent to the panel. Members were asked to respond to the new information, and to make any changes, additions, and/or deletions that might make the composites more acceptable to them.

The actual choices presented consisted of several composite definitions, derived from analysis of Round One questionnaire responses. Care was taken to ask the questions in a way that respected the individual characteristics of original answers.

Panel members' responses to Round Two were returned to the researcher and read. A second round of composites was then constructed by conducting a conceptual analysis of these responses.

[Round Three]

5. These composites were sent to the panel members in a Round Three questionnaire for final additions, changes, or deletions. After the second set of responses was received, final definitions were formulated. These were sent to the panel members who were asked to select their single favorite response to the definitional question.

[Round Four]

The entire paper was sent to panel members with requests for their comments. These responses compose Round Four.

Analysis

A stepwise format for conducting conceptual analysis of verbal qualitative data, as elucidated by Tesch (1980) in *Phenomenological and Transformative Research: What They Are and How to Do Them* was used to analyze the data. We will present a brief summary of the steps in this type of analysis to give the reader an overview of the process before we elaborate on the actual findings.

Step 1. First, each respondent's complete answers to the questionnaires were read, thereby enabling the researcher to develop a sense of the entire picture before beginning the actual analysis. The data were sorted according to the organizing themes presented in the answers. *Themes*, in this study, refer to clusters of ideas that panel experts may have held in common in their definitions of paradoxical intervention.

Step 2. Each theme was studied to determine what the panel members were saying about paradoxical intervention. Some helpful study questions suggested by Tesch include:

> Which comments seem to express the same idea or opinion about the theme? What is this idea or opinion, in your own words? Is there unity about the theme (i.e., most people say something similar), or is there controversy? What is the nature of the difference of opinions, and how many people take the one or the other stance? Is the language passionate, strong, personal, or matter-of-fact, uninvolved, general? The answers to these questions are recorded in the form of a summary of the theme substance. (Tesch, 1980, p. 32)

Step 3. The themes were compared with each other to see if any were sufficiently alike to be grouped together. For example, the answers to the question about operational definitions of paradoxical intervention produced several different themes, some of which were combined due to similarity; a few distinctly different themes evolved from the experts' responses to this question.

Step 4. The major themes culled from the initial analysis were compiled in a second round questionnaire and sent to the panel members, who were asked to read them and select the one that they thought came closest to their own definition. (Panel members were also asked to make comments, additions, or suggestions for possible deletions that would bring the definition closer to their own ideas.)

The experts analyzed the responses to the themes (presented to them as feedback), again looking for common meaning units. Here the researcher examined the panel's comments, additions, and so on, as well as their actual choices of most acceptable definition.

Step 5. Based on the initial and feedback responses, three literature definitions and six operational definitions were formulated for the concept of paradoxical intervention. These were sent to panel members for a final selection of the definition that came closest to their own views.

DEFINITION OF PARADOXICAL INTERVENTION

Round One

Step 1. The participants' answers to the first question in this study were read through twice to enable the researcher to get a sense of the responses before beginning the actual analysis. The data were sorted according to organizing themes presented in the answers.

Step 2: Summary of Theme Substance. The request for an operational definition of paradoxical intervention was: "What elements are necessary for an intervention to be categorized as a paradoxical intervention?" Eighteen responses were analyzed. (Four of these responses were received after the first analysis of Round One responses and subsequent sending of Round Two questionnaires.) Brief summaries of the answers to the definitional question are presented below to give the reader a sense of the variety of approaches taken to define paradoxical intervention. Five answers were similar in that they centered on the theme of "countering" the presenting symptom. One response was matter-of-fact in defining a paradoxical intervention as that which produces second-order change; a *therapeutic* double bind used to treat individuals trapped in a *pathogenic* double bind. One respondent stated that paradoxical intervention is defined from the client's perspective, in that the client must perceive the intervention as not addressing his/her therapeutic goals in a common-sense manner: The intervention may be illogical, opposed, or irrelevant to the goals of therapy.

Another member defined paradoxical intervention as an approach with an element of surprise which resolves a paradox by changing the epistemological frame of reference. One respondent emphasized that the specific frame of reference is the therapist's prescribing of the symptom. The paradoxical statement implicit here is: "Do what you were doing, and it will be different." (From a process perspective, doing now what you were doing, because you are now being told to do it, *is* different.) Another respondent saw paradoxical intervention as the therapist communicating on a more encompassing level of abstraction than the client, in order to change the client's frame of reference. Yet another respondent defined paradoxical intervention as the communication of two apparently contradictory messages which, when introduced into a rigid idea framework, disrupt the rigidity and allow for individuation and great creativity. One expert preferred the term *restraint from change*, seeing it as more descriptive than paradoxical intervention. And another participant defined a paradoxical intervention as a global positive connotation of the behaviors of all participants "in that context and history." Three panel members submitted no definition.

Two distinct, broad themes emerged from the definitional question in Round One, each of which contained subthemes. These themes are as follows:

Theme 1.   Paradoxical intervention is a term for what the therapist does in response to client/family behaviors (especially resistant behaviors). Specifically, s/he:

a.   Restrains the family from change.
b.   Sends two contradictory messages: One is the context of the therapeutic relationship, which implies that change is to take place; the other, given directly by the therapist, says "don't change."
c.   Exaggerates some client/family behavior, or uses surprise to shock the family out of rigid frame of reference (as in some of the Zen koans).
d.   "Counters" the family's paradoxical ways of looking at their problem with a "therapeutic" paradox.
e.   Locates the possible function of a problem behavior or any behavior and prescribes it (behavior and function) as a homeostatic maintainer (referred to as second-order change).
f.   Positively connotes behaviors of all participants in a particular context and history.

Theme 2.   Paradoxical intervention can be viewed in terms of the client's/family's perception.

a. It is paradoxical when a client/family sees the therapist's intervention as illogical, lacking in common sense, or irrelevant to the goals of therapy.

b. The intervention isn't paradoxical per se—the family's chosen perception of the behavior creates the paradox. Paradox is in the eye of the beholder.

These broad themes represent two very different perspectives on paradoxical intervention: One sees it in terms of the therapist's response to client behavior, the other in terms of the client's/family's perception of the therapist's intervention or of the behaviors presented.

Round Two

Step 4. Nine composite responses to the Round One question (operational definition of paradoxical intervention) were compiled in a Round Two questionnaire and sent to panel members. Members were asked to read the selections and choose the one or two which they thought came closest to their own definition. In addition, members were given nine different literature definitions and asked to choose the one or two they thought came closest to their own operational definition.

Summary Results from Round Two Questionnaire

Nineteen panel members responded to the Round Two questionnaire. The favored definitions are given below, in addition to the number of respondents who chose each of them. There are two parts to this definitional question: Part A contains the favored responses to the *literature definition* of paradoxical intervention. Part B includes responses to the composites formulated by the researcher, based on *Round One responses* from the panel of experts.

Part A: Literature Definitions. The literature definitions favored by most panel members stated:

> A paradoxical intervention can be defined as follows: "Within a context where the client comes to therapy in order to change, the therapist asks him to produce more of the behavior that the client wants changed, and within a context of acceptance of the involuntary nature of the client's behavior, the therapist requests that the patient produce this behavior voluntarily." (Madanes, 1981, pp. 7–8)[1]

---

[1]References to the literature definitions were not provided in the study.

The second most favored definition from the literature was 9, with *nine* respondents choosing it. This definition reads as follows:

> A paradoxical order is one which, if correctly executed, is disobeyed; if disobeyed, it is obeyed.
>
> A paradoxical intervention then, is any intervention, command, prediction, request that, if followed or accepted, will accomplish the very opposite of what it is seemingly intended to accomplish. It is dialectics as applied to psychotherapy, consisting of seemingly self-contradictory and sometimes absurd therapeutic interventions which are always constructively rationalizable, although sometimes very challenging, and which join rather than oppose symptomatic behavior, leading to increased social interest. (The notion of dialectical thinking can be summarized in the idea that things are not what they seem.) The success of the paradoxical intervention depends on the family's defying the therapist's instructions or following them to the point of absurdity and then recoiling. "If a family continually defies compliance-based interventions, it can be safely assumed there is some hidden interaction in the system that undermines their usefulness—some secret alliance, contest, or coalition that the family is reluctant to reveal or change. The target of the systemic paradox is this hidden interaction that expresses itself in a symptom." (Papp, 1980, p. 46)

The third most favored definition, with *six* panel members choosing it, was 5, which reads:

> Paradoxical intervention refers to any intervention designed to produce what Watzlawick et al. (1974) called second-order change as opposed to first-order change. (Second-order change refers to change in the system itself, e.g., the rules of the system, and is called paradoxical change.) (Weeks, 1979, p. 62)

Part B. Operational Definitions from Panel Members. The favored operational definition in Part B, chosen by *eight* panel members, was no. 3, which states:

> A paradoxical intervention is the prescribing of the symptom or presenting problem; i.e., it is to commend that the client (individual, couple, or family) do something they are already doing, without first making explicit that they are doing it; and so they should do this, as if, as it were, they were not *already* doing it. Secondly, they should do it (as if they were not already) because in the therapist's view, doing it (i.e., doing what they were doing) will bring change. The paradoxical statement implicit is: "Do what you were doing, and it will be different." Process-wise, doing now what you were doing, because you are now being told to do it, *is* different.

The second most favored operational definition, chosen by *seven* respondents, was no. 2, which reads as follows:

A paradoxical intervention is one that has an element of surprise (i.e., is contrary to context-bound expectations) and resolves a paradox by changing the epistemological frame; it is an unexpected exaggeration of a pattern of behavior that has been previously resistant to other forms of intervention.

In addition, five experts presented new ideas for the definition of paradoxical intervention. Three of these were included in the Round Three questionnaire, as they represented totally different approaches to the definition of paradoxical intervention. A fourth response was received after the Round Three questionnaire had been sent. It represents a different view and is presented here verbatim:

To me, the archetype of the paradox is most effective when it is the by-product of the striving for consciousness. And that striving leads to a confrontation with the paradox in question simultaneously with an awareness of the paradox in all life.

There is a challenge in the statement, "You can't get there from here." To contrive to precipitate an awareness of a paradox prematurely or as a technique is oppositional and destructive to the patient.

A paradox functions like a Zen koan. It thrusts you back on *deeper resources*. The famous example, "What is the sound of one hand clapping?" confronts you with the futility of the ordinary intellectual defensiveness.

Round Three

Step 5. The favored responses from Round Two plus three of the new definitions were presented to the panel of experts in the Round Three section containing operational definitions of paradoxical intervention. Panel members were again asked to choose which definition came closest to their own (choosing only *one* definition each). In addition, three definitions from the literature, which were favored in Round Two, were presented and each member was asked to choose *one* which best fit his/her own definition.

Summary of Results from Round Three Questionnaire

Sixteen responses to Round Three questionnaires were received. In the first section on the definition of paradoxical intervention *(from the literature)*, two definitions were favored.

Definition A was most favored, being chosen by six panel members. It reads as follows:

A.   A paradoxical intervention can be defined as follows: Within a context where the client comes to therapy in order to change, the therapist asks him to produce more of the behavior that the client wants changed, and within a context of acceptance of the involuntary nature of the client's behavior, the therapist requests that the patient produce this behavior voluntarily. (Madanes, 1981, pp. 7–8)

It refers to any intervention designed to produce what Watzlawick et al. (1974) called second order change as opposed to first order change. (Second order change refers to change in the system itself, e.g., the rules of the system, and is called paradoxical change.) (Weeks, 1979, p. 62)

Definition C was second favorite, being chosen by five respondents. It read as follows:

C.   Paradox is inherently an epistemological phenomenon. The "existence" of paradox requires the premises and beliefs of an observer. There are no phenomena which are paradoxical in themselves—apart from an observer. The major premise that generates "paradox" is the (false) assumption that we live in an Aristotelian universe. This premise requires that self-recursive phenomena be considered to be somehow unreal or illusory. (Self-recursiveness is cybernetic feedback wherein a statement, organism, or system alters its own behavior because its previous output feeds back to it and modifies its subsequent behavior.) Such epistemological (and ontological) disqualification of self-recursive phenomena leads to a variety of consequences, perhaps the least of which is "paradox."
  . . . There is no such thing as "a paradox." Rather, all "paradox" exists only in the mind of the beholder. Accordingly, all attempts to explain paradox either as an entity or as a therapeutic intervention are fundamentally flawed and can lead only to further conceptual confusion. (Dell, 1981, p. 127)

Responses to the *operational* definitions (Section II) were spread among three of the six choices. Definition B received the most agreement, with five respondents choosing it. This definition read:

B.   A paradoxical intervention is one that has an element of surprise (i.e., is contrary to context-bound expectations) and resolves a paradox by changing the epistemological frame; it is an unexpected exaggeration of a pattern of behavior that has been previously resistant to other forms of intervention.

The second favored response was chosen by four panel members and read as follows:

A.   A paradoxical intervention refers to a counter-intuitive instruction or request made by the therapist, bypassing the patient's demonstrated tendency to discount, criticize, forget, postpone, or mis-understand simple, straightforward directions or neutralize them by claiming *inability* to comply. Thus, if a person says he/she is helpless to *stop* a symptom, by definition he/she is *not* helpless to continue performing the symptom if that is what is prescribed. (Counter-intuitive, in this instance, means "against the direction prescribed by common sense.")

The intervention is not a "thing," is not the "change agent." The change agent is within the process which encompasses the "fit" between the patterns of the client/family and the pattern of the inter-vention.

A third favorite was one of the new responses, included in Round Three because it represented a new approach. This re-sponse received three votes of agreement from panel members.

D. There exists an interpretation or instruction to the family that restrains them from the change they have come to therapy to ask help for, or from any change at all. Since this is done within a context that implies that the family's request will be honored, a contradiction is set up. This contradiction is often called a "paradoxical interven-tion." As the intervention only *seems* paradoxical or illogical from the point of view of client expectations, the descriptive term, "restraint from change," may be used to refer to the situation mentioned.

Telling a person/family to continue with a problem, and giving a rationale that is validated by at least some of the family's percep-tions, is not "paradoxical." It is contrary to expectation. The ra-tionale may be trivial or incomplete. Using such a trivial rationale to restrain the family from change may seem absurd. But it is not paradoxical because at the system level it makes sense from many angles; it has justifications any one of which one might choose to use as a rationale for restraining the family from change. Which one, of course, is the essence of the art.

Perhaps, just as in dreams and animal communications, there is no way to say "not" to people caught in a symptomatic configura-tion. To say *don't change* within a context that implies change seems to be analogous to Bateson's description of an otter communicating "play" to another otter by pretending to fight. By biting an ear but not biting it hard, one otter signals to the other "this is play." Peo-ple get the message when it is put this way where they often don't when told to change directly.

In addition to the above three choices, there was one distinc-tively new approach to the definition question. In this approach, paradox is seen as "syntax" of a certain type. In other words, you can speak in paradox language or in ordinary English just like you can speak in prose or poetry. Quoting the panel member further, "I have yet to work out what the rules are but they deal mostly with valuing and giving directions. Instead of saying in prose, 'That is bad. Do this instead,' in paradoxical syntax you first assign levels and then say, 'It is good that that is bad.' A similar form would be used for the command."

Quoting further, "an operational definition of a syntax is a grammar. The element of surprise and noncoerciveness would be probably the same if one spoke in rhyme or in elaborate flowery gestures, etc."

This last definition emphasizes the language *form* as important in understanding paradox, especially as it compares with *straight* interventions.

Conclusions

Paul Dell (1981) mentioned in a recent article that any attempt to define paradox either as an entity or as a therapeutic intervention leads to further conceptual confusion. Giving credence to this statement, we can proceed to "make sense" of the wide variety of responses to the first question in this study—how to define paradoxical intervention. What seems even more perplexing is attempting to define an intervention in which paradox is either spontaneously or purposively used in communications with clients, or is at least recognized as being present in such communications. It is helpful to keep in mind that the term *paradoxical intervention* is very new in the literature of therapeutic communication.

The rationale for seeking a definition was that by first learning about the operational definitions of panel members, the researcher would be able to grasp more of the meanings in responses to another question: What are the criteria in deciding to "use" or not to "use" paradoxical interventions?

The final analysis of the various definitions for paradoxical intervention showed that experts used several conceptual categories in thinking about paradoxical interventions. We will discuss these categories, starting with the more general and abstract conceptualizations and proceeding to the more specific and concrete ones. As one might well imagine, the categories were not cut-and-dried. Rather, several of the conceptualizations overlapped. In addition, some panel members defined paradoxical intervention with differing emphases. The three major areas of emphasis consisted of message components, process components, and more theoretical aspects.

There were seven major approaches to defining what was

meant by a paradoxical intervention. They are listed below and a discussion of each follows (P.I. = paradoxical intervention).

1. P.I. is in the mind of the beholder.
2. P.I. is intuitive and experiential.
3. P.I. is an archetype symbolic of paradox in all of life.
4. P.I. is connected closely to concepts of circularity and the systemic nature of interventions.
5. P.I. is dependent upon client's perception of a specific intervention.
6. P.I. is a term for something specific the therapist does.
7. P.I. is specific syntax.

Paradoxical intervention, when viewed as "in the mind of the beholder," represents the most abstract way of understanding this concept. Its message can be summed up in the statement: What is paradoxical to you may not be paradoxical to me; no two "realities" are alike.

The second approach to a definition considers paradox intuitive, experiential, and a product of the therapist's personality and lifestyle; thus it cannot be explained or defined without "killing" it (just as a good joke loses its punch upon elucidation). This approach, though still somewhat general and elusive, does give one a flavor of the koan-like nature of paradoxical communication in therapy. It acknowledges that the therapist's primary "lever" for change is his/her own personality (which is a totally different view from the one in which the therapist follows a strategy or format based on specific hypotheses formulated earlier, as in the Milan team's approach). Additionally, this approach implies that the therapist is *in* the situation or paradox *with* the client; it is clearly not therapist as guru conceptualization.

The third approach is somewhat similar to the second, although several distinctions are noted. This approach acknowledges (a) the archetypal nature of paradox, (b) the connectedness of the paradox archetype with the striving for consciousness (in therapy), which (c) leads to a confrontation with the paradox in question and simultaneously to an awareness of the paradox in all of life. This definition also makes a strong statement about the intuitive nature of paradox in therapeutic communication. Quoting one respondent, "There is a challenge in the statement, 'You can't get there from here.' To contrive to precipitate an awareness of a paradox prematurely or as a technique is oppositional and destructive to the patient." This approach also acknowledges the fact that the therapist's personality is crucial to the therapy process. The therapist might handle a therapeutic situation differently on any day of the week, but it is clear that in this approach to a definition, "the therapist and client are in there struggling in the same soup."

Additionally, the resolution of a paradoxical intervention requires a change of stance. The individual must search for solutions of a totally different nature from those previously tried and they must come from the person's whole being. The paradoxical intervention is not to be contrived. It evolves—from the shared reality which therapist and client create together within the therapeutic environment. The theme present in both the second and third response is that paradox and interventions termed *paradoxical* are not explainable in the realm of intellect. They surpass logic and encompass one's whole being: they are not to be understood through "thinking." These responses give credence to and appreciation for the deeper levels of existence involved in the "solving of paradoxes." They also demonstrate the relative absurdity of trying to explain or define, with logic, phenomena that exist in a different realm from that of everyday conscious thought.

The latter two conceptualizations about paradox lend themselves to a wide range of useful and potent linguistic forms—myths, fables, poetry, and other similar mediums—within which therapeutic communications may be framed.

The fourth approach is connected with systems theory, and, more specifically, to the therapist's understanding of the way systems work. Quoting one panel member, "If the therapist has understood the family system correctly, then what the therapist does will work. This is true whether an observer would label what the therapist uses as 'logical' or 'illogical,' 'straight-forward' or 'paradoxical'." Another way of saying the above is that an intervention may appear paradoxical when one does not understand the system context and the "logic" in which the particular intervention is made: if one understands these, the particular intervention does not seem paradoxical at all, but rather, well fitted to the therapist-family relationship context.

A continuation of the theme which connects the concept of paradox with systems thinking is a view that suggests a change in the language used when referring to what have been previously called paradoxical interventions. One panel member stated:

> There exists an interpretation or instruction to the family that restrains them from the change they have come to therapy to ask help for, or from any change at all. Since this is done within a *context* that implies that the family's request will be honored, a *contra-*

diction is set up. This contradiction is often called a "paradoxical intervention." As the intervention only *seems* paradoxical or illogical from the point of view of client expectations, the descriptive term, "restraint from change," may be used to refer (more appropriately) to the situation mentioned.

Telling a person/family to continue with a problem, and giving a rationale that is validated by at least some of the family's perceptions, is not "paradoxical." It *is* contrary to expectation. The rationale may be trivial or incomplete. Using such a trivial rationale to restrain the family from change may seem absurd. But it is not paradoxical because at the system level it makes sense from many angles; it has justifications any one of which one might choose to use as a rationale for restraining the family from change. To determine which one, of course, is the essence of the art.

This systems-oriented view puts much more emphasis on the quality of the therapist-family relationship.

Some panel members emphasized the importance of capturing the circularity and/or process nature of paradoxical interventions. Two examples of this emphasis follow.

1. The definition of paradox belongs to the world of logic. But the term *paradoxical intervention* usually refers to reverse psychology, not necessarily to an intervention designed to bring about second-order change (as previously defined by Watzlawick). One need not succumb to the temptation to view paradoxical intervention as "what you use when the client is 'oppositional' to tip the homeostatic balance. That just makes the client into an object. The key is in the *process interface* between therapist and client. It's in that in-between. You can only create something at the interface."

2. "A paradoxical intervention is not a 'thing,' is not the 'change agent.' The change agent is immanent within the process which encompasses the 'fit' between the patterns of the family/client (as described by the therapist to himself) and the pattern of the intervention." [*sic*]

These general comments about the term "paradoxical intervention" point out the circularity involved in conceptualizing about paradox and change when one takes into account the existence of systems—family systems as well as the therapist-family system interface.

Some of the more "concrete" responses to the definitional question fell into three general areas:

a. Paradoxical intervention as a term which specifies something the therapist does.

b. Paradoxical intervention as a term for defining the client's perception of an intervention.

c. Paradoxical intervention as a term used to describe the specific syntax of certain communications.

There were several responses which are subsumed under the heading "something the therapist does." These will be listed briefly to give the reader an idea of the variety of responses. A paradoxical intervention can be seen as one in which the therapist:

Attempts to alter the frame of reference in which the problem is conceptualized by the patient.

Within a context of the client coming to therapy in order to change, (the therapist) asks him or her to produce more of the behavior that s/he wants changed.

Prescribes the symptom or presenting problem, that is, the therapist commands that the client do something s/he is already doing. The paradoxical statement implicit is "Do what you were doing, and it will be different." Process-wise, doing now what you were doing, because you are now being told to do it by the therapist, *is* different.

Gives a global positive connotation of the behaviors of all participants in the particular context and history. S/he prescribes the symptom, or defines the symptom as positive, and defines others' behavior as positive.

Does something or says something that has an element of surprise (i.e., is contrary to context-bound expectation) and resolves a paradox by changing the epistemological frame. If the therapist can change the frame around, s/he can get a bit of leverage which could not otherwise be attained.

Communicates in a way that allows for two apparently contradictory messages. Introducing a paradoxical intervention into a rigid idea framework disrupts the rigidity and allows the possibility of individuation and group creativity.

The second, more concrete approach to a definition emphasized the client's perception of the intervention as being the deciding factor about whether it is paradoxical or not. If clients perceive the intervention as not fitting with their own commonsense views of how their problem should be solved, then the intervention is paradoxical. With this definition one may note a connection with the more abstract statement that "paradox is in the mind of the beholder."

The third definition belongs on a level totally different from the others. This particular formulation forced us to think more than any others (perhaps because it was so new). This definition is more of a creative searching than a black-and-white here it is. It states that "paradox is syntax of a certain type. In other words, you can speak in paradox language or in ordinary English just like you can speak in prose or poetry."

The rules "deal mostly with valuing and giving directions. Instead of saying in prose 'That is bad. Do this instead,' in paradoxical syntax you first assign levels and then say, 'It is good that that is bad.' A similar form would be used for the command." [*sic*]

This definition places paradox on a plane with poetry, fables, and myths. Poetry is a useful analogy. People's responses to it are as varied as are responses to the use of paradox. Some view poetry as nonsense, a waste of time, word magic, and cryptic communication. Others view it as sublime expression, language of the gods, mythic, soul food, the language of free expression. What makes the difference? The language of poetry has been called the language of the "unconscious." Poetry says what prose dares not—what prose cannot, in some instances. So also with paradox language. "The elements of surprise and non-coerciveness" allow for the suspension of conscious thought and the emergence of "intuitive perspectives."

A well-known story illustrates the idea.[2]

> "Laws do not make people better," said the Wise Man to the King; "they must practice certain things in order to become attuned to inner truth. This form of truth resembles apparent truth only slightly."
>
> The King decided that he could, and would, make people observe the truth. He could make them practice truthfulness.
>
> His city was entered by a bridge. On this he built a gallows. The following day, when the gates were opened at dawn, the Captain of the Guard was stationed with a squad of troops to examine all who entered.
>
> An announcement was made: "Everyone will be questioned. If he tells the truth, he will be allowed to enter. If he lies, he will be hanged."
>
> The Wise Man stepped forward.
>
> "Where are you going?"
>
> "I am on my way," said the Wise Man slowly, "to be hanged."
>
> "We don't believe you!"
>
> "Very well; if I have told a lie, hang me!"
>
> "But if we hang you for lying, we will have made what you said come true!"
>
> "That's right: now you know what truth is—YOUR truth!"
> (Shah, 1972, p. 23)

---

[2] © 1966, Mulla Nasrudin Enterprises Ltd. Used with permission.

Round Four

The entire study, including results from three rounds of questioning, was sent to the 26 panel members who had participated. Each was asked to comment on the study and comments were incorporated in Round Four. Responses were received from 23 persons. Of these 23, 17 responded with favorable comments about the study process with remarks such as "well done," "congratulations," and "favorably impressed." The remaining responses were cards accepting acknowledgment for participation in the study. Eight panel members sent articles or references to articles they had written on related topics. Five participants contributed additional comments based on the entire study. One panel member suggested adding three relevant experimental studies (which he would send references for). Another stated that he was shocked by the negative arguments of other participants regarding ethics and paradox in therapy. In disagreeing with them, he suggested that with many destructive and repetitive episodes (such as truancy or excessive drinking) one framework would be that of planning a "probable" relapse. For example, one might say to the client, "When do you think the relapse will happen this time? Who will say what so that you will relapse again? What will you be doing before you have your next relapse?" This probable plan approach does not prescribe the destructive behaviors; it calls attention to the patterns involved and the feelings connected with such behaviors.

A third participant described her own experience of working paradoxically. She stated, "I don't know how I do it. Cases do not become clear to me until I have a metaphor for them." This expert noted that paradox in therapy seemed very similar to drawing a picture. Citing the book, *Drawing on the Right Side of the Brain* (1979) by Betty Edwards, this respondent noted that what is necessary is to so confuse the left brain that it shuts off. For example, when one draws a hand with the left brain one draws the symbol of a hand. When the left brain is shut off and the right brain is functioning (the right brain being able to flow freely with details), the picture really looks like a hand and not merely a symbol. Second, this panel member agreed with comments made by another participant—that the problem of glibness of attitude regarding paradox does seem to exist. She noted that this seems to be the case with therapists in the learning stage, and less so with more seasoned therapists. Last, this expert posed an important question: Can paradox really be taught? Or is it somehow absorbed through experiencing of spiraling paradoxes within a supervisory or therapeutic relationship?

One expert elegantly verbalized her experience of the whole picture as follows:

> I have been tilting crazily in and out of your finished product. This "delphi" is fascinatingly circular in its process and seems to move collectively along from Position 1 to Position 2, as earlier ideas accumulate and push people on to new contexts from which to operate. I myself am interested in tracing what I think is a genuine movement from one "state of the art" sense to a newer one. The process of facing folks with their old thoughts and feedbacks from anonymous others about these thoughts, is in itself a statement about how Mind works. It is like the Milan methods for generating a hypothesis and their technique of circular questioning. I like it as a refreshingly non-scientific instrument. Brad Keeney would call it scientific in the sense of a "context for discovery" as opposed to a "context for research."
>
> Anyway, I would love to know who said what, but I guess that would blow everyone's mind if you divulged your secrets. People would find themselves matching up with their least favorite others, if not their veritable enemies. And it would be even worse it they didn't. So keep it all to yourself.
>
> ...My new slogan will be: Stamp Out Paradox, but the upshot is to move me along in a conviction of a growing division in the field, and how the two sides look. (Of course, as we shall soon know, there are never real oppositions, but only apparent dualisms, and imbrications of one side recursively into another, the Zig a context for the Zag and vice versa. In each generation the old Zag becomes the Zig for the next Zag. It's not better or worse, just how things change.)

A fifth panel member expressed excitement at the diversity of approaches, being amazed that the problem could be perceived from so many different angles. One of the critics of paradox roused this respondent's interest: he wondered if the critic was someone who hadn't worked much with families in which the more usual situation is one in which one family member is a "good" patient, while the others are not interested in therapy. This type of many-faceted psychosocial situation requires multilevel skills and attentiveness, or the family therapist can easily burn out in two or three years.

In summary, Round Four feedback elicited responses to the entire study process and results. Highlights of these responses include disagreement between two panel members regarding critics' comments, an example of a probable plan approach, emphasis on intentionally confusing left brain functioning so it shuts off and permits the right brain's creative function to operate, a comparison of the process to the work of the Milan team, and viewing the Delphi process itself as a statement about how "mind" works.

RECOMMENDATIONS

There are several areas that are relevant to furthering the research on paradox in psychotherapy. A broader historical perspective on paradox is needed. Much has been written on the ancient use of koans as ways fostering "enlightenment." Western therapists know little about the artful use of these koans and how their process relates to paradox; an in-depth historical elucidation is needed. Clearer understanding of the relationship between conscious manipulation and human caring within the therapeutic relationship is urgently needed as is more in-depth study of the short- versus long-term value of using paradoxes for change. Phenomenological studies of clients who have experienced paradox in their therapy relationships are needed; these could lend invaluable insights into what is useful and meaningful about paradox in the therapy process. The use of paradox in therapy needs to be studied and measured with respect to its potency and usefulness. Carl Whitaker (1982), in a personal communication, highlighted this issue with, "One of the great paradoxes is long, continued therapy with the assumption of change that is not taking place. Ten years of therapy with no effective change is by itself a powerful paradox" (personal communication). Last, the process-research method itself needs refining; its usefulness is becoming more apparent as more and more clinicians/researchers grapple with the fluctuating elements involved in change.

CONCLUDING REMARKS

Several observations from a more general perspective are relevant. First, the meanings inherent in the differing definitions are important. It would be easy to assume that all clinicians speak the same language and that each has the same definitions of terms, concepts, and methods. But such an assumption would be wholly unrealistic. People bring their own associations, ideas, memories to a term or concept: so it is with the defining of paradoxical intervention. Granted this evolving process (associations, ideas, etc.) has its base in some original definitions of Watzlawick, Haley, and Erickson. But each new "user" of the concepts forms a new, idiosyncratic, and in many cases, creative understanding of that concept.

This process of conceptualizing poses an interesting challenge for communicators. Each has a specific definition or set of associations to the words and each of these definitions is meaningful and useful. Nevertheless, in talking about paradoxical intervention, it is important that each knows the other's definitions, grants that there is no wrong or right one, and acknowledges that, to the extent possible, agreement among communicators on what is most useful in understanding the concepts is essential.

The variety of definitions of "paradoxical intervention" in this study reveals the process of creative discovery within one particular group of therapists/researchers. None of the experts in this study copied what someone else had said before. Each seemed involved in sharing his/her own creative search.

To conclude, a quote from Erickson, Rossi, and Rossi's book, *Hypnotic Realities* (1976, p. 63), seems fitting:

> Ideally, our therapeutic double binds are mild quandaries that provide the patient with an opportunity for growth. These quandaries are indirect hypnotic forms insofar as they tend to block or disrupt the patient's habitual attitudes and frames of reference so that choice is not easily made on a conscious, voluntary level. In this sense a double bind may be operative whenever one's usual frames of reference cannot cope and one is forced to another level of functioning. Bateson (1975) has commented that this other level can be "a higher level of abstraction which may be more wise, more psychotic, more humorous, more religious, etc." We simply add that this other level can also be more autonomous or involuntary in its functioning; that is, outside the person's usual range of self-direction and -control. Thus we find that the therapeutic double bind can lead one to experience those altered states we characterize as trance so that previously unrealized potentials may become manifest.
>
> In actual practice, there is an infinite range of situations that may or may not function as binds or double binds. What is or is not a double bind will depend very much on how it is received by the listener. What is a bind or double bind for one person may not be one for another. . . . Humans are too complex and individual differences are simply too great to expect that the same words or situation will produce the same effect in everyone. Well-trained hypnotherapists have available many possible approaches to hypnotic experience. They offer them one after another to the patient and care-

fully evaluate which actually lead to the desired result. *In clinical practice we can only determine what was or was not a therapeutic bind or double bind in retrospect by studying the patient's response.* [Emphasis added.]

In my opinion, usefulness of double binds or paradoxical interventions does depend on how each person and/or each family perceives the bind. And another element involves the therapist's attitude toward strategic thinking. That is, what happens for the therapist who decides to plan a certain strategy to help the client? One important idea is that part of the power in the pradoxical approach lies in the therapist's "thinking about" the system and planning strategies based on his/her observations. This does not imply that the therapist hasn't "joined" the family: It *does* imply the therapist's recognition and use of a somewhat paradoxical position in the therapist-family system. S/he can join the family and establish rapport and also recede to "think about" the system dynamics and plan possible strategies. S/he can operate with flexibility in two important dimensions of therapeutic functioning.

In summary, the therapist's ability to move in and partially out of the system, the client's perception of the particular paradox, and the quality of the therapist-client relationship operate as essential criteria for acceptance and/or use of paradox in therapeutic communication.

REFERENCES

Bateson, G. *Steps to an ecology of mind.* New York: Ballantine, 1972.

Dalkey, N. *The Delphi methods: An experimental study of group opinion.* Santa Monica, Calif.: Rand Corporation (RM-588-PR), 1969.

Dell, P. Paradox redux. *Journal of Marriage and Family Therapy.* 1981, 7.

Edwards, B. *Drawing on the right side of the brain.* Los Angeles: J. P. Tarcher, 1979.

Erickson, M., Rossi, E., & Rossi, S. *Hypnotic realities.* New York: Irvington Publishers, 1976.

Hoffman, L. *Foundations of family therapy.* New York: Basic Books, 1981.

Madanes, C. *Strategic family therapy.* San Francisco: Jossey-Bass, 1981.

Palazzoli, M., Bascolo, L., Cecchin, G., & Prata, G. *Paradox and counterparadox.* New York: Jason Aronson, 1978.

Papp, P. The Greek chorus and other techniques of family therapy. *Family Process,* 1980, *19.*

Shah, I. *The exploits of the incomparable Mulla Nasrudin.* New York: E. P. Dutton, 1972.

Tesch, R. *Phenomenological and transformative research: What they are and how to do them.* Santa Barbara, Calif.: Fielding Institute, 1980.

Watzlawick, P., Weakland, J., & Fisch, R. *Change.* New York: W. W. Norton, 1974.

Weeks, G. & L'Abate, L. A compilation of paradoxical methods. *American Journal of Family Therapy,* 1979, 7, 61–76.

Weeks, G., & L'Abate, L. *Paradoxical psychotherapy.* New York: Brunner/ Mazel, 1982.

Weiner, N. *The human use of human beings: Cybernetics and society.* New York: Avon, 1967.

Whitaker, C. Personal communication. March 1982.

Williamson, D. Personal authority in family experience via termination of the intergenerational hierarchical boundary: Part III—Personal authority defined, and the power of play in the change process. *Journal of Marital and Family Therapy,* 1982, 8, 309–322.

Part Two

Approaches to Paradoxical Intervention

2

Unpredictability and Change: A Holographic Metaphor*

by Brian W. Cade, CSW

"It's time for you to answer now," the Queen said, looking at her watch: "open your mouth a little wider when you speak, and always say 'your Majesty.'"

"I only wanted to see what the garden was like, your Majesty—"

"That's right," said the Queen, patting her on the head, which Alice didn't like at all: "though, when you say 'garden'—I've seen gardens, compared with which this would be a wilderness."

Alice didn't dare to argue the point, but went on "...and I thought I'd try and find my way to the top of that hill—"

"When you say 'hill,'" the Queen interrupted, "I could show you hills in comparison with which you'd call that a valley."

"No I shouldn't," said Alice, surprised into contradicting her at last: "a hill can't be a valley, you know. That would be nonsense—"

The Red Queen shook her head. "You may call it 'nonsense' if you like," she said, "but I've heard nonsense, compared with which that would be as sensible as a dictionary!"

Lewis Carroll, *Through the Looking Glass*

---
*I wish to acknowledge the members of my team without whom none of this would have taken place: Bebe Speed, Philippa Seligman, and Philip Kingston. The chapter is dedicated to the late Dr. Harvey Jones whose influence brought me into this field.

HISTORICAL INFLUENCES

A colleague and I were once asked by Lynn Hoffman how we had arrived at our Marx Brothers style of therapy. My answer was that I was on the road to Damascus when a green book called *Strategies of Psychotherapy* fell out of the sky and hit me. As is probably true of many in our field, it is hard to overestimate the influence of Jay Haley on my professional development, not the least of which was his introduction to me of the work of Milton H. Erickson (Haley, 1963, 1973). The other major influences on my development have been the work of the Brief Therapy Centre, M.R.I., California (Watzlawick et al., 1967, 1974; Weakland et al., 1974), and the work of Mara Selvini Palazzoli and her colleagues at the then Centro per lo Studio della Famiglia, Milan (Palazzoli et al., 1975, 1978). During recent years, I have also developed a growing fascination with the indefinable and unpredictable work of Carl Whitaker (see Neil & Kniskern, 1982).

My early interpretations of Haley's work led me to construe therapy as a kind of contest in which paradoxical techniques were power tactics that could be used to prevent a client or family from using symptomatic behaviour to control and define their relationships with me. Later, pardoxical work became more of an intellectual exercise, a kind of chess game. Attempts would be made, meticulously, to construct interventions with all potential loopholes blocked, thus forcing the client or family to move outside of the rule-governed "symptomatic game without end, which up to that moment, had no meta rules for the change of its own rules" (Watzlawick et al., 1967, p. 237).

At this time, much effort was devoted to trying to answer the question, "Is this a true paradox?" and interventions were measured against external yardsticks from the fields of mathematics and logic. However, it became increasingly clear to my colleagues and me that a central ingredient in our "paradoxical" work was the unexpectedness of the position taken by the therapist (or therapy team) or of the interventions given. We began to talk less and less about paradoxes (Is it? Isn't it?) and more about introducing difference or new information into systems through unpredictability. As Palazzoli has declared, "People are most influenced when they expect a certain message and receive instead a message at a totally different level. . . . anything predictable is therapeutically inefficient" (1981, p. 45).

Interventions began to be designed and measured by yardsticks more integral to the process of therapy. More time was spent attempting to ascertain how the client or family were expecting, or apparently wanting us to be, and then taking a position, or making a response, including our interventions (the more formal closing statements or prescriptions), that was isomorphic enough to connect with the client's/family's expectations (see de Shazer, 1982[a]). Yet, with sufficient, unexpected, sometimes absurd, even shocking elements come *difference*. As Erickson and Rossi (1979, p. 5) observe, "Any experience of shock or surprise momentarily fixates attention and interrupts the previous pattern of association. Any experience of the unrealistic, the unusual, or the fantastic, provides an opportunity for altered modes of apprehension." However, many of the approaches, and interventions—or aspects of the interventions—that we have developed will fit the criteria for the definition of paradoxical, as elaborated, for example, by Weeks and L'Abate (1979, 1982) or Rohrbaugh et al. (1977).

THE CLINICAL SETTING

The work to be described took place in a small family therapy agency set up in 1971 in Cardiff, South Wales. This was the first such agency in the United Kingdom. Individuals or families are either self-referred or referred by the myriad of social, medical, or psychiatric services in the area; they present with the whole range of emotional, behavioural, or psychological problems. The Family Institute offers free services and is funded primarily by a major British charity, Dr. Barnardo's.

As with most major British cities, Cardiff is fairly cosmopolitan: Referrals to the institute come from all social classes and reflect a range of cultural strands. Breunlin et al. (1983) examined some facets of British culture that have influenced our tendency toward the more indirect approaches to therapy. The British tend to be much more cautious about change, suspicious of "technical" solutions to family and other social problems, and pessimistic about the potential benefits of talking as a way of approaching problems.

> The American tendency to "let it all hang out" and to form personal relationships quickly is regarded by the British as a sign of superficiality, transience, and egotism, and even as a breach of etiquette. The British value "keeping oneself to oneself." When a problem exists, it should be handled within the family, as it is important "not to wash one's dirty laundry in public."
>
> The British are far less direct about their interpersonal relationships, seldom making direct statements about how they function or

how they wish them to be different. They maintain a "proper" distance when relating, and avoid strong displays of affect. (Breunlin et al., 1983, p. 99)

Although the above represents a rather drastic oversimplification of British societal values, it can offer a useful backdrop against which to view the attitudes of the average British family towards the idea of psychotherapy. There will, of course, be differences among various subcultures. Yet most families can generally be expected to demonstrate this backdrop of culutral injunctions against the openness required in the process of psychotherapy.

Judicious care is taken not to imply premature familiarity. The therapist avoids the suggestion that therapy may provoke rapid or extensive change.... The therapist reassures the family that change should not imply throwing out the baby with the bath water, that is, unwittingly removing qualities of life valued by the family, or creating new problems by oversimple formulations and hasty action.... Levels of intensity are adroitly monitored, because of the societal emphasis on avoiding undue proximity, affect-laden revelations, or statements that directly define or redefine relationships. (Breunlin et al., 1983, p. 100)

A TEAM APPROACH

Much has been written about the use of paradoxical techniques by a single therapist. This chapter will concentrate on a team approach to therapy in which one member acts as therapist while the others observe from behind a one-way mirror. The observers can intervene in a variety of ways: by telephoning in, calling the therapist out, sending messages via the therapist, and occasionally entering the room (see Breunlin & Cade, 1981; Speed et al., 1982).

Our use of teams evolved partly from our training programs, through which we discovered the potential richness of live consultation as a way of increasing therapist maneuverability and stimulating creativity. The team approach was also particularly helpful with those individuals and families adept at incorporating a therapist into their systems—of both thought and action—thus quickly rendering him impotent. A family could achieve this end by raising the therapist's level of anxiety; making him increasingly angry or frustrated; making him care for or overprotect them; making him competitive (either with them or other involved professionals, past or present); uncritically "cooperating" with him but never changing; seducing him into an interesting and stimulating social relationship or intellectual exercise; inviting him to join the "reasonable and motivated" versus the "unreasonable and unmotivated" factions within their ranks; or sometimes simply overwhelming him. With such families, the team attempted to reduce the predictability of the social transactions around therapy, thus throwing the family off balance and in various ways avoiding such pitfalls.

At first, this unpredictability was seen primarily as a way of freeing the therapist, allowing him to get on with the therapy. However, we increasingly found that the unpredictability itself was a powerful promoter of change. It is the latter phenomenon that this chapter will explore and elucidate.

Initially, the observers saw themselves as advisors, whose role was to help the therapist intervene to change the family as quickly and effectively as possible. Gradually, we began to see more clearly how a family and a therapist would construct, conjointly, a "reality," in ways such as those elaborated above, which would often inhibit the process of therapy. More and more, the observing team found itself intervening on the family's and the therapists' system. Frequently, the therapists would resist the family's inputs, sometimes consciously but more often quite unaware that they were doing so (e.g., by adopting a posture, gestures, facial expressions, or a tone of voice that subtly undermined or contradicted the input).

We also found that the team tended to be drawn into a number of families' "game without end," with the result that we would begin feeling bogged down, frustrated, angry, overanxious, overwhelmed, and so forth. Sometimes, the team would squabble unproductively, different members identifying strongly with different individuals or factions within the family. At other times, we would become bored and "switch off," both emotionally and intellectually, leaving the therapist to sink or swim. (The latter would mainly happen when the therapist seemed stubbornly aligned with the family and against the team.)

It soon became clear that just as the therapist could not be an objective observer of the family, the team could not be an objective observer of the therapy. The family, the therapist, and the observing team were all involved in the process of constructing a reality, which could, through the process of reification, inhibit the process of change. As observed elsewhere:

> Gradually the implications began to appear broader than in the earlier explorations with triangulation and paradox. The context of

therapy, through the medium of the screen, had become more complex again. Therapeutic change was increasingly conceived as a phenomenon that grew out of the evolving nature of the relationship between therapist, team and family, and the "definition" of each only "existed" in terms of each element's "ideas" about the nature of the others and of the relationship between them. Variation in any one element could bring about change in the other two. (Cade & Cornwell, 1983, p. 78)

We began to experiment with changing the reality of the therapy context. Thus it became much more difficult for families to define the rules of the "game." Information, opinions, news of events in the team, shifting alliances, criticisms or approval, and so on could be transmitted to the family in a variety of ways. "As with Alice's mirror in *Through the Looking Glass*, a new world of possibilities, sometimes vivid, simetimes strange or illogical, had unfolded. Though never invited to pass, like Alice, through the mirror, such families could be offered glimpses which, combined with what each family member might project from his or her own beliefs, could begin to disrupt their habitual patterns of thought and behaviour" (Cade & Cornwell, 1983, p. 78). It was during these team experiences that I found myself concerned more with the unexpected and unpredictable than with the "paradoxical," seeing the latter as one aspect or class of the former.

A META-THEORETICAL FRAMEWORK

Karl Pribram (1976) of the Stanford Medical School has proposed that the brain works along holographic principles. Before considering the implications of this theory for therapy, I will briefly describe holography.

In 1947 Denis Gabor invented a new photographic process for which he received a Nobel prize in 1971. A photographic plate is exposed to two sources of light, one reaching it directly from a source, the other reflected off the object(s) to be photographed. The resultant interference pattern caused by the meeting of the two light sources is recorded on the plate. When, subsequently, the plate is exposed to a light source of equal intensity to, and from exactly the same direction as, the original direct source, a three-dimensional image of the object(s) is "recovered" and appears, floating in space in the position of the original object(s).

Unlike the normal photographic negative, there is no direct correspondence between the shape of the object(s) and the image on the holographic plate, which appears as an apparently meaningless pattern of swirls. Each part of the plate carries information about every part of the object(s) and therefore each part can be used separately to form an image of the whole object(s) by shining a light onto it (though it will lack some of the sharpness of detail that can be recovered from the whole plate).

Another important feature of the holographic plate is that it can be used to store a vast number of different images. Changing the frequency of the light source and the direction of the beam will allow a different image to be laid down and subsequently recovered by a recreation of the original conditions (i.e., frequency and direction of beam). Also, if the two light sources are reflected simultaneously from two different objects (rather than one source reaching the plate directly), the interference pattern laid down will relate to both and reilluminating the plate with light reflected from either one of the objects will recover the image of the other. Each image will be permanently "associated" with the other. Thus, the hologram represents a sophisticated information storage system, second only to the human brain. Recreating the original conditions will recover any image or group of images.

The "Holographic Brain"

The human brain can be seen as sharing a number of important features with the process of holography. First, it appears that each memory may be distributed evenly throughout the brain rather than localized in any one part. Earlier in this century, Lashley's experiments showed that removing successively larger parts of the brains of experimental animals, though impairing performance, did not eradicate memories. Russell has proposed (1979, p. 154), "Any one memory would be encoded as a pattern of chemical changes over trillions of synapses—and possibly glia cells as well—and each synapse would be involved in billions of different memories."

Another vital feature of the brain is its ability to associate experiences and to store patterns of association. Thus, access to part of a pattern leads to an almost instantaneous completion of that pattern based on learned associations. As with a holographic plate, but in a far more complex and sophisticated way, when the original conditions under which a memory or group of memories were laid down are recreated, the experience, or significant parts of it, can be recovered. The process of association also means that with access to a small part of the original conditions the brain can recover much or all of the memory or group of memories.

In any given situation potentially limitless facets of the total gestalt of externally and internally derived experiences exist that can serve to recreate the original conditions. These, in turn, can cause a whole range of memories and associations to be recovered. Which of these facets of experience become highlighted at any particular time, given the huge backdrop of potential associations, depends on the particular conscious (or less conscious) concerns occupying us at that point in time. As Wellwood comments (1982, p. 130), "Applying a frame to the implicit (i.e., the whole gestalt) is somewhat analogous to deblurring a blurred photograph by highlighting the major contours or spatial frequencies, so that particular shapes can emerge from the blur." In other words, our particular concerns—the specific focuses derived from our frameworks for applying meaning—will, through intensification, separate out certain features or aspects of experience from the implicit or potentially rich associations possible. As our patterns of association become established in a particular way, they will tend to influence the processing of subsequent experiences. As De Bono has suggested (1971, p. 124), "Patterns are picked out of the environment solely on the basis of familiarity, and through such selection become ever more familiar." In this way we develop belief frameworks or mental "sets" that determine how we see ourselves and our world, and how we ascribe meaning, and thus respond to, those experiences. In our relationships with others, we then develop patterns of behaving together, that both reflect our mental sets and those of the people with whom we interact, and tend by repetition to be confirmed—though such patterns rarely develop consciously.

Wellwood talks of the relationship between the conscious and the unconscious as follows:

> We are continually processing many kinds of interactions or interference patterns and can only pay attention to a very few. The organismic processing that we do not attend to becomes part of an unconscious background, holographic blur. This background blur, which has an implicit structure to it, is surely what the concept of the unconscious refers to. However, the traditional model of the unconscious in depth psychology makes it appear as though the unconscious has an explicit structure to it, as though drives, wishes, repressions, or archetypes exist in explicit form, as though the unconscious were a kind of autonomous alter-ego.... What is unconscious are holistic patternings, which may be explicated in many different ways and at many different levels of the organism/ environment interrelationship. (Wellwood, 1982, p. 133)

Thus, we can be seen as becoming like holographic plates on which the same range of lights (i.e., same range of frequencies, directions, and intensities of beams) tend repeatedly to be shone, thus recovering the same range of images and associated images and leaving unrecovered a myriad of other possibilities. Those lights shone with a greater intensity (because of our current concerns) will lead to particular images and their associations will stand out more sharply in a figure/ground relationship to the others.

Completing this metaphor, the process of therapy can be seen as analogous to changing the lighting directed at a holographic plate by (*a*) increasing the number of potential light sources, and (*b*) varying their direction, frequency, and intensities, such that a greater range of images and associations can be recovered and different facets highlighted, allowing for different figure/ground relationships.

Health and Dysfunction

From this framework, health can be considered the availability and possibility of complex potential association patterns, and of potential framings for interpreting the "reality" of experience that leads to a wide range of possible affective and behavioral responses.

Dysfunction will thus be seen as the converse. Association patterns become limited and belief frameworks increasingly reified and rigidified, allowing for ever more limited possibilities for interpreting reality, which lead to a more restricted range of affective and behavioural responses.

However, the terms *healthy* and *dysfunctional* are not used here as predicates. We do not argue that certain people or groups *are* healthy or dysfunctional, but that in specific contexts and with respect to particular functions, either pattern of thought and behaviour can develop.

Symptoms are those affective, behavioural, or physiological responses that develop and become maintained through the rigid application, in any area of functioning, of reified frameworks for defining and responding to reality. They are particularly likely to develop or intensify where it becomes necessary for the individual, family or other system significantly to change or adapt patterns of belief and response due to developmental or other changes either internal or external to the system.

Because symptoms tend to become the focus of considerable attention, they may serve to draw attention away from other areas of distress and dysfunction. This phenomenon may lead to an apparent vested interest in symptoms being maintained. Yet I think it an error to assume that they thus have "a purpose" (though as a way of framing certain interventions, this formulation has certain uses). I regard symptoms as *outcomes* of certain patterns, which subsequently may *apparently* come to serve a purpose. Why, in any given situation, a particular class of symptoms occurs, and how the bearer is "selected," usually depends on a wide range of variables. One analogy is that, as with a balloon, the symptom reflects a weak spot where, under pressure, the breakdown occurs. Such weak spots can include tendencies towards physical ill health in one member, potentials for stress between particular members, one member's involvement in particular peer groups (e.g., gangs of youth on the fringes of delinquency, drinking fraternities), tensions between families of origin, and many others. In any gestalt, there may be tensions and potential difficulties at various levels of functioning, and an increased focus on a particular issue that, at a particular point, stands out from the others. These tensions can lead to the evolution of a "problem" surrounding that issue relative to which other issues remain in the background.

This process of problem formation is described most eloquently by Watzlawick et al. (1974). Wrong, or inappropriate solutions (whether acts of commission or omission), that derive from particular belief frameworks applied to certain difficulties can result in no change or an exacerbation of those difficulties. A problem may then evolve as "more of the same" attempted solutions (or class of solutions) are repeatedly or increasingly applied or intensified. This can lead to more of the same problem, and so on.

Symptoms and Holograms

Symptoms, whether seen as residing in the individual, the family, or any other system, tend to be the focus of considerable preoccupation by the symptom bearer, his or her intimates, and often of other systems—legal, medical, psychotherapeutic, school, neighbourhood, work, and so forth. Such preoccupations will consist of frameworks for thinking about the symptom and its meanings, affective responses, and behaviours for dealing with the symptom and its various effects. As the symptom becomes entrenched, one can see the presence of a holographic gestalt in which certain beliefs, attitudes, and responses are continually highlighted and repeated and thus reinforced. Through the process of association, the highlighting of any one part of this gestalt will tend to recover the other parts; as the process becomes self-perpetuating, other patterns of thinking and responding become less and less available.

In holography, if one keeps shining the same frequencies of light at the same intensities and from the same direction, one will repeatedly recover the same images and associated images with the same figure/ground relationships, even though the potential range of possible images and associations on the plate may be considerably wider. Similarly, and perhaps through a related process, if the same range of attitudes and behaviours are repeatedly focused on a problem and the processes that surround it, the same interlocking pattern of responses will tend to be recovered from those involved in the process and the same association patterns will be highlighted.

Therapeutic inputs can become part of such a process if the therapist's orientation, both personal and professional, leads to a particular way of thinking about and approaching a problem. The more of the same approach or class of techniques, deriving from the therapist's particular frameworks or models, can lead to more of the same problem, and so on. It is as though s/he is shining the same range of lights, as described above, onto the situation, thus continually recovering the same images and associated images with the same figure/ground relationships.

The following case example should clearly demonstrate this process. A thirteen-year-old girl was described by her father as disobedient, uncouth, and out of control. The man was in his midfifties and was described by his wife and by the therapist involved as rigid, Victorian in his ideas about discipline, and totally resistant and lacking in motivation. The man saw all psychiatrists and social workers as "worse than useless." Arguments in the family were frequent and the mother, who was in her late thirties, identified with her daughter, frequently defending her from the father's unreasonable attitudes and expectations. The therapist considered the girl to be quite healthy, but driven by her father's rigidity to act out her frustrations and rebel. She had been unable to get the man either to "see" his contribution to this process or to cooperate with her attempts to persuade him to be less severe. The therapy became deadlocked.

One can see how each member of this group acted out of beliefs held about the others, and how those actions had the effect of recovering specific responses from the others. Such a system served to continue the "game" and to confirm each member's beliefs.

The father's attempts to control his daughter would lead immediately to her fighting back. His wife would "attack" him and defend the girl, and the therapist would be brought in to try to get him to "own" his responsibility and "see" that he needed to change his ways.

The mother's attempts to moderate her husband's views and

encourage her daughter's development would serve to make the father angry with both of them, at which point he would try to impose further restrictions. The girl would fight back and the therapist would be called in to "deal with him."

The girl's defiant attempts to find some space for herself would anger her father and her mother would have to defend her; the therapist would again attempt to get the man to change his attitudes.

The therapist's efforts to have the father see that he was far too severe would anger him and he would blame his daughter and wife. The girl would fight back, the mother would defend, and so on.

Although this familiar process can be viewed and "explained" through a range of different frameworks, one can see how each person's inputs into the process tended both to recover and be recovered by the inputs of all the others. Thus, a reality had been created which, through the process of reification, inhibited the possibility of change.

A THEORY OF CHANGE: PREDICTABILITY AND UNPREDICTABILITY

One important feature of "stuckness" in any context is the predictability of responses on the part of the participants. Obviously, a degree of predictability is important in any context. Only thus can we negotiate and establish the many patterns that must go into the forming of any stable relationship or set of relationships. However, adaptability to changing circumstances requires the possibility of renegotiating reality, of responding in an unpredictable way; that unpredictability must then lead to a renegotiation of how we view ourselves, our relationships, and the meaning of experiences.

This process of creating "realities" can be represented in a circular fashion as shown on the following page.

As with any circle, this process has no beginning or end. It should be possible for change to be elicted by a significant variation at any point in the process. Of course, what will represent a significant variation will change enormously from situation to situation, as will the location in the circle of the point at which introduction of a variation might be most influential. The important factors will be (a) the nature and flexibility of the various attitudes and belief sys-

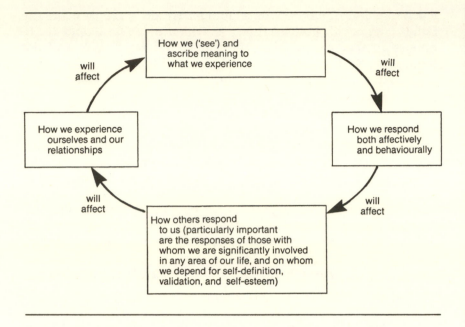

tems being focused onto the situation, and (*b*) the number of different systems or themes that can be seen as having influence on, or investment in, the continuation of how things have been. Any context can include variables involving repetitive patterns among significant participants that limit the ease with which an individual or group can change behaviours and belief frameworks. Such limitations on change can occur where, for example, parental overinvolvement impedes an adolescent's ability to differentiate; a heavy investment in their immediate extended families makes it difficult for a couple to negotiate an improved marital relationship; and a family with children deemed "at risk" remains under constant surveillance by relatives, neighbors or professional agencies, in spite of its attempts to change. Feelings of impotence and inadequacy are thus perpetuated—the same feelings that may have led to the emergence of the original problem.

As suggested earlier, symptoms can be seen as arising from the rigid application of reified frameworks for defining and responding to reality. In such frameworks, there will be a high level of predictability with respect to the ways participants focus upon and respond to the problems. As shown in the earlier case example, therapy became *stuck* when the therapist became predictable in *his* approach to the problem. Through a reciprocal process of verbal and particularly nonverbal negotiations, a reality becomes constructed that reflects the attitudes, beliefs, and responses of all participants, but serves to inhibit change.

Trying to change a system while oneself remaining the same, in terms of how one views a situation and thus responds to it, seems (if the difficulty does not become quickly resolved), only to recover more of the same responses from the other members of the system (however correct or logical a position appears to be one's own viewpoint). The implication here seems to be that to change or increase the adaptability of a system, it is necessary to be able to change oneself and the position one takes—to become, as it were, unpredictable. In terms of the holography metaphor, adaptability seems to require the possibility of varying what is focused (i.e., both ways of thinking and the actions that reflect *and communicate* the thinking) onto any situation in order that new images, associations, and figure/ground relationships can be recovered from a background that will already contain potentially limitless possibilities for reconstructing realities.

For example, in the earlier case example, the approach taken was to completely change the focus that had been adopted by the previous therapist. I commented to the father on how difficult it is to bring up children in these more permissive times, and on how many of the older values of respect and self-discipline seem to have been lost. I declared my belief that parents, not children, should decide what is appropriate behaviour in their family and that youngsters need the greater experience of their parents—even though they may see them as old-fashioned. "Of course," I ended, "good parents will obviously become more flexible and negotiate more as their children grow up." The man's attitude changed almost immediately. And after a short period of thoughtfulness, he began to insist that his daughter was really "not a bad kid," that perhaps he was being too hard on her and needed to change his approach.

The man had doubtless come to the therapy anticipating a further attack on his position. Initially, he seated himself with his back turned towards me; his counterarguments had doubtless been well rehearsed. Expecting an approach inconsistent with his apparent beliefs and attitudes, he was met instead by an approach that validated his position and he thus seemed immediately able to accept the suggestion, "Good parents will obviously become more flexible and negotiate more as their children grow up." In the face of my continued expressions of caution and reluctance to let him blame himself, he increasingly generated his *own* arguments as to why he should become more tolerant. He agreed to a short series of sessions: The outcome of the case was a considerable improvement in the situation.

The previous therapist had concentrated totally on trying to change the man's position. I concentrated on changing *my* position, in order that new possibilities could be recovered from potentials that *already existed* in the family.

The main features of this intervention were:

1. The position I took was *sufficiently isomorphic* to that of the father for him to feel validated and accept the suggestion that good parents become more flexible.
2. The father's attitudes were given a *different meaning* and relabeled as virtues.
3. I had taken a totally *unexpected position* in the father/therapist process, a process that had become nodal in the previous stuckness.

These three features—sufficient isomorphism, different meanings, and the unexpected position on a nodal issue—are central to this approach and will be expanded on in the following section.

Thinking differently about things does not appear to require insight into what previously was "wrong." In fact, as a therapeutic approach, giving insight tends to focus attention back to what *was* or *is* rather than to what *might be*, and thus tends to recover responses that relate to past or present patterns rather than future possibilities. My own opinion is that where insight seems to work, it does so through the process of reframing or giving new meanings to experience, which leads to the client or family seeing and experiencing things differently, in turn responding differently, and so on.

It is interesting to compare this approach with that of Carl Whitaker who never appears to directly try to influence families. He seems to concern himself primarily with his own growth during the therapy experience and refuses to let the family define his position on any issue. He behaves unpredictably in that he always reflects back to the family a different and sometimes surprising or absurd perspective on the nodal themes with which they are struggling.

"Unpredictable" Therapy

Over the door of the Pasteur Institute in Paris is the inscription, "Luck Comes to the Prepared Mind." To be creatively but relevantly unpredictable requires that a number of areas be sufficiently assessed. It is not enough just to be unpredictable; it is necessary that the unpredictability relates to nodal issues and themes, both in the family and the therapy process. With increasing experience, more and more of the assessment process may be made unconsciously. Therapists such as Whitaker can act from intuition largely because, with many years of experience to draw on, they can trust that they are doing their basic processing, from which their "intuitions" emanate.

Having elicited clear descriptions of problems in terms of actual behaviours and events rather than predicates, and information about how often, when, where, and in relation to whom they most occur, it is also important to discover what attempts the client, family, or other involved parties have made to solve the problems. From this information it should be possible to begin making assessments about the interlocking patterns of belief underpinning the attitudes and responses of the various participants—those elements that perpetuate recovery of more of the same problem behaviours. Symptoms can be seen as embedded in a hierarchy of themes and contexts and it is necessary to identify—from the participant's various responses and from the words and metaphors they use—the nodal issues and processes that may be contributing most to the stuckness. Decisions about who and what should be included in the therapist's frame of reference will partly reflect themes and processes imminent in the problem context, and partly the frameworks (individual, family, network, etc.) from which the therapist functions and thus selects and orders information.

It is also important to assess the position the client or family (and sometimes the referring professional) seems to expect, want, or seems to be maneuvering the therapist to take, particularly with respect to those nodal issues or processes or towards the symptom. If there have been previous therapies, expectations will obviously be based on those experiences, and a therapist can sometimes be faced with considerable upset or anger if s/he does not behave like a previous therapist, even though that therapy may have been unsuccessful in solving the problems.

In both the position that the therapist or team adopts and the interventions offered, significant facets of the participant's beliefs, attitudes, responses, or the symptomatic behaviour itself should be reframed or relabeled, usually so that what previously has been seen negatively is presented positively. New connections can be made between particular aspects or processes, and *different meanings* can lead to different experiences and responses.

For an intervention to impact usefully, it must be sufficiently isomorphic to the belief patterns and attitudes of the individual or family or subgroup chosen as the focus of the intervention. That is, there should be sufficient direct or analogic correspondence between important facets of the position taken in the intervention and nodal beliefs, themes, events, or structures in the family, individual, or subgroup. If the intervention can make sufficient connections, both cognitively and affectively, that can be recognized, identified with, and responded to, then the therapist and individual or family can become engaged together, albeit briefly, in a reality. These subsequent reframings and other unexpected aspects of the intervention can have maximum effect in that they evolve, as it were, from "familiar territory" or from perceived similarity in beliefs and attitudes.

The intervention must then include an unexpected attitude, explanation, request, or injunction with respect to a nodal issue or theme, so that a different light is focused (either directly or through analogy) on an area of particular significance and preoccupation for the client or family. This unexpected aspect need not be dramatic or shocking; it can be gentle and relatively unprovocative.

It is important continually to monitor the feelings, attitudes, and responses elicited from the therapist or team by the client's or family's beliefs, attitudes, and responses to the therapy. These will reflect the frameworks underpinning what the therapist or team will give to the situation. Therapists can become quickly committed to a particular diagnosis, especially once they have made an emotional investment. The diagnosis can thus become reified so that, even in the absence of change, the same therapeutic approaches are applied and more of the same problem behaviour(s) are recovered.

For most of us, when therapy becomes stuck our training leads us to look harder and harder at the individual or family. This approach suggests that the opposite is as important: When stuck, the therapist or team should look to the framework from which the approach being used has evolved. It is often not enough to appear to change position tactically while in reality remaining committed to a particular diagnostic formulation. It is arguably impossible for therapists, over any extended period of time, to disguise our basic diagnosis; it will inevitably be betrayed, albeit at an unconscious level, via the many nonverbal behaviours through which information can be exchanged. This is especially true where we hold a strongly negative or blaming view of a particular individual or group.

The choice, at any point in therapy, of which behaviour or

theme, which individual or subgroup on which to focus an intervention is a matter of therapeutic judgment, as is the choice of the unexpected component, and the degree of attention paid to issues of engagement and maintenance. While standardized assessment procedures can give useful guidelines, particularly about what positions to avoid, it is also important that a therapist or a team member be able to trust his/her intuitions. As Milton Erickson observed, "I always *trust* my unconscious. Now, too many psychotherapists try to *plan* what thinking they will do instead of waiting to see what the stimulus they receive is and then letting their unconscious mind RESPOND to that stimulus" (Gordon & Meyers-Anderson, 1981, p. 17).

WHAT IS PARADOXICAL THERAPY?

Weeks and L'Abate (1982) refer to the problem of defining paradoxical interventions. They comment, "The definitions either seem so broad and abstract as to be meaningless or not broad enough to include all the techniques asserted to be paradoxical in nature" (p. 94). It may be that the problem lies in the attempt to measure what happens in therapy against criteria from the fields of mathematics and logic.

From this framework, paradoxical interventions can be seen as one class of unpredictable positions or approaches that can be taken by a therapist or a therapy team in which, given a client's or family's expectations, a *reversal* of the usual approach to a symptom or to related processes is proposed. This is not to deny that it is possible to demonstrate how certain techniques can answer the formal definitions of paradox, nor to suggest that paradox cannot be a useful metaphor and that the various compilations on paradoxical techniques do not offer valuable guidelines for making therapeutic choices and decisions. My argument is that the holographic metaphor can offer an alternative framework for considering stuckness and the process of therapy and change based on a theory of how the brain processes and responds to experience—albeit a theory that has by no means found universal approval.

De Shazer has asserted, "Any intervention, paradoxical or not, can be seen as built on a mirror image of the family patterns; thus it is erroneous to consider paradoxical interventions as something in a class by themselves. This view permits us to discard another notion that has not been too useful, namely, that it is the *thing* paradox that is the change agent" (1982[b], p. 82).

It is easy to see how the best known and perhaps most common paradoxical technique, symptom prescription, involves, in its various forms, a reversal of an expected position or approach. Whether compliance or defiance based approaches are being used (Rohrbaugh et al., 1977; 1981), the client or family expects to be helped to *decrease* or be rid of a symptom and is instructed or advised to *increase* it. In this and other approaches, what usually is perceived as negative and harmful can be framed as positive and helpful, even vital. "Slow down" can be recommended rather than "improve." The therapist is expected to be helpful and an expert. Yet s/he may define the situation as hopeless or declare impotence rather than encourage change. Or the therapist may accept or exaggerate a position taken by the client or family on a symptom or related processes.

It is not my intention here to elaborate on the various kinds of paradoxical techniques or to translate them into this framework: If necessary, the reader can do this quite easily for him- or herself. Such compilations can be of great help, particularly for beginners to an approach. My reservation, however, with lists of techniques, together with indications and contraindications for their use, is that they can become reified and lead to clients or families being classified and 'fitted' into preconceived categories. As Gordon and Meyers-Anderson (1981) observe, "Very often the kind of changes that a particular therapist will pursue with clients are those that are consistent with the *therapist's* model of the world (professional training and personal experiences) rather than a function of, and related to, the *client's* model of the world. The point is that our private and professional beliefs/standards/rules do not encompass what is possible, but instead LIMIT what is possible." They go on to point out that this tendency "...is dependent upon the presuppositions that what is effective for one person can be effective for another, that problem situations that share a common name and experiential description are structurally isomorphic" (p. 12).

I have used unpredictable reversals of expected therapeutic positions in a whole range of situations, including many that have appeared in various listings of contraindications, and achieved positive results. One such intervention with a chaotic and potentially violent family (see contraindications listed by Fisher et al., 1981) will be described in the next section. A careful analysis of any situation, with particular reference to the assessment framework described earlier, should help ensure that interventions fit with a client's or family's beliefs, anxieties, fears, and expectations, and so on. As Erickson observed, "In dealing with people you try not to fit them into your concept of what they should be

...you try to discover what their concept of themselves happens to be" (Gordon & Meyers-Anderson, 1981, p. 34).

Team Interventions

A number of papers have addressed the use of teams in therapy and have elaborated on a variety of techniques, many based on the transmission of "expert" opinions, or the utilization of the potentials for triangulation inherent in the approach (Breunlin & Cade, 1981; Cade, 1980; Cade & Cornwell, 1983; de Shazer, 1982[a], 1983; Hoffman, 1981; Palazzoli et al., 1978; Papp, 1980; Speed et al., 1982). In this section, I will concentrate on those interventions in which the team reports or demonstrates changes in its position or dynamics, with the therapist usually adopting a neutral position or, on some occasions, identifying with the client's or family's position. A reality is projected, as it were, through the one-way mirror, which in part mirrors facets of a client's/family's beliefs or processes, and often addresses aspects of the therapy process.

A woman sought help with her fifteen-year-old daughter who she said was out of control and an inveterate liar. The mother claimed to hate the daughter who, in turn, claimed to hate her mother. The only thing both could agree upon was that the mother's cohabitant of some four years duration and a younger, thirteen-year-old daughter were in no way involved in the problem and should in no way be involved in the therapy.

In the first interview, the couple fought bitterly and viciously over every issue, often screaming at each other, leaving the therapist confused and, unable to steer the interview into a more constructive channel, feeling totally impotent. The therapist vainly sought some positives in the relationship, but to no avail: The couple often ignored her attempts to calm things down and to seek further information.

After about one-half hour the team called the therapist out for a consultation and evolved the following intervention. The therapist returned looking angry and confused, slamming the interview room door behind her. She apologized for coming back feeling somewhat "ratty" and reported that the consultation had been most unhelpful because there had been a lot of disagreement among the team.

> Some of my team feel that I have not listened carefully enough to you nor understood the depth of feeling going on between you, and how deep-seated the feelings of hatred are. They feel I've been trying to look for positive feelings between you where they, in fact,

do not exist. My team has left me totally confused. One of my colleagues, with a lot of experience working with potentially violent or violent families, has told me that it is often surprisingly the two members of a family who are, deep down, the closest to each other who seem to get locked into battles such as you've described. He says there's nothing you can do but go on struggling with each other. That sounds very confusing to me but that is what they said.

The mother immediately asked whether it would be helpful if she gave a complete history from the time of her daughter's birth (something the therapist had tried to take earlier without success). Mother and daughter then began to muse together over how very close they had been through the many difficulties they had shared, first as unsupported mother and child and then bringing up the younger girl together. They smiled frequently at each other and cooperated to give the therapist a comprehensive picture of how good things were until four years ago, each building on the other's contributions. As they discussed more recent events, they again started to bicker. Immediately the team called through to the therapist and advised her to look angry, to repeat into the telephone that she had not the slightest idea of what the team was talking about, and then to leave the room.

After a gap of some ten minutes the therapist returned, again looking angry and confused and slamming the door.

Therapist: I don't know what's got into my team today; they are totally at sixes and sevens.

Mother: [With a wry smile] I think they need a bit of therapy.

Therapist: Perhaps they do; they're certainly giving me lots of mixed messages and have succeeded in confusing me more. In fact I feel that the most help I've had during the last hour or so has been from you two, and not from them. Because we now have no time left, all I can do is share with you my confused impressions of what they have given me, and then arrange a further appointment. So I will be left with my confusion and must try to clarify and make sense of things.

One colleague keeps on insisting that you two must have loved each other very deeply to be behaving as you are now.... There's a very strong feeling in the team, and this is confusing to me, that... er...they seem to have some catastrophic expectation that something dreadful would happen if things changed. They seem to feel that if you two were not having terrible fights, hating each other the way you do, that things would go wrong for other members of the family, perhaps between you [*indicating the mother*] and your younger daughter, or between you and your man, or between you [*indicating the daughter*] and your grandmother [with whom she was apparently very close]. I need to go away and think about this and try to sort things out. I'll see you both at your next appointment.

The therapist then quickly ushered the puzzled couple out of the room, the woman saying she would discuss this with her cohabitant, the girl saying she would discuss it with her sister.

At the following session, four weeks later, all four members of the family arrived and reported dramatic improvements. The mother explained these changes as probably being the result of the daughter's sudden decision about four weeks ago to join a youth club and to take a Saturday job to supplement her pocket money. The family in no way related the changes to the therapy nor was any responsibility claimed by the therapist who remained cautiously pleased for them that things seemed to have sorted themselves out.

Two years later, a follow-up visit by a researcher found that the improvements had been maintained, there had been no recurrence of the problems between them, nor had any other problems developed. The girl was now in full-time employment and her relationship with her mother was described as good. When asked about the therapy team, the woman smiled and said that while she felt they could doubtless have been of help to many families, "I think we just had them completely confused." This highlights a major problem with the follow up of cases in which such interventions are used. The client or family is usually unaware that an intervention has been made and changes are rarely attributed to the therapy. Perhaps all that can be shown with certainty is that sometimes, after many years of symptomatic behaviour, things begin to improve "coincidentally" just after a particular kind of intervention has been used.

A chaotic family with multiagency involvements, who had been the subject of regular case conferences, was brought for a series of consultations by their social worker. She felt totally stuck, knew she had become overinvolved, but was unable, because of official concerns, to disengage herself.

The family consisted of Enid, a 33-year-old "depressed and severely agoraphobic" mother with three children, William, 14, Sally, 11, and Cristopher, 4. Sally had become a truant from school and there were suspicions that she was also being sexually promiscuous: In the sessions she certainly behaved in a provocative manner. The mother had an older sister, Joanna, 35, an alchoholic who slept in rough derelict houses but regularly visited the family, often extremely drunk: At such times, Enid would carefully bath her and put her to bed. There was also a younger brother of 30 who was mentally subnormal, prone to violent outbursts, and a patient in a local psychiatric hospital situated immediately behind the family's house. This brother would come over the wall nearly every night and often caused havoc. The family lived in considerable fear that he might harm one of the children because of his extreme jealousy of the attention they received from Enid. The hospital claimed they could not restrain him because he was a voluntary patient (though they sent a burly orderly with him for the first two therapy sessions "in case he were to become violent"). A lodger also lived in the house, a 50-year-old subnormal man who was suspected of having some sexual contact with the children, but was otherwise seen as "quiet and harmless."

The social worker had managed, thus far, to keep this chaotic family together, despite considerable opinion that the children should be removed from the house for their physical and moral safety.

Though in the initial sessions reasonable contact was made with the various members of this family, the therapy hour was always chaotic. The noise level was high and increased dramatically whenever an intervention was attempted, family members often arguing together and occasionally striking out at each other.

The team learned gradually that Enid's older sister had been very close to their father and that her brother had been their mother's favorite, in spite of the trouble he caused her through his aggressive behaviour. Enid had, in many ways, been the Cinderella of the family; she had worked hard to care for them all, yet had never been or felt recognized or loved. The father had died many years earlier, at which point *Joanna* had begun drinking more and more heavily. The mother had died two and one-half years earlier, at which point *Enid* had become increasingly symptomatic.

The family's attitude towards therapy alternated rapidly between anger that so many professionals were attempting to interfere and tell them how to run their lives, and desperate appeals—particularly by Enid—for someone to help. The social worker would receive frequent emergency telephone calls from or about the family: Upon arriving at their house, she would find them resistant or puzzled as to why she was there.

At the end of the fourth consultation session with the family, I entered the room after a period of consultation with my colleagues. I looked distressed and reported that my team had had a big argument. One side had asserted that the family members were doing quite well and did not need the continual interference of so many social agencies. The other side felt that Enid particularly needed considerable help to carry out an important task she had undertaken on behalf of the whole family since the death of her mother. Enid had recognized how much the family needed and missed her mother (who herself had rarely gone out of the house) and, even though Enid had to sacrifice many aspects of her own life, she had decided to become her mother—to stay at home and always to be available when needed. Since this was an extremely difficult task, Enid required the constant help and support of the social worker to carry it out. Her brother and sister and, particularly, daughter Sally were viewed by this side of the team as sensitive to the whole family's needs, and their troublesome behaviours were, in a way, a help in that they kept Enid continually worried and depressed and thus unlikely to think about going out and not be constantly available to the household.

Enid soon began to reject this idea and to say she did not want the responsibility of being this mother figure. I agreed with her and claimed I had tried to tell my team the same thing but they had insisted that it was important, not only that she continue to take her mother's place for her sister and brother, but that she also assume a grandparent role for her children, all of whom had been very close to and missed their grandmother.

"I cannot step into my mother's shoes," Enid protested, "My mother was an old woman!"

"That's what *I* told them," I said, "but they insisted that it was vital that you continue to fill these roles—mother to your brother and sister and grandmother to your children."

Enid began to protest more vehemently, insisting that she should be able to have a life of her own. The more Enid expressed determination about not wanting to take on this responsibility, the more I claimed that I had tried explaining this to my team, but that they had persisted in emphasizing the importance of her remaining responsible, and that she thus needed the help of the social worker to continue with this difficult but necessary task.

Finally, I promised Enid that I would try to sort things out with my team. I stated repeatedly that I was feeling confused as to what they expected and thus was unable to give any advice. I said I would be in touch with the social worker if I succeeded in making any sense of what had been said. As she prepared to leave the interviewing room, using the one-way mirror to adjust the head scarf she was putting on, Enid, as though she suddenly recognized how wearing it the way she did made her look much older, started to laugh and said, "Well, I suppose I might as well put on this old scarf."

A few months later, the social worker wrote to report that Enid had become far more independent. She had undertaken her own negotiations with the Social Security department, was going out much more and looking far less dowdy, and had coped with a particularly trying period during which two of her children had been hospitalized. Though under great stress, Enid regularly visited both children in their separate hospitals; one such visit required a fifty-mile bus journey. The social worker wrote, "I have a feeling that Enid's newfound independence is increasing her confidence and she seems at the moment to be making all positive attempts to resolve her own situation." Enid had written to both her member of parliament and a local counselor about the psychiatric hospital's unhelpful attitude toward the family's fears about her brother's disruptive behaviour and potential for violence. The social worker was careful to point out to me that her "only involvement in this was to supply her [Enid] with a pen."

In another case, a couple was referred by their general practitioner for marital therapy. The husband was simultaneously receiving outpatient treatment for "schizophrenia," following a series of psychotic breakdowns over the previous ten years during each of which he had been hospitalized and treated primarily with drugs.

In an early session, the team had framed his *illness* as his attempt, on behalf of his family of origin, to keep alive the memory of a sister who had died several years before his birth. The man had not only been born on his sister's birthday but at the same time of day, a coincidence that had always been seen by his parents as somehow having special significance. As far back as he could remember, the man's birthday had always been, for his family, a day of mourning.

This framing produced an initial improvement but, during the fourth session, the man began to exhibit many of the symptoms described earlier as the first signs of an impending and usually rapid breakdown. He was becoming increasingly preoccupied with the meaning of life as *revealed* to him during his previous psychotic episodes. He was excitedly sharing these revelations with the therapist in an increasingly agitated manner, talking volubly over her frustrated attempts to seek further information about the couple's wider family context.

As the man's thought processes became more and more disordered, his wife, a nurse by profession, looked on with calm concern. Finally, with a look of anguish, he said despairingly that anybody who is not a schizophrenic could never understand what he was trying to communicate. Shortly after this interaction, the therapist came out for a consultation: The man continued talking excitedly to his wife.

The therapist was advised to return to the session with a look of agitated concern and report that one of her colleagues had just begun to understand what the man had been saying and had become quite disturbed. The therapist was further advised to say that her colleague felt it extremely important that she ask some questions concerning the couple's wider family context. The man became instantly calm and for the rest of the session cooperated in answering all of the therapist's questions without any further sign of his "disturbed" behaviour.

During this second part of the session it was ascertained that in the man's family of origin and his wife's family, there were relationship problems about which he often worried. During his breakdowns each family would visit him and express caring and concern. When "sane," however, both families rejected him, and any expressions of concern *by him* for their various problems would lead to angry denials and claims that his worries stemmed from his psychiatric condition, a claim echoed by his consultant psychiatrist.

At the end of the session, the following intervention was devised. The therapist returned, again looking concerned, and reported that the colleague who had begun to understand what the man had been expressing had, during the consultation, attempted to convince the rest of the team of the importance of the man remaining unsuccessful and a psychiatric patient. He had warned them that, if the man let go of his dead sister's memory or became successful in leading a normal family life, serious problems could possibly arise in either his or his wife's family. She further reported that the more this colleague tried to convince the team, the more they became upset and angry and rejected his warnings.

The colleague became increasingly agitated as he continued trying to convey his worries to the team, who in turn became increasingly angry with him, defining his ideas as crazy. "At this point," said the therapist, "I called the consultation to a halt, and so I can only leave you with this confused account of what has happened in my team and I will see your in four weeks time." The couple politely thanked the therapist and left without comment.

In the next session, the couple reported considerable improvements in both the man's state of mind and their relationship. Therapy was discontinued after two more sessions. Two years later the couple's family practitioner reported continued improvements. The man had been working, and would call into the surgery occasionally for a chat and sometimes for a mild tranquilizer to help him through a particular period of stress.

In all three examples of unexpected team interventions, the *reality* presented as existing behind the one-way mirror had replicated and evoked, analogically, nodal issues or struggles in the families or the process of therapy. These realities were based on the team's observations of how family members repeatedly dealt with each other and the therapy, and its hypotheses about the underlying rules and beliefs through which family members interpreted their experiences. The therapist then expressed and acted out the feelings that had been evoked in him or her by the way(s) in which the family had thus far been dealing with the therapy.

As suggested earlier, families can often evoke strong responses in a therapist by their behaviours: Often more of the same behaviours by family members will recover more of the same responses from the therapist and vice versa. These responses, however, must in no way be blamed on the family but rather on the team's internal struggles, and no overt or impled linkup should be made for the family between these realities and their own attitudes and behaviours, which must in no way be negatively connoted.

Through reframing or relabeling, new meanings were placed on nodal issues. The therapists, usually by remaining neutral with respect to the team's interventions, or sometimes by identifying with the family's or a family member's position, stepped out of the framework that had been eliciting the more of the same responses. The sorting-out of the issues evoked was presented as the responsibility of the therapists and their team; and it was implied that, for the time being, therapy would come to a halt until these issues had been resolved.

As I have commented elsewhere:

> At the following session, regardless of how effective the intervention appears to have been or not to have been, it is usually best to make no mention of the "struggle" unless specifically asked. In the author's experience, it is rare for a family to inquire. If, however, an inquiry is made, it is best that the "struggle" be reported as not having been resolved, even though the "feelings" may, if necessary, be reported as having diminished or settled. This is because to resolve the "struggle" in favour of one side is likely, by implication, to negatively connote the other. (Cade, 1980, p. 261)

Interestingly, as highlighted at the follow-up interview with the mother in the first example, the families will be unaware that any therapeutic intervention has been made; thus, even though considerable change may occur following their use, family members can only assume they have brought about such change themselves. At follow-up interviews, when asked about their experiences of the team behind the one-way mirror, families have never, in our experience, "remembered" such interventions.

These interventions, we have found, tend only to be effective where an impasse has been reached in the therapy. When we have used them as techniques to shortcut the process of therapy, they have had little effect. It is as though the potency of the interventions arises out of the experiences of deadlock from which the team derives the necessary, and perhaps often unconscious, information for their construction.

Some of the basic "unexpected" maneuvers upon which such interventions can be devised and built have been elaborated elsewhere (Cade & Cornwell, 1985). Briefly, they include:

a. The criticisms by the team of some aspect(s) of the therapist's behaviours, and/or apparent beliefs and attitudes that can be seen as underpinning his/her approach to the family. Such criticisms will reflect and express directly, or by analogy, aspects of the family's more resistant responses to and apparent feelings about the therapy. Thus, development of a symmetrical struggle between family and therapist can be diverted or blocked and the interview often moved in a more constructive direction, the family's position having been understood and also powerfully expressed by the team.

b. The reporting by the therapist of opinions, advice, cautions, and so on sent through by the team about which s/he remains neutral, by claiming, for example, incomprehension, puzzlement, or total confusion. The therapist can, in this way, avoid being pulled into a struggle over the content of an intervention. S/he can claim to be unable to explain the message, yet remain sympathetic to the family's struggles to understand and deal with what has been said.

c. A declaration of impotence by the therapist or by the team. No blame must be attached—either directly or by implication—to family members, and no hint of challenge, disapproval, or sarcasm must be betrayed.

Maneuvers such as these tend to reverse the flow of a session in which the therapist's previous approach has been recovering increasing levels of resistance to the incorporation of new information on the part of the family or particular family members.

ETHICS

There will always be critics for whom such techniques will be seen as manipulative, controlling, and dishonest, particularly the presentation of manufactured realities, as described above. However, this framework raises an interesting ethical issue. If stuckness in families and therapy can be seen, in part, as a function of a reified diagnostic framework repeatedly focused on the situation, so that the same associations and responses continue to be recovered, is it ethical to adhere to that framework in the face of no change occurring, or even to find a way of "blaming" the family by defining them as lacking in insight, resistant, or untreatable?

I will always remember the case of a forty-five-year-old man who had been told by a psychiatrist that no help was possible at his age because he would need five years of intensive analysis before it would be possible even to begin addressing his sexual problems. No doubt the psychiatrist concerned was being "honest" from his framework. Unfortunately, this honesty prevented the man from seeking further help. He had believed the diagnosis and it had become part of his own belief framework that he was untreatable.

I am in agreement with the view of Watzlawick et al. (1974) and Haley (1976) that it is impossible *not* to manipulate. The question can never be whether or not to manipulate, but rather how much and in what way will be most helpful in any particular case. The myth that it is possible to avoid manipulation is at best a utopian self-deception; at worst, and particularly when coupled with the belief that there is a *correct* view of reality, it can add considerably to the distress of individuals and families as they are forced, sometimes subtly, sometimes through the power of medical or legal authority, to accept the therapist's view of reality, especially when defined as unmotivated, resistant, defiant, untreatable, inadequate, and so on.

My view is that it is possible to see these interventions as introducing, through analogy, a range of alternative perspectives that will refer to more significant truths for the family in that they are usually framed with respect to underlying and often denied themes and struggles. If there is deceit, it is only in the trappings surrounding the transmission of the essential framework of ideas. The effectiveness of any intervention will depend on the validity of the offered perspectives and their relevance to the individual or family, rather than on the means by which they are introduced.

Weeks and L'Abate (1982) have highlighted the importance of not using such techniques as gimmicks, or out of frustration when therapy seems flat or families uncooperative. They underline the importance of making responsible decisions based not only on intuition but also on careful analysis of each case.

CONCLUSION

Although, throughout this chapter, I have been using principles from holography as a *metaphor* to help consider the processes of stuckness and change, there are those, particularly Karl Pribram (1976), who believe that our brains do work on such principles.

A recent paper in *New Scientist* (Zuccarelli, 1983) has proposed that, in hearing, the ear not only receives sound but also transmits it and then analyzes the resulting interference pattern or "acoustic hologram." Some scientists, notably the physicist David Bohm (1980), have gone further and proposed that the whole universe is constructed on holographic principles.

REFERENCES

Bohm, D., *Wholeness and the implicate order.* London: Routledge & Kegan Paul, 1980.

Breunlin, D. C., & Cade, B. W. Intervening in family systems using observer messages. *Journal of Marital and Family Therapy,* 1981, 7, 453–460.

Breunlin, D. C., Cornwell, M., & Cade, B. W. International trade in family therapy: Parallels between societal and therapeutic values. In C. J. Falicov (Ed.), *Cultural perspectives in family therapy.* Md.: Aspen Systems Corp. 1983.

Cade, B. W. Resolving therapeutic deadlocks using a contrived team conflict. *International Journal of Family Therapy,* 1980, 2, 253–262.

Cade, B. W., & Cornwell, M. The evolution of the one-way screen. *The Australian Journal of Family Therapy,* 1983, 4, 73–80.

Cade, B. W., & Cornwell, M. New realities for old: Some uses of teams and one-way screens in therapy. In D. Campbell & R. Draper (Eds.), *Applications of systemic family therapy.* London: Academic Press, 1984.

de Bono, E. *The mechanism of mind.* Middlesex, Eng.: Pelican Books, 1971.

de Shazer, S. *Patterns of brief family therapy: An ecosystemic approach.* New York: Guilford Press, 1982. (a)

de Shazer, S. Some conceptual distinctions are more useful than others. *Family Process,* 1982, 21, 71–84. (b)

de Shazer, S. Some bonuses of using a team approach to family therapy. In L. R. Wolberg & M. L. Aronson (Eds.), *Group and Family Therapy, 1982.* New York: Brunner/Mazel, 1983.

Erickson, M. H., & Rossi, E. L. *Hypnotherapy: An exploratory casebook.* New York: Irvington Publishers, 1979.

Fisher, L., Anderson, A., & Jones, J. E. Types of paradoxical intervention and indications and contraindications for use in clinical practice. *Family Process,* 1981, 20, 25–35.

Gordon, D., & Meyers-Anderson, M. *Phoenix: Therapeutic patterns of Milton H. Erickson.* California: Meta Publications, 1981.

Haley, J. *Strategies of psychotherapy.* New York: Grune & Stratton, 1963.

Haley, J. *Uncommon therapy: The psychiatric techniques of Milton H. Erickson, M.D.,* New York: W. W. Norton, 1973.

Haley, J. *Problem solving therapy.* New York: Jossey-Bass, 1976.

Hoffman, L. *Foundations of family therapy.* New York: Basic Books, 1981.

Neil, J. R., & Kniskern, D. P. *From psyche to system: The evolving therapy of Carl Whitaker.* New York: Guilford Press, 1982.

Palazzoli, M. S., Boscolo, L., Cecchin, G., & Prata, G. *Paradox and counter-paradox: A new model for the therapy of the family in schizophrenic transition.* Paper presented to the 5th International Symposium on Psychotherapy of Schizophrenia, Oslo, 1975.

Palazzoli, M. S., Boscolo, L., Cecchin, G., & Prata, G. *Paradox and counter-paradox.* New York: Jason Aronson, 1978.

Palazzoli, M. S. Comments on Paul Dell's Some irreverent thoughts on paradox. *Family Process,* 1981, *20,* 37–51.

Papp, P. The Greek chorus and other techniques of family therapy. *Family Process,* 1930, *19,* 45–58.

Pribram, K. *Consciousness and the brain.* New York: Plenum, 1976.

Rohrbaugh, M., Tennen, H., Press, S., White, L., Raskin, P., & Pickering, M. *Paradoxical Strategies in Psychotherapy.* Paper presented at the American Psychological Association, San Francisco, Calif. 1977.

Rohrbaugh, M., Tennen, H., Press, S., & White, L. Compliance, defiance and therapeutic paradox. *American Journal of Orthopsychiatry,* 1981, *51,* 454–467.

Russell, P. *The brain book.* London: Routledge & Kegan Paul, 1979.

Speed, B., Seligman, P., Kingston, P., & Cade, B. W. A team approach to therapy. *The Journal of Family Therapy,* 1982, *4,* 271–284.

Watzlawick, P., Beavin, J., & Jackson, D. D., *Pragmatics of human communication.* New York: W. W. Norton, 1967.

Watzlawick, P., Weakland, J. H., & Fisch, R. *Change: Principles of problem formation and problem resolution.* New York: W. W. Norton, 1974.

Weakland, J. H., Fisch, R., Watzlawick, P., & Bodin, A. Brief therapy: Focused problem resolution. *Family Process,* 1974, *13,* 141–168.

Weeks, G., & L'Abate, L. A compilation of paradoxical methods, *American Journal of Family Therapy,* 1979, *7,* 61–76.

Weeks, G., & L'Abate, L. *Paradoxical psychotherapy: Theory and practice with individuals, couples and families.* New York: Brunner/Mazel, 1982.

Wellwood, J. The holographic paradigm and the structure of experience. In K. Wilber (Ed.), *The Holographic Paradigm: and Other Paradoxes*, Boulder, Colo.: Shambhala, 1982.

Zuccarelli, H. Ears hear by making sounds, *New Scientist*, 1983, *100*, (1383), 438–440.

3

Beyond Paradox and Counterparadox

by Klaus G. Deissler, Diplompsychologe

Now this going with the wind or the current, plus the intelligence pattern of the human organism, is the whole art of sailing—of keeping wind in your sails while tacking in a contrary direction.

Alan Watts

FOREWORD

Much has been thought and written about paradoxes—indeed a whole type of therapy has been named after it. In my opinion, so much has now been written about therapeutic paradoxes that I get the feeling I am dealing with a "gnawed and old bone" about the state of which there is very little left to write. The most important articles and books have already been written (for detailed bibliographical notes, see Weeks & L'Abate, 1982).

The question is then: What is there left to say?

I. HISTORICAL INFLUENCES

A. People Who Have Directly Influenced My Thinking

When I maintain that paradoxical communication is an everyday phenomenon (Sluzki & Ransom, 1976), this in itself says just as much or as little as Milton Erickson's statement that trance is an everyday phenomenon. It is only when we come to define such statements more closely that it becomes possible to draw conclusions about their usefulness (on trance as an everyday phenomenon, see, e.g., Erickson & Rossi, 1979).

I was first introduced to paradoxes by my maternal grandfather. He was regarded as a kind man in our family, but he could also do mysterious things, for example, take away the sting from burns. It was this grandfather, too, who would offer my sisters and me one deutsche mark if we had hiccups and could deliberately produce at least 10 repetitions. Our efforts were usually in vain.

On other occasions he gave us "riddles": he would ask, "What is it? It hangs on the wall and goes tick-tock, and if it falls down the clock is broken." The answer to this riddle is so obviously implied—it is a clock. What I did not notice as a child, though, was that my grandfather created an interrogatory attitude or soft confusion. The answer to the riddle is so obvious that the person trying to solve it has to ask himself subconsciously, "What's the point of this silly riddle?" or "What answer does this person want by asking a question such as that?" The trick in this case is to evoke an inquisitive or searching attitude. Of course, as a child I missed the point of the next suggestion from my grandfather. For example, he would say, "Come on, finish your dinner, we want to go to town." However, it gets worse: The paradox with which he confronted me that influenced me most was the fact that he could make me inquisitive about all the mysterious acts he could perform. When as a teenager I asked him to explain, for example, how he could take away the pain from burns, he would not give me an answer. This had a tremendous effect on me: I became even more inquisitive and, disappointed, I resolved to find my own answers. In any case, it was my grandfather who aroused my interest in indirect interpersonal influence, and who more or less directly suggested that I go into psychology and later study indirect suggestion. I had an "aha experience" when I read Haley's book on Erickson in 1974 (Haley, 1973).

B. Works Which Have Influenced My Thinking

I had long forgotten about the stories with my grandfather. However, after I obtained my degree in psychology in 1974, having found the course rather boring, I realized I was dissatisfied with what I had learned up to then. Toward the end of my degree work I became acquainted with an older doctor from whom I was learning autogenic training (see Schultz, 1966; Thomas, 1972). This doctor apparently also mastered other hypnotherapeutic techniques, but was not willing to teach them to me as he wanted to reserve them for other medical doctors. My further attempts at finding out about hypnotherapeutic methods in German-speaking countries were rather disappointing: The procedures were authoritarian; they had the hallmark of a "white-coat mentality"; and they were heavily ritualized. What I was looking for were indirect, more flexible procedures that stood out through their artistry.

Just before I took my degree I read Watzlawick's classic, *Pragmatics of Human Communication* (Watzlawick, Beavin, & Jackson, 1967). This book was for me the starting point for intensive studies that went in two particular directions: (1) the practice of psychotherapy—effect patterns that circulate in therapeutic communication; and (2) the theory of human systems—higher connections or process patterns that are able to provide the instruments of analysis in therapeutic processes.

I came across a further puzzle, or "koan," when dealing with pathogenic and also constructive or creative double binds (see, e.g., Haley, 1963; Bateson, 1969; Berger, 1978; Erickson & Rossi, 1975). This "koan" concerned me until about 1979, the year in which I met both Mara Selvini and her team, and Gregory Bateson. At that point in my therapeutic work, I became a systemic family therapist; at the same time, my work has been committed to Ericksonian hypnotherapy since 1976. The interim end of my therapeutic development consisted of combining Erickson's practical genius with Bateson's theoretical genius: Perhaps we can call the result "contextual psychotherapy."

II. PARADOXICAL THERAPY—A CONCISE TERM FOR SELF-REFLEXIVE THERAPEUTIC CONFUSION?

A. The Double Bind Theory

The double bind theory was originally conceived by Bateson et al. (1956) as a way of freeing the term *schizophrenia* of its biological and intrapsychic implications and finding an explanatory model for schizophrenic behavior with a more social base. Whether this function has been fulfilled is open to discussion. In psychotherapy, however, the double bind theory did turn out to be a "branching criterion" or parting of the ways for the therapeutic mind. Some therapists dealt with the double bind theory without being able to master it; they remained loyal to their old mechanistic epistemology. Others left this theory behind and turned to systemic and cybernetic thinking and action models (see Bateson, 1969). The most influential development and adaption of Bateson's ideas were carried out in Milan (see Selvini-Palazzoli, 1978).

However, let us stay for the moment with the double bind theory. Watzlawick et al. (1967) and Erickson & Rossi (1975) in particular used the double bind theory explicitly for therapeutic purposes by constructing situations that helped their clients out of the context of negative alternatives and put them in the position of not being able to lose. I need not stress the fact that construction of such double binds requires practice, skill, and precise knowledge of the client's problems. If a therapist manages to persuade a couple who have not been on holiday for 20 years that they have a choice of going to Spain or the Alps, this is a classical form of double bind—even if the couple finally decides to go to Italy.

B. Criticism of the Double Bind Theory: "Paradox"

Discussion about expressions, concepts, and theories in psychotherapy are often, in my opinion, hairsplitting or a "war with words" (see Shands, 1971). An example of this war with words was, for me, the discussion of Dell's (Dell, 1982) and Keeney's (Keeney, 1982) articles in the journal, *Family Process*. The attempt to bring about conceptual clarity only results in more confusion than there was before. (In principle, articles like these are relationship offers or definitions themselves. Perhaps a few clear statements offer clarity, which may be used as suggestions by some readers (see Erickson, 1964). In the light of these remarks what follows should not be taken too literally or seriously.

1. The Need to Differentiate. When human beings are not in a state of meditation, trance, or confusion, they are dependent on making decisions in order to come to terms with their world. Among the most important differentiations they must make are figure and ground, text and context, and element and class. These differentiations can be scrambled or resigned; for example, figure and class, text and ground, and element and context. Sometimes such reassignments are useful; however, they change nothing of the basic need to make differentiations. As is implicit in the above considerations, one of the most important possibilities for making differentiations is to define units that are parts of higher units. Of course paradox can be defined as the situation in which a unit is a part of itself. Bateson has formulated this thought in various connections following Whitehead and Russell (see, e.g., Bateson, 1972).

If in this connection we prevent an element from being a part of itself, we thwart the possibility of a creative solution. Unfortunately, the theory of "logical types" recommends this prevention and most thinkers who have dealt with paradoxes have accepted it uncritically. On the other hand, it is equally foolish to replace the interdiction of confusing element and higher unit with a new one, that is, to forbid differentiating between different context levels or extensions. In so doing, one robs oneself of the newly won freedom by replacing an old restriction with a new one.

2. The Need to Consider "Time."   I will restrict myself to remarking that the problem of the "self-including unit" could be claimed as partially resolved through the factor *time*. Astute thinkers might argue as follows: The classical form of paradox implies two presuppositions: (1) There is a differentiation between class and element; and (2) A defined order category can be class and element of itself at the same time.

The second presupposition thus relies on simultaneity. If one were to allow time to enter the consideration, one could disentangle confusion or avoid paradox by avoiding simultaneity. *First* a defined unit can be considered as a class that includes a number of elements. *Then* this class can be considered as a unit which is an element of a higher class; thus this defined unit can be class and element depending on what order category one selects *successively*. If one were to now oscillate between the two functions of this defined unit (class and element), one could postulate that this was the class that includes itself or the element that was its own class. This simple but exhausting trick is also often used when the linearity of language is applied to describe patterns of action which are recursive. In this case, the linear-causal *if-then* chain of logic is attached to or equated with the linear-successive *first-then* chain of time. If we proceed in this way, however, we rob ourselves of a perception, which was suggested by cybernetics through the term *feedback* which means recursive processes (*re* is a Latin prefix meaning *back*).

A way of better understanding the human "self" (understanding oneself) is thus to consider recursiveness. The perception *self* implies of course recursivenes: What I am doing feeds back (recurses) to myself. Thus considering time can help to avoid confusion by oscillating between the two functions of a defined unit—class and element—but this oscillating process is rather strenuous and time-consuming. Additionally, the perception of the unit which includes itself is a rather solid and static one. So it is necessary to postulate more fluid patterns, processes influencing themselves through recursiveness.

3. The Need to Consider Self-reference, Recursiveness, or Autonomy. Living beings are characterized by something which has been described in different terms: self-reference, self-monitoring, self-organization, and so on—in brief, autonomy. Maturana and Varela have looked into this question in great detail (see, e.g., Maturana, 1982). Varela (1975) took Spencer-Brown's indication logics further and developed the "calculus for self-reference." At the same time, he added the "need to consider that of recursiveness" to the "need to consider difference."

In therapeutic terms this raises the question of the significance of recursiveness for living beings. Basically, we can differentiate between two possible types of recursiveness:

a. A planned action can be completed independently of contextual feedback. Living beings that act in this manner behave as if they were "closed, hard-programmed, autonomous systems."

b. Results or interim results have an effect along with other context variables on one's own actions and those of others. Living beings that act in this manner behave as if they were "open, soft-programmed, autonomous systems."

Maturana described the first case of recursiveness—the "machine model" of autonomous living beings. An example of such behavior would be a racing driver who does not care about the lives of others, who drives on, relentless toward victory. This kind of behavior is usually considered as "re-lentless [re (Latin) = back], straightforward, and powerful." It can be called "biological autonomy": All options of behavior are biologically programmed and easy to predict.

I should like to call the second type of behavior "contextual autonomy." Here, the social context of the action is taken into consideration. This kind of behavior is generally called "re-spectful, re-sponsible" and possibly even systemic humility" (see Bateson, 1972).

4. Conclusions for a Therapeutic Model. Contextual autonomy, described until now, implicitly focuses on one person, the context itself not being further described. Every family therapist knows, however, that there is a vital difference in speaking about individuals, relationships of individuals, or systems (of relationships of individuals). If we accept the need to differentiate, we can, when including recursiveness or autonomy, differentiate between different contextual extensions, that is, individual, relational, and systemic (composed of three or more persons).

It is also possible to differentiate between different contextual extensions and simultaneously attribute relative autonomy to them. Elsewhere I have called this process "recursive contextualization" (see Deissler, 1983). See Figure 1.

Each of these contextual extensions—individual, relational, or systemic—is taken in its own right, that is to say recursively, self-referentially, or self-inclusively. This way there is no longer paradox in the classical sense because the positing class that includes itself is essential for autonomy.

The next step consists of processes, which run through time in the model. Hoffman (1982) has suggested a model which she calls "Time Cable." This model includes time processes. If we try to transfer this model to the therapy process, we can introduce, for example, change of interlocutor as a "relationship parameter" in order to illustrate systemic processes in time. Figure 2 is a model of this kind of therapy session.

C. Conclusions

Room for confusion remains: an autonomous subsystem (e.g., member of family) is not identical with the higher autonomous system (e.g., family) of which it is a constituent subprocess. Even if we allow the possibility of transcendence, both types of process must be kept separate to avoid confusion. At the same time the following can be said of paradoxes in the classical sense:

1. The system that includes itself as a subprocess is by definition autonomous. Such systems are the rule rather than the exception in the field of living processes. Systems which do not have this recursiveness are "dead." Systems which are in addition self-productive or self-maintaining are called *autopoietic* by Maturana and Valera.

   When several autopoietic systems combine to form higher level systems, we can speak of self-organizing systems (see Jantsch, 1982).

2. If we then place the autopoietic system and self-organization of several such systems at the same level, we confuse the defined hypothetical differentiation limits between at least two system levels, which is useful in encouraging meditative exercises, induction of trance or, ecstatic states. On the other

FIGURE 1

The Recursive Contextualization of Natural Processes*

Systemic
process level

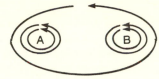

Any 3-person (or more)
   system
4 process extensions:

systemic	(1: ABC)
relational	(3: AB, BC, CA)
psychological	(3: A, B, C)
somatic	(3: A', B', C')

examples: family or couple
   therapy

Relational
process level

Any 2-person subsystem
3 process extensions:

relational	(1: AB)
psychological	(2: A, B)
somatic	(2: A', B')

examples: couple, individual
   therapy

Psychological
process level

Any 1-person subsystem
2 process extensions:

psychological	(1: A)
somatic	(1: A')

examples: member of family,
   member of therapeutic
   team

Somatic
process level

Any somatic subsystem
1 process extension:

somatic	(1: A')

examples: woman, man

*Graphical illustration within synchronic process perspectives, i.e., temporal processes are ignored. A diachronic illustration including time would have resulted in a multiple complex helix.

Source: Illustration from K. G. Deissler, "Die rekursive Kontextualisierung natürlicher Prozesse," *Familiendynamik* 1983, *8*, p. 145.

hand, a differentiation is useful if, for example, it is a question of understanding symptoms of autonomous individuals in self-organizing eco-groups (e.g. families).

3. Whether we call this kind of confusion (of at least two systems) a paradox depends on whether one allows oneself to be

FIGURE 2

The Person-Space-Time-Model of an Ongoing Self-Organizing Human System*

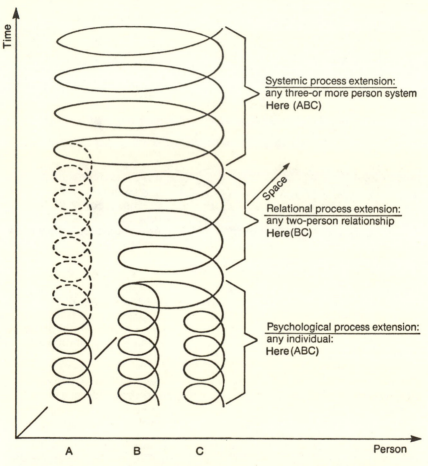

*As distinct from the synchronic illustration of the *recursive contextualization* (see Figure 1), the *diachronic* illustration considers *time* and *space* additionally. This means that the recursion model is extended to form a *multiple helix*.

I call this helix the *person-space-time-model* (PST) or co-relational-space-time-model of an ongoing self-organizing human system. The advantage of this model is that it allows specification of *systemic effect patterns* (which form a certain communication), *space* (where this communication takes place), and *time* (when this communication is enacted). These variables are considered necessary to define a human system.

confused or not. In my opinion, confusion is useful in the therapeutic process, for example, to encourage creative solutions, so the term *paradox* is no longer important. I prefer to follow Erickson and speak of utilizing systemic processes in a therapeutic context.

D. Systemic Utilization—An Alternative Model

Erickson is known as the person who introduced the utilization approach into psychotherapy—especially into hypnotherapy. If you want to help a client with his problems, it is necessary to know the exact nature of his problems, that is, the things he complains of. Moreover, it is also advantageous to know something of his positive resources, for example, the things he does not complain of. If you know both levels, it is possible to suggest two ways of getting the client to help himself: (1) The positive points can be used to displace those described as negative; and (2) Those described as negative can be "used" in such a way in therapy that the client is triggered to displace himself.

The second part is one which I should like to define here as the utilization approach and is closest to what is meant by paradoxical intervention. The following example may serve as an explanation:

A 10-year-old boy who lives with his mother and 2-year-old sister steals from his mother by taking money from her wallet and then spending it on toys and candy. The mother has tried unsuccessfully several ways of stopping the boy from stealing. The therapist decides to implement the utilization approach by using what is available to get the persons concerned to solve their problem. He observes the following conditions: (1) the relationship between mother and son; (2) The symptomatic relationship pattern: The son steals from the mother who tries in vain to solve the problem.

The therapist tells the mother to get a "theft bag." At the beginning of each week she is to put in five deutschemarks in one-mark coins. The son is told to steal a maximum of two marks a week from the theft bag. If he fulfills this condition, he receives an additional two marks pocket money as a reward. But if he takes more than two marks he gets no pocket money. This procedure should be continued for at least four weeks under the mother's supervision. In order to understand the task, it is necessary to know the following implications:

> The task has the mother make the theft possible. The mother has in addition the responsibility for carrying out the exer-

cise. Moreover, she has to get the theft bag. Finally, she has to put the money in the bag.

The stealing is redefined and by implication desirable.

The boy either steals the prescribed amount of a maximum two marks and is then rewarded by the mother with an additional two marks or he takes the money and forgoes the additional pocket money from his mother by rewarding himself for stealing.

Mother and son report at the next meeting that the son has taken no more than two marks per week and has regularly received two marks pocket money. At the same time, the son reports that it is no longer fun to take the money. In the next meeting, mother and son report that stealing is no longer an issue. They agreed in front of the therapist that the boy would get two marks a week pocket money and that the other two marks would be put into a savings account for larger purchases (for example, a bicycle). Thus this relationship between mother and son, with the therapist part of the therapeutic system, showed relational autonomy by parent and child deciding among themselves that the boy would no longer steal from his mother. Moreover, with the therapist's help mother and son found a new definition of their relationship.

This brief example describes a systemic process in which three persons are involved: mother, son, and therapist (see Figure 1). The therapist utilizes the relational process between mother and son by:

Accepting their definition of their relationship.

Prescribing symptomatic behavior, thus defining the relational process between mother and son as desirable, so that stealing is still described as such, but by implication a new definition of the relationship between mother and son is created.

In this way the son's symptom is utilized to redefine the relationship between mother and son. This is done by putting the mother in a benevolent, affirmative role towards her son, which allows him to do that which was previously forbidden or for which he was punished. This "permission" removes the son's opportunity to protest by stealing, and an opportunity to protest against this redefinition of the relationship is given by stopping the child from stealing. Through this therapeutic process, individual, symptomatic behavior is extended to a relational recursive context.

The most frequently-used term for this process is *reframing*. I prefer to call it *recontextualization*, since this term can be defined more precisely (see below).

The systemic utilization technique is composed of:

1. *Acceptance of the family's definition of their problem,* whether the problem is seen as an individual symptom, a relationship, or a multiperson conflict (see Figure 1).
2. Redefinition of one part of or the entire stated problem in a systemic-recursive context, by declaring it as positive, desirable, sensible, or useful in the frame of a recontextualization *(positive connotation).*
3. Implicit or explicit *recontextualization* by: (1) changing the "recursive context" (contextual extension. how many people are involved in the problem?); (2) changing the temporal context, if necessary; and (3) changing the spatial context, if necessary.
4. *Prescribing* in part or as a whole the *recursive patterns which affect* the problem or a further additional part.

E. Summary

1. Effective interventions always seem *paradoxical* when:
   a. Different contextual extensions are confused and thus we cannot differentiate between them.
   b. The behavior defined as a problem and the interventions aimed at this behavior are explained without considering time.
   c. The recursiveness of the different contextual extensions and thus their respective relative autonomy are disregarded; in other words, interventions seem paradoxical when linear explanatory models are used.
2. *Systemic utilization* provides an alternative. In the process, it is taken into account that symptoms and human behavior in general can be described on identical levels. From a therapeutic point of view, this involves choosing a process level for intervention which will most readily trigger an autonomous solution to the problem. These may range from habitual cognitive patterns of an individual to systemic effect patterns of a multiperson system. Thus possible interventions range from indirect hypnotherapy (see Erickson, 1980) to those methods derived from systemic family therapy (see Selvini-Palazzoli et al., 1978, 1980; Hoffman, 1981; Penn, 1982; de Shazer, 1982). It is the therapist's duty to accept the person-space-time continuum of which he has become a part and the subprocess to which it belongs—to learn to understand its essential systemic patterns. Using these ongoing processes in such a way that they can remove or solve themselves, the therapist or the therapy team contributes to the *autosystemic transformation* of the family (see Deissler & Gester, 1983).
3. Thus the purpose of systemic utilization is to allow the group

with the problems (see Haley, 1976), after a stage of systemic confusion to solve those problems through autonomous reorganization, in which the systemic effect patterns are reorganized. From this perspective, systemic utilizations intervene in the self-organizing of the human system by triggering solutions, evoking, suggesting, or preventing them which—paradoxically—strengthens the autonomy. Solutions that the family finds themselves are best, as each family is its own expert.

F. Final Metaphor

In situations in which parents push their children away, the children are particularly apt to cling to them. If parents, however, reciprocate (to excess) to the clinging of their children, the child will remember that it does not want to be clung to. S/he will strive to be free. Parents who love their children and value their own and their children's autonomy, give a little counterpressure at the right time or let them free themselves.

III. PSYCHOLOGICAL WELL-BEING AND PSYCHOLOGICAL SUFFERING

Somatic illness aside, the question arises as to whether psychological suffering is, like physical suffering, an illness—perceivable, objectifiable, measurable. Thomas Szasz, *The Myth of Mental Illness* (1974), is the person who has most emphatically pointed out the metaphorical nature of the term *mental* or *psychological illness*. However, if psychological suffering is a social and thus systemic phenomenon, relationships and systems of relationship are the focal points on which the observer—including oneself—must concentrate his attention (see Ruesch & Bateson, 1951). If the observer includes himself in his observations, he automatically defines himself as an autonomous subprocess of a larger observation unit. Thus the question of recursiveness once again enters our discussion.

The vital question in this context is: What is the epistemology of the person who calls himself a therapist with reference to the social phenomenon psychological suffering? (Thomas Szasz raises important questions here as well.) I should like to summarize my position using the following six basic points:

1. Psychological suffering is a systemic phenomenon involving at least the persons sharing the problem or those who consti-

tute it. We refer here especially to the closer ecological group whose member bears the symptom. When such a group enters a therapeutic relationship, the therapeutic organization shares the problem (see Haley, 1976). This group and the therapeutic team form a larger unit. This unit is the equivalent of an eco-systemic approach to human problems (see also Keeney, 1979; de Shazer, 1982; or Deissler, 1981).

2. According to the recursive contextualization model, those contextual extensions to social processes can be determined which constitute a psychological problem, maintain it, or can contribute to its solution. It is useful for therapeutic purposes to choose that contextual extension which is best able to provide an autonomous transformation of the systemic effect or relationship pattern. In most cases, this will be the contextual extension that includes close partners, that is, the family or eco-group.

3. Wherever possible, the therapist should avoid a *dualistic position* in which s/he appears as a member of a system of healthy relationships as opposed to a system of sick relationships, called upon from a position of health to "cure" the "illness" of the other system. Instead therapist and team should see themselves as a seam in the social interlacing with other eco-systemic subsystems. This method enables the therapist to become an autonomous part of the "consensual space" shared with a family seeking help (see Maturana, 1982). This way both parties—therapist and family—contribute to the solution of complex social problems, which avoids such juxtapositions as: therapist good, healthy, responsible—client bad, ill, guilty.

4. Psychotherapy, in particular systemic therapy, does not serve to enforce social control or power and thus adherence to social conventions, but to encourage *novelty*, that is, the creation of new information in relationships. Thus therapy may serve—indeed only within a small context—social variety. The old view that psychotherapy should serve to maintain social conventions and thus prevent transformational processes comes from linear cause-and-effect thinking, especially as used in custodial psychiatry.

5. The hypothetical construction "power in relationships" is seen by some authors as being central to the understanding and maintenance of psychological problems (see especially the work of Haley, e.g., 1959 or 1980).

   On the other hand some authors (see Bateson, 1972), suggested that it was not power itself but the *belief* in or epistemology of power that causes certain groups of people to become caught up in this model (see Stierlin, 1982). The therapist's job is to manipulate these "power games," to encourage or prescribe them in such a way that they become superfluous. Thus the family is helped to abandon its epistemology of power by implication in favor of a systemic epistemology which in turn can strengthen the family's autonomy.

Therapists who accept this point of view are *beyond the power construct:* If families behave according to the power construct, the therapist is accepting, but works with the family to transcend this construct by planning the power game, thus making it superfluous for the family.

6. The most abstract and general formulation of what accompanies psychological suffering in human relationships is that relationship systems are fluid (ongoing), systemic patterns that effect an accelerated evolution, and two conditions restrict the evolutionary nature of this effect pattern process. We can differentiate between these two diametrically opposed processes.

   a. The system that is in a permanent state of development, change, and reorganization has slowed its development rate due to specific events or the course of specific processes. We can call this changed speed of development *anachronic.* An example of this phenomenon is the family that cannot let its children become autonomous.

   b. The reverse situation in which development is too great is equally possible. For example, the severing of a child from the family happens too quickly or the members of the family have no reliable basis for a relationship, thus systemic effect patterns change more rapidly than those involved can tolerate. In such cases as above, family members compensate with symptoms. This kind of accelerated development can be called *metachronic.*

   c. In both cases, those involved have good reasons to accept the anachronic or metachronic developmental rate of change. It is the therapist's task to find these reasons—through an appropriate exploratory process—in order to use them effectively in therapy (an exploratory process which is a further development of "circular questioning" is described by Deissler, 1983).

IV. THERAPEUTIC METHODS

The following case is presented to give the reader closer insight into therapeutic process as practiced and taught by the Institut für Familientherapie Marburg. The examples can be called *typical,* in that they are based on a detailed analysis of "problem-forming effect patterns" and further describe the systemic utilization technique. To make our methods easier to understand, I should first like to define more closely the basic therapeutic framework.

A. Therapeutic Framework

The Institut für Familientherapie Marburg is a private institution not financed by any public body. It is thus free from regulations or restrictions that could hinder its therapeutic methods. The Institut's aims consist of: (1) investigating "problem-forming systemic effect patterns" in naturally occurring human groups—whether families, communes, groups of residents, or other groups—in order to develop and apply the most efficient, appropriate, therapeutic strategies to these natural forms of human self-organization; and (2) examining these strategies for short- and long-term effects.

The therapeutic process is as follows: All the basic data for the problem group are available before the first interview; these data are noted during the first telephone contact with a member of the problem group (see basic data form, Appendix I).

All therapy meetings are prepared via teamwork and conducted under live supervision. After a minimum of 45 minutes, the therapeutic session is interrupted for further deliberation by the team. These *interim deliberations* take at least 15 minutes, but in difficult cases last up to 90 minutes. During these interim deliberations, we attempt to develop a hypothetical explanatory model of the problem-forming effect pattern and, as far as possible, evolve an appropriate intervention. If, following the interim deliberation, the team does *not* agree about the problem-forming effect patterns, further explorations are made according to the different hypotheses or the family is asked without explanation to come back for the next session.

If the therapeutic team *agrees* on the problem-forming effect patterns, the family is asked to return to the next session and the intervention is applied immediately or disclosed as a written process diagnosis with or without prescription within the following days. Another possibility is for the therapeutic team to announce its conclusions at the end of the following session (this form of intervention gives the family an opportunity to make its own decisions about the internal search processes and possibly to prescribe something itself). The interventions are planned and carried out based on the systemic utilization technique. At the end of the session the therapeutic team discusses the anticipated effects with a view toward intervention. The entire therapeutic process (preparation, application, intervention, anticipated effects) is noted on a specially developed therapy process form. This procedure is also used with respect to the effects actually perceived in the following session (see checklist for therapy process form, Appendix II).

The therapeutic technique used in an individual case depends on the course of the therapy and has to be redecided from case to case; too much space is required to describe this procedure in detail here. A checklist (see Appendix III) may be used to decide on the therapeutic procedure. It should be pointed out, however, that before each intervention, the hypothetical explanation model has to be developed and consolidated (where possible) by circular questioning. The intervals between each session average three to six weeks in order to give the commentary, tasks, and so on an opportunity to take effect (see Selvini-Palazzoli, 1980).

There is no official upper limit to the number of sessions: Thus, the family is under no pressure to improve or not improve in a fixed number of sessions. The aims of the therapy are stated by those seeking help, and the therapy team accepts them. However, the team reformulates these aims by converting them to *systemic process level*. This can, for example, mean that the team sees the family's problem as one of organization, whereas the family merely sees a daughter having a somatic problem. The therapists do not declare their systemic construction of the problem unless doing so is specifically planned as a therapeutic measure. Neither does the team discuss the way the therapy works with the family unless they come to the conclusion that, for research reasons, such a discussion will be useful. For example, to discover the negative effects of a particular procedure, the team encourages it.

B. A Case of a "Pathological Craving for Marriage"

As the title suggests, I am exceeding the bounds of the remarks above about psychological suffering and poking fun at psychopathological categorizations. However, I would like to point out the following: If the therapy team had used this diagnosis as a basis for treatment, the therapy would have been unsuccessful. This kind of categorization contains three decisive errors:

We pretend that the problem-forming effect pattern is caused by one person.

We pretend that this cause is a negative entity within the person said to be ill.

We define the problem more or less explicitly as being insoluble— either for the therapist or the system itself (see also Haley, 1980).

There is, however, a problem in describing clinical cases which have been successfully treated. If we omit "declarations of illness" from a collegial point of view, we quickly find critics of our own work who claim, "The case you're telling us about has nothing to do with illness. That's why it's so easy to treat." Still, let us look at our concrete example.[1]

A young, unmarried couple, Lars, a 33-year-old lawyer, and Marie-Ann, a 29-year-old social worker, have known each other for about five years and have been living together for three. Lars, who had been married for eight years (until shortly before he started therapy), had been separated from his former wife for five years; he has a 12-year-old son by this wife. His contacts with his former wife are sporadic and contingent on his contact with his son. However, his former wife has contact with his parents, especially his mother. He is fairly close to his own family and has regular contact with them. Marie-Ann hardly has any contact with her family whom she partly rejects. While living with Lars, she often expressed the wish to get married. Lars usually rejected this; he was still married. Then, about one and one-half years ago, Marie-Ann presented Lars with an ultimatum: "Either you divorce your present wife or we split up." Lars capitulated and got divorced.

Shortly after the divorce, Marie-Ann confronted Lars with another, more or less ultimative request: "Either we get married or we split up." Lars rejected this second ultimatum. As the situation deteriorated and the couple became increasingly bogged down in a vicious circle of quarrels based on demands, refusals, accusations, and counteraccusations, they came to us.

The therapy team constructed the problem-forming effect pattern in the first interview just as it was described. We acquired the additional information that Marie-Ann described the relationship between Lars and his mother as very close; she also felt his parents had a negative attitude toward her. Lars stated that he would not consider marriage after his recent divorce, and denied a close relationship to his mother.

In the interim deliberation, the team considered what could be done to encourage the couple to find an autonomous solution to their problems. We had little difficulty with the positive connotation of the problem, when a good *correspondence* between the team and both the partners became apparent during the session.

In order to make a solution possible, it became necessary to put the problem into a new context. We decided to transfer the prob-

---

[1]In this case the therapeutic team consisted of: Klaus G. Deissler, therapist; Peter W. Gester, live supervisor; and Dorle Engel, minute taker. Therapeutic interventions are always a result of joint efforts.

lem from the partners to their parental families; that is, to make the problem one of their need to sever themselves from their parental families. Thus we implicitly gave the problem of marriage—which was of primary importance to the couple—a secondary position.

In addition, we accepted Marie-Ann's desire to get married as the "official" problem and finally, we gave consideration to the fact that Lars frequently discussed his problems with his parental family. To avoid antagonizing the partners, we decided to give them a task which would take both parts into consideration. Thus we were able to prescribe the problem-forming effect pattern. This session was concluded with the following intervention:

1. The therapist led the partners to understand analogically (with voice tone, gestures, etc.) that the team accepted the couple's relationship and supported them in finding a solution to their problems (analogical or implicit *positive connotation*).

2. He told both partners that the quarrels about whether to get married or not were affecting their relationship *(acceptance of problem definition)*, but that the therapeutic team saw the major problem as their not having settled the question of their relationships to their parental families and the marriage issue as a way to avoid sorting out these family problems. If there was to be a solution, the contexts would have to be clarified *(recontextualization)*.

3. For the above-mentioned reasons, the following task seemed appropriate: They were to write a joint letter to their relatives in which each would give his/her point of view about marriage; each was to give three of their arguments. They were both to ask for help in solving the problem and request that the relatives respond within a reasonable time (utilization of the marriage problem, especially in relation to Marie-Ann, and utilization of the family ties in relation to Lars) to trigger multiple systemic effects. Aim: *Autosystemic transformation* of effect patterns in part by the mutual writing of a letter to the relatives, so that Lars and Marie-Ann would be regarded implicitly as a couple. They both accepted the commentary and the task: The therapy team had the impression that Lars was affected because he quietly asked further questions about the task, whereas Marie-Ann sighed and thought aloud what effects of carrying out the task might be. All in all, both Lars and Marie-Ann seemed satisfied with the advice they were given.

A few weeks later, Marie-Ann called us and said they didn't need to keep their next appointment; the problem had been solved. Some family turbulence had led to Lars severing himself more from his mother and his ex-wife and becoming closer to Marie-Ann. They were both happy with the result: Marie-Ann didn't want to marry Lars now that she realized he was closer to her.

We asked both partners to let us know about reactions to the letter. We have copies of Lars's and Marie-Ann's letter as well as the replies. Together, they constitute 20 handwritten pages. This is the text of the letter that Marie-Ann and Lars sent to their relatives:

> Dear
>
> You will certainly be surprised to get a letter from us. We are writing you to ask your advice on a problem that has been bothering us for some time.
>
> Marie-Ann wants to get married and Lars doesn't.
>
> This is Marie-Ann's point of view:
>
> I am convinced tht Lars is the "right" man for me. I am also for marriage because it's an official and recognized step for living together. I also think that marriage puts the seal on growing up because children finally leave their parental family in order to found a new one. I think the ceremony of marriage is important and necessary in this context.
>
> Lars rejects marriage for the following reasons:
>
> I don't see why the state should give its O.K. to our relationship and I don't want the state's and attendant expectations and rules associated with it.
>
> I don't think that marriage would bring about the changes Marie-Ann wants—also regarding her own family. What's more, I don't want to make the mistake again of saying "yes" out of consideration to a step which I can't stand by.
>
> Many discussions have not helped us to find a solution or to come to an agreement. So we would like to ask you to write to us by...with your advice. As we would like to hear your own point of view, please write without consulting other people. We are looking forward to hearing from you.

The answers—as you can imagine—were varied. I will present only the gist of the responses here to give the reader an impression of the "systemic effects" of the letter:

> *Lars's mother* wrote two letters in quick succession: She told Lars that she could understand his doubts, suggested separation, and added that each should look for a new partner. In a further letter, she supported marriage suggesting sterilization for one partner to facilitate a compromise of "no family."

Lars's aunt suggested living together as man and wife as legal marriage caused enough problems.

Marie-Ann's mother, answering also for her father, supported Marie-Ann's wish for legalizing marriage. At the same time, she apologized for her two "lazy" sons who are not going to reply.

Lars's grandmother believed both partners would find a solution and was sorry she couldn't help any further.

Lars's father didn't believe in marriage; he wished them both a good time together.

Lars's sister, already twice divorced, advised against spoiling the good relationship through a half-hearted marriage.

Lars's ex-wife—herself a therapist—wrote in great detail about the "reactionary nature" of marriage. She tried to set some things straight about her marriage to Lars, for example, she sent Lars the bill for the divorce. As far as Lars and Marie-Ann were concerned, she thought they were both aiming for a separation.

Marie-Ann told us in writing that there had been an argument between Lars and his mother after the letter in which Lars emphasized his autonomy and took Marie-Ann's side. Marie-Ann said that was all she wanted; marriage was no longer important to her. Furthermore, her relationship to Lars had changed. He did more housework and had assumed responsibility for contraception. Lars confirmed these changes with the qualification that the argument with his mother was less dramatic than described by Marie-Ann.

C. A Case of "Psychotic Loss of Identity"

This neologism shows that the inventivenss for psychopathologizing knows no bounds. I do hope, though, that not all readers will take offense at this further irony.

The family to be described here was sent to us by a school psychologist who had heard of our work. She worked in a town about 140 kilometers from Marburg, where the family came from. The father of the family got in touch with us to make an appointment. He was asked to tell us about the problem in writing before the start of the therapy. A good month before the therapy started, we received the following letter:[2]

---

[2]The letter is very hard to read and contains many orthographical and grammatical mistakes. To make it easier to understand, a corrected version is reproduced here.

Esteemed Mr. Gester,[3]

We have already spoken on the telephone. I shall now try to describe our problem.

We are family W.: Father Helmut, 49 years old (civil servant, fire brigade); Mother Gertraud, 45 years old (housewife); Berthold, 15 years old (secondary school); Uwe, 13 years old (secondary school).

Married 1966.

My wife had to leave her home town and move to R. (had difficulty in settling down, many quarrels during the first years of marriage).

After a miscarriage, birth of Berthold, 1968—small apartment, no nursery.

Berthold was a restless child, cried a lot. I often shouted at the boy and smacked his bottom.

Berthold was timid towards other children. Two years later, Uwe was born. At first, Berthold always wanted to push the baby away, but then he got used to him and played with him—especially as my wife and Berthold always had and still have a close relationship. As a small boy, Berthold was always interested in electric wires, his favorite occupation was switching lights on and off.

A little cushion, his "heia" was his constant companion; it then became so unappetizing that I threw it away on the advice of the grandmothers. This was a shock for Berthold. A few days later he looked for a doll he could take to bed or on journeys and even now, at 15 years of age, the doll always has to be there at bed time. Until he was 12, he often spoke to the doll, especially before he went to sleep.

When he was four, Berthold had to go into hospital for 4 days for a throat operation—he went to his bed with much screaming and struggling—visiting was not allowed in those days. When I was able to collect him 4 days later, he was lying there quite apathetically. It was only when he saw his things that he dressed quickly and left the hospital like a whirlwind. At home, he clung to my wife's dress and followed her wherever she went.

1972—move to a larger apartment. The children got a room of their own.

Berthold started kindergarten; Berti just sat quietly in a corner and didn't play with the other children, then a year later, when Uwe started kindergarten, things got better. On our many visits to the grandparents, where there were a lot of children whom Berthold knew, he played with them gladly and lively.

School: To start with he had great difficulty in getting on with the teacher and other children. Difficulties with writing and drawing (illegible), even now an urge to use only the right-hand side of a piece of paper. Favorite subjects—physics and biology—good

---

[3]In this case the therapeutic team consisted of: Peter W. Gester, therapist; Klaus G. Deissler, live supervisor; and Andrea Böhnke, Dieter Heim, and Hilde Krott, minute takers.

grades there too. Between the ages of 7 and 13, we took Berthold to the education advice centre, then to the schools' psychologist in R. (conversations with the therapist helped us the parents, and working in the group helped Berthold a lot).

Berthold's school results got better and he became more open towards others.

A year ago, the group work finished. At the same time he got a new teacher. Berthold related well to this teacher, a motherly, but determined woman who understood him. The new teacher, young, energetic, strict—and the class was reorganized (few old classmates)—this put a lot of pressure on Berthold.

During the next school holidays I took my boys on a cycling trip and noticed some strange behavior in Berthold: before going to bed he would fold his trousers over and over again to get them into a particular position. Before, when eating, he would sometimes make movements with his hands as if to lift the food through the gaps. When he felt he wasn't being watched, he made head movements as if he wanted to pull up an object. When he got on his bicycle and rode off it looked as if he wanted to pull the object behind him. After a lot of asking, Berthold said he had built up little walls.

His school results deteriorated, his behavior was strange there too: when he sat down or stood up, he would swing his legs over the back of the chair as if he had to climb over a wall.

On his way home from school, Berthold walked as if on a marked line. After many talks with Berthold and the teacher, who takes a lot of trouble over him, and who we get on well with, he gave this habit up, or substituted another one: the doors to rooms had to be closed, open doors bothered him—and washing his hands, 5–6 times in succession isn't unusual. You have to be insistent to stop him.

His interests: intense playing with Lego, building bridges, aerial railways, gears, reading, asking questions about something that has aroused his interest—in detail and intensively.

Esteemed Mr. Gester, I shall stop now, until our appointment on. . . .

                                        With best wishes, Helmut W.

In principle, this letter gives enough information about the family to enable the team to work out an intervention from it, although the father's description is centered strongly on the symptoms of the son Berthold.

In the preliminary interview, the letter and the information it contained were used to establish investigative directions that would lead to concrete information. The interview revealed the following analogical information:

1. The father answers nearly all the questions, including those not directed at him.
2. The mother is extremely retiring, almost shy. She leaves it to the father to answer the questions—including those directed at her—by claiming to have forgotten something.
3. Berthold hardly answers any questions; Uwe answers but often indirectly hands things over to the father.
4. Berthold sometimes acts as if he hasn't even heard the questions he is being asked; he stares ahead or looks blank.
5. The mother seems to be suffering and the father becomes active.
6. During the interview, Berthold makes several imaginary movements, as if to carry out certain actions.

The interview produced the following additional information:

1. Berthold had undergone play therapy for three years—from 1979 on—but his symptoms were still present. His father explained the imaginary actions: Berthold wanted to build a protective wall around himself.
2. The parents married relatively late (he 32, she 28), because the wife didn't want to leave home—about 70 kilometers from her parents' home. (She was very attached to her parents.)
3. According to the father, Mrs. W. got on better with Berthold in the past than now. Mr. W. is equally fond of both sons.
4. Four years ago Mrs. W.'s father died. Mrs. W.'s mother then lost the will to live: Her children and grandchildren couldn't comfort her after her loss.
5. According to Mr. W., his wife suffered the most during her father's illness; she worried that if he died she would go mad.

During the interim deliberation, the therapeutic team discussed extensively the additional information they had gathered. With respect to the information that the interview had essentially confirmed, the problem seemed clear: The team members did not differ in their reconstruction of it. The team was concerned, however, that the family might disqualify a directly-given verbal comment. They thus decided to send a written, elaborated, hypothetical, explanatory model as "process diagnosis" to the family. After doing so, they told the family that the next appointment would be in about seven weeks: Only the parents were invited. After the family was told about the process diagnosis, they were immediately dismissed.

The diagnosis elaborated and written by the therapeutic team was sent five days after the session. The letter is reproduced here verbatim, after which the elements of the systemic utilization technique used for this intervention are summarized. The elements can be further resolved with the aid of the checklist (see Appendix III).

First we gave instructions with written interventions including how, when, and by whom the letter should be read. Our instructions were as follows:

Dear Mr. W.,

As promised we are sending you our diagnosis for your family.

We ask you to proceed as follows: wait until Saturday evening before handing each member of the family the sealed, individually addressed envelopes. This should be done shortly before supper when the whole family has gathered to eat. Only then should the envelopes be opened. This applies to yours as well.

As soon as each member of the family has taken their letter out of the envelope, read your letter aloud, slowly. Please make sure that you are not interrupted. After reading the letter you can have your supper.

Yours sincerely,
Peter W. Gester, for the therapy team

This is the text of the letter itself:

Dear W. Family,

As promised during your visit to Marburg, we are sending you our diagnosis.

You, Mr. W., love your wife and family very much. You care for them in big and little matters in a way that only very few fathers do. You have been doing this since the start of your married life.

You, Mrs. W., are the same. Through your marriage, you were separated from your family, and especially the separation from your father (grandad) has caused you much pain. You made the sacrifice of leaving your beloved parents for the sake of your husband's job.

You, Mrs. W., were always quiet, like your father (grandad) and so as not to disturb your husband you never told him how much you were suffering through the separation from your parents, especially your father (grandad).

You, Berthold, noticed this even as a small child. Therefore you decided early on to comfort your mother during this separation. Doing this without considering yourself, you sacrificed your own development.

When you, Mrs. W., suspected your father was going to die, you were afraid of going mad, because you feared you wouldn't be able to bear the grief of the bereavement. In addition, you were worried whether your mother would survive your father's death. After grandfather's death you decided to bear this stroke of fate quietly.

You, Berthold, noticed all this exactly and took the only possible decision, namely to comfort your mother and your grandmother: this meant going mad instead of your mother and being like your grandfather; adopting his characteristics and behavior (making things, being quiet and withdrawn). Your constant hand and finger movements also express the fact that you took on your grandfather's manual skill to comfort your mother and grandmother.

You, Uwe, decided to help your parents with their problems by being the family sunshine.

The therapy team is deeply impressed by the mutual concern in your family. We especially respect the sacrifice made by Berthold to console mother and grandma.

Therefore we cannot ask that you, Berthold, change your behavior or even abandon it, but on the contrary: *We want to set you the task of maintaining your sacrifice, at least in your mother's and grandmother's presence, behaving like your grandfather until no one can tell the difference.*

Yours sincerely,

Peter W. Gester, for the therapeutic team

The systemic utilization technique used here is composed as follows:

1. The instruction to read the letter out loud implies a *ritualized prescription* that utilizes the *pattern of action* (speaking/silence pattern) of the family.
   The father reads the letter, the others have to listen.
   The following supper ensures that they all "swallow" the prescription together and then "mutually digest" it over a longer period (metaphorical or symbolic utilization).
2. The entire communication pattern of the family is given a *positive connotation:* mutual affection, father's activity, mother's pain at separation, Berthold's sacrifice, Uwe's efforts, and so on.
3. The problem as defined by the family is accepted, but *recontextualized* by including the mother's parental family—grandparents, parents, Berthold.
4. Finally, the *recontextualized problem-forming effect pattern is utilized by prescription:* In the presence of at least his mother and grandmother, Berthold is to behave like his grandfather "until no one can tell the difference." This implies an increased demand with the implicit continuation of Berthold's behavior.

About a week later, the colleague who had sent the family to us called and said that Mr. W. had been to see her and had shown her our letter. He had told her that the family was completely confused by it, especially Berthold. For example, Berthold was asking if he was mad and would have to go into a mental hospital. Mr. W. was also surprised that only the parents should attend the next session.

In our colleague's opinion we had hit the nail on the head. She had had the same hypothesis for years but had been unable to communicate it to the family. She said she had asked Mr. W. not to talk to her about the content of the letter, but only to us.

As previously agreed, the couple came to the second session alone. They didn't seem at all confused; on the contrary they were rather balanced. Possibly the weeks in between had lessened the effect of the letter. Their spoken contributions were more evenly distributed. Without being asked directly, Mr. W. mentioned that Berthold had calmed down, wasn't fidgeting or "messing around" anymore (imaginary actions). The grandmother, whom they were visiting at the time, had noticed this too. However, Berthold was shocked that, according to the letter, he was behaving like his grandfather, and asked on occasion whether he was mad.

Mrs. W. confirmed her husband's observations, but pointed out that the improvements could be due to the present school holidays and that Berthold's behavior could occur again when school reopened. But, she concluded, Berthold really had become quieter.

Mr. W. added that he thought his wife had been shocked by the letter too. Mrs. W. confirmed this; the word *mad* had been so "odd." Further themes of the session were: (1) how the partners had got to know each other; (2) their present relationship to Mrs. W.'s mother; and (3) their sexual relationship.

The interview didn't bring any important new information to light: The hypotheses were confirmed that Mrs. W. was still sad about leaving home. Mr. W. continued trying to ease his wife's separation from her parents at considerable cost to his own psychological well-being, and they were virtually unable to discuss their sexual relationship.

After the second session, the family received a further intervention. It was similar to the first, but emphasized more directly Mrs. W.'s comforting function for *her* mother, as well as Berthold's for *his*. In addition, relapses were predicted for Berthold. The family was also advised to discuss this letter with the school psychologist and ask for advice.

The children were invited to attend the next session at which time the effects elicited by the first letter were confirmed. Therapy ended after the fourth session. The school psychologist reported further improvement in Berthold's behavior, which was confirmed by several of his teachers.

In drawing a conclusion from this therapy, we can assume that the first intervention released systemic confusion (compare the school psychologist's reports). The therapy team further hypothesized that the confusion was started by an *autonomous reorganizing of the patterns which effect* in the family (autosystemic transformation).

V. FUTURE RESEARCH

In 1978 I carried out an investigation in a school, the object of which was a quantitative check of paradoxical interventions on speech anxiety before classmates. For various reasons, I have yet to publish the results, the most important being that to a certain extent I concluded that quantitative investigatory methods are completely unsuited to the precise evaluation of the systemic effects of therapy. To explain this further, I should first like to summarize the most important conclusions that I, personally, have drawn from the results:

1. Quantitative tests for measuring gradual differences in the degree of fear parameters are easy to construct and, when well prepared, provide accurate results.
2. Standardized paradoxical procedures used with groups of people assembled based on quantitative criteria (using statistical parameters of comparable control groups) cannot be more precisely analyzed because of their *qualitative* effects. The quantitative effects of these standardized procedures deviate widely, but do not show any significant *mean* differences. Among other things, they do not take into consideration the relevant qualitative conditions of the test persons, but merely the degree of certain parameters.
3. Inexperienced therapists, even if they have been taught individual techniques and had several practice lessons in using them, are not able to compensate for the standardization effect (see no. 2 above). On the one hand, these therapists are tied to the standard procedure, and on the other they are unable to estimate the effect of other possible positive influences that they might use constructively.
4. The most significant disadvantage of standardized paradoxical procedures is the fact that the relational or systemic context is

not considered and thus the concept "systemic patterns which effect," whose essential components are individual symptoms, is neglected as an influencing network. These contextual effect patterns need to be considered in paradoxical procedures if one is to work efficiently: The systemic utilization technique is a procedure that meets this requirement. Thus I conclude that quantitative investigations conceived according to the "isolated variation in variables" model and attempting to separate effect variables are, for therapeutic purposes, of little value.

If we accept the above conclusion as being correct, the question of how these systemic effect patterns can be exactly evaluated arises. Let us remember that we are evaluating fluid, ongoing relationship patterns. I believe that we are at the beginning of a scientific development within this field, but I suspect that the first steps toward evaluating systemic effect patterns have already been taken. I should simply like to cite some models that I believe will codetermine future research: Spencer-Brown (1979), Varela (1975), Taylor (1979), and Pearce & Cronen (1980).

These models have one thing in common: They make it possible to show isomorphic recursive process patterns, thereby helping to show ongoing relationship patterns in natural groups. The above-mentioned models have not been sufficiently developed to make them directly usable for practical purposes. Thus their further development is necessary.

Finally, I should like to point out that the therapist as well as the participating observer must include themselves in the consideration of these models to achieve a circular or recursive consideration of ongoing effect patterns. This means, in principle, that the therapist must direct his own behavior, that is, his therapeutic skill toward the effect patterns of which he is a constituent part.

VI. THERAPEUTIC ETHICS

No therapeutic procedure has been or is so attacked from an ethical point of view as the so-called paradoxical procedures. Why? The answer is simple: The problem is complicated. The more efficient the therapeutical procedures, the more they are suspected of being manipulative. In German-speaking countries, people are especially cautious in this respect. The original language of psychoanalysis is German. Thus in Germany, many analytically oriented psychotherapists see their thinking and actions threatened when new, efficient procedures—like paradoxical ones—start displacing traditional therapeutic methods. It is not surprising that critics of paradoxical procedures attack them at their most sensitive point—efficiency. Paradoxically, a decidedly weak point of efficient procedures is their efficiency: Or, the strength of these procedures is their weakness.

Let us take an example: One can use a knife to carve wood, cut bread, carve meat, or—and nobody can deny it—kill people. Therapists concerned about efficiency are confronted sooner or later with a central question, the significance of which only few people have reflected upon. What type of person considers using himself as a means for change—a trigger for change in other people—in such a way that someone seeking help really feels better after therapy? Moreover, the uninitiated will ask what is occurring when an intervention prescribes the very thing that is contrary to one's thinking: This is immoral or underhanded, is it not?

My own therapeutic work has been called "technization," "cold intellectualism," or "contempt of human beings"—even when clients felt much better after therapy. The *effectiveness* of my therapeutic work did not play any part in its criticism. My values were questioned: Is it permissible to intentionally manipulate people therapeutically so that they will feel better afterwards?

I am not sure how I would convince someone observing my therapeutic work and doubting my integrity that I respect natural processes—and human life in particular. I try to be as unprejudiced as possible—neutrally concerned—toward the clients who come to me.

In my opinion the gist lies elsewhere. Thomas Szasz pointed out in his book, *The Myth of Psychotherapy:*

> Franz Anton Mesmer nowadays may be considered as the father of modern psychotherapy. This is a late acknowledgment of his work. But Mesmer made some mistakes in his therapeutic endeavors—and therapists in these days still do. Let me remind the reader of Mesmer treating Maria Theresa Paradies. This girl—an excellent piano player—suffered from "hysterical blindness." Mesmer treated her successfully, but he did not respect two contextual aspects concerning this case:
>
> — her family (the ecological context of his patient)
> — his own colleagues (his own professional context)
>
> Therefore the result of his success was—in short—that this case was his greatest failure. His envious colleagues warned her family that their daughter might lose the pension given to her by the empress, the family got angry at him, the girl felt worse after having regained her sight, she played worse piano and a campaign against Mesmer was started by his medical colleagues. Finally Mesmer left Vienna.

What does this Paradies-metaphor tell us? I think it is the following: Therapists who try to gain power through their therapeutic work, e.g., their successes, are doomed ultimately to fail. We can paraphrase Bateson and say that they don't realize that they themselves are only parts of higher-level evolving systems that cannot be manipulated unilaterally and linearly according to the construct of power.

APPENDIX I: BASIC DATA

Date:

Referred by:

Family doctor:

Medical insurance:

I. Caller

1. Name:
2. Address:
3. Reason for call—
   current problem:
4. Date of birth:
5. Profession:
6. Phone:

II. Partner

1. Name:
2. Address:
3. Start of partnership:
4. Date of birth:
5. Profession:
6. Phone:
7. Marriage:
8. Separation:

III. Children

1. Name:
2. Date of birth:
3. Profession:
4. Phone:

IV. Further Partners (Living Together)

1. Name:
2. Date of birth:
3. Profession:
4. Phone:

V. Parents of Caller

1. Name:

2. Date of birth:
3. Profession:
4. Phone:

VI. Parents of Partner

1. Name:
2. Date of birth:
3. Profession:
4. Phone:

VII. Siblings of Caller

1. Name:
2. Date of birth:
3. Profession:
4. Phone:

VIII. Siblings of Partner

1. Name:
2. Date of birth:
3. Profession:
4. Phone:

IX. Pets

X. Previous Psychotherapeutic or Psychopharmacological Treatment

XI. Future Notes

XII. End of Therapy

XIII. Result

APPENDIX II: CHECKLIST FOR THE COMPLETION OF A THERAPY RECORD

A. Planning of Therapy

1. *Formal Data*
   a. Date.
   b. Name of the family.
   c. Which people were required to attend.
   d. Members of the therapy team present.

2. *New Information before the Session*

3. *Hypotheses*
   a. Systemic—the entire defined problem-bearing system.
   b. Relational—various relationships within the system.
   c. Psychological—the individuals.
   d. Somatic—the individuals.

4. *Therapeutic Measures*
   a. Joining.
   b. Recursive creation of information.
   c. Intervention at end of session.

B. Therapeutic Procedures

5. *Formal Data*
   a. Date.
   b. Members of family present/absent.
   c. Length of session.
   d. Video—audio—live.

6. *Effects Triggered by the Therapeutic Intervention of the Previous Session—Observed or Reported*
   a. Systemic (see above).
   b. Relational.
   c. Psychological.
   d. Somatic.

7. *How Is the Therapeutic System (Including Therapist) Tuned during the Session?*
   a. Systemic (see above).
   b. Relational.
   c. Psychological.
   d. Somatic.

8. *Which Therapeutic Measures Were Carried out Compared with Those Which Were Planned?*
   a. Joining. (How did the therapist actually join the family?)
   b. Recursive creation of information. (Which questions did the therapist actually put to the family; how did he do this?)
   c. What effects did the therapist evoke through *a* and *b*?

9. *How Was the Interim Discussion?*
   a. Length.
   b. Team in agreement?
   c. Which interventions did the team decide on?

      No intervention (reasons).

      Further exploration in next session (reasons, fields).

      Verbal commentary at end of session with or without task (brief formed and context sketch).

      Preparation of written intervention (brief content and formal sketch).

10. *End of Session*
    a. Was the session terminated by the therapist as planned by the team; did he make important changes?
    b. Did the final intervention bring new information to light?
    c. How did the family, in general, take the final intervention?

11. *Next Appointment*
    a. Date.
    b. Persons required to attend.

12. *Mistakes and Difficulties Noted at the Session*

13. *Anticipated Long-Term Effects of Intervention*
    a. Systemic (see above).
    b. Relational.
    c. Psychic.
    d. Somatic.

14. *Prepatory Considerations for Planning Next Session*
    a. Are there any special points that were not dealt with during the session?
    b. Are there new directions for probing in the next session?

APPENDIX III: CHECKLIST FOR DESIGNING SYSTEMIC UTILIZATIONS

A. Phases in the Designing of Systemic Utilizations

The formulation of systemic utilizations assumes that the therapists are familiar with the basic premises of systemic thinking and practice. In addition formulating systemic utilizations can be useful for exercises or beginners to aid in differentiating between the following phases of the team consultation:

1. The Cathartic Phase. In this phase, every member of the team should be allowed to express his feelings—whether negative or positive—even if they do not contribute to the solution of the problem. Each team member thus has the opportunity to express first impressions of the family. Since this phase is called "cathartic," we can understand the role of expression of feelings for therapeutic interventions.

2. The Analytic Phase. This phase immediately follows the cathartic phase. It enables the team to collect analytical elements (mosaic stones) and to develop new hypotheses about the problem. Every member of the team can express his thoughts, assumptions, constructions of the problem, and so on.

3. The Positive-Connotative Phase. The analytic phase often produces the result that most analyzed elements of the problem are seen negatively by the people who express them. It is often amazing to observe how hard a team must work to wrest positive aspects from a problem. However, serious aspects of problems should not be softened, even in this phase. Usually, it is possible to develop a positive connotation of the problem, which implicitly evokes the family's cooperation and at the same time suggests solutions to the problem.

4. The Systemic Phase. Only when the team has developed a positive aspect of the whole problem spectrum is it able to reach the systemic level. In this phase, an understanding is developed based on a review of connected effect patterns. The problem-forming effect patterns can be constructed by the therapeutic team, which defines itself as a "participating ecological partner."

The team is aware that in so doing it is *constructing reality* and not describing *objective reality*.

5. Planning an Intervention on the Basis of the Systemic Construction of the Problem: Systemic Utilization. In this phase, a utilization of the problem-forming effect pattern is put into action. In so doing, the team is not interested in the *reality of things* but in *Wirklichkeit*. Here *reality* means that which is effected—as the German word so precisely describes it—that which has an effect: effect connections, effect patterns, relationship patterns, systemic processes, and so on. The next section gives a few suggestions for the construction of systemic utilizations.

B. Suggestions for the Development of Systemic Utilizations

1. *Positive Connotation and Systemic Approach*
   These are prerequisites for systemic utilization: They imply that the family will find its own solution to the problem.

2. *Redefinition or Redesignation of the Problem-Forming Effect Patterns*
   The aim of a redefinition lies in the implicit opening up of possible solutions or options for the family. We can differentiate between the following kinds of redefinition: (*a*) *Relabeling* (exchange of labels, changing a name); (*b*) *Recontextualization* (regarding persons, space, time); and (*c*) *Refunctionlization* (allotment of new effect or function of process patterns).

3. *Utilization of the Problem-Forming Effect Patterns*
   a. *Solution-Oriented Prescriptions in Phases of Simple Cooperation:*
      Simple prescriptions of the problem-forming effect patterns as they appear to the therapist.
      Prescription of a worsening of the problem-forming effect patterns (regarding frequency, length, intensity).
      Prescription of the problem-forming effect patterns by modifying the context (compare with 2(*b*); persons, space, time).
      Prescription of the problem-forming effect patterns by division of intention and effect.
      Prescription of problem-forming effect patterns by division into different effects.
      Prescription of new, ritualized, formal patterns without link to contents.

b. *Prescription by Preventing or Reversing Changes in Phases of Inverse Cooperation:*

> Emphasis of negative consequences of change.
>
> Emphasis of the advantages of relating the problem-forming effect patterns.
>
> Direct prevention or banning of changes.
>
> Prediction or prescription of a relapse.
>
> Taking back effected changes.
>
> Announcing an intervention without ever giving it, so that the family develops a prescription for itself.

c. *Prescriptions by Indirect Utilization:*

> Problem-referential metaphors which open up new options (jokes, proverbs, stories).
>
> Metaphorical (symbolic) tasks (tasks with formal analogies to the problem but nonetheless open up options).
>
> Direct or indirect suggestions interspersed at will into conversation, making solutions possible.
>
> Indirect communication, through proxy, when somebody else is meant.
>
> Creating confusion, then offering practical suggestions that are gratefully accepted to lessen the confusion.

d. *Written Interventions Which Make Use of the Techniques a.–c.*

C. Criteria for the Prognosis of Success of Therapeutic Utilizations

1. Do the therapeutic team and the family meet at their corresponding levels of evolution (coevolutionary interface)?
2. Has the right contextual extension of the family been chosen?
3. Have the problem-forming effect patterns been accurately described?
4. How well or how elegantly has the therapeutic team connoted the positive problem-forming effect patterns?
5. How well has the therapeutic team formulated a redefinition of the problem-forming effect pattern implying a solution?
6. How well has the therapeutic team managed:
   a. To construct the therapeutic double bind in such a way that only a positive solution is possible? (This intervention does not allow the problem group any comment or leaving the field; it is the equivalent of a discontinuous change.)

   b. To construct the therapeutic double binds in such a way
   that a continual glide into new possibilities for a solution
   are initiated? (This procedure relies on comment, i.e.,
   reaction from the problem group; it is the equivalent of
   continuous change.)
7. Is the utilization close enough to the family's own epistemology to be accepted by them?
8. Is the utilization far enough away from the family's own epistemology to be regarded as inventive and proficient, that is, as
   opening up options?

REFERENCES

Bateson, G. The birth of the double bind. In M. Berger (Ed.) *Beyond the double bind.* New York: Brunner/Mazel, 1972.

Bateson, G. *Steps to an ecology of mind.* New York: Ballantine, 1972. (b)

Bateson, G., Jackson, D. D., Haley, J., & Weakland, J. Toward a theory of schizophrenia. *Behavioral Science,* 1956, *1,* 251–264.

Berger, M. M. (Ed.). *Beyond the double bind: Communication and family systems, theories, and techniques with schizophrenics.* New York: Brunner/Mazel, 1978.

Deissler, K. G. Anmerkungen zur ökosystemischen Sichtweise der Psychotherapie. *Familiendynamik,* 1981, *6,* 158–175.

Deissler, K. G. Die rekursive Kontextualisierung natürlicher Prozesse. *Familiendynamik,* 1983, *8,* 139–165. (a)

Deissler, K. G. Rekursive Informationsschöpfung. Regeln zur Entwicklung problemrelevanter Fragen im kokreativen Prozeß der systemischen familientherapie. In preparation, 1983. (b)

Deissler, K. G., & Gester, P. W. Autosystemic transformation: Trance phenomena, systemic transformation or utilization in family therapy. Paper presented at the 2nd International Congress on Ericksonian Approaches to Hypnosis and Psychotherapy. Phoenix, Ariz., November 30–December 4, 1983.

Dell, P. F. Beyond Homeostasis: Toward a concept of coherence. *Family Process,* 1982, *21,* 21–41.

de Shazer, S. Patterns of brief family therapy: An ecosystemic approach. New York: Guilford, 1982.

Erickson, M. H. The confusion technique in hypnosis. *American Journal of Clinical Hypnosis,* 1964, *6,* 183–207.

Erickson, M. H., & Rossi, E. L. Varieties of double bind. *American Journal of Clinical Hypnosis,* 1975, *17,* 143–157.

Erickson, M. H., & Rossi, E. L. *Hypnotherapy: An exploratory casebook.* New York: Irvington Publishers, 1979.

Family Process, 1982, *21,* 391–434.

Haley, J. The family of the schizophrenic: A model system. *Journal of Nervous and Mental Disease,* 1959, *129,* 357–374.

Haley, J. *Strategies of psychotherapy.* New York: Grune & Stratton, 1963.

Haley, J. *Uncommon therapy: The psychiatric techniques of Milton H. Erickson.* New York: Ballantine, 1973.

Haley, J. *Leaving home: The therapy of disturbed young people.* New York: McGraw-Hill, 1980.

Hoffman, L. *Foundations of family therapy: A conceptual framework for systems change.* New York: Basic Books, 1981.

Hoffman, L. A co-evolutionary framework for systemic family therapy. Unpublished manuscript, 1982.

Jantsch, E. Die Selbstorganisation des Universums. Vom Urknall zum menschlichen Geist. München, Germany: dtv, 1982.

Keeney, B. P. Ecosystemic epistemology: Critical implications for the aesthetics and pragmatics of family therapy. *Family Process,* 1982, *21,* 1–19.

Keeney, B. P. Ecosystemic epistemology: An alternate paradigm for diagnosis. *Family Process,* 1979, *18,* 117–129.

Maturana, H. F. *Erkennen: Die Organisation und Verkörperung der Wirklichkeit.* Braunschweig, Germany: Vieweg, 1982.

Pearce, W. B., & Cronen, V. E. *Communication, action, and meaning: The creation of social realities.* New York: Praeger Publishers, 1980.

Penn, P. Circular questioning. *Family Process,* 1982, *21,* 267–280.

Rossi, E. L. *The collected papers of Milton H. Erickson* (Vols. I–IV). New York: Irvington Publishers, 1980.

Ruesch, J., & Bateson, G. Individual, group and culture: A review of the theory of human communication. In J. Ruesch & G. Bateson (Eds.), *Communication: The social matrix of psychiatry.* New York: Norton, 1951.

Schultz, I. H. *Das Autogene Training. Versuch einer klinisch praktischen Darstellung.* Stuttgart: Thieme, 1966.

Selvini-Palazzoli, M. Why a long interval between sessions? The therapeutic control of the family-therapist suprasystem. In M. Andolfi & I. Zwerling (Eds.), *Dimensions of Family Therapy.* New York: Guilford, 1980.

Selvini-Palazzoli, M., Boscolo, L., Cecchin, G., & Prata, J. *Paradox and counterparadox.* New York: Jason Aronson, 1978.

Selvini-Palazzoli, M., Boscolo, L., Cecchin, G., & Prata, J. Hypothesizing-circularity-neutrality: Three guidelines for the conductor of the session. *Family Process*, 1980, *19*, 3–12.

Shands, H. C. *The war with words*. The Haag: Mouton, 1971.

Sluzki, C. E., & Ransom, D. C. (Eds.). *Double bind: The foundation of the communicational approach to the family*. New York: Grune & Stratton, 1976.

Spencer-Brown, G. *Laws of form*. New York: E. P. Dutton, 1979.

Stierlin, H. Familientherapie—Wissenschaft oder Kunst? (Engl.: Family therapy—science or art?) Opening lecture at the 4th Annual Meeting of the German Association for Family Therapy (DAF), Marburg, Germany, October 6–10, 1982. In *Familiendynamik*. 1983, *8*, 364–377.

Szasz, T. *The myth of mental illness*. New York: Harper & Row, 1974.

Szasz, T. *The myth of psychotherapy: Mental healing as religion, rhetoric and repression*. Oxford, Eng.: Oxford University Press, 1979.

Taylor, W. R. Using systems theory to organize confusion. *Family Process*, 1979, *18*, 479–488.

Thomas, K. T. *Praxis der Selbsthypnose des Autogenen Trainings*. Stuttgart: Thieme, 1972.

Varela, F. A calculus for self reference. *International Journal of General Systems*, 1975, *2*, 5–24.

Watzlawick, P., Beavin, J., & Jackson, D. D. *Pragmatics of human communication*. New York: Norton, 1967.

Weeks, G. R., & L'Abate, L. *Paradoxical psychotherapy: Theory and practice with individuals, couples, and families*. New York: Brunner/Mazel, 1982.

4

Paradoxical Intention

by Viktor E. Frankl, M.D., Ph.D.

The purpose of the following chapter is to present the details of the logotherapy position regarding the use of paradox in therapy. Although the material will not be new in the sense of offering previously unpublished facts, it is our intention to provide a definitive statement regarding this therapeutic issue based upon a review of the significant logotherapy literature in the area. A discussion of relevant research will not be undertaken in this report as the information is available elsewhere (Solyom et al., 1972), in addition to Chapter 8.

Paradox in logotherapy is largely subsumed under "paradoxical intention," a technique developed by Frankl in 1929 at the psychiatric hospital of the University of Vienna Medical School and first discussed by him in a Swiss neuropsychiatric journal (Frankl, 1939). Frankl coined the term *paradoxical intention* in 1947 in a book that he published in German (Frankl, 1947).

Frankl explains this technique's therapeutic effectiveness by referring to the phenomenon known as anticipatory anxiety.* The

---

*Editors note: Logotherapy has been extensively used in the treatment of obsessions and compulsion, phobias, and sexual neuroses. However, it can be used in the treatment of many other disorders.

erythrophobic individual, for example, who is afraid of blushing when he enters a room and faces a group of people, will actually blush at precisely that moment. A given symptom in a patient evokes a phobia in the form of "fearful expectation" of its recurrence; this phobia actually provokes the symptom's recurrence; and the recurrence of the symptom reinforces the phobia (Figure 1).

FIGURE 1

**The First Circle
Formation: Phobias**

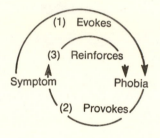

In order to demonstrate on what theoretical grounds the practice of paradoxical intention had been based, I would like to quote the following passage from the book I wrote 37 years ago.

> All psychoanalytically oriented psychotherapies are mainly concerned with uncovering the primary conditions of the "conditioned reflex" as which neurosis may well be understood, namely, the situation—outer or inner—in which a given neurotic symptom emerged the first time. It is this author's contention, however, that the fullfledged neurosis is caused not only by the primary conditions but also by secondary conditioning. This reinforcement, in turn, is caused by the feedback mechanism called anticipatory anxiety. Therefore, if we wish to recondition a conditioned reflex, we must unhinge the vicious cycle formed by anticipatory anxiety, and this is the very job done by our paradoxical intention technique. (Frankl, 1947, p. 91)

There are cases in which the object of the fearful expectation is fear itself. Our patients spontaneously speak of a "fear of fear." Upon closer interrogation it turns out that they are afraid of the consequences of their fear: fainting, coronaries, or strokes. As I pointed out earlier, they react to their fear of fear by a "flight from fear" (Frankl, 1953). In 1960 I had arrived at the conviction that "Phobias are partially due to the endeavour to avoid the situation in which anxiety arises" (Frankl, 1960).

Along with the phobic pattern which we may describe as a flight from fear, there is another pattern, the obsessive-compulsive one, characterized by what one may call a "fight against obsessions and compulsions." Patients are afraid they might commit suicide[1] or homicide or that the strange ideas haunting them might be the precursors—if not symptoms—of a psychosis. In other words, they are not afraid of fear but rather of themselves.

Again, a circle formation is established. The more the patient fights his obsessions and compulsions, the stronger they become. Pressure induces counterpressure, and counterpressure in turn increases pressure (Figure 2).

FIGURE 2

The Second Circle Formation: Obsessions and Compulsions

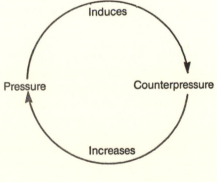

---

[1]Perhaps a special comment should be made with respect to the application of paradoxical intention to situations involving suicidal ideas and impulses. It cannot be too strongly stressed that it is to be used only when suicide is the content of a true obsession being *resisted* (and reinforced by this resistance) by the patient. In a situation where a patient is prone to *identify* himself with the suicidal impulse (as may be the case in endogenous depression), paradoxical intention will serve to increase the danger and is therefore absolutely contraindicated. Let me summarize: Paradoxical intention should not be applied in psychotic depressions, but only in cases in which an individual is haunted by the obsessive idea that he might attempt suicide. The obsessive individual doesn't wish to commit suicide, but rather fears to do so. That is the type of patient whom the therapist may encourage (ironically of course) to attempt suicide.

In order to unhinge all the vicious circles discussed, the first thing to do is take the wind out of the anticipatory anxieties underlying them, and this is precisely the work of paradoxical intention. It may be defined as a procedure in whose framework patients are encouraged to do, or wish for, the very things they fear—albeit with tongue in cheek. In fact, an integral element in paradoxical intention is the deliberate evocation of humor, as Lazarus (1971) justifiably points out. After all, a sense of humor is one of the specifically human capacities, namely, the capacity of "self-detachment" (Frankl, 1966). No other animal is capable of laughter.[2]

In paradoxical intention, the pathogenic fear is replaced by a paradoxical wish, thereby unhinging the vicious circle of anticipatory anxiety. We will cite the following case as an example. A woman, Mary B., had undergone various methods of treatment for 11 years yet her complaints, rather than decreasing, had increased. She suffered from attacks of palpitation accompanied by marked anxiety and anticipatory fears of a sudden collapse. After the first attack, she began to fear it would recur and consequently it did. The patient reported that whenever she had this fear, it was followed by palpitations. Her chief concern, however, was that she might collapse in the street. After her admission to the neurological department of the Polyclinic Hospital, Dr. Kurt Kocourek advised her to tell herself at such a moment, "My heart shall beat still faster! I would just love to collapse right here on the sidewalk!" Furthermore, the patient was advised deliberately to seek out places which she had experienced as disagreeable, or even dangerous, instead of avoiding them. Two weeks later the patient reported, "I am quite well now and feel scarcely any palpitations. The fear has completely disappeared." Some weeks after her discharge she reported, "Occasionally mild palpitations occur, but when they do I say to myself: 'My heart should beat even faster,' and at that moment the palpitations cease."

Another woman, treated by Dr. Michael Ascher, complained of a fear of contracting genital herpes following the appearance of a feature article on this topic in a national magazine. She was a 32-year-old secretary in a large law firm and lived by herself. She began wearing gloves from her departure from home in the morning to her return in the evening. She stopped eating lunch with her friends and ate at her desk, only consuming food brought

---

[2]Hand et al. (1974), who treated chronic agoraphobia patients in groups, observed that they spontaneously used humor as an impressive coping device: "When the whole group was frightened, somebody would break the ice with a joke, which would be greeted with the laughter of relief" (pp. 588–602). One might say these patients reinvented paradoxical intention.

from home in sealed pouches, and only when she had thoroughly cleansed and prepared the area. Her time outside of work was spent mostly in her apartment with a few close friends or her parents. She never permitted anybody to enter her apartment, and never wore clothes in her home that she had worn outside; these "contaminated" articles were kept in a special closet. She consulted a therapist when she began carrying a sheet which she used to cover any chair she sat on outside of her apartment. Finally, the client was encouraged to remove her gloves, throw the sheet upon which she was sitting into a corner, and try to "catch" herpes. The therapist modeled and the client initiated "herpes-catching" behavior, that is, sitting on all chairs, touching various places in the office (desks and various places on the floor), touching her face and body with her ungloved, "contaminated" hands. Throughout the session, which was quite lengthy, the therapist and eventually the client joked about their activities, about the client's concern regarding catching herpes, and about herpes in general (it was quite funny; the reader should have been there). Naturally, the client was reluctant to participate at the beginning of the exercise, but by its conclusion modeling was unnecessary for she was initiating the required behavior. At the conclusion of the session, the therapist suggested that the client continue to try to "catch" herpes throughout the next week. That is, she was not to use her gloves or sheet; she was to wear the "contaminated" clothes throughout her apartment, use public lavatories whenever possible, eat lunch with her friends in local restaurants, and in general, do everything possible to "catch" the disease. Upon her return the following week, she reported that she had carried out the therapist's instructions and felt a good deal better, but was "sad" to report that she had not contracted herpes. In fact, she still had periods of discomfort and retained some ritualistic behavior. However, she was completely comfortable in the therapist's office and further "contamination" there was unnecessary. She was instructed to continue to try to catch herpes during the week prior to her third session. When she returned, she reported that she felt better than she had in many years and that no rituals remained. Therapy continued with a focus on other issues; her concerns regarding contracting genital herpes did not reappear at a one-year follow up.

Paradoxical intention may be effective even in severe cases. Let us turn to an illustrative case history:

> Mrs. Elfriede G., a 35-year-old woman, was a patient in the Neurological Department of the Polyclinic Hospital when I presented her

at one of my clinical lectures. She reported that as a child she was meticulous and while her friends were playing in the park, she stayed at home scrubbing and cleaning. For three years, the patient had been virtually incapacitated by an extreme fear of bacteria; hundreds of times a day she had washed her hands. Fearing contact with germs, she no longer left the house; fearing exposure through outsiders, she excluded all visitors. She would not even allow her husband to touch the children for fear he would transmit germs to them. Finally she wanted a divorce because she felt she had made her family unhappy.

She had been institutionalized because of several attempts at suicide. After unsuccessful treatment in various clinics and hospitals, she had finally been taken to the neurological department of the Polyclinic Hospital by ambulance, for she had become completely helpless. In the lecture hall of the hospital, in the presence of a class of students, I spoke to the patient for the first time. I asked her: "Are you accustomed to check the door many times before leaving home, or to check whether a letter has really fallen into the mailbox or not, or to check several times whether the gas valve is really closed before going to bed?" "Yes, that is my case," she said anxiously. I then proceeded by pointing out that this meant she belonged to a certain type of character structure which in traditional European psychiatry was conceived of as "anankastic," and that this meant immunity to psychoses. A sigh of relief was her response, relief after long years of suffering from the fear of becoming psychotic.

Because of her fear that the obsessions had been psychotic symptoms, the patient had fought them. By this very counterpressure, however, she had increased the pressure within herself. I then remarked: "You have no reason for such a fear. Any normal person can become psychotic, with the single exception of people who are anankastic character types. I cannot help but tell you this and destroy all your illusions in this respect. Therefore you need not fight your obsessive ideas. You may as well joke with them." Then I started paradoxical intention. I invited the patient to imitate what I did. I scrubbed the floor of the lecture hall with my hands and said: "After all, for the sake of a change, now, instead of fearing infection, let's invite it." Stooping and rubbing my hands on the floor, I continued: "See, I cannot get dirty enough; I can't find enough bacteria!" Under my encouragement, the patient followed my example, and thus she began the treatment which, in five days, removed ninety percent of her symptoms.

An incapacitating pattern of three years' standing was broken up in a matter of a few weeks. She spoke jokingly of all her former symptoms. She asked her fellow patients whether any of them could provide her with "some more bacteria." She cleaned postoperative patients in the laryngological department. She was in steady contact with bloody things. She washed her hands only three times a day although she frequently handled putrid material. She wanted "to make as much acquaintance with germs as possible." She spontaneously declared: "I want to let the poor beings live and not wash them away." On the sixth day she left the hospital to buy wool to knit a pullover for her youngest child, to knit it "here in an environment full of bacteria." "On each loop of the sweater," she said humorously, she wanted "one bacterium sitting." She was beaming with joy and felt completely healthy. When she went home for Christmas her behavior was, for the first time, as normal as it had been before the onset of her neurosis three years before.

There was no longer any need to apply paradoxical intention. The patient embraced the children, caressed them without the slightest fear of infecting them. She resolved deliberately: "Now I will transfer the bacteria onto my children." The washing compulsion had disappeared. "I am the happiest person on earth," she declared. She was able to do everything in the normal routine including tasks that formerly she had not been able to finish. She did all of the housework and devoted herself to her children as she had not been able to do since her neurosis became full-fledged. She was able to devote herself to her youngest child for the first time in his life! Some time later I asked her about the washing compulsion. She replied: "I have to laugh at that now. It seems quite unreal to me that I ever had to suffer from anything like that. Now at ten o'clock in the morning my housework is finished. Before, I got up at 3 o'clock in the morning and even by night my housework was not completed." (Frankl, 1975, pp. 226–237)

Compare this type of intervention with the technique of symptom prescription. Symptom prescription and paradoxical intention are two different things. When I apply symptom prescription, I want the patient to increase, say, anxiety. When I use paradoxical intention, however, I want the patient to do, or wish for, *that whereof* he is afraid. In other words, not fear itself but rather its *object* is dealt with. Let me invoke a case published by the logotherapist Byung-Hak Ko (1981), a professor at the National University of Korea. The patient had been suffering from fear of death. Treating him by paradoxical intention, the psychiatrist did in no way recommend him to increase the thanatophobia but, to quote from the paper, the respective instruction read: "Try to be more dizzy, have faster palpitations, and choke more. Try to *die* in front of the people." And the next time, in fact, the patient entered the psychiatrist's "office cheerfully and reported success."

Or, to quote another example to demonstrate the difference between paradoxical intention and symptom prescription: A professor at the University of Nebraska, discussing paradoxical intention (in an unpublished paper), explained it as follows: "For example, a person who has an obsession to wash his hands ten times a day will be invited to do so 30 times a day." I would say such a procedure is unequivocally representative of symptom prescription: The patient was advised to exaggerate the symptom! Along the lines of this technique, Mrs. Elfriede G., whose case history I presented above, would have been advised to wash her hands not "hundreds of times a day" but rather thousands of times a day; in other words, to exaggerate her bacteriophobia. Instead, however, an attempt was made—and, as we saw, successfully—at converting her fear of germs into the ironical wish "to make as much acquaintance with germs as possible." In contrast to symptom prescription, paradoxical intention does not focus on the symptom and its increase but rather on the fear underlying it and—rather than its increase—its inversion.

The paradoxical intention technique lends itself to the treatment of sleeplessness. The fear of sleeplessness results in a hyperintention to sleep which prevents the patient from sleeping since sleep presupposes the utmost of relaxation. But how can one remove the anticipatory anxiety that is the pathological basis of hyperintention and brings about a vicious circle that increases the disorder? The hyperintention to fall asleep must be replaced by the paradoxical intention to stay awake.

In order to take the wind out of the sails of his fear of sleeplessness, we advise the patient not to try to force sleep, since his body will provide the minimum amount of sleep it really needs by itself. Therefore, he can safely try to do just the opposite—stay awake as long as possible. In other words, the hyperintention to fall asleep, arising from the anticipatory anxiety of not being able to fall asleep, should be replaced by the paradoxical intention *not* to fall asleep, which soon will be followed by sleep.

The following report was written by a student at Duquesne University and also illustrates the use of paradoxical intention.

> For 17 years I stuttered very severely; at times I could not speak at all. I saw many speech therapists, but had no success. One of my instructors assigned your book, *Man's Search for Meaning*, to be read for a course. So, I read the book and I decided to try paradoxical intention by myself. The very first time I tried it, it worked fabulously—no stuttering. I then sought out other situations in which I would normally stutter, and I applied paradoxical intention and it successfully alleviated stuttering in those situations. There were a couple of situations thereafter when I did not use paradoxical intention—and the stuttering quickly returned. This is a definite proof that the alleviation of my stuttering problem was due to the effective use of paradoxical intention. (Frankl, 1978, pp. 129–130.)

The principle underlying paradoxical intention is sometimes used unwittingly and even unwillingly. This story concerns a client of my former student Uriel Meshoulam of Harvard University, who reported it to me as follows:

> The patient was called to the Australian army, and was sure he would avoid the draft because of his stuttering. To make a long story short, he tried three times to demonstrate his speech difficulty to the doctor, but could not. Ironically, he was released on grounds of high blood pressure. The Australian army probably does not believe him until today, that he is a stutterer.

Of the three pathogenic patterns distinguished by logotherapy, two have now been discussed: the phobic pattern, characterized by flight from fear, and the obsessive-compulsive pattern, distinguished by the fight against obsessions and compulsions. What then is the third pattern? It is the sexual neurotic pattern, which again is characterized by the patient's fight. Here, however, the patient is not fighting *against* anything, but rather *for* sexual pleasure: It is a tenet of logotherapy that the more one aims at pleasure the more one misses it.

Whenever potency and orgasm are made a target of intention, they are also made a target of attention (Frankl, 1952). In logotherapy the terms we use are *hyperintention* and *hyperreflection* (Frankl, 1962). The two phenomena reinforce each other so that a feedback mechanism is established. In order to secure potency and orgasm, the patient pays attention to himself, to his own performance and experience. To the same extent, attention is withdrawn from the partner and whatever the partner has to offer in terms of stimuli that might arouse the patient sexually. As a consequence, potency and orgasm are in fact diminished. This in turn enhances the patient's hyperintention and the vicious circle is completed (Figure 3).

In order to break it up, centrifugal forces must be brought into play. Hyperreflection can be counteracted by the logotherapeutic technique called *dereflection* (Frankl, 1955), that is to say, the patients, instead of watching themselves, should forget themselves. But they cannot forget themselves unless they give themselves.

Again and again, it turns out that the hyperintention of sexual performance and experience is due to the patient's sexual achievement orientation and tendency to attach to sexual intercourse a "demand quality." To remove it is the very purpose of a logotherapeutic strategy that (in addition to the dereflection technique) I described first in German (Frankl, 1946). To illustrate the logotherapeutic approach to sexual neurosis, let me quote from the first pertinent publication in English (Frankl, 1952):

FIGURE 3

The Third Circle Formation: Sexual Dysfunctions

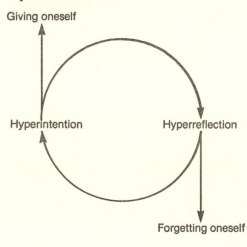

The following trick was devised to remove the demand placed on the patient by his partner. We advise the patient to inform his partner that he consulted a doctor about his difficulty, who said that his case was not serious, and the prognosis favorable. Most important, however, is that he tell his partner that the doctor also has absolutely forbidden coitus. His partner now expects no sexual activity and the patient is "released." Through this release from the demands of his partner it is possible for his sexuality to be expressed again, undisturbed and unblocked by the feeling that something is demanded or expected from him. Often, in fact, his partner is not only surprised when the potency of the man becomes apparent but she goes so far as to reject him because of the doctor's orders. When the patient has no other goal before him than a mutual sexual play of tenderness, then, and then only, in the process of such play is the vicious circle broken. (pp. 129–130)

The report from which I am now going to quote concerns a patient of mine suffering from frigidity (Frankl, 1962). The technique used in treating this case was dereflection.

The patient, a young woman, came to me complaining of being frigid. The case history showed that in her childhood she had been sexually abused by her father. However, it was not this traumatic experience in itself that had eventuated in her sexual neurosis. It turned out that, as a result of reading popular psychoanalytic literature, the patient lived all the time in fearful expectation of the toll that her traumatic experience would someday take. This anticipatory anxiety resulted in both excessive intention to confirm her femininity and excessive attention centered upon herself rather than upon her partner. This was enough to incapacitate the patient for the peak experience of sexual pleasure, since the orgasm was made an object of intention and an object of attention as well. Although I knew that short-term logotherapy would do, I deliberately told her that she had to be put on a waiting list for a couple of months. For the time being, however, she should no longer be concerned about whether or not she was capable of orgasm, but should concentrate on her partner, better to say whatever made him lovable in her eyes. "Just promise me that you won't give a damn for orgasm," I asked her. "This we'll take up discussing only after a couple of months, when I start treating you." What I had anticipated happened after a couple of days, not to say nights. She returned to report that, for the first time not caring for orgasm, she had experienced it the first time. (pp. 194–195)

Claude Farris once treated another type of sexual neurosis and did not apply dereflection but rather paradoxical intention:

Mr. and Mrs. Y. were referred to me by Mrs. Y.'s gynecologist. Mrs. Y. was experiencing pain during intercourse. Mr. and Mrs. Y. had been married for three years and indicated that this had been a problem from the beginning of their marriage. Mrs. Y. had been raised in a Catholic convent by sisters, and sex was a taboo subject. I then instructed her in paradoxical intention. She was instructed not to try to relax her genital area but to actually tighten it as tight as possible and to try to make it impossible for her husband to penetrate her and he was instructed to try as hard as he could to get in. They returned after one week and reported that they had followed instructions and had enjoyed painless intercourse for the very first time. Three more weekly sessions indicated no return of the symptoms. Paradoxical intention has proved effective in many cases in my experience, and at times almost works me out of business.

The logotherapeutic technique of paradoxical intention lends itself to the treatment of a variety of neurotic conditions, in particular, those in which anticipatory anxiety (nowadays often referred to as performance anxiety) plays a decisive role as a pathogenic factor.

Last but not least, I would like to emphasize that opportunity remains for both therapist and patient to develop creative modifications of this technique: Such accommodations to a given case are even mandatory. For not only in logotherapy, but in psychotherapy in general, it is imperative to individualize according to the person with whom the therapist is confronted, and to improvise according to the situation with which the patient is faced.

REFERENCES

Frankl, V. E. Zur medikamentosen Unterstutzung der Psychotherapie bei Neurosen. *Schweizer Archiv fur Neurologie und Psychiatrie*, 1939, 43.

Frankl, V. E. *Arztliche Seelsorge*. Vienna: Deuticke, 1946.

Frankl, V. E. *Die Psychotherapie in der Praxis*. Vienna: Deuticke, 1947.

Frankl, V. E. The pleasure principle and sexual neurosis. *International Journal of Sexology*, 1952, 5.

Frankl, V. E. Angst und Zwang. *Acta Psychotherapeutica*, 1953, 1, 111–120.

Frankl, V. E. *The doctor and the soul: From psychotherapy to logotherapy*. New York: Knopf, 1955.

Frankl, V. E. Paradoxical intention: A logotherapeutic technique. *American Journal of Psychotherapy*, 1960, 14, 520–535.

Frankl, V. E. *Man's search for meaning: An introduction to logotherapy*. Boston: Beacon Press, 1962.

Frankl, V. E. Logotherapy and existential analysis: A review. *American Journal of Psychotherapy*, 1966, 20, 552–560.

Frankl, V. E. Paradoxical intention and dereflection. *Psychotherapy: Theory, Research and Practice*, 1975, 12.

Frankl, V. E. *The unheard cry for meaning: Psychotherapy and humanism*. New York: Simon & Schuster, 1978.

Hand, I., Lamontagne, Y., & Marks, I. M. Group exposure in vivo for agoraphobics. *British Journal of Psychiatry*, 1974, 14.

Ko, Byung-Hak. Application in Korea. *The International Forum for Logotherapy*, 1981, 4, 89–93.

Lazarus, A. A. *Behavior therapy and beyond*. New York: McGraw-Hill, 1971.

Solyom, L., Garza-Perez, J., Ledwidge, B. L., & Solyom, C. Paradoxical intention in the treatment of obsessive thoughts: A pilot study. *Comprehensive Psychiatry*, 1972, 13.

5

Paradoxical Techniques: One Level of Abstraction in Family Therapy

by Luciano L'Abate, Ph.D.

This chapter presents paradoxical techniques as one level of abstraction among at least four different therapeutic approaches. Paradoxical techniques are also the first step in the process of therapy. They function to reduce stress and conflict, provide symptomatic relief and crisis reduction, and engage the family in the process of learning to trust the therapist enough to find new ways to negotiate problems.

HISTORICAL BACKGROUND

The major emphasis in a paradoxical approach to therapy stems from a variety of sources (L'Abate, 1969). Those who have most influenced a circular approach (in this context, *circular* is synonymous with *paradoxical*) are Dewey and Bentley (1949), Ruesch and Bateson[1] (1951), and von Bertalanffy (1968). Incidentally, Rychlak

---

[1] I consider J. Ruesch and A. F. Bentley the two unsung pioneers of how general systems theory preceded family therapy theory. Perhaps someone will someday trace their contribution more fully than I can.

(1968) is one whom I credit with clarifying my thinking on dialectical versus demonstrative approaches. Other influences are so heterogeneous as to defy pinpointing.

My particular position can be called positivistic in that I use a constructive, positive approach in response to the negatives presented at the outset by most families (L'Abate & Kearns, submitted for publication). One could say that my thinking has been influenced by families themselves, as they (mostly children in my original practice of clinical child psychology) presented their referral problems (L'Abate, 1973). Some of my thinking has of course been influenced by Rogers (1951)—positive regard; Ginott (1965)—intimacy; and the Bible—specifically the "Sermon on the Mount" paradox.

Most clients responsible for my conceptualization of a paradoxical approach (L'Abate, 1975) were seen in the context of my part-time private practice, my supervision of graduate students in a university clinic, and in my supervision of private practitioners seeking further professional training to qualify for AAMFT membership. Consequently, the cases submitted to me by supervisees or seen directly range from schizophrenics to normals. The most common symptoms in my practice have been school underachievement, learning disabilities, lack of motivation in studying (L'Abate & Baggett, in press), and a variety of family problems that can be subsumed under family depression (L'Abate, in press). As a whole, my practice has not included extreme cases of drug abuse (though I have dealt with some), alcoholism, or extreme psychiatric pathologies.

My thinking on paradox came about through dealing with the original referral (L'Abate, 1975, pp. 63–75). I became literally sick and tired of listening to families scapegoating via the child's underachievement, lack of motivation, learning problems, and the whole host of negatives that were practically overwhelming the child. So, over time, I found myself shifting more and more in the direction of contradicting the family about the reason for referral, essentially finding a positive reason (love and care) instead of accepting the family's negatives. I began to seek positive reasons for the referral which I generaled to the whole of the negativity (L'Abate & Kearns, submitted for publication) that families bring with them to therapy sessions. In counterposition to the family's negativity, I learned to develop a positive stance basically the same as what various authors have called *positive reframing*, with the same characteristic—a positive rather than a negative outlook on family functioning (L'Abate, 1975). Because I felt effective in using a positive approach to the referral symptom, I generalized this approach to anything and everything negative that a family or a client brought to my office (Weeks, 1977).

Regarding the specifics of paradox, I found that paradoxical techniques fit within a framework of therapy consisting of at least four different levels of abstraction: (a) structural, (b) linear, (c) circular, and (d) metaphorical. The paradox stems first from an appreciation of the variety of levels of abstractions in therapy and a dialectical view of behavior.

The structural approach, best represented by Minuchin (1974), is understood to mean dealing with nonverbal aspects of family living, that is physical arrangements for sleeping, eating, chores, responsibilities, and routines. This is clearly the most concrete, probably the primary, level at which a therapist needs to intervene. The linear approach is the straightforward one used by the majority of family therapists. It consists of a gradual, step-by-step sequence of confrontations, interpretations, homework assignments, and exercises (L'Abate, submitted for publication 1983[a]), all of which derive from a gradual, step-by-step view of behavior.

Circular approaches consist of more tangentially indirect, cryptically paradoxical reframing of symptomatic behavior in positive terms. They are best illustrated by the work of Weeks and L'Abate (1982), Madanes (1981), and de Shazer (1982), which will be elucidated in this chapter. Metaphoric approaches are perhaps best illustrated by the work of Carl Whitaker (Neill & Kniskern, 1982) and some members of the existential school (Kempler, 1981). They are at the highest level of abstraction because they extract dimensions and issues from behaviors that are not clearly evident to the naked eye and ear. They cannot be classified as either linear or circular because they function in a completely different modality—the metaphor. Hence, they need to be classified under a separate heading.

WHAT IS PARADOXICAL PSYCHOTHERAPY?

The therapeutic paradox consists of (a) a variety of ways of intervening without appearing to intervene and of helping (without appearing to control) a family learn to control what they are doing; and (b) contradicting a family's ideologies and mythologies without appearing to contradict. The paradox, understood to be a contradiction, lies in the therapist's contradicting what the family does without appearing to contradict (lest the family feel discounted). Therefore, the paradoxical stance supports a family as a group of *individual* human beings; the therapist never criticizes or judges what they do. The therapist needs to help them break dysfunctional patterns of behavior without increasing their feelings of inadequacy to the point that they flee from treatment, and avoid confrontations that increase either "resistance" or feelings of inadequacy to the point that they discontinue treatment.

The theory that underlies paradox is based on a view that behavior is inherently variable—intra- as well as interpersonally. The many facets of variability can be condensed into two aphorisms or truisms: "One person's trash is another's treasure," which speaks to interpersonal variability; and "Our assets can be our worst liabilities," which speaks to intrapersonal variability. Once we accept the inherent variability of human existence, we can accept the idea that psychopathology consists of wide swings from one extreme of contradiction to the other within and among individuals in the family. The goal of therapy is to decrease such variability, and to decrease contradictions and inconsistencies as much as possible (the goal of reducing variability will, of course, be elaborated further).

The paradox can be an approach, a technique, or a method, depending on its replicability. As an *approach*, paradox is a metatheoretical view, one that relates mostly to variability: It represents a philosophical position about human nature. Basically, a *technique* is peculiar to the individual and relates to the style of the therapist. A *method* can be replicated, regardless of the particular style of the therapist (Haley, 1976; Hansen & L'Abate, 1982; L'Abate et al., in press).

The intended effects of a paradox are of course to help a family change by decreasing either the anxiety level (if you prefer, intrapsychic concepts) or the variability and turmoil that exist among family members, helping them find new ways to relate after the turmoil and crisis have been reduced (L'Abate, submitted for publication 1983[a]). Obviously, this goal is achieved in a variety of ways; the paradox appears in as many forms as do other treatments.

HEALTH AND DYSFUNCTION

My theory of family pathology has evolved over a period of time (L'Abate, 1964, 1976, 1983[a]) and is currently composed of four major aspects: (*a*) styles, (*b*) components, (*c*) levels, and (*d*) power and negotiation.

Styles

The three styles in intimate interpersonal relationships (L'Abate, in preparation 1983[b]) pertain to apathy (*A*), reactivity (*R*), and conductivity (*C*).

Apathy consists of all kinds of behaviors that pertain to abuses—atrophied, aggressive, avoidant, aversive—that is, destructive relationships. Reactive relationships represent the polarities of negative complementarity, in which the dialectic is same-opposite and of which repetition is the main characteristic: yes-no, black-white, true-false, right-wrong—immediate reactions of one individual to what another says or does. Reactive styles characterize a great many husband/wife, parent/child intimate (close and prolonged) transactions. One individual reacts to the other. Then, because the second individual reacts to the first, counterreactions and escalations ensue.

The conductive style represents commitment to constructive change through change of self. It represents the ability to delay reacting until much more information (both internal and external) is obtained and processed and a response can be constructive and positive. Clearly, psychopathology is present in all abusive, apathetic, avoidant relationships. A slightly lesser degree of pathology (but still dysfunctionality) is present in reactive relationships, while "health" is found in conductive relationships.

Components

Interpersonal relationships can be represented through a circular information-processing model based on five components: Emotionality, Rationality, Activity, Awareness, and Context. These five terms stand for, in traditional psychological language, structure, process, outcome, correction mechanism, and context. In information-processing language, these components would be called input, throughput, output, feedback, and context. These five components perform a variety of classificatory and diagnostic functions, which have been elucidated elsewhere (L'Abate, 1981; L'Abate & Frey, 1981; L'Abate et al., 1982; Ulrici et al., 1981).

This model indicates that, for health, all five components need to be present on an equal basis. Pathology represents an overreliance on one of the five at the expense of the others. For instance, an overreliance on emotionality may bring about a decrease in rationality, producing a sequence that goes from emotionality to activity, thereby bypassing and short-circuiting rationality. By the same token, an overreliance on rationality may delay activity and push emotionality into a secondary or tertiary position, one in which emotionality is not used as a resource but is seen instead as a liability. The same applies to awareness, defined as reflection on one's behavior. The context could be denied, overemphasized, or misinterpreted. Balance among all the components and equal, flexible use bring about health; overreliance on one at the expense of the others brings about pathology.

Levels

The third aspect of this theory consists of levels and patterns of congruence in functioning (discussed in greater detail in L'Abate, 1964, 1976, 1983 [a]). There are two levels of interpretation—the descriptive and the explanatory. The descriptive level is composed of two sublevels: The self-presentational, which refers to the facade or public image; and the phenotypical, which describes how we actually behave in our more private moments. The explanatory level also consists of two sublevels: the genotypical, which refers to the underlying, attributionally inferred, abstract constructs that we use to explain (redundantly, one might add) individual or systemic behavior (e.g., anxiety, guilt, self-esteem); and the historical, which is the generational, life-cycle view of how behavior came to be. Health represents a certain degree of consistency among all levels; that is, one level is not overemphasized at the expense of another.

Power and Negotiation

The fourth aspect of this theory considers power sharing and negotiation. The power-sharing model defines power as who makes the decisions and responsibility as who carries them out. The two levels of task assignment are orchestration (i.e., large decisions, such as moving, changing jobs) and instrumentation (i.e., the picky, everyday decisions). Negotiation Potential (NP) is based on (a) the degree of functionality (ill-health), (b) the motivation to negotiate (will), and (c) the ability to negotiate (shall). This particular aspect of the model is summarized by a formula: NP = ill × skill × will. The negotiation model consists of the 'having,' 'being,' and 'doing' model (L'Abate et al., 1980), which speaks to a family's modalities of living (what is to be negotiated). The content of negotiation can be based on services and information (doing), goods and money (having), or love and status (being). Conflicts in doing or having are pseudo issues that distract us from our inability to deal with issues of being.

Theory of Personality

Health and pathology are based on the differentiation of relationships. Change and growth result from our ability to be conductive. Change is based on three multiplicative requisites: (*a*) doing something positive and constructive, (*b*) doing something new and different from what one has done in the past, and (*c*) doing it frequently or intensely enough for it to withstand the impulse to maintain the status quo. The three requisites of change, then, are positivity, differentness, and strength. We fail to grow when we behave abusively or reactively; that is, when we continue to do either the same as or the opposite of the other persons in the family. In conductive relationships, two pluses equal a multiplication (growth) in the relationship. In reactive relationships, there is one plus and one minus (same-opposite), which equal zero and thus repetition of the same relationship over time. In abusive relationships, two minuses divide or split energy to the point of destruction (L'Abate, 1976).

More helpful than the view of health and pathology as a continuum is the bell-shaped curve view. That is, health is in the middle of the curve with pathology on both its sides (one side being too much and the other too little; one too frequent and the other too infrequent; one too intense and the other not intense enough). Health thus represents the middle of the road on the four components previously described (L'Abate, 1964, 1976; L'Abate & Kochalka, in press).

Health is properly represented by the whole concept of conductivity; it is our ability to be committed to change, to be creative and constructive. Normalcy would be properly represented by reactivity because, if we consider normalcy just a statistical concept of frequency, it appears that most human relationships are reactive. Normal, however, would be neither health nor dysfunction; dysfunction is represented by the apathetic relationships already described.

Symptoms are usually produced by generational patterns in which an inability to express hurt in conductive, appropriate, constructive ways brings about pathology (L'Abate, 1977; L'Abate et al., 1979). Symptoms then are produced by our inability to express properly, constructively, and conductively our genotypic feelings of hurt, despair, grief, loneliness, inadequacy, helplessness, vulnerability, fallibility, and neediness, and by our inability to resolve these feelings by sharing them with our intimates, who in turn reassure us of our worth and our importance to them (L'Abate & Sloan, in press, [a], [b]). Of course, we first have to be convinced of our own inherent worth as human beings and aware of our need to let those we love know about our hurts and our fears of being hurt.

A symptom is any behavior that over time brings pain, hurt, and grief to the family and decreases the family's functioning to the point of increasing dependence on outside others (L'Abate & Kochalka, in press). The purpose of a symptom is to keep the system unchanged, to freeze it in repetition or in increasing abusiveness and apathy, which leads eventually to its complete breakdown. A system redresses the balance of power within a family: The least powerful and most vulnerable individual, usually the symptom bearer, holds the upper hand and has control and power over the rest of the system. The symptom is usually metaphorical of relationships, and allows the most vulnerable and supposedly weakest individual to achieve some degree of supremacy over the rest of the family system.

One of the many characteristics of dysfunctional families (L'Abate & Kearns, submitted for publication) is acontextuality; that is, most families are unable to see the symptom in context. Thus they evidence linearity (concreteness in particular causes/effects), digitality (at the expense of analogic thinking), uncontrollability of the symptom, defeating behavior, conflicts in distance regulation, lack of intimacy, and lack of laughter. The symptom, therefore, represents a double bind: The most vulnerable and uncontrollable individual, who is the symptom bearer, through his uncontrollability, achieves control of the system. The major paradox of the system—the achievement of power without appearing to achieve power—is the inherent contradiction in most dysfunctional families. This contradiction also applies to the therapist's behavior; that is, the therapist needs to achieve control without appearing to control.

THEORY OF CHANGE

Change occurs when the symptom is restructured in a positive context. When reframing is strong and frequent enough, the family can successfully work as a system. The most important condition in the process of change is a cognitive restructuring—a reframing of the symptom from a negative to a positive context.

Change occurs when a therapist helps a family achieve control of the symptom through either a straightforward prescription of the symptom, or positive reframing plus prescription of the symptom: The symptom is ritually and systemically linked to the rest of the family (Weeks & L'Abate, 1982). The client does not need insight into why and how change has taken place. In fact, it can be argued that in some cases insight will be harmful. Instead, the therapist can use positive restructuring to explain how a symptom works. A full explanation should be given in a variety of positive attributions rather than in the one attribution acceptable to the client (L'Abate, in press).

Cognitive restructuring in and of itself is not sufficient to effect change. Even if thinking is altered in dysfunctional systems, changes in thinking cannot be directed toward behavioral change per se: by the very nature of reactive and apathetic behavior, one person's more positive thinking will be contradicted by the more negative thinking of others who are frightened by any possible change in the system. Thus thinking or rationality would actually be counterproductive. It is important, therefore, that positive reframing, multiple or otherwise, be followed by a precise prescription for altering the behavior of the family, a prescription that links the symptom ritualistically—through repetitive manifestations of the dysfunctional behavior in which the whole family system is involved. With this particular framework (positivity, differentness, and frequency), change can occur. Eventually, of course, the ultimate goal in family therapy is to help the system achieve intimacy, an area that most paradoxical, structural, and systemic therapists have ignored (L'Abate & Sloan, in press, [a], [b]).

How rapidly paradoxes will produce change is difficult to predict. When a paradoxical direction, or injunction is given in terms of *multiple positive attributions* and symptom *repetition* that is *ritualized* and *systemically linked* to the rest of the family, change can be very rapid. This change, however, represents only the first part of therapy (L'Abate, submitted for publication [a]). I agree with Alexander and Parson's (1982) view that therapy consists of three separate phases. The first is symptom alleviation, crisis reduction, turmoil decrease; the second is skill training; and the third is termination. Most paradoxical techniques are to be used in the beginning phases of treatment to help the system achieve a degree of stability. After this goal has been achieved, a variety of linear procedures (task assignments, structured enrichment) may be followed (L'Abate, submitted for publication [a]). Therapy is not based on a single, simple use of one technique or method.

Families are interested in procedures that work; their orienta-

tion toward help is very pragmatic. The family orientation becomes philosophical only in family systems that are too rationally
oriented, systems that use rationality to avoid emotionality, or
'having' and 'doing' to avoid 'being.' When the paradox is positively administered, the reactions—in addition to what is called
the paradoxical face—are delight, pleasure, enthusiasm, relaxation, and enjoyment. These responses should be the outcome of
any therapeutic procedure and should especially occur when the
family learns to control and conquer the symptom.

It is useless to consider conscious-unconscious levels in family
functioning. In some cases paradoxical directives work without
any explanation at all; in others they function best when a full
explanation is given. Whether or not (and how much) the therapist should explain depends on the family: some families neither
want nor care for explanation; others crave, demand, and need a
full, logical explanation of whatever is being done. It is important
then that the therapist understand how the family functions best
in order to meet their expectations.

Sometimes amnesia occurs; that is, the family is completely unaware of what happened during the first session. For instance in a
blended family that had been able to defeat a therapist after two
years of treatment, rapid change occurred when the 13-year-old
daughter's misbehaviors were relabeled as "protection" for her
mother's depression. The daughter was congratulated for all the
care she had shown in protecting her mother and being so very
sensitive to the mother's needs. These positive verbal interpretations were all that was needed to bolster this girl's feelings of sag-
ging self-esteem and failure and turn her into a delightful, happy,
and successful teenager, one who brought about a new level of
functioning in the rest of the family. Of course, other directives
and other interventions were needed. Yet the family, including
the former identified patient (I.P.), repeatedly indicated their complete unawareness of how this "miracle" had been achieved.

In some cases, the family is perfectly aware of all the steps that
have taken place. A key to the human condition, when considering behavior from a viewpoint of individual differences, is that it
is difficult to condense or to generalize the importance of a single
dimension.

Change can only occur in context. It is almost impossible to
obtain an isolated change, one that does not affect the rest of the
system. I am not aware of (nor can I imagine) any situation in
which symptomatic relief was not accompanied by some change
in the rest of the system.

The therapist who wants to make a living needs to produce

change. I am aware that many individually oriented therapists have successful practices by helping individuals "to feel good" even though no external change seems to be taking place, especially in the client's family relationships. For a marital and family therapist, however, behavioral change is the measure of effectiveness. The therapist need not behave in any specific ways, but needs such a combination of expertise and humanness that expert interventions can be administered without appearing expert. Perhaps this is another paradox: The way a therapist needs to act is perhaps important to the therapist's internal consistency; that is, being an expert without appearing to be one.

The importance of always being human is in contradiction to the "expert" position taken by the Milano Group (Hansen & L'Abate, 1982), who like to maintain some distance between themselves and the families. The paradox here is to achieve closeness without losing distance—to be just close enough and just distant enough to be objective and effective. Paradoxical interventions need to be imparted in a context of personal humanness, which is what makes almost every method a technique, and technique must always be grounded in some methodology. If one equates methodology with expertise and techniques with humanness, it is the combination of the two that produces change. Overreliance on method is as counterproductive as overreliance on humanness. Effective therapy is always a combination of the two.

Paradoxical therapy may be necessary at the beginning of therapy, but it is not sufficient to effect change. Effective therapy consists of a variety of structural, linear, circular, and metaphorical procedures that need to be interwoven in the therapy process. In some cases, paradoxical therapy may function as a placebo, in that it decreases "anxiety" thus decreasing variability and improving the stability of the system. If this is what the placebo does, it could be that paradoxical therapy makes the system more amenable to linear interventions. Whether it works as a placebo to provide temporary relief or as a "real cure" to provide long-range changes, a therapist can often make hay out of either outcome (L'Abate, submitted for publication [a]).

Change can be lasting when a positive spiral takes place; on the other hand, there may be regressions. The therapist must always take the position that the family is responsible for change ("I do not want to be praised because I don't want to be blamed"). Thus, any intervention needs to be evaluated by the test of time. As therapists, we cannot rest on our immediate observations and accept positive change as permanent. We need to question whether the change is indeed lasting and whether it has produced a positive spiral of other changes and offshoots to indicate that the interventions have been truly successful.

Paradox is not a religion: there is no question of believing or not believing the paradox. The only belief necessary is the acceptance of alternative positive explanations (i.e., positive reframing), worded in a way that makes sense to the family. The family's belief may not be necessary; following the directives, regardless of belief, is necessary. The reorganization in thinking that derives from the positive reframing may take some time. Furthermore, different family members need different interpretations or they will interpret differently regardless of what the therapist says. What is important is that the family members behave in new ways that are in agreement with what the therapist has said. They may follow the directives and change may not occur, indicating that a different paradox may be needed or that the therapist missed the boat at that particular time and needs to use other kinds of directives. This is why the therapist must always qualify directives with tentativeness, with uncertainty: "I'm not sure whether this will help; it may sound crazy"; "I don't know whether or not this will work, but let's try"; "I don't know anything else to do at this point—but let's see what happens if..." These qualifications make the therapist more acceptable and the intervention much more human than it might otherwise be.

The best way to prevent a relapse is to predict one. The relapse should always be interpreted as a natural regression; the therapist needs to be ready for regressions at any level and stage of therapy. Without regressions, we might question whether the system is really alive and struggling. One should not only be very tentative in giving prescriptions but should wonder whether they will work, whether something else may be necessary. In fact, I routinely say from the very beginning of therapy, "Things are going to get worse before they get better," or, "If I'm doing you any good, things are gonna have to get worse so that the system can explode and existing, traditional ways of behaving can be given up for new, different ways." Any kind of relapse or regression can be positively interpreted as the system's way of returning to familiar, past behaviors due to the difficulty of finding new ways of relating to each other ("The devil I have is better than the devil I may get").

When there is a symptom substitution, the same approach is necessary; it may indicate that the therapist has erred in dealing with the symptom to begin with or has miscalculated the dysfunctionality of the system. There are multiple-problem families whose degree of dysfunctionality is such that all the therapist can do is fix the leaks. When one leak is fixed, another springs up elsewhere. This, however, is not an indication of symptom substitution but an indication of the degree of dysfunctionality. There are families whose homeostasis is predicated on continuous uproar and turmoil. These are systems that not only resist intervention but are not interested in intervention (apathy). There are systems that survive through turmoil, systems that in fact would not know how to deal with each other because they would face such a degree of internal depression that homicide, suicide, or psychosis could be the outcome of stirring up such extreme underlying (genotypical) dysfunctionality. In some cases, these families might be let alone until they break down completely. This may be a heartless thing to say, but if help is not sought and no change is forthcoming, there is very little that a therapist can do.

INDICATIONS AND CONTRAINDICATIONS

Assessing the degree of dysfunctionality is impressionistic and intuitive, and is based chiefly on whether the system will or will not follow directives, homework assignments, tasks. The degree of conformity with or opposition to a homework assignment is one of the basic clues by which we can evaluate the appropriateness of the assessment. Psychiatric labels may sometimes help to indicate the degree of severity of the dysfunctionality; however, if the labels are used to deemphasize a systemic perspective, those labels are not only useless but can be destructive to a systemic understanding of a family. Assessment, then, is mostly subjective, inferential, and attributional. How much the family can or cannot take the interventions that are given during the initial sessions is one way to assess the degree of dysfunctionality or functionality. The symptom, the strength of the symptom, and the degree of rigidity of the family—all these characteristics are present. An informal checklist (L'Abate & Kearns, submitted for publication) plus a variety of other paper and pencil tests and questionnaires (L'Abate, in preparation [b]; L'Abate & Wagner, in press) about the characteristics of dysfunctional systems are used to assess the system multidimensionally.

The first three sessions are thus devoted to assessment in which the family evaluates the therapist(s). It is up to the family to decide after the third session whether they want to enter a therapeutic contract. The first three sessions are strictly diagnostic in terms of present and past situations. History and a genogram are sometimes useful, even though they may be taken sketchily at the beginning and filled in during the course of therapy. Tasks are used to check on the degree of functionality of the family system. If a family is able to comply directly with structural changes and complete homework assignments, there is no need to go on to a circular or a metaphoric approach.

If tasks are not completed or not even undertaken, a more circular approach may be necessary. Which kind of intervention is decided strictly on the basis of cooperation or inability to cooperate. Cooperation suggests use of structural and linear approaches; lack of cooperation or inadequate cooperation suggests use of circular or metaphoric approaches.

In the diagnostic assessment of a family, the theoretical framework presented earlier through the models of Apathy-Reactivity-Conductivity (A-R-C), Emotionality-Rationality-Activity-Awareness-Context (E-R-A-Aw-C), and power sharing and negotiation are all used. The framework is diagnostic as well as therapeutic. The levels of abstraction in therapy serve as a framework for specific treatment guidelines. Go structural if possible; if not, go linear; if linear does not work, go circular; and if circular does not work, try metaphorical. Sometimes, one reasons quickly and intuitively that the metaphorical might be used. These are not absolute guidelines; it is very difficult to give any guidelines that could not be contradicted (see Weeks & L'Abate, 1982, for contraindications for the use of paradox).

The paradox in and of itself is just one approach, and it has to be mixed with all the other approaches. The more techniques and methods the therapist knows, the more flexible and better off the therapist is in meeting the various needs of families. Thus the therapist shifts always from one level of abstraction to another. The level of abstraction and flexibility of the therapist in meeting the family's demands could range across all four different levels. There is no one treatment of choice: In certain cases, paradox may be the only treatment of choice; in some cases, it is never the treatment of choice. There should be as many ways to meet families as will allow us and them to succeed.

STRUCTURE AND PROCESS OF THERAPY

In terms of sequence of interventions, the level of abstraction already outlined indicates how we can work with a combination of approaches. Sometimes, especially if one knows from the first session that the symptom bearer is hostile and negative and will oppose any task assignment, it is clearly important that the task assigned from the beginning session be paradoxical. If the symptom bearer and the rest of the family respond positively to the therapist, demonstrating very few signs of opposition, structural and linear approaches are more appropriate.

The stage for a paradoxical intervention is set in terms of the family's readiness to interpret reality in different, positive, and strong ways, through multiple attributions (L'Abate, in press). In preparing the stage, the therapist is extremely tentative about how the intervention will work and very clear about if, when, and how the intervention is to be given. That is, the therapist uses the four basic aspects of paradoxical intervention—*positive reframing*, leading to a *prescription* that is *ritualistically repeated* and *systemically linked* to the rest of the family.

Deciding which technique to use is mostly intuitive, in the sense that it is done very quickly and the therapist must feel confident about the chosen intervention. But when there are many indications of potential resistance and rigidity in the system, a paradoxical approach clearly seems in order. The first three diagnostic sessions are used to decide which techniques to use, when and how to use them.

No intervention is ever given unless there is a follow-up. A diagnostic contract for three sessions needs to be reached before a therapist can give the next assignment. An intervention is given for the purpose of diagnosis rather than improvement of the system. The family is told that, except for specific directions given by the therapist, the system is not to change but to continue as usual.

When an intervention does not work, we have to decide whether it was poorly structured, whether there was someone in the system who sabotaged it, or whether a more relevant intervention is needed. (The whole issue of defeats and failures in therapy is considered in L'Abate & Baggett, in press; L'Abate & Kochalka, in press.) If the family is truly bound by defeat, they enjoy defeating each other and are set in defeating. If they know how to relate only by defeating each other through discounting, contradicting, reactivity, and apathy, the therapist must take hold of the fear that s/he will be defeated. When the defeat is clear, it needs to be positively reframed: "You need the defeat and you need to defeat each other [by not doing assignments, or not doing homework, or not carrying out whatever directives are given] to be together and to keep the family close; It is important that you continue defeating each other; let's see how many ways you can find to defeat."

When defeat seems to be the key theme of a family's functioning, it is important that the therapist prescribe the defeat, allowing the family latitude to continue to defeat each other but starting the defeats at certain times, in certain places, and in certain ways (frequency and intensity), all of which allow the therapist to achieve control over the defeats. Linearly, one can deal with the defeats by having every family member list how each defeats others and how each is defeated by others. After this assignment, a master list is developed by having each person share their individual lists with the entire family. Everybody then knows how the family succeeds through the defeats. The family is exhorted to continue defeating each other, because if they do not do so they may fall apart and break down. Thus, appreciation of how defeats keep the family together is important. Although such an explanation may sound paradoxical to the family, it is not paradoxical from the therapist's viewpoint. The paradox is that prescription of the defeat allows the therapist to achieve control over self-defeating and other-defeating behaviors.

Prescriptions must be given with time, place, and frequency constraints. For instance, siblings who are experiencing sibling rivalry ("loving each other") are assigned to bicker and fuss at each other—at certain times, in certain sequences, and in certain places, with links to the rest of the family. If they are going to fight, they should do it for 30 minutes on Monday, Wednesday, Friday, or for 15 minutes on Tuesday, Thursday, Saturday. These are part of the ritualization that helps the therapist achieve control over the system. Ritualization makes the assignment specific, but the therapist must keep always in mind that positive reframing should come before the assignment is given to the system: "You care enough to fight with each other. If you did not care for each other, you would not fight. Fighting is, after all, a form of lovemaking."

The goal of treatment is to help families function more productively and constructively and to feel better about themselves and each other. The goal of therapy is to help families negotiate issues; thus, no matter what issues they want to negotiate, they need the skills to negotiate (L'Abate et al., in press). This is an area in which paradox is limited. In other words, paradox is limited at the beginning of therapy when there is a crisis or an uproar. Eventually, the initial phase of treatment, as mentioned before, needs to be followed up by skill building. Skill building consists of giving families a paradigm by which they can learn (through rules, regulations, and guidelines, including, eventually, family conferences) how to negotiate (L'Abate, submitted for publication [a], [b]).

The goals of treatment—what they want to get out of therapy—should be decided by the family. They may decide the specific content. The process, however, is decided by the therapist; the process then results from the structure provided by the therapist. The specific issues that the family wants to deal with are the content. It is up to them to learn to negotiate those specific issues. Some of the process goals—to become much more conductive, more balanced in functioning, and much more congruent at levels of functioning, to learn how to share power, and to learn to negotiate—are appropriate for all families. I cannot think of any families for whom these goals are not useful. The specificity of the content is the business of the family; the generality of the process is the business of the therapist.

Paradoxes are fully explained to some families, which allows them to think differently about the system. The level of explanation, however, is limited strictly to how much a family can take. If a family includes a six-year-old child, it is going to be very difficult to explain certain aspects to that child. The level of explanation has to be geared to the lowest common denominator of understanding in the family, which may sometimes limit what a family can understand. It is more important, however, for families to change for the better than to understand.

Clients try to avoid some practices by not following the task or by indicating that they do not buy the positive reframing, thus continuing to do what they have been doing. At this point, the therapist needs to be aware of being defeated and use the defeat to explain how the family needs to defeat each other. Termination is complete when the family feels they have achieved their goals—that they feel better, that they are more functional, more relaxed, more satisfied with each other, and that they have achieved some constructive modus operandi to indicate that they are in charge (e.g., family conferences in which they negotiate issues more constructively).

According to the therapeutic contract, cancellations must be made 24 hours in advance or the family is charged (except for dire emergencies). Termination must take place in the therapist's office, not by telephone. The agreement to terminate needs to include everybody in the family. The whole issue of termination is an important one in ascertaining whether the family is indeed ready for termination. Sometimes, one member of the family does not want to terminate because s/he remains dissatisfied. In such an instance, how much freedom is that individual given to express an opinion? An agreement that is satisfactory to the individual who does not want to terminate can be made to terminate within a given number of sessions. Here, the therapist needs to be sensitive to unfinished business, intimacy typically being one of the most important (L'Abate, submitted for publication [a]).

Success is determined by the family's happiness in being alive, their feelings of joy and success in negotiating, completing issues, being in charge, and their reported satisfaction with services rendered.

TECHNIQUES

Paradoxical techniques should be organized as follows: (a) "Things are gonna get worse before they get better"; (b) "I'm not sure this is gonna work, but let's try it and see"; (c) positive reframing through prescription of the symptom, which is (d) ritualistically and (e) systemically linked for the whole family.

I continue to rely on written (I believe very strongly that letters can be used with children) as well as verbal communications, and I believe that more linear techniques should be developed before one goes on to the paradox. If there are any common errors in the use of these techniques, they lie in using them too stereotypically and generally, without considering the specific case and the specific context of specific families. Using paradox rigidly and uncritically will, I think, produce severe disappointments for both families and therapists (L'Abate, 1977; Wagner et al., 1980).

CLINICAL ILLUSTRATIONS

Some uses of the paradox in an inpatient children's setting have been reported by Jessee and L'Abate (1980) and in other publications (L'Abate & Farr, 1981; L'Abate & Samples, 1982; Soper & L'Abate, 1977; Weeks & L'Abate, 1982). This section will describe isolated cases in which I consulted on a one-shot basis and stayed in touch with the therapist about the long-range results of the intervention.

In one case, treated by Don Laird, I consulted over a period of three years. A young man of 22 had a long history of hospitalization and incarceration for sudden, seemingly unprovoked and explosive temper tantrums that ended in destructive or aggressive outbursts against property and people, especially members of his family. During previous hospitalizations, he had at various times been diagnosed as paranoid schizophrenic and given other, similar labels. He was seen in the fourth session during a treatment that spanned three years. The aggressive outbursts were explained to him as his way of expressing himself. As positives, they were accepted as part of his style. Perhaps he might want to achieve control over these outbursts (he did). But it would be very difficult, if not impossible, not to have them because he used them, instead of emotionality (which he avoided diligently), as his mode of self-expression.

Consequently, a plan was laid out: He should have aggressive outbursts at specific times with specific family members with whom he was involved and in whose presence he was in the habit having temper tantrums. He was also told to call the therapist after each outburst to describe the outcome for the family; he called to indicate that he did not feel like having a temper tantrum but that he would try again. The therapist expressed amazement at his inability to follow instructions, especially in view of his long history of aggressive outbursts. He was told to try again at the specified times. He should have them in the houses of both his grandmother and his parents. He did have one or two minor half-hearted, half-baked aggressive outbursts.

Eventually, the outbursts disappeared completely. He was able from then on to start writing letters to members of the opposite sex, with whom until then he had been unable to establish any relationship. Ultimately, he was able to apply for a job, which for the first time he maintained for longer than one year. He is now contemplating marrying the girl he has dated for more than a year, and he has kept his current job for two years.

The next case, which also concerns temper tantrums, was a 10-year-old boy, from an abusive, incestuous family, who had been farmed out to a foster family for possible adoption. Therapy was conducted by Dr. Margarett S. Baggett; I was again the one-shot consultant. The boy's temper tantrums were quite explosive and threatening, especially to the foster mother; he also exhibited them in school. The tantrums were positively reframed as his own method of expression. A specific place was chosen where he was encouraged to have his tantrums on a regular basis. The principle here is that *the undesirable, symptomatic behavior should be made to occur when and where it does not naturally or spontaneously occur* (L'Abate & Kearns, submitted for publication). In this case, a basement room (which contained only empty boxes) was designated for the temper tantrums. The foster father was encouraged to get a couple of old inner tubes, fill them, and ask the child to go to the basement on a regular basis to have his tantrum. We agreed that Saturday morning, when the foster father would also be present, would be the best time. The boy was then to have a tantrum for at least 15 minutes. He was to report back to the therapist when he had finished his assignment. The foster parents were to encourage him to have the temper tantrum from 10 A.M. to 10:15 A.M. every Saturday morning. The child reported to the therapist (Dr. B.) that he had failed to do the assignment and that he was not planning to have any more temper tantrums. The therapist expressed surprise at his inability and unwillingness to carry out the assignment and also noted that Dr. L. would probably be very disappointed that he had not carried it out: He was encouraged to continue having temper tantrums, especially at the time and place specified. This case was followed up after a few months, during which time the temper tantrums, especially at home, had subsided to zero, even though the boy still had a few tantrums at school. Unfortuantely, however, the foster parents changed their minds about adopting the child because of the stress he seemed to place on their marriage. To decrease the pain of loss when the boy left, Dr. Baggett organized a farewell party to make the leavetaking a joyous occasion.

In spite of his considerable improvement and exemplary behavior, this child did continue to exhibit occasional fits of oppositional behavior, which displeased his foster parents a great deal. Consequently, plans were made for his return to his family of origin, who, in the meantime, had received therapy and counseling from another therapist. Although the battle of the temper tantrums was won, the war—to keep this child in the foster home and be adopted—was lost. Nevertheless, the child did show considerable improvement in his self-control, even upon returning to his family of origin.

Another case was a couple, married for 25 years, referred to us (Dr. L and Mrs. L) by their son, who was concerned that they stayed at home all the time. During those 25 years, the mother had developed a complete phobia about housework. The father was employed full time but had learned to cook and do the household chores, while the wife went shopping and spent her time in nonproductive activities. She had become completely phobic about going outside (except for shopping) and enjoying life. Theirs was a rather miserable existence, with no friends, no travel, no vacation—all because of the wife's continuous need to control all situations. Eventually, she was verbally congratulated for the way she had achieved control over everybody (without, of course, having appeared to achieve control) and for how much she cared for the whole family, especially the husband. She kept him busy all the time to help him (a refugee and victim of the holocaust) avoid dealing with his depression and his own hurt. After receiving this interpretation, the couple reported having gone on a work-vacation holiday (the first in years). She had begun to do housework and cook (in spite of the husband's resistance!). They discontinued treatment after the seventh session because they had not gotten anything out of therapy. I agreed with them and offered to refund their money, an offer they refused.

CONCLUSION

Paradoxical techniques are but one level of abstraction in at least four levels of therapy. They are especially relevant in the initial phase of therapy to induce symptomatic relief and reduce stress and emotionality. These techniques are not the end of therapy but rather, the beginning. To achieve success, a therapist needs a variety of linear approaches that will help families attain greater intimacy and learn to negotiate problematic issues.

REFERENCES

Alexander, J., & Parsons, B. V. *Functional family therapy.* Monterey, Calif.: Brooks/Cole, 1982.

Bertalanffy, L. von. *General systems theory.* New York: Braziller, 1968.

de Shazer, S. *Patterns of brief family therapy: An ecosystemic approach.* New York: Guilford Press, 1982.

Dewey, J., & Bentley, A. F. *Knowing and the known.* Boston: Beacon Press, 1949.

Haley, J. *Problem-solving therapy.* San Francisco: Jossey-Bass, 1976.

Hansen, J. C., & L'Abate, L. *Approaches to family therapy.* New York: Macmillan, 1982.

Jessee, E., & L'Abate, L. The use of paradox with children in an inpatient setting. *Family Process,* 1980, *19,* 59–64.

Kempler, W. *Existential family therapy.* San Francisco, Calif: Jossey-Bass, 1981.

L'Abate, L. *Principles of clinical psychology.* New York: Grune & Stratton, 1964.

L'Abate, L. A communication-information model. In L. L'Abate (Ed.), *Models of clinical psychology.* Atlanta, Ga.: Georgia State College School of Arts and Sciences Research Papers, No. 22, 1969. 65–73.

L'Abate, L. Psychodynamic interventions. A personal statement. In R. H. Woody & J. D. Woody (Eds.), *Sexual, marital, and family relations: Therapeutic interventions for professional helping.* Springfield, Ill.: Charles C. Thomas, 1973. 122–180.

L'Abate, L. A positive approach to marital and familial intervention. In L. R. Wolberg & M. L. Aronson (Eds.), *Group therapy 1975: An overview.* New York: Stratton Intercontinental Medical Book Corp., 1975. 63–75.

L'Abate, L. *Understanding and helping the individual in the family.* New York: Grune & Stratton, 1976.

L'Abate, L. *Enrichment: Structured interventions with couples, families, and groups.* Washington, D.C.: University Press of America, 1977.

L'Abate, L. Toward a systematic classification of counseling and therapy theorists, methods, processes and goals: The E-R-A model. *The Personnel and Guidance Journal,* 1981, *59,* 263–265.

L'Abate, L. (Ed.). *Family psychology: Theory, therapy, and training.* Washington, D.C.: University Press of America, 1983. (a)

L'Abate, L. Styles in intimate relationships: The A-R-C model. *The Personnel and Guidance Journal,* 1983, *61,* 277–283. (b)

L'Abate, L. The paradoxical treatment of (marital) depression. *International Journal of Family Therapy,* in press.

L'Abate, L. *Toward a systematic approach to family therapy.* Manuscript submitted for publication, 1983. (a)

L'Abate, L. *Toward a technology of marriage and family evaluation and intervention.* Manuscript in preparation, 1983. (b)

L'Abate, L., & Baggett, M. Failure to keep a father in family therapy. In B. Coleman (Ed.), *Failures in family therapy.* New York: Guilford Press, in press.

L'Abate, L., & Farr, L. Coping with defeating patterns in family therapy. *Family Therapy,* 1981, *8,* 91–103.

L'Abate, L., & Frey, J., III. The E-R-A model: The role of feelings in family therapy reconsidered: Implications for a classification of theories of family therapy. *Journal of Marital and Family Therapy,* 1981, *7,* 143–150.

L'Abate, L., Frey, J., III, & Wagner, V. Toward a classification of family therapy theories: Further elaborations and implications of the E-R-A-Aw-C model. *Family Therapy,* 1982, *9,* 251–262.

L'Abate, L., Hansen, J. C., & Ganahl, G. *Key concepts and methods in family therapy.* Englewood Cliffs, N. J.: Prentice-Hall, in press.

L'Abate, L., & Kearns, D. *The tenets of paradoxical psychotherapy.* Manuscript submitted for publication, 1983.

L'Abate, L., & Kochalka, J. Clinical training in family psychology. In B. Okun (Ed.), *Training issues in marriage and family counseling.* Ann Arbor, Mich.: ACES, in press.

L'Abate, L., & Samples, G. T. Intimacy letters: Invariable prescription for closeness-avoidant couples. *Family Therapy,* 1983, *10,* 37–45.

L'Abate, L., & Sloan, S. Z. Intimacy. In L. L'Abate (Ed.), *Handbook of family psychology and psychotherapy.* Homewood, Ill.: Dow Jones-Irwin, in press. (a)

L'Abate, L., & Sloan, S. Z. Intimacy workshops to increase intimacy in couples. *Family Relations,* in press. (b)

L'Abate, L., Sloan, S., Wagner, V., & Malone, K. The differentiation of resources. *Family Therapy,* 1980, *7,* 237–246.

L'Abate, L., & Wagner, V. Theory-derived, family-oriented test-batteries. In L. L'Abate (Ed.), *Handbook of family psychology and psychotherapy.* Homewood, Ill.: Dow Jones-Irwin, in press.

L'Abate, L., Weeks, G., & Weeks, K. Of scapegoats, strawmen, and scarecrows. *International Journal of Family Therapy,* 1979, *1,* 86–96.

Madanes, C. *Strategic family therapy.* San Francisco: Jossey-Bass, 1981.

Minuchin, S. *Families and family therapy.* Cambridge, Mass.: Harvard University Press, 1974.

Neill, J. R., & Kniskern, D. P. (Eds.). *From psyche to system: The evolving therapy of Carl Whitaker.* New York: Guilford Press, 1982.

Ruesch, J., & Bateson, G. *Communication: The social matrix of psychiatry.* New York: W. W. Norton, 1951.

Rychlak, J. *A philosophy of science for personality theory.* New York: Houghton Mifflin, 1968.

Soper, P. H., & L'Abate, L. Paradox as a therapeutic technique: A review. *International Journal of Family Counseling,* 1977, *5,* 10–21.

Ulrici, D., Wagner, V., & L'Abate, L. The E-R-A model: A heuristic framework for classification of skill training programs for couples and families. *Family Relations,* 1981, *30,* 307–315.

Wagner, V., Weeks, G., & L'Abate, L. Enrichment and written messages with couples. *American Journal of Family Therapy,* 1980, *8,* 36–44.

Weeks, G. Toward a dialectical approach to intervention. *Human Development,* 1977, *20,* 277–292.

Weeks, G., & L'Abate, L. *Paradoxical psychotherapy: Theory and practice with individuals, couples, and families.* New York: Brunner/Mazel, 1982.

6

Ericksonian Styles of Paradoxical Treatment

by Stephen R. Lankton, MSW, and Carol H. Lankton, MA

We came upon a fortune cookie while writing this chapter that read: "Always remember: if you tell the truth, you never have to remember anything." The master paradoxologist is the person who says only the obvious, thus suggesting great meaning. In fact, Lao Tzu (c. 550 B.C.) wrote that "Words that are strictly true seem to be paradoxical" (1976, p. 168). In this chapter we will not discuss the content of pardoxical truth but the impact and use of paradoxical interventions. More specifically, we will relate our understanding of an approach that makes use of paradox both in symptom prescription and in metaphor.

THE VALUE OF PARADOX

Our interest in paradox resulted from contact with Milton Erickson, a phenomenal paradoxologist. Gregory Bateson, after studying Erickson, defined paradox as a contradiction in conclusions that were correctly argued from consistent premises (Bateson, 1972, p. 223). He observed that some clients responding to

Erickson would produce trance phenomena to resolve problems posed by contradictory commands which could not be discussed. He cited this observation as an illustration of a double bind situation being resolved via a shift in logical types (1972, p. 223). Webster's *Third New International Dictionary* defines paradox as: "1. a tenet or proposition contrary to received opinion. 2a. a statement of sentiment that is seemingly contradictory or opposed to common sense and yet perhaps true." Bateson's definition appears at 2(b): "a statement that is actually self-contradictory and hence false even though its true character is not immediately apparent" (1976, p. 1636). It is this usage that we refer to in the following case transcript, which includes paradox delivered explicitly in words (paradoxical binds), in the logic of indirect suggestions, in the context of a metaphoric story line, in symptom prescriptions, and in paradoxical intention for interview management.

Following his contact with Erickson, Bateson introduced paradoxical interventions to Haley and the MRI group who were influential in studying and popularizing this approach. Richard Fisch, director of Brief Therapy at the Mental Research Institute (MRI) informed us recently, however, that a trend among the MRI group is to abandon the notion of paradox in therapeutic intervention (Fisch, December 2, 1982). This trend results from the idea that the interventions formerly called *paradoxical* are not actually paradoxes at all. Instead, the MRI group views them as perfectly logical given the family system in which they are delivered. It seems to us, however, that the descriptive term *paradox* (and related concepts) need not be abandoned simply because its use in a disordered family system is often eminently logical. Obviously, we wouldn't be using these interventions unless there were some logic in doing so, even if the logic is only apparent to the family or individual receiving them.

Perhaps the ultimate value in paradox rests in the understanding that ideas have cycles of existence. This is true for the momentary thoughts we each entertain and for groups of individuals. When groups discuss a topic, the topic is given longer existence. But the consensus beliefs and sets of beliefs associated to *core* beliefs all have a duration and a cycle, both in the culture and in history. The value of paradox may result from the role it plays in reminding us, albeit sophistically, that these cycles exist. With the paradox, the listener is reminded of the wisdom illustrating that what we do now is part of the cycle of what we do later, or, at the very least, shall we say: What we *think* and *believe* now is cyclical, and in some way each seemingly polarized part allows for the existence of its opposite. We all know that winter makes way for summer; day makes way for night; the moon sets and the sun rises; we can get angry and later be more loving; we can decide affirmatively and negatively about the same incident in a matter of years, months, even shorter periods. Each of us recognizes these truths to contain a certain natural reminder, but we often fail to put the wisdom of that knowledge into practical application. Paradoxically, it is true that the moon rises so that we can enjoy sunlight, winter comes so that summer will find us, and so on.

We will take a short tangent to illustrate this point. Part of the value of this natural wisdom is the colloquial (day-to-day) application of its principle. For instance, we often hesitate to act on a decision to follow an impulse until we examine that impulse from other perspectives or otherwise think it over, give some time to find out how we feel about it over time, and so on. Each of us has hesitated on a purchase, held back something we might have said prematurely, restrained our vocal tone, gone somewhere to "think over" a concern, and so on. Such behavior is preventative problem solving, and often preventative mental health. As a case in point, Fritz Perls introduced a Gestalt therapy exercise that consisted of examining the exact opposite of one's urge, wish, impulse, fantasy, feeling. In so doing, the individual learned to maintain a "creative precommitment." "The ability to achieve and maintain an interested impartiality between imagined opposites, however absurd one side may seem, is essential for any new creative solution of problems" (Perls et al., 1951, p. 53).

But in the case where a problem already exists, the application of the principle of cycles comes too late (or was preempted by the problem). In these cases, the logic of restraint, acting in an opposite way, or tapping an opposite goal has not already been considered. The application of the principle finds value in that doing the same thing to get the opposite result has not usually been considered. The paradox introduces this consideration by appealing to an understanding (no matter how well developed) of this wisdom. Jung wrote: "And just as the conscious mind can put the question, 'Why is there this frightful conflict between good and evil?' so the unconscious can reply, 'Look closer! Each needs the other'" (1959, p. 153). The paradox then is one of the symbols of this wisdom. Alan Watts stated that paradox is the truth standing on its head to attract attention (Watts, 1953).

If, however, the paradox does not express profound truth, it can at least be expected to capture attention and provoke thought. Parmenides of Elea (515 B.C.) and his student, Zeno (490–85 B.C.) were among those intrigued by the complexities of paradox. Plato, in his *Dialogue of Parmenides*, referred to Parmenides and

Zeno as the originators of the several paradoxes posed by Socrates, which have become known as the Achilles paradox, the Arrow, and others. You may recall Zeno as the man who originated the idea that anything in motion is stationary. (Of course, that idea went nowhere!) Socrates was at an impasse about Parmenides' reasoning that things do not change, because indeed things do change and reasoned explanation to the contrary presented an attention-capturing and thought-provoking dialogue.

A paradox used in treatment is less likely to convey a profound truth than to capture attention; yet the use of paradoxical interventions ought not be considered a trick. With paradoxical interventions, as with all interventions, we suggest they be offered with sincerity. We agree with the MRI group in the understanding that a paradox is not illogical in the context of a client system. In the case of a paradoxical symptom prescription, for instance, we *really* mean for the client to continue the behavior for his or her own benefit; we are not trying to trick the client. A paradoxical trick is actually a sophism, or a conspicuous paradox, it often alerts the listener to an intention to convey an elusive meaning. Sophisms such as Zeno's are clever manipulations that are false and have knowingly been committed. A true paradox, on the other hand, is knowingly committed but *true:* As such it may lead the listener to a disquieting conclusion or absurd conclusions, but it is not fallacious. That is, a genuine paradox is a conclusion based on valid reasoning at every step.

A paradoxical intervention then may be used to help produce several results that can be of value in treatment. It symbolizes the natural wisdom of impermanence; it captures attention and may provoke new thought. Most of all, it illustrates a line of reasoning to reach its conclusion. Therefore, it arrests attention, overloads consciousness, and causes the listener to question axioms, postulates, beliefs, reasoning, facts, memory, congruity checking, and so on. In short, it stimulates thinking in general, and elicits responses that are exactly the social and psychological results sought for and created by paradox.

SOCIAL HYPNOSIS, PATHOLOGY, AND PARADOX

We are all aware of the significance of a transaction for the individual, and the health or pathology that is transmitted, elicited, shaped or reinforced in an individual. But the effect of a transaction on the social network has an equally important causational influence on mental health. A transaction is a model for all observers in that it provides a map, and thereby socializes others. When others operate from the map, the transaction reinforces in that it predicts (roughly) how the person upon whom the map is used will respond. For instance, someone makes a joke and in some way puts another person down. When this transaction is observed, the role and behavior of joking are associated and memory provides a partial map of conduct for the observer to use when faced with a similar situation, person, or set of prompts: Thus the social network is simultaneously socialized to treat the "odd" or "hostile" child as if s/he were odd or hostile. The map predicts the results the user can get from the real world and thus forms part of the user's self-system and ultimately part of his or her belief system.

The role taken by the therapist when s/he uses paradoxical symptom prescription with a family or family member confuses (at least temporarily) all members in the social network regarding their roles and behavior related to the symptom. Therefore, paradox may be used to stop the deleterious social transmission, reinforcement, and shaping of the symptom. In moments when the usual pattern of social interaction and transmission of roles, rules, affects, and ideas are stopped, the therapist gains an entry into the broader areas of the client(s) personality(ies) and has an unparalleled opportunity to help rearrange new combinations of personal experiences, perceptions, and maps of conduct. We demonstrate in the transcript that follows several areas in which therapeutic outcomes are created, using paradox to impede usual thought association processes and metaphor to convey both the paradoxical logic or directive, and to stimulate mental search and retrieve novel experience. First, however, we want to examine the social effects of paradox on both social transactions and personality.

PARADOX AND PERSONALITY

Although it has become fashionable to take only a systems approach—as we have done above in analyzing transactions—we think there is also much to be gained by looking at several commonly acknowledged aspects of personality and asking what might be happening with respect to feelings, imagination, and expectations. In the case example presented in this chapter, the client alters his expectations and his perceptions. In fact, he increases and concentrates attention in a slightly different way as ongoing behavior continues. As a result, he has an opportunity for novel experience that is of course therapeutically directed. This socially or transactionally created "opening" to the client emphasizes that alterations in internal behavior are possible as a result of communication containing paradoxical features.

If we assume that drives, urges, and bodily impulses must in some incipient way be involved in movement and consequent roles taken by the person, then we might ask what about the change in desires, urges, impulses, and so on that has been set in motion or otherwise involved by the paradox. What change in impulses and drives might explain how the person comes to confide in the therapist slightly more as a result of the changed frame of reference that has been cocreated with the therapist? As confiding and risk taking are seen as measures of self-esteem (Yalom, 1970), we might ask how drives and urges might have been affected such that self-esteem and risk taking have been altered. The answer of course is that the client's creativity is subjectively increased due to the symbolic value of paradox. Further, depending upon the subsequent communication, the client may experience expanded options for previously unnoticed behaviors, feelings, and perceptions.

When a person hears a paradox, s/he does not know what expectations will be sanctioned. S/he must suspend the customary frame of reference and therefore the predisposition to a particular feeling state. A great deal of bodily and psychodynamic experience is temporarily altered when a person is engaged in response to paradox and much of this alteration becomes the foundation for therapeutic learning.

An impulse is a wave of excitation passing through certain tissues. An urge is a force that rouses activity from an otherwise dormant state. Urges, drives, impulses, and the like, as bodily experiences, are affected by the state of the body; they occur in relation to nutrition, stimulation, sleep, and chemistry. But ultimately, they are woven into the map of historical experience and channeled into what the individual would call the way s/he "feels," the "mood," or more scientifically, his or her self-system. Usual emotions, whether healthy or pathological, are the combined result of these phenomena. Affect, then, is created as the gestalt of bodily urges, desires, and drives interacting with the match (or mismatch) created between perceptual reality and anticipated images.

SEARCH PHENOMENA

Our synthesis of the personality consists of a redundant or recurring blend of perceptions, expectations, and urges, all of which combine to produce particular affects. Consciousness and deliberate thought in imagery occur secondary to this otherwise primary process and only in varying degrees do individuals exercise the ability to inhibit, direct, or modify the impact of these affective states voluntarily and experimentally. More often, the social system is created to exert control in cases where the individual has not.

There is predictability to a personality even though it operates dynamically within a living and changing person. An individual, until s/he changes, continues to expect a finite variety of experiences in the world (e.g., the postman will be anonymous, the fish store personnel will be friendly, Sally will be eager, our son will like this and that, etc.). This colloquially noticed personality is of course a result of the predictability gained by the redundant occurrence of relatively similar urges, expectations, perceptions, and subsequent states of affect.

In the absence of conditioned responses to paradox (a highly unconditioned stimulus), the person has no established map to follow from previous learning and will consequently respond with searching behavior designed to produce an appropriate response. The person attempts to construct a new map to guide behavior, affect, and expectations regarding likely consequences for both self and others. Specific indicators of such internal searching are flattened cheeks, decreased movement, slowed reflexes (breathing, blinking swallowing), pupil dilation, eye scanning, and increased pallor. These search phenomena are considered to be signs of light trance in that the person's attention is at least temporarily internally concentrated.

To the extent that searching for a logical map to follow is not successful, the person can be expected to become increasingly receptive to external direction from the therapist which stimulates the co-construction of a map containing and detailing new options. Working from an Ericksonian approach to treatment, we find that deepening the naturalistic trance initiated by the paradox and then presenting metaphors to the client provides him or her an opportunity to entertain novel experiences in a nonthreatening way, examine them as possible options, evaluate them from a personal perspective, and expand the map to include those metaphors judged personally relevant by the individual.

Though what will be personally relevant to the individual is ultimately decided *by* the individual, the therapist is obligated as a professional to diagnose and assess the client and the social network, make a carefully considered estimate of which therapeutic outcomes are likely to be relevant, and design a treatment plan which provides the client an opportunity to learn the affect, transactions, attitudes, and so on compatible with achieving such outcomes. We list in some detail six therapeutic outcomes which we consider essential in any complete treatment. Though the presenting problem and the greatest deficit in logical maps may seemingly be confined to one area, we would want, in the interest of thoroughness, to metaphorically address possible changes in each of the other areas that might be related to integrating new behaviors. In the case transcript presented in this chapter, we metaphorically address four of these six outcomes in the first interview. But, prior to discussing therapeutic outcomes, we will briefly summarize several guidelines for creating effective paradoxes to be used in Ericksonian approaches.

ELEMENTS OF EFFECTIVE THERAPEUTIC PARADOX

Recognizing that there are many and varied ways to intervene paradoxically, we offer the following elements of paradox as flexible guidelines for therapists to use in initially formulating and delivering paradoxical interventions, as well as in examining why a particular paradoxical intervention was not effective. We do not imply that all of these elements must be evident in any effective paradoxical intervention, but that each element is important to consider and address in some way, though not necessarily in an obvious fashion or in the order in which they are discussed here.

Empathic Activity and Establishing Rapport

Establishing rapport is a foundation goal in most therapies; it is particularly crucial in a therapy in which clients are not encouraged or expected to have a conscious understanding about the manner in which therapy is proceeding. In fact the opposite is typical, namely that clients are expected to experience a good deal of conscious confusion and perhaps even anger at the therapist for behaving in such an unorthodox manner. An angry reaction may be subdued, accepted by the client, or avoided entirely if sufficient rapport is established prior to the therapist behaving paradoxically. Occasionally, however, offering paradoxical behavior prescriptions is itself a way of establishing rapport, at least with that part of the client that is generating the behavior being prescribed. For example, in the case to be discussed later in this chapter, the client presents himself for therapy because of his oppositional attitudes and resulting difficulties with "authority." Rapport was facilitated by beginning a trance induction with the instruction that the client was to rebel against our words to the extent necessary for him to be certain that he followed only those instructions that were in his best interest. It was quite likely that he would rebel in some way to what we said to him and by suggesting that he do so, with good reason, we expected to stimulate his feeling of being understood at one level and simultaneously confused (therapeutically) at another.

More frequently this element of building rapport and helping the client feel understood is accomplished more conventionally. Erickson would often demonstrate his understanding of a client's presented difficulty by restating almost verbatim the client's complaint. Reflective listening training has prepared most therapists to almost automatically paraphrase the client's expressed or implied feelings. This training allows the therapist to "automatically" respond emphathically to the client's expressed difficulty while at another level enabling him or her to begin formulating paradoxical interventions which will eventually help the client reframe the difficulty and resultantly conceptualize new solutions.

Providing a Positively Framed Reason for Paradoxical Instruction

Since clients typically present problems that seem to them nothing but problems, paradoxical interventions that suggest continuing the problem are more likely to receive therapeutic response if some seemingly logical, albeit completely unexpected "reason" for doing so is presented. Giving such a positively framed reason for continuing and even increasing a problem behavior accomplishes several things. At the social level, it encourages the client to go along with the therapist in doing something unexpected and not immediately understandable. At the psychological level, the client is helped to accept the problem itself as serving some useful purpose, to recognize it as an ally that may actually become an unexpected means of achieving far more than symptom removal. Once the client accepts the notion that there may be some benefit in having and/or continuing the "problem," an atmosphere is established in which the client, by shifting the previous frame of reference, can begin to generate possible solutions never considered before. These solutions may take the form of how the positive result accomplished by the problem might instead be accomplished in some creative, new way.

When offering positively framed reasons for following paradoxical prescriptions, we do so sincerely bearing in mind the Ericksonian principle that clients, at any given time, are always making the best choice for themselves that they have so far learned to make. All behavior, even problematic behavior, was learned for some good reason and is continued in the absence of a better choice in a particular situation. Of course the "reason" underlying the problem posed by the therapist may not always be accurate, but will at least stimulate the client to consider that some positive reason exists for having and therefore continuing the problem behavior in order to accomplish some therapeutic aim.

Altering the Symptomatic Behavior

When the client has agreed to voluntarily continue engaging in the problem behavior, the previous routine, in which the problem was felt to be uncontrollable and completely negative, has already been disrupted: The client will not be able to engage in the problem in the same way once it is being viewed positively and done volitionally. But to go several steps beyond this natural disruption of the problem routine, it is very often desirable to alter the symptomatic behavior in a therapeutic direction by either splitting the client's experience of the problem, adding another (therapeutic) behavior upon which the problem behavior is contingent, or modifying the occurrence of the problem along such dimensions as timing, location, intensity, and so on.

One initial goal of such alteration is to provide the client with a new sense of hope and control. Perhaps an even more important goal is to create a context in which therapeutic alternatives can be taught. The first step in teaching such alternatives often involves a process of stimulating the search phenomena described earlier by suggesting something not readily understood by the client such as, "Go ahead and have the ringing in your ears, but I wonder if you can tune yourself so that you don't hear it." This directive, paraphrased from one of Erickson's cases, suggested splitting the client's experience between physiologically "having" and psychologically "hearing" the ringing. Though, upon hearing such a suggestion, a client may have some vague notions about what the therapist is implying it is more likely that intensive internal searching will be initiated in which the client reviews experiences to find some specific, personal understanding of the therapist's casually offered suggestion. We would consider this a search for therapeutic alternatives; that is, for personal resources that can be applied in new ways to solve an established problem.

Illustrating and Retrieving Needed Experiences with Metaphor

Having confused the client's customary frame of reference concerning the problem with the paradoxical directive and having initiated an internal search for specific ways of cooperating with the suggested alteration, the therapist is in a position to stimulate the client to retrieve needed resources and create a new map to follow that includes therapeutic alternatives—an association of those personal resources to the context of the problem. In this regard, we find that metaphor or a series of metaphors logically follows the paradoxical directive and suggested alterations. Metaphorical speaking indirectly stimulates the client's own thinking about needed resource experiences and may model a possible map for the client to interpret, modify, assimilate in part or whole, or reject if not relevant. It is not enough to simply disrupt the client's routine with respect to the problem and consider therapy complete. We have only set the stage for the real work of therapy to begin, to help the client develop a personally relevant and satisfying map of conduct in which desired resources are available and associated to stimuli in his or her social and problem network. The case to be presented in this chapter thoroughly illustrates this element of paradox utilization.

Delivering the Paradox at the Beginning or End of the Therapeutic Sequence

The logic of presenting a paradox at the beginning of a therapeutic sequence has probably become apparent from the preceding discussion which emphasized that delivering a paradoxical intervention will cause the client to shift frames of reference and initiate an internal search. When this searching does not result in a readily understandable meaning for the client, search phenomena increase and the client displays signs of light trance. Receptivity to additional direction from the therapist is increased at that point; thus it is an optimal time for the therapist to present a series of therapeutic metaphors. These metaphors may also contain elements of paradox and confusion to overload the conscious mind and allow the client to entertain novel experiences.

Delivering a paradox at the end of a therapeutic sequence is often desirable as a way of reorienting the client and distracting the conscious mind from excessive analysis of the preceding work. At the same time, the paradox allows the conscious mind something to analyze and retroactively frames the series of metaphors in a compelling manner. The client attempts to understand the metaphors based on the concluding paradox and at the same time attempts to unravel the paradox's possibilities and implications. We refer to this type of concluding paradox as one which facilitates closure, an increased sense of meaningfulness about what went before based on the final paradox's compelling nature.

Delivering in a Manner That Is Not Authoritative or One Up

We offer this consideration about delivery of paradox based on research by Weakland et al. (1974) which indicated that a confused, ignorant stance on the therapist's part (one down) seemed to facilitate greater compliance by avoiding a high pressure approach that might arouse client resistance. We tend to modify this conclusion by recommending that therapists generally refrain from being one-up or authoritative. Being indirect or metaphorically paradoxical is certainly one way to accomplish this goal. There are, however, those clients for whom binding conditions at the outset or a challenging stance from the therapist will be the most effective way to proceed.

SEEDS WITHOUT SUNSHINE? THERAPEUTIC OUTCOMES IN METAPHOR

We have mentioned that the paradox provides a stimulus that reminds the listener of certain philosophical wisdom and possibilities of applying something previously unconsidered to the solution of a problem or completion of a task. Simultaneously, the paradox enters a slight confusion when a paradoxical situation is posed or paradoxical logic or directives are given. The rules of experience and combining experience that once applied no longer apply. Logic is arrested and unconscious process and search are stimulated. Presenting paradoxes designed to stimulate unconscious search without directing or stimulating that search in some manner would be similar to planting seeds in an area where they do not receive sunshine. Therefore it shouldn't be surprising to find here a discussion of another important technique to be used along with Ericksonian paradox: metaphor. Aristotle said this about metaphor: "The greatest thing by far is to be a master of metaphor....and it is also a sign of genius, since a good metaphor implies an intuitive perception of the similarity in dissimilars" (1954, p. 255). Metaphor provided a means by which Erickson could gently guide the development of the growing seed-ideas. More technically, we might say that metaphor provides *controlled elaboration* of ideas that are the subject of unconscious search.

A strategic therapist begins the therapeutic process by assessing the individual and family system. This assessment is most useful when it includes a decision about what therapeutic outcomes are desirable. The therapist must reach a tentative decision on which life experience or growth process to elaborate. This decision is reached by combining what the client specifically requests with the therapist's observations of related changes indirectly requested in the client's manner of presentation. This assessment is not necessarily shared with the client; it is only a point of reference for the therapist. It is important to emphasize, however, that the client is the ultimate judge as to whether a goal is relevant or how any metaphor that may depict a possibility of change will be interpreted or acted upon.

Once the therapist has formulated those goals that, according to careful clinical assessment, seem desirable and relevant for a particular client-system, s/he is ready to design interventions to facilitate those goals. These interventions will very likely include paradox, especially as a means to "open a doorway" of experience and temporarily confuse and suspend the client's normal frame of reference with regard to the problem or goal. It is at this point, as mentioned earlier, that each individual client is likely to be most receptive to new possibilities or information about how to proceed. As Ericksonian therapists, we find that the most effective and respectful way of communicating with such clients is indirectly, with metaphor and anecdotes. In this way, we insure that we do not impose our values or goals on the client but only offer the client a stimulus to do his or her own thinking. Each client who hears the same story, for example, will interpret it differently according to his or her personal understanding. The metaphors and other interventions selected and designed will of course depend on the therapeutic outcome goals formulated by the therapist before the delivery of the paradox.

We have grouped these goals into six broad areas of therapeutic outcomes: (1) family structure and social network changes; (2) changes in age, appropriate intimacy, and task behaviors; (3) attitude restructuring; (4) affect and emotional role changes; (5) changes in self-image; and (6) changes related to self-discipline and enjoying living. As we examine each individually, it will be useful to bear in mind that often the client-system may only request change in one area and may do so indirectly by asking for symptom removal. As therapists, however, we consider therapy to be complete only after we have seen evidence of change in each area. Often this involves our specifically addressing each area with metaphors designed especially to facilitate change in that area.

Family Structure and Social Network Changes

Many problems presented in therapy clearly indicate the desirability of change in this area. These include marital problems, family difficulties, discomfort entering, dealing with, or appropriately separating from a particular phase of a family cycle. Goals here are usually stated in terms of dealing more appropriately with demands of the current or next logical stage of family development. Desired change in the family structure depends on the unique culture, history, and goals of each family but generally includes several features:

Changes in who is involved in the network.

Changes in who speaks to whom.

Changes in what is spoken about.

Changes in the affect typically present and exchanged.

Changes in the subgroups that form and what they do.

Changes in role sharing and role support.

Changes in how needs are expressed.

Changes in how expressed needs can be responded to.

Changes in clarity of communication.

Implementation of communication aimed at relationships.

Implementation of communication aimed at goals.

Implementation of solution- and resolution-oriented communication.

Changes in the use of direct and indirect communication.

Changes in the use of reinforcement and punishment among members.

Other problems brought to therapy do not as readily indicate that a family or individual expects change in the family or social network. We contend, however, that even therapy with individuals for specific symptoms such as smoking, pain control, and so on will be most beneficial when we help each individual client and his or her family members prepare for logical changes in family structure or social network that will likely be stimulated as a result of the symptom resolution. When we have only an individual in treatment, we help that individual create a helpful interface as s/he returns, changed in some way, to the environment of significant others who in turn will also be stimulated to change and support changes made by the individual in therapy. Erickson was very thoughtful about how even his individual clients would operate at interface points with others in their families and/or social network systems, since the success of changes begun in any area will depend on how well they are integrated into the client's environmental circumstances. This is, then, the rationale for using metaphors that sensitize even the individual client to the roles, expectations, behaviors, feelings, and so on that will be called for in the family and social network.

The Individual and Change

Regarding an individual as the client in family therapy, Erickson did not take the psychoanalytic view (as did Akerman) as justification for seeing the individual while doing family therapy. Erickson was both practical and ingenious. As most therapists know, many symptoms presented in therapy which would seem to be isolated from family structure matters are really only the superficial request for a much more pervasive therapy which frequently deals specifically with hidden problems in family structure not yet disclosed. The nature of these familywide and indeed social, networkwide changes need not be mysterious. Frequently theorists attempt to propose neat, systemic, homeostatic, cybernetic, and rule-bound frameworks to analyze the tensions and changes in a family system. Although we would be very pleased to impose any neat and concise framework on families to cast an air of scientific respectability onto our profession, Erickson frequently reminded us to treat each case uniquely. He went so far as to say that he made a new theory for each individual.

He didn't consider symptom removal in one individual to always result in a dysfunction in others (or the same person) in the family. In fact, we expect that often the entire family improves dramatically when the identified patient recovers from difficulty.

Often a valiant effort at recovery in one person is an inspiration to others to move ahead and grow. To assume in every case that there is a sinister, systemic pathology at work in the family is to bring to family therapy the same morbid attitude toward difficulty that the medical model helped foster in the early theories of individual personality.

There is, however, a logic of dynamic interplay which must be recognized at the level of systems theory, and that is by virtue of nothing more (and nothing less!) than the interdependence of each person on another. So we might best characterize Eriksonian attempts to intervene in a family as explained by the practicality of the unique family and how the persons in that family necessarily depend upon one another. The social play occurring at the interface points created between members is typically examined by asking the following types of questions: Does the husband support roles needed by the wife and vice-versa? Is there a role complementarity? Do the changes being stressed, shaped by, or expected of one family member enjoy a supportive other? The role behavior that may or may not be supported shapes the sanctions that will befall the family and hence shapes its destiny because in the process of growth the members will meet others and meet them with altered emotional flexibility, altered behavior, altered self-image expectations, altered attitudes, and so on. These alterations became opportunities for others to support, reject, interfere, model, reinforce, punish, and more. Thus in working with the individual only, Erickson was certain to help that individual interface with important others and maximize those meetings through the changes s/he was making or had made. In other words, Erickson would help an individual change in order to foster systemwide changes.

Family conflict is often viewed in light of the incongruities created by role taking within the family and extending beyond the family to interfaces with the broader social network. The way the person forms and uses interfaces is the key to doing family therapy with the individual in an Eriksonian style. The boundary between separate individuals in the client's world can be shaped in many ways. First, the individual's feelings, behaviors, expectations, and perceptions with respect to any particular other can be changed directly as the hypnotherapist deals with him or her. Further, the behavior of, say, a wife can be shaped by the selective behavior of the husband when only the husband is willing to come to therapy. This latter case is of course more difficult. But the behaviors, interpretations, emotions, and perceptions of the wife toward the husband are not as difficult to change via the husband's selective behavior when he has changed in therapy. This is true for any combination of persons in the network. For example, when working with an elderly woman for the reduction of psychic pain, we simply suggested that she entice her avoiding daughter in a particular manner: By so doing, she easily created in the daughter and son-in-law a change in their perception of her from malingering to inspiring. The mother also found a way to shape new approach behaviors in the daughter and son-in-law and new feelings of togetherness were experienced by all. In this case, working to change the family via the identified patient was probably quicker and more successful than a family therapy and insight-confrontation approach would have been. The daughter and son-in-law considered it their idea to approach the elderly mother in a new manner. They did not lose face, feel evaluated, find it necessary to defend the previous avoidance, or any other such eitrogenic response, because they were never even in the office!

To help clients accomplish changes in perception, emotion, and behavior to the extent that necessary interface maneuvers will be learned, it is important for therapists to be effective in ways that extend beyond the focused awareness of the family therapy metaphors. The five additional categories that follow are briefly explained and will then be illustrated in the case analysis to come.

Age Appropriate Intimacy and Task Behaviors

Related to changes in family structure and social network are changes in specific behaviors necessary for age appropriate intimacy and age appropriate developmental tasks. Goals are frequently stated in terms of change in perceptions, experiences, and transactions involved in approximating the chronological age appropriate intimacy and task situations that could be achieved by the client. Again, presenting problems may or may not point to obvious changes in this area. Complicating this matter is the therapeutic task of determining an individual's psychological age with regard to specific areas of functioning. As the psychological age is assessed, logical behavioral deficits will usually be apparent. These deficits will often be clearly related to the presenting problem. In the case discussion to follow, the client's presented difficulty with "authority" was so pervasive that he couldn't relate appropriately to his boss, peers, or wife and one could easily assume that this difficulty would soon be evident with children he might father. It was also clear from his adolescent manner and his description of competitive relations with his own father that behaviors related to trust, openness, making mistakes, and expressions of vulnerability had not been learned naturally and were not available to him in those situations and relationships he considered problematic.

Once psychological age and typical behavioral deficits are assessed, the therapeutic task is to systematically teach and model desired behaviors, usually in metaphor. By so doing, those behaviors (perceptions, experiences, transactions—either internal or externally observable) which were not learned in natural development are made available to the client as s/he experiences, identifies with, and assimilates them such that they can be used at appropriate times and in appropriate situations.

In some cases, the behaviors to be learned, determined by assessing developmental age and associated tasks, may not be as clearly related to the presenting problem. Such might have been the case if our client had asked for help managing physical pain. Still, we assume that making more mature, age appropriate behaviors available through metaphor will expand the client's options with regard to any problem, though perhaps in ways beyond those which we can anticipate.

Attitude Restructuring

Central to any lasting therapeutic growth are changes in perception and in the belief system, at the very least in those perceptions and beliefs that supported the problem. Change is often facilitated by helping the client alter the priority of perceptions and the weight or cognitive interpretation given to perceptions. This includes changes in the client's assumptions which may have been used previously to justify or make predictions about the problem and its continuation.

Attitude restructuring is necessary whether the problem is primarily somatic or more overtly interpersonal in nature. Believing that a skin condition is genetic and therefore incurable is an attitude that needs to be changed to enable the person to congruently retrieve and apply the personal abilities that might result in cure. And, changing that attitude enables the client to look for and find evidence of the expected change. With respect to the client to be discussed in this chapter, his limiting belief was that success or winning were only possible through superiority or rebellion against authority. Here the attitude change indicated was one that allowed the client to comfortably incorporate and utilize the new behaviors and affects addressed by the other metaphors.

For this client, paradoxical intention was useful to confuse his typical attitude and present a contrasting one whose logic was not immediately apparent.

Affect and Emotional Flexibility

In this category goals are usually conceptualized in terms of the client's understanding and use of emotions necessary to achieving the contracted therapy goals, including supporting perceptions of internal physiological components of the emotions. We begin from the assumption that any client has, by virtue of having lived, some experience of or at least the potential for experiencing all the emotions. The difficulty often lies in the area of emotional *flexibility* or the ability to use personal capabilities in particular situations. Erickson summarized it this way when he said: "Psychological problems exist precisely because the conscious mind does not know how to initiate psychological experience and behavior change to the degree that one would like" (Erickson & Rossi, 1979, p. 18). So, our therapeutic task is one of first retrieving and then associating these "psychological experiences" to situations where they are needed in order to facilitate flexibility of this "initiation" process. The purpose of initial metaphors, however, is simply to retrieve, build components of, or stimulate the desired experiences or affective states, preferably by discussing situations far removed from those areas in which the client ultimately wishes to use them. (The association step is usually managed by other metaphors from categories such as self-image thinking, family structure change, or age appropriate intimacy behaviors.

A factor that influences the content of metaphors designed specifically to retrieve affect is the psychological age of the client. Telling stories about experiences common to (or prior to) that age will run no risk of being too psychologically sophisticated for comprehension and congruent identification. With the "authority" client who follows, for example, metaphors designed to retrieve comfortable dependency feelings, trust, and a sense of competence were constructed bearing in mind the developmental period of adolescence, since this seemed to be the stage of development in which he was fixated. Thus we talked to him about dependency experiences every adolescent enjoys (riding in the front of a canoe, playing team sports) and appealed to his sense of competence and trust from even younger periods in "a boy's life" (learning to dress himself and tie knots) to enable us to proceed with utmost confidence that we were describing experiences he could powerfully experience.

Self-Image Thinking Enhancement

Goals here are generally stated in terms of improvement in the client's ability to anticipate him- or herself using new options in various situations, either privately or with significant others. This requires the ability to imagine, formulation of an awareness of the self as worthwhile, and a belief that certain new situations would be beneficial, or that it would be desirable to have certain behaviors and qualities ("psychological experiences") newly available in situations that have been typically problematic.

Metaphors or more direct methods designed to stimulate and direct these abilities are an almost essential component of any effective therapy. They provide an opportunity for clients to practice or mentally rehearse enacting in professional, familial, or social situations those learnings that have been stimulated by the therapy. They help the client to literally make a new map that can be depended upon to shape future performance. Images guide performance and self-image thinking provides a thoughtful alternative to automatically relying upon residual images from the past.

And finally of course, self-image thinking metaphors, by stimulating fantasies of typical situations in the client's future paired with new behavioral and emotional options, become an important associational link that helps clients accomplish the step of "initiating psychological experiences and behaviors" in situations where this had previously been difficult or impossible. This is clearly illustrated in the transcript to follow when the client listens to a metaphor which indirectly stimulates him to visualize himself in a new way, that is, with those behaviors and affective states that weren't typical in his interactions, and to study this new image of himself through a variety of situations in which he had previously behaved inappropriately. In this mental rehearsal, however, he was led to visualize himself interacting in new ways which "pleased and surprised him." The metaphoric content involves another client who is studying his reflection in the window of a train.

Enjoyment and Discipline in Living and Changing

Clients typically come to therapy for help in solving some problem and they often phrase goals in terms of what they want to *not* do or behaviors they want to "get rid of." Very few come to therapy specifically in order to enjoy life more, though in the instance of depressed clients, this goal is often clearly indicated. But regardless of the presenting problem, every client can benefit from interventions designed to stimulate processes leading to greater enjoyment in life.

Involved in the process of enjoying life is the matter of self-discipline, though this may sound paradoxically illogical to some. Erickson was an avid proponent of both enjoyment and discipline and frequently paired the two activities. He explained to one client ("Nick") in no uncertain terms that life's gifts are earned and merited: "You reach an understanding that every happiness is earned and, if given to you, it's merited. Because there is no such thing as a free gift; you have to earn it or you have to merit it. And merit requires labor and effort on your part" (Erickson in Lustig, videotape, 1975). We observed Erickson working with a client who was eventually stimulated to laughter (enjoyment) in the trance state. At the moment the client was laughing hardest, Erickson introduced the matter of discipline, suggesting that he "have that experience (the enjoyment) next time you *make up your mind about what you're going to do*" (Erickson, August 7, 1977). This example illustrates that self-discipline needn't necessarily be drudgery or a burdensome responsibility, but something that can be accomplished with enjoyment.

Erickson frequently enjoyed surprising clients and students with his own very well-developed sense of humor and in that way modeled enjoyment for them. Very little needs to be mentioned about the way in which Erickson modeled an exacting self-discipline. His entire life and many accomplishments—despite his physical infirmity—are testimony enough of that. Metaphors designed to stimulate an appreciation of living, even during the process of change, can also include associations to the necessary and proper amount of discipline that a client needs to acquire in order to achieve defined or implied goals. The ratio of these two elements to one another will vary considerably of course from client to client. With the client to follow, for example, though discipline/enjoyment wasn't specifically addressed in the one session presented here, a good bit of self-discipline needed to be modeled and stimulated in therapy in order to help him learn to have enjoyment by cooperating and being responsible. Other clients may be neglecting enjoyment of life by being overly responsible not only for themselves but for others. In cases like this, the task may be something akin to what Erickson told the wife who was overprotecting her handicapped husband. He indicated to her that her most important task was to teach him that he didn't need her: "And I wanted your husband to realize that *there is a lot he can do for himself*... And it isn't right for me to tell him, 'You learn this or you learn that!' *Let him learn whatever he wishes, in whatever or-*

der he wishes" (Erickson & Rossi, 1979, pp. 113, 115). With the same woman, who expressed her love for her husband by worrying over him, Erickson shared a personal anecdote, that he (also handicapped) encouraged his wife to show her love for him by enjoying herself since there was no real need to waste time being concerned: "I'm just in a wheelchair. That's all! I want her to put her energy toward enjoying things" (Erickson & Rossi, 1979, p. 109). At the end of their session, he emphasized this learning again: "And neither of you need to be concerned about the other. You need to enjoy knowing each other. *And enjoying what you can do as meaningful to you*" (Erickson & Rossi, 1979, p. 119).

CASE EXAMPLE

We have covered various elements of paradox that illustrate its significance and importance. We now want to turn to examples of actual interventions and their effects. We discuss their selection and the design of a treatment plan in which they can be thoughtfully delivered. Since much of the literature about paradox addresses symptom prescription in the context of strategic family therapy, we will focus on Erickson's style involving the use of lesser noted forms of paradox in other therapeutic contexts. We are emphasizing the use of paradox for both interview management and therapeutic outcome. Specific interventions include binds, confusion techniques, indirect suggestion, and especially therapeutic metaphor. Ericksonian hypnotherapy is a therapeutic modality particularly well suited to illustrate both variety and frequency of these interventions while carefully examining the client's response to them. For this reason, we have selected a case for analysis in which hypnosis was the primary modality.

History

Frank (male, age 29, married) requested treatment to solve his problem with "authority." He said that he had difficulty taking orders and following rules, and could not accept feedback, even constructive feedback from his wife. As a professional therapist himself, he was aware that this situation was not appropriate. He needed to be comfortable with criticism and he realized that his reflexive rebellion was out of his control. He revealed that he had a number of traffic and parking tickets which he had not paid, had served a brief jail sentence in this regard, had broken marijuana laws and been caught, and had arguments with his wife, peers, and employer. He smiled and attempted to induce laughter throughout the interview. He in fact did not merely laugh; he attempted to have us laugh with him as he "cutely" related his difficulties. Finally, when asked about his father, he said that their relationship had been strained, that his father had been openly competitive with him, and frequently "motivated" him with challenge and provocation.

Frank was either one down in the challenged and ridiculed position or he behaved in a manner typified by an overt mild hostility and coldness. He said usual conversation between himself and his father centered on a shared attitude of disgust about "stupid rules" imposed on themselves and others by "ignorant people." In these cases, again the affect was hostile and in no case did the relationship establish roles that would support the sharing of dependency needs, fears, weaknesses, scares, doubts, and reassurances so common in most developing children. Weaknesses were hidden, taken to be attributes of others instead of the self, and in most cases were exploited as a basis of ridicule.

Initial Treatment Plan

Our initial planning included interventions to stimulate Frank's comfort with his dependency needs, an alteration in his self-image thinking in order to enable him to implement his own use of those feelings, and an acceptance of himself not based on his father's provocation and encouragement of rebellious behaviors. Thus new maps for his experience would provide a basis for Frank to make changes in his relationships and better approximate an age appropriate intimacy. To help him accept feedback from others, we needed to promote in him a sense that his needs were actually socially acceptable. He would need a map of conduct about expressing those needs and he would need to conclude that compromise does not mean loss. A new sensitivity to acceptance of some of his dependency needs paired with a rehearsal of how he might express those needs openly and even enjoy doing so could be effected by stimulating his own thinking through the use of metaphors.

Initial planning completed, we were ready to induce trance and share metaphors about succeeding in enjoying the game of life by breaking the rules and winning, about learning and rehearsing self-acceptance, and about the fantasies, emotions, and self-talk that a man could have when a father was close and supportive. Each metaphor, however, would contain an element of paradoxical logic. We would therefore take nothing away from the client but rather follow Erickson's directive: "One always tries to use whatever the patient brings into the office. If they bring in resistance, be grateful for that resistance. Heap it up in whatever fashion they want you to—really pile it up. But never get disgusted with the amount of resistance" (Erickson & Rossi, 1981, p. 16).

Orientating the Client to Trance

C: Have you been in trance before, by the way?

F: Well, er, ah, yeah...

C: You say that with some incongruence. What?

F: Well, I've never had someone who knows what they're doing.

S: So I'd suggest you lean back in your chair...

C: to find out how comfortable you can be in the cool air with your feet flat on the floor.

S: A lot of times a person goes into a trance by staring at something.

C: There are plenty of things out there you could stare at, a few feet in front of you...

S: And just find some one spot.

C: ...or far away.

S: You don't need to move.

C: It doesn't really matter what you think about or what you notice.

S: I wonder if you're going to fail to succeed at not going into trance at exactly your own speed or whether you won't.

C: And hypnosis, as you know, is a way for a person to learn from himself and so I hope that you succeed in rebelling to the proper extent against those suggestions we give so as to make certain that you only follow those suggestions that are relevant for you to follow. And just staring at one spot, beginning to feel the comfortable relaxation that you know how to feel, listening to one thing we say, being aware of the people, the place, the context. It doesn't matter whether you go into trance with your eyes open or close your eyes. Wait until the proper time to close your eyes, but you can begin to enjoy the freedom of having precisely your own thoughts in response to those stimuli that we offer.

S: And I think it would be very interesting if you try to keep your eyes open throughout the entire trance.

C: So enjoy the freedom to rebel because you can't help but rebel and do what is uniquely appropriate for you to do. You can wonder about that.

The initial paradoxical instruction to Frank stated that it is important for him to rebel and have his own thoughts. This was expressed in the sentences: "Hypnosis, as you know, is a way for a person to learn from himself and so I hope that you succeed in rebelling to the proper extent against those suggestions we give so as to make certain that you only follow those suggestions that are relevant for you to follow." What is paradoxical about the suggestion is of course best illustrated by studying the options available to Frank at that point. Frank could follow the suggestion and have his own thoughts rather than ours or he could rebel against the suggestion that he have his own thoughts (not follow our suggestion) and therefore be thinking a thought of his own. This paradoxical symptom prescription is a bit like the classical paradox: "Everything I say is a lie." But better, the latter sentence is extremely personal to Frank and he is *bound* to consider it.

How is this therapeutically useful for Frank? Perhaps it is not useful to *him* therapeutically, but it is useful to the therapeutic process as a device for interview management. We have addressed Frank at several levels. Consciously, we have increased rapport to the extent that he recognizes the acceptance of his rebellious behavior. We have reduced his need to be defensive and encouraged him to continue his defensive behavior; we have allowed him to protect himself if he deems it necessary to so do. Below the level of consciousness, we have accomplished at least two things. We have stymied his most familiar manner of resisting feedback from others by the logical overload on his conscious association process and thus encouraged unconscious search. In a subtle manner, we have focused his awareness on our words and his personal reaction. We have defined the area of experience to which attention must be given: Whether he rebels or complies with our instruction, he can only determine the difference by noticing our words and his reaction. Thus we have helped him accomplish several things that will deepen his trance experience: intensified rapport, accomplished fixation of his attention, and intensified concentration on internal experience.

To effect the paradoxical nature of the induction then we asked him to "fail to succeed at not going into trance" at his own speed, to "succeed in rebelling," to "enjoy the freedom of having precisely his own thoughts," and to "try to keep your eyes open throughout the entire trance." Intimately tied to the paradoxical nature of the instructions was the construction of and effects created by indirection, confusion, and the therapeutic bind aspect of the communication.

Some other features of the induction, although not paradoxical, are worthy of attention if for no other reason than to underscore the point that the use of paradox does not singularly constitute a treatment. Rather, paradox is a tool that must be considered against a background of treatment methodology. While this methodology is explained at length elsewhere (Lankton & Lankton, 1983), we will discuss these features briefly here as a point of reference for further study and as indication of the numerous other aspects of interpersonal influence. These aspects, as we have previously stated, exist to support the impact of paradox in an Ericksonian approach. In this discussion then, we attend to the conveyance of paradox through the use of indirect suggestions and therapeutic binds as well as metaphor.

Conscious/Unconscious Dissociation

In the course of creating an induction it was important for Erickson to maximize the degree of dissociation between the conscious and the unconscious and establish a dissociated hypnotic personality. "Only in this way can there be secured an extensive dissociation...which will permit a satisfactory manipulation of those parts of the personality under study" (Erickson, 1980, p. 7). In order to achieve such a dissociation we frequently structure our speech in the manner that follows.

C: Your conscious mind has a certain line of thought. You bring various concerns, various interests and they have nothing to do with your unconscious processes.

S: Your conscious mind is in the process of wondering, watching what is going to happen...

C: But try as you might...

S: while your unconscious mind is in the process of taking care of a lot of things for you that you don't appreciate.

C: ...you have very little control over just what those things are and how your unconscious goes about taking care of them.

S: It would be a good idea for you to take control of your responses to the things that we say and sooner or later you develop your own trance.

C: Your conscious mind has one idea about the depth of trance, wonders...

S: Your unconscious mind has some other idea about the depth of trance that you need or may need.

C: ...whether or not you're responding appropriately.

S: And thoroughly understand the depth of your own experience.

C: But your unconscious mind automatically finds that depth of trance that's relevant...

S: Now somewhere in the back of your mind are your thoughts...

C: ...and your conscious mind discovers later.

S: . . .you haven't known that you were going to think.

C: Of course you know that it's impossible not to have thoughts. You have thoughts as we speak about one think. . .

S: I don't know whether you remember or not. . .

C: . . .and perhaps another thing simultaneously.

S: . . .that there are billions of brain cells and you've only had enough time, at the speed of thought, the speed of electricity. . .

C: And listening to Stephen's voice, you can wonder. . .

S: . . .to notice some of those thoughts.

C: . . .just what he's getting at, what you can learn, learning things that perhaps you already know, things you've known all along but didn't know that you know.

The reader will note that the transcript reveals an intertwining of suggestions from both speakers. In fact, there are moments when one speaker completes the suggestion begun by the other. More often, each speaker continues to deliver his or her suggestion completely but in sectioned phrases. The aspect of dual induction was achieved here as one and then the other speaker alternated speaking and thus alternated the delivery of first one and then the other section of the complete suggestion. The paradoxical directives at the initial stages of the induction depotentiate the normal critical aspect of Frank's conscious mind. This conscious-unconscious induction now unencumbered by that usual framework helps the client intensify his awareness for and sensitivity to his different thought processes. His heightened appreciation for unconscious processes thereby creates a situation of expectancy. He has observed a difference in his ability that he may not have previously noticed. This perceived ability becomes the seedbed for developing therapeutic resources that are the real meat of therapeutic change.

Ratify and Deepen Trance

The stage of induction that typically conveys to the client an awareness that an altered state has been achieved is referred to as ratifying trance. You want the client to select one bit of trance phenomena out of many and confirm it. "When [the client] does that, [the client] is also confirming or validating the others, and that's what you want your patient to do" (Erickson & Rossi, 1979, p. 371).

S: Your heart is pounding and there are a lot of other things that are beating. And while we've been talking, your cheeks have flattened out.

C: You haven't moved.

S: And you can only notice some of those thoughts.

C: You've closed your eyes but your unconscious continues to maintain your balance, breathing, and you can consciously alter your breathing, take a deeper breath...

S: But you should notice the enjoyment because as your thoughts come out of the back of your mind, the more relaxation you feel, the deeper you go into trance. And they'll come out of your mind.

C: ...but your unconscious automatically resumes the process of regulating your breathing rhythmically in a way you can forget about completely.

S: Going into a trance should be a matter of noticing that you can be aware of a lot of things that come out of your mind. And there's no reason to worry about taking in ideas that will make you go out of your mind.

C: Your conscious mind might enjoy being able to monitor your progress into your trance by noticing how you can go one twentieth of the way into trance with each count. Not much difference between 20 and 19.

S: Sometimes you might want to find out that you're failing to go into trance by increments.

C: Eighteen, 17, 16.

S: You're failing to know that one of your hands can get lighter.

C: And how can you really be sure...

S: Are you aware of which of your hands will fail first to get lighter?

C: ...that you really aren't going one twentieth of the way, 15, 14, 13...

S: And at least one of your hands is going to fail to raise up to your face in small increments of cataleptic movement.

C: ...or that one of those hands really isn't becoming lighter.

S: Now you have a number of various ways you can do that.

C: And a hand can become lighter, even heavier, but the first thing you notice is that altered sensation. And just what area will you notice that sensation first?

S: It's lightening to know that altered the sensation and you were pleased to find out. There are a number of ways in which you can fail to let one of your hands. You can fail to notice one of your hands getting lighter.

C: Will it be in the fingers? The elbow? Or maybe you'll notice it by the change in pressure that your thigh can sense as your hand rests less and less against it, 10.

S: Your hand can get lighter and you can fail to notice. Your hand can fail to get lighter and you can notice. Your hand can fail to get lighter and you can fail to notice or your hand can get lighter and you can notice.

C: Seven, 6.

S: Maybe your hand is going to feel lighter as it raises halfway to your face or maybe a quarter of the way to your face. Maybe it's going to get heavier and fall down to the side of the chair.

C: And that would be another interesting adaptation, another interesting way to follow your own rule, 4, 3.

S: And perhaps it's going to stay where it is. So we're just going to have to find out.

In this segment the typical alterations of initial trance are observed and described to the client: heartbeat alterations, cheeks flattening, lack of movement, deeper breathing, and relaxation. Following this summary of obvious occurrences, we began deepening trance by suggesting more uncommon trance phenomena. Since Frank was oppositional, we continued to use paradoxical behavior prescriptions, challenging him to deepen his trance. This is found in the lines "Find out that you're failing to go into trance by increments"; "You're failing to have one of your hands get lighter"; and finally, "At least one of your hands is going to fail to raise up to your face." Again, the paradoxical element lies in the binding quality of the situation. We have appealed to the common motivational relationship that his father created with him—challenge. Thus we have appealed to his transference need to both please and rebel against us. If he rebels he will have achieved a deepening by creating the trance phenomena. If, contrary to our expectation of failure, he does fail, then he has followed our suggestion. Following our suggestion will thus lead to deepening because we subsequently suggest that he doubt his ability to not raise a hand, not go deeper, and that he dissociate further. The sentences used for this are: "You're failing to know that one of your hands can get lighter"; and "How can you really be sure?" "There are a number of varieties of ways in which you can fail to let one of your hands." "You can fail to notice one of your hands getting lighter." And finally, a series of all possible alternatives of the above was suggested ending with "Your hand can fail to get lighter and you can fail to notice."

S: And you don't need to listen to the things a hypnotist says. You have a lot of your own thoughts.

C: Your conscious mind may be interested in analyzing the structure of what we say and why...

S: And your thoughts are worth examining.

C: ...but that has nothing to do with your true purpose in coming and presenting that difficulty...

S: Slowly, still lighter, and thoroughly.

C: ...and your conscious mind had no way of predicting ahead of time just what you'll learn but you can wonder and be interested or maybe your conscious mind won't be interested at all in what we say...

S: And your thoughts are worth sharing and responding to but since they are your thoughts, it's an opportunity to go into trance and examine your own thoughts...

C: ...because your own thoughts are so much more your own.

S: You use the hypnotist's words to stimulate your own thinking...

C: Three, 2.

S: ...and you accept those suggestions you think would be useful, but otherwise, the rule is to discard those suggestions and do things your own unique way for your own betterment.

We completed the deepening begun in the earlier segment by suggesting incremental changes which themselves were too small to detect. In the first sentence of this segment we again prescribed the resistive behavior that we expected the client to automatically engage: "You don't need to listen to the things a hypnotist says"; and "Your conscious mind may be interested in analyzing the structure..." If Frank uses these usually defensive maneuvers he has done so under our direction and we therefore have control. If instead, he rebels against them then he is listening and cooperating and we again have control of the therapy. This paradoxical bind is continued at every phase of the treatment to maintain our ability to manage the interview in the therapeutic direction. It is continued up to the final sentence that defines in Frank's own vocabulary "The *rule* is to discard those suggestions and do things your own unique way" but true to the add-on aspect of the Ericksonian style continues with the subtle phrase "for your own betterment."

It is again notable that the Ericksonian form of paradoxical symptom prescription is not viewed as an end but a means to the therapy. We maintain the control and focusing of attention throughout the interview while accepting Frank's rebellious independence and frame his behavior as "for his betterment." We thus gain and fixate rapport and become indispensable (as well as credible) sources of information. After all, he needs to pay attention to us in order to discover how he has been doing the correct thing by doing what he thought was incorrect.

Multiple Embedded Metaphors

Goals for the following set of metaphors included helping Frank gain an experiential understanding of the feelings, role, attitude, and self-image foundations of cooperation. These are of course in keeping with the client's request, but achieving this personality goal is contingent upon his learning to understand and accept dependency needs, experience parental acceptance, rehearse specifics of cooperation, create an emotional connection with his wife, and build certain behavioral skills. The several metaphors chosen were expected to help Frank build an experiential map of conduct in each of these areas. Each was designed to appeal to his need for rebellion and each, therefore, contained paradoxical elements to facilitate the learnings or gains; they are summarized as follows:

1. Prepare him to have dependency needs (affect) and examine them in relative comfort.
2. Learn to express such needs in intimacy encounters (age appropriate intimacy behavior) with significant others.
3. Create an expectation of normal parenting to help prepare him for his role in fatherhood (family structure change).
4. Learn to conceive of new roles and feelings with pleasant anticipation in several areas of life (self-image thinking enhancement).
5. Prepare him to change his understanding (attitude restructuring) about how cooperation rather than competition results in success.

Commentary is interspersed throughout the development of the metaphors in this continuing transcript. Consistent reliance on paradoxical intention in suggestions to maintain trance is obvious as are the more novel elements of paradoxical logic within the metaphoric drama.

Begin Matching Metaphor

C: And so just waiting, we can talk about anything. You know only a fool would fail in such a way as to fail...

S: ...but a wise man fails in such a way as to succeed.

C: Now Fred couldn't have been more clear about this fact at 40 years old...

S: ...but when he came to see us at 30, he had a good deal of bad deals he needed to deal with. And we made a deal with him. If he would put his cards on the table, we would see his bet and up the ante. And the more deeply he went into trance, the more deeply we put him into trance.

C: Fred had enjoyed those affairs a great deal. It was a different story after his wife found out.

S: He came to therapy perplexed with the idea that he had had a number of affairs for a number of years which were no difficulty to him emotionally, so it was incomprehensible to him that when he decided firmly and resolutely to stop the affairs, he felt guilty.

C: He knew the game was up. He wasn't going to have the affairs but he didn't want to have the guilt.

S: So he came to psychotherapy after he decided he had been punished long enough and it wasn't going to go away. He came for our help. It was a good reason to see him for therapy. We accepted the case. We asked him to go into trance.

C: It was a pleasurable activity to go into trance even with concerns on your mind.

S: And to develop the depth of trance you think you want or may want is an easy matter in the therapist's office.

C: And the last client we put into trance didn't realize how fully he was in trance until we asked him to come out of it.

This opening metaphor sets the stage for Frank to begin the process of questioning his prevailing attitude about competition. It also contains six major points of interest with regard to paradox. First, "Only a fool would fail in such a way so as to fail... but a wise man fails in such a way as to succeed," defines the story as paradoxical in nature. The comment about how a "fool" fails should hook Frank's need to rebel when challenged. If he is hooked, we have furthered the trance by facilitating his fixated attention and internal concentration. We have increased the likelihood that Frank will become interested in the story in order to determine his position on the issue of foolishness, success, failure, and rule breaking. The key element in such a "bull's eye" story is the contradiction of succeeding by failing—hence the metaphoric paradox.

Second, "Fred couldn't be more clear about this fact at forty years old," challenges Frank to understand or admit he is still "young." Or perhaps Frank will be motivated to "beat" Fred by learning whatever it was that Fred learned (which is yet to be revealed) much faster than it was learned in the story.

Third, "The more deeply *he went* into trance, the more deeply *we put* him into trance," denies our control of the hypnotic situation. This is a paradoxical bind for trance maintenance. If he rebels he gives us control; if he complies, then he follows suggestions and definitions created by us and hence he goes into trance more deeply.

Next, "He had a good deal of bad deals" is an oxymoron—a combination of contradictory or incongruous words. As such, it will subtly stimulate a new examination of what really constitutes a good or bad deal. It plants a seed for more detailed illustrations to follow about how what initially seems negative (like dependency) is a necessary and positive aspect of mature functioning.

Also, "When he decided firmly and resolutely to stop the affairs, he felt guilty" (and not vice versa), is another paradox. It defines the situation as one involving rules of marital commitment and intimacy.

And finally, "The last client we put into trance didn't realize how fully he was in trance until we asked him to come out of it" is again a paradoxical bind for trance maintenance. He can rebel and realize now that he is in trance or if he does not realize this, he implicitly complies with the suggestion that he not realize now but rather later. Compliance now of course sets him up for compliance later. So, whether he now believes he is in trance or now believes he is not, he must admit that he is following our suggestion.

Begin Resource Retrieval

S: Now he was a person who, going into trance, exhibited the degree of scare that he had in a number of interesting ways that your unconscious would know more about than your conscious knows. I don't even think that his conscious mind could stomach the awareness. And we never brought it to his conscious attention. He had had a belly full of that in his life and he didn't need any more.

In this transition segment we refer to the possibility of repressed fear that Frank experiences due to the constancy of pressures brought on by the situation of rebellion and rule breaking referred to in the previous segment. We focused his awareness on his stomach and presented an altered interpretation that this repressed fearfulness constituted (no pun) a belly full of distress. This may be his first indication that we are "on his side" in an effort to relieve the distress he has endured. In light of this new interpretation we now continue to shift the client's framework even further by temporarily suspending the matching metaphor and pursuing another metaphor about another client that will allow Frank to experience the resources needed for achieving the goals summarized earlier.

C: And speaking of that symbolic representation of his difficulty...

S: ...we began to speak to him about another client we had worked with.

C: Phil had had an ulcer for five years. He had never spoken about it to anyone.

S: He was a medical resident who was well known in his community.

C: He had a lot of responsibility professionally, and besides that, he was the father of five children.

S: In the intake interview it became apparent that his ulcer problems had begun when he found out that his wife was pregnant with the fifth child.

C: It seemed as if there was absolutely no time in Phil's life when he got to be the one taken care of. He was always taking care of somebody—from the dog or the child or that inexhaustible supply of psychiatric patients.

S: Building additions onto the house, reading professional journals.

C: If it wasn't this, it was that. There's never enough time, he had been heard to say.

S: All those ideas.

C: He wanted to relax. He thought that would be a great idea. But I just can't afford the time, he would say.

S: It was very clear that the matter of self acceptance is a result of the way the child comes to understand himself in the process of developing personality that we bring with us into adulthood.

C: We asked Phil to conserve time by focusing on his tension as a way of going more quickly into trance.

S: There is a good deal of integrity you have when you learn to tie your shoes. You might be interested in the double bow the first week, how children have the ability to tie knots with manual dexterity. You think that you can tie a square knot, you can tie a half-inch knot, you can tie fishing line together so that it won't come apart under pressure and uncles are interested in this. Neighborhood boys and girls are frequently impressed with this ability. Tying a knot takes on entirely different meaning to that girl later. You don't even need to think about that because your unconscious learns about the appreciation for your manual dexterity. Every child learns you have ten fingers and it's just another way of focusing the growing child's awareness on nimble fingers.

C: A child who becomes tired of doing things the same old way with his ten fingers tries to figure out how he can accomplish that task even using his toes. "Look Ma, no hands" is something every child enjoys.

The latter segment emphasized lessons of self-worth and self-acceptance, learned as a child learns to tie his shoes, tie a bow, tie various knots, and increase manual dexterity. Frank had indicated by his general preadolescent disposition that his psychological development was arrested. We would not attempt to focus his awareness on mature forms of self-acceptance that he may not have mastered. We could, however, depend upon the fact that a competitive child would have learned to compete by attempting to outdo his peers; one possible area for the expression of competition is knot tying. We expanded upon this by mentioning the ability to impress others and even impress a parent with "look ma no hands." All these skills were framed as "Self-acceptance is a result of the way the child comes to understand himself in the process of developing personality that we bring with us into adulthood."

We continued our appeal to Frank's rebellion with suggestions containing paradoxical intention such as, "We asked Phil to conserve time by focusing on his tension as a way of going more quickly into trance." Finally, the entire metaphor was framed around a theme calculated to appeal to Frank's rebellion toward authority and apparent fear of growing up in a world of responsibility—a client who worked so hard and was so responsible that he had an ulcer, a secret trouble. The true nature of the secret trouble, which was not yet revealed to our client, was that the trouble resulted from his inability to be dependent on others, to be cared for, to recognize dependency needs, and to transact in such a way so as to get his needs noticed and met. These are in fact the same dynamic roots that seem to create anxiety for our client, Frank.

S: Now you're in trance yourself. You probably wonder why your unconscious doesn't know anything about moving your fingers up off your lap.

C: And that's an interesting thought. You know that you know how to lift your fingers up off your lap. You've known all along, even before you knew that hand belonged to you. You knew how to raise it up to your face and transport that rattle to your mouth.

S: But the fact that your hand fails to demonstrate that rapid response doesn't mean it won't do it in its own good time as your hand is lifting up toward your face even as I speak.

C: And it's important to do it in your own way. You knew that.

S: Your arm is resting slightly on your thigh, your wrist is demonstrating that jerky movement because your unconscious moves isolated muscle groups.

C: Minute muscle movements.

S: Elbows, and soon a finger will probably demonstrate the jerky movement because unconscious ideas of a finger will tend to stimulate a movement in the muscle of that area cortex and you'll be pleased to find out whether or not you're going to do that.

C: And on the same subject, we reminded Phil of that experience that most midwestern children have had at summer camp or on vacation, the idea of going on a canoe trip. You can have any fantasy you like out on the freedom of that river.

S: You can feel the alteration in the tension of the index finger which began to relax, and still lighter, that's right. And soon your thumb will rest more lightly on the pants.

C: Nothing to remind you that you are in this time or this place but you can be anywhere. Your own thoughts and imagining can be real. And when two boys go on a canoe ride together, there is always the question of who's going to sit in the front of the boat and who's going to ride in the back. Now everybody knows that the person sitting in the back has ultimate control about just which direction the canoe will take...

S: But the conscious mind can notice the extreme slow speed of that right hand raising off of your lap doesn't prevent your unconscious mind from knowing that you learn to use your fingers in a variety of ways as a child.

C: ...how fast the canoe is going to slide through the water, and yet only a fool would want to ride in the back of the canoe all the time because the vantage point from the front of the canoe is so much more conducive to your own imagination. The view is much better and it's a pleasure to just relax in the front of the boat...

S: You may call it manual dexterity or you may call it good with your hands but the conscious mind can be proud of the fact that you accept yourself. You learn to stand in a certain posture to button your shirts, or select which notch you use in your belt.

C: ...and leave all of that steering and all of that effort up to someone else. And that way when the canoe gets snagged in low branches you can joke to the one in the back "you idiot, why did you steer us into the branches." You can be proud knowing that you could have done a better job but you can still enjoy allowing someone else to enjoy making their own mistakes, giving you a free ride.

S: And how many people realize as grown men that when you fasten your belt buckle your conscious mind feels proud of the notch in which you are able to get your belt to buckle but your unconscious mind has allowed you to have that feeling of your pride moving your fingers.

C: And you have a lot of pride. Your conscious mind frets because you notice your hand and wonder whether or not it's gotten off of your leg or whether it ever will. Sooner or later it will.

S: Now another matter is your fingerprint.

C: And just what depth of trance have you reached and what's important to notice about that?

S: You couldn't look at your fingers and find out but you are as unique as your fingerprint and you can't change your fingerprint.

C: Your fingerprint has a right to be here and you have a right to be attached to it.

S: And so you should enjoy always being you. ... And so Phil had no idea about why we were speaking about those things in the context of dealing with that stomach ulcer.

C: He knew he enjoyed it when we spoke about ball games and those teams on which most boys have had a chance to play at some time or another in their life.

S: But he did know unconsciously that what was presupposed behind those stories was related to that stomach ulcer because his stomach became more relaxed when he listened to them.

C: We reminded him about playing in a game and being very proud about the role you play in the game and we also mentioned the relief a player can feel when he hears the coach delegate responsibility to another player: "Go in for Phil." It's not a failure in any sense but a pleasure to have that relief. It's all part of team spirit.

S: And his ability to relax there in the chair while the gang was out improving their skill on the court...

C: ...being proud of their progress, proud of his progress.

S: It was because he had the kind of background that he had that nobody needed to ask him to notice how he was relaxed in his legs. Nobody needed to tell him your relaxation is in your arms and stomach.

C: He didn't need to learn that achievement is something that you can have even when you're not doing anything.

S: They didn't need to say relax your neck and your back and your eyes. He had a good coach and because he had a childhood experience of that kind of relaxation being accepted you grow into adulthood using those experiences. Now his stomach ulcer indicated that he hadn't learned to have that response automatically in adulthood. So we asked him to just consciously let your confusion of your dialogue forget about the, have amnesia automatically...

C: Time passes...

S: Because it's a possibility that you'd like to use the experience of not remembering...

C: ...in interesting ways.

S: I didn't know whether or not he'd forget about what we said because of the amnesia or fail to remember it because he could retrieve his own ability at failing to not remember something that had been forgotten...

C: Maybe he only failed to remember that he thought about what we said.

S: ...in such a way that his unconscious mind kept it and his conscious mind listened to something else. Your hand is rising off your lap.

C: And that's an interesting thing to focus on. The pressure has definitely lessened on your thigh and there's a little contact remaining between the ring finger and the knee.

S: And you memorize the client's dissociation in the hand and arm...

C: You don't really know as it clears the thigh whether it's going to float higher or out to the side or halfway up.

S: ...so that you could even watch a movie while you're feeling dissociated. Your dissociation experience sitting there watching the movie...

C: ...listening to one thing...

S: . . .you can hardly care what you're seeing on the movie screen. . .

C: . . .having your own thoughts. . .

S: . . .is a common experience that he had had before, up toward your face. . .

C: . . .much like the feeling that your hand experiences whether it's rais-ing up or pressing down, it's doing something separate and apart from what you're doing.

S: It's nice to know when a conscious mind is confused. . .

C: . . .and up and down. . .

S: . . .you can do a lot of things that you didn't consciously know. You had a right hand moving up to your face. Again soon, the confusion of the conscious mind.

Begin Direct Work Metaphor While Reinforcing Dissociation

Our goal at this most intense phase of the multiple embedded metaphor was to teach Frank a new behavioral role which would allow him to deal more appropriately with his peers, boss, wife, and eventually with his children. Specifically, he needed to un-derstand and accept his dependency needs, sense of vulnerability, ability to trust, and the behavioral transactions involved in the manifestation of these needs and abilities. To solidify the role of a man his age who possesses and is responding appropriately to the resource feelings just retrieved, we used a story that provided a context for an imaginary encounter between a boy and his father.

Frank's personal encounter was stimulated by listening to the metaphorical one between protagonist and father. It was an op-portunity for us to help him build more suitable associations to his tender, dependent feelings, by altering what he could expect form proper parenting by a father figure. Frank can benefit from this experience in two ways. He can "receive" some of the accept-ance that was never offered in real transactions with his father and thereby be "reparented" to some extent. And he can incor-porate the behaviors of proper parenting, thereby supporting his own changes with internal dialogue and having these responses available when the time comes for him to literally interact with his own children. It is important to remember that Frank is likely to resist, compete with, and rebel against our rules, but his competi-tiveness and need to take a challenge can really be considered pre-dictable therapeutic assets so long as we rely upon the use of par-adoxical intention and paradoxical logic to utilize the reversal re-sponses that can be expected from him at every turn.

C: When Bill approached us in Australia at a treatment marathon he told us that he was a sheep farmer.

S: You could think about your hand...

C: He struck us as a very naive therapy client. He didn't know the first thing about really having his feelings.

S: ...amazed moving up to your face, why your unconscious...

C: He didn't even know that a man has feelings.

S: ...mind takes that feeling of dissociation you have in your arm...

C: He didn't know how he'd have an arm raise up toward his face. He didn't even know it was possible to go into trance.

S: He complained that there were two wc.lds, the work world and the world at home and his wife didn't like his inability to separate them and he asked for therapy about that.

C: He wanted to make his wife happy and he wanted to be happy at work.

S: He had missed out on his entire childhood. His father hadn't spent any time with him at all.

Once again resistance was utilized by paradoxically stating the opposite of what was intended. We stated that the Australian client was naive and we expected that Frank would condescendingly assume himself superior to the Australian. Actually, it was possible for Frank to be naive and still realize he could gain from the therapy, or to rebel and consider himself smarter (and thereby be expected to gain even more). Further, if Frank disidentified with the type of person in the story, he would create a situation in which he could be less defensive when the painful relationship that character had with his father was mentioned. So again, we have seemed to fail to be correct in order to be even more effective with Frank's therapy.

Next, dissociation is suggested. The following segment helps Frank develop the ability to view himself at a dissociated distance. We expected that the intensity of the dependency and tenderness feelings we would be suggesting to him might be overwhelmingly threatening, unless we "diluted" them with dissociation and splitting of affect. We considered examination of the feelings, even with dissociated splitting, to be better than his characteristic repression and suppression.

S: You get the feeling of dissociation developed some place in the body, convince the client at the conscious level it doesn't matter if you're paying attention to that or not.

C: But in the same way you have that dissociation in the body, make a transition, to psychological dissociation.

S: And we asked him to realize that he could see a movie with an itch and he wouldn't feel an itch in his body.

C: And on the other hand, if you're not interested in that movie, you don't even notice what's going on there because you're having your own thoughts and they are so much more interesting.

S: Somebody could be crying in the movie and you could be laughing. I know it's the context that makes a difference. When I saw *Night of the Living Dead* at the drive-in, I left twice. It was too scary for me to see then, but when I saw it in graduate school we all laughed at the monsters and I could deal with that.

C: Meanwhile, the people on the screen were still very frightened. It was no laughing matter to them.

S: Likewise, you could watch somebody having a love scene on television and you're not interested in that.

C: So you can have your own reactions no matter what the characters on the screen have or know.

Describing laughter at a movie known to be scary would be still another illogical conclusion reasoned paradoxically were it not for the manner in which the change of context was revealed. By allowing a client to understand the leap to the next logical level, a possible paradoxical statement is made logical. Viewing the movie in a room full of sarcastic college students changed the impact of the images. So too, being in a room filled with professionals viewing him in trance will alter the importance of his feelings; in this situation, his feelings will likely become more intense. We shared with Frank the secret of frame change in the film, but obfuscated the logical level of frame change in the actual relationship with us. The metaphor allowed a natural context for the paradoxical bind to enhance therapeutic success.

S: You don't realize your own self sitting here in the trance listening to our stories with your eyes closed. You don't know that a lot of people have their hands up in the air. But if you had your eyes open and saw, you'd still have your hand down on your thigh, because you don't need to have a reaction to things you see.

C: The intensity of your response is enough for you to know that you can have that dissociation. Your conscious mind can be interested in how your unconscious mind creates it.

S: You have reactions to your own unconscious processes that develop a dissociation so you could watch yourself winning the award for the best-stuffed fish.

C: Watch yourself hitting that golfball the farthest.

S: Watch yourself getting a paper in school.

In the segment above, the stuffed fish was mentioned as a ludicrous image to appeal to Frank's sense of "making fun of" or being "one up" on others. How easy to get his conscious mind engaged by jerking him to an image as laughable as a stuffed fish! In the segment to follow, we continued to appeal to this need to be "one up" by expanding that *even* a sheep farmer could picture himself. We could have further insured that he would picture himself by using paradoxical intention as well, by saying something like: "There is an interesting way in which you will fail to make a clear image of yourself." However, we expected we could satisfactorily elicit his visualization at this point by relying on his need to be superior.

S: You could imagine yourself sleeping, riding a bicycle, speaking with your parents, and all the while your unconscious allows you to have your own... Sitting here in the chair, you're relaxed, shoulders down, hand on your thigh for now...

C: ...face muscles smoothed out, your eyes are closed. There's no need to do anything. But we asked Bill to do something very complex, despite being naive and despite not having a father that he could respect.

S: See himself with his father but even though he had had no father who had developed good feelings in him as a child, he could picture himself interacting with what he would imagine to be a father.

C: He was quite able, even a sheep farmer could picture himself and picture that father that we described.

S: We reminded him that as a grown man we didn't need to remind him what it would be like had his father said "I'm proud of you." We didn't have to tell him what it was like to have a father say, "You've worked very hard. You deserve a rest."

C: And he didn't know how, but he responded in a way that we didn't have to explain when we told him that a father could say, "That's alright son, that's an interesting mistake. What can you learn from that mistake?"

In this segment, the interaction with a father constitutes a learning for Frank but in a context in which we denied that we were in any way educating him (or the protagonist). This was accomplished with statements that denied an aspect of responsibility of the communication (Haley, 1963, p. 31), such as: "We didn't need to remind him," "We didn't have to tell him," and "We didn't have to explain." In this manner, Frank could take credit for knowing the parenting information (which in some way, he most certainly did) and for applying it to himself, without rebelling against our authoritative knowledge. Finally, we made the decisive point that framed mistakes as opportunities for learning and improvement rather than proof of inadequacy—an existential polarity to the point repeatedly taught in Frank's competitive relationship with his own father. Likewise, the possibility that a mistake is a chance to learn and change supports (but doesn't fully explain) the logic of the original paradoxical metaphor: You can lose in such a way as to win. The learning will bridge the gap between the emotional experience in this present stage of trance and the eventual conclusion that will be brought to that original—now suspended and postponed—metaphor.

S: Your conscious mind is doing quite well thinking about your own responses, no reason to pay attention to our words consciously when your unconscious can pay attention and learn something. We didn't need to tell Bill you can see an embrace. We did have to remind him, because he wouldn't have thought of it on his own, to picture his father crying.

C: He seemed to go into a dream in order to picture that.

S: But it was a new thought for his unconscious mind to realize that...

C: So we directed the dream, suggesting that he watch the softness on your father's face; see that tear roll out of his left eye or was it his right eye first. Notice that he doesn't seem to be ashamed of that at all.

S: We were tricking him. We told Bill to first imagine seeing his father place his hand on his son's hand and say "You know how hard it is for me to tell you I love you."

With the preceding segment, we continued to use denials to educate Frank. We commented about the father, who is of course sought after by both the protagonist and Frank in real life. The father was described by us as demonstrating softness, crying, tenderness, and so on to help Frank experience association to a new male role. We hoped Frank would accept those parts of himself, and accept them as part of the role he would come to play in the not too distant future with his own children. Perhaps the most important aspect of this segment is the continual dissociation of conscious and unconscious functioning to support amnesia, and the conscious confusion about this reassociation of experience. With the assistance of such trance phenomena, Frank would be less likely to interfere with his changes by criticism, analysis, and his usual condemnation. (It was, by the way, revealed upon reorientation that he did have amnesia for this portion of his therapy experience.)

S: And then suggest that he experience what it'd be like for an Australian sheep farmer to caress his son and say "I do love you."

C: Now, then, so far back in the past. *[Client coughs.]* And it wasn't difficult at all the way that Bill was able to imagine it, though it had never happened he had the experience *[Client coughs again.]* and it choked him up. *[Client's stomach muscles visibly shake.]* He visibly shook. A tear came out of his eye.

S: And his conscious mind didn't even know what we were talking about, wasn't even interested, because Bill's ability to develop a dissociation let his unconscious learn a great deal or *[Client coughs again and raises hand to cover mouth—noticeably becoming increasingly uncomfortable.]* maybe changed his mind. And that's not the only way you know you can raise your hand to your face.

At this point, we had obtained the parasympathetic clues that indicated success in getting Frank's response for tenderness, risk-taking feelings, and dependency.

To briefly restate our goal regarding these feelings, we saw Frank's authority and rebellion problem being rooted in an inability to accept his dependency needs. Since he did not feel comfortable with his dependency, Frank had not learned to trust. Instead of having learned to ask for help, he had learned to compete. He had not learned to take advice about his feelings of weakness, but rather to project those feelings and condemn others. Therefore, we regarded Frank's coming to terms with his dependency needs as the foundation for change in the area he presented to us and contracted with us to change.

Link Resources to Immediate Social Situation

In the next segments, the client's attention is abruptly directed back to the previous metaphor storyline, without associative links to the story just completed. Switching storylines rapidly and without reference can be expected to produce amnesia or similar trance phenomena in most subjects. Always, it is necessary to appeal to the client's unique personality and in this case Frank's rebellious, contrary nature was addressed in such a way as to include an outlet for his pseudoanger, with phrases such as "damn bus" and "damn Lanktons" in the linking segments that follow.

The general goal at this stage of the multiple metaphors is to link the resources that were retrieved and organized to family roles and relevant situations in the social network. This linking is accomplished with imagery that we expect will facilitate Frank's having several thoughts about how to apply the new resources in his immediate social situation after therapy. Here, Frank's self-image thinking is fostered through visual fantasy rehearsal in the context of completing the suspended metaphor about the ulcer client.

S: When Phil left our office he was confused.

C: Besides that he was late. He was late for the bus he intended to catch for home.

S: He didn't know that he was catching the wrong bus.

C: He ran for it, ran and ran.

S: He later reported that he ran two blocks.

C: He saw the bus about to pull off as the doors began to close.

S: He banged his fist on the bus, "damn bus." The bus driver stopped.

C: The bus had already rolled a foot but did stop.

S: He hoped the bus driver hadn't heard him say "damn bus." He got on the bus and fell onto the leather seat.

C: You can imagine how relaxed he really became as he sank into that seat with the relief—knowing that he had caught the bus and could leave the driving to someone else. He was exhausted from running and his heart was pounding.

S: And in the hours where the heart is weak and memory is strong and it just seems that time stands still...

C: And when the bus pulls off jiggling along...

S: ...his thoughts went to various things, inluding our posthypnotic suggestion he'd never intended to follow.

C: And what an excellent context to have your own thoughts, jiggling along on a bus.

S: We had been certain he would catch the bus that would go through the tunnel.

C: At first you look out the window, things are happening out there that have no special interest to you and you just watch life passing by effortlessly.

S: When the lighted bus goes into a tunnel, you see reflections in the window. And we knew that he was going to be staring blankly into the window in trance because that was the posthypnotic suggestion.

In the preceding segment, Frank's rebellion toward authority was addressed with the protagonist's condemning and remorseful reaction to the bus driver. It was concluded with an ambiguous mention that "his heart was pounding," which was true in both the protagonist's experience and for Frank, who had become anxious in response to the previous metaphor. In the context of mentioning anxiety, associations to feeling relieved and relaxed were suggested. When Frank appeared to be relaxing again, we returned to the paradoxical twist of the metaphor: "His thoughts went to various things including our posthypnotic suggestions *he'd never intended to follow."* We could be certain that Frank would recall the discussion of posthypnotic suggestions to follow. He would also expect himself to be clever enough not to follow them since he typically censors, monitors, and competes with suggestions from others. Thus when he sooner or later comes to think about these suggestions, he will have followed them, since we stated that his thoughts went to the posthypnotic suggestions "he never intended to follow." The use of past perfect tense allows the possibility that he folllowed or did not follow the posthypnotic acts; either way they corectly highlight his intention. Therefore, he must come to admit that we predicted his thinking and his intention. Thus we gain more credibility and increase the likelihood that Frank will expect to follow the posthypnotic acts.

C: And so when the bus did, in fact, enter the tunnel, his own reflection was so striking that he couldn't help but notice it.

S: In the trance we had explained that you're going to see your hair is combed nicely, you have relaxed lips, your cheek muscles are flat...

C: ...you're breathing quite comfortably...

S: Your face is red, your posture is erect, shoulders are square and your head is somewhat tilted.

C: You have every opportunity to be relaxed on that bus, no responsibility really. For Phil that was quite unusual not to have responsibility.

S: He tried to move and he realized that he was fixated on that picture of himself breathing relaxed.

In the above segment, we began describing Frank's actual facial appearance. The switch in pronouns to *your* created a convenient ambiguity. It was likely that Frank would begin to wonder what the posthypnotic thoughts might be: Only by knowing our suggestions could he be sure to avoid them.

C: And he thought, those damn Lanktons, they've got me looking at myself in a way that I don't know how to look at myself.

S: They wanted me to pay attention to my face but that was only half of the story he consciously understood.

C: He thought he had the whole thing figured out.

S: But the unconscious mind was learning something entirely different he didn't even understand.

C: But despite that thought his conscious mind had over and over his unconscious, as if running a projector, flashed on the screen of that window a scene from his life.

S: Every time he passed one of those little booths that separate the tunnel, the scene would change.

C: And in those scenes the background would change to include those situations that he'd been in before and he knew he would encounter again, such as those with his wife—a most difficult situation and yet, he was interacting with her in a way he really could be pleased about. He could see her appreciation of those changes, her appreciation of his softness, her appreciation of his vulnerability.

S: Breathing relaxed, looking her in the eyes...

C: And he watched that reflection and was just fascinated by it, fixated on it.

S: And he had no intention to change that picture.

In the segment above, various scenarios were painted in which Frank's self-image interacted in new ways, using the resources just retrieved in the previous metaphors. Now, since Frank was given something of a challenge, he probably thought consciously that he knew what was meant when we said such things as "that was only half of the story," and "he didn't even understand." In fact, this was another purposeful way for us to seemingly fail at distracting him (from the posthypnotic aspects of the suggestion) while actually succeeding, at another logical level (as Bateson would say), to distract him from the association of the previously revitalized feelings of risk taking, dependency, tenderness, and pride. It is easy to see how this paradoxical approach distracts the client's conscious mind in this example.

In the following segment, the same approach is expanded but the visual scenarios include other interactions. Each time care is taken, by monitoring his physical demeanor and nonverbal behavior, to associate his fantasies to his novel feelings. He thus learned to think of himself with the addition of new feelings and new, available, and organized behavioral options.

C: But then another bump in the road and he'd shake his head and try to shake the image thinking again, those damn Lanktons, what do they have me doing and why?

S: They think I'm going to stare at that image of myself in the window and see myself.

C: I know what they're up to but it's not going to work.

S: And he was only half right because his conscious mind was questioning the suggestions but his unconscious was still learning something else.

C: And despite that conscious thought once again another background emerged and there he was with his boss...

S: Chest was relaxed, stomach was relaxed, breathing was quite relaxed...

C: ...the chief psychiatrist and he was being criticized constructively for failure to succeed completely with a patient.

S: And he was smiling incongruently because he was smiling at the thought that the Lanktons have got me picturing myself relaxed here on this bus and I can't move a muscle but the face was quite relaxed.

C: And then he found to his surprise that in the image of himself interacting with the boss, he was smiling there while receiving criticism and interacting in a very appropriate way that he could be pleased about, curious about.

S: He knew that the sounds on the bus had very little to do with the voice he was hearing in the back of his head that was saying "I understand." Or was it him hearing his own voice? And his conscious mind didn't understand at all.

C: And another jiggle of the bus, another shake of his head, another image.

S: He found out that in adulthood you use those childhood learnings that have stayed with you...

C: It didn't matter how irritated he became thinking about his doing something that was actually instigated by us because he was still learning something even though he only knew the half of what it was that he was learning.

S: ...and your conscious mind needn't pay any attention to them but you can appreciate your own ability to use that and there he was seeing himself appreciating himself while he was watching himself interact with that fifth baby that had created that tension all along.

C: And so when the bus came out of the tunnel it was a shocking change. He realized at that moment the bus he was supposed to be on didn't even go through a tunnel. It was at that moment he realized he had been on the wrong bus.

S: Suddenly his attention was disrupted and "those damn Lanktons" was the thought that didn't even get finished because he had amnesia for what he thought he had not remembered about before and was certain of it at this time.

C: And everyone knows that certain surge of panic that comes when you've realized you've made a terrible mistake that's going to cause a lot of inconvenience. But just as that familiar tension began to rise and register in his stomach he thought to himself "I don't give a damn if I did catch the wrong bus. I enjoyed what happened here even if those Lanktons were behind it.

S: And that was the end of the growing tension that had created the ulcer.

C: And he knew he had learned something even though he didn't know what he had learned, he still had that relaxation.

End Matching Metaphor

In the following segment, we finally return to the original metaphor and bring closure to that long suspended paradox about failing in such a way as to succeed.

S: And that's the only thing that we really had to share with him. So when the first baby was born it finally dawned on him and he didn't let us know until he was 40 years old the meaning of that phrase he had heard in therapy, "Only a damn fool would fail in such a way that he fails. It takes a wise person to fail in such a way that he succeeds." We had explained in great detail that it's an *absolute rule* of social contract, that you define your behavior and when you operate outside of that...

C: ...guilt is an automatic result...

S: ...definition of yourself you feel guilt.

C: ...and you can't help but have guilt. It's a rule.

S: So we explained in great detail that you operate within your self-system and have the feelings you think you're entitled to and the expression of guilt is merely the understanding that when you operate out of your defined and accepted roles you feel an unusual feeling called guilt and it's simply the rule. We explained very carefully and it was the only thing he remembered when he left the office until that child was born and then it dawned on him...

C: He'd had his own way of doing things. He had managed to break the rules by following the rules without having any guilt. It wasn't necessary in his case.

S: He wasn't having any affairs, but he had broken the rules and he was free of the guilt and that was a very wise way to prove that any fool can fail by failing but it takes a wise man to succeed by failing.

C: And it was his own way of failing in such a way as to succeed.

Since Frank's proclivity for breaking rules was well known, we reminded him that the "absolute rule of social contract" is to feel guilty for having affairs. We purposely shifted emphasis away from the actual (unspoken) rule that one does not have affairs, and instead stressed that part of the rule that concerns guilt. This provided Frank an opportunity to break a rule and have neither guilt nor affairs.

Once again, we want to state that Frank was not known to have had affairs, but the value of metaphor is that it is a symbolic reflection into which the client projects actual and literal meaning. If Frank thinks the metaphor refers to *real* affairs and that we have correctly guessed, that is fine. If, on the contrary, he thinks "In my case this is like rebelling against authority," that too is fine. In the latter situation, the meaning becomes something like "I'm supposed to feel foolish that I have broken rules and rebelled so I won't." The presupposition is that he will break the rule and avoid unpleasant feelings, but he will *not* continue to rebel. However, this is probably much more apparent to the reader than it was to Frank, who remained in trance listening through the filter of his rebellious personality.

In the final segment, the client was also referred to his next logical stage of family or social development. In this case, we mentioned children, stimulating Frank to think about making this likely change in his family structure. (He had indicated to us in the interview that he and his wife did hope to have children at some point in the future.) We did so, keeping in mind the importance for Frank of paradoxical intention. By suggesting that the protagonist didn't come to realize the point until the birth of his first child, we encourage Frank to take exception and conclude something like: "I can figure it out now. I don't have to wait until my first child."

In other words, Frank will attempt to compete with the protagonist in terms of achieving the understanding more quickly and in this story more quickly is measured against the time necessary to have a child. Thus Frank will be less inclined to challenge the act of having a child and will *begin* to consider the possibility of fathering children and comfortably expanding the roles that he can imagine himself filling. These few references to fathering are only a beginning. But this beginning is a very tidy addition to the therapy. It is the generative change, the future change, that will support the larger changes Frank has learned to make.

Reorienting the Client

S: Now you don't need to wait as long as he did in order to express a learning. Thursday night is a very good night...

C: ...as is Tuesday but you might prefer to do it on Wednesday.

S: We had a client we really wanted to change on Wednesday and he thought we wanted him to change on Wednesday so he'd show us...

C: ...he did it on Monday.

S: And while we've been talking you can realize that your hand raised up off of your lap to let you know that your unconscious really wants to demonstrate your ability to you...

C: Change is constantly occurring in your body, your thoughts, your conscious thoughts going one way and your unconscious thoughts going another way.

S: ...and your hand is rising up off your lap again now.

C: You don't even know how your unconscious responded.

S: I don't know if it will get off of your lap by the time you come out of trance.

C: You may know about the images your unconscious mind allowed your conscious mind to notice but you don't know what rate you're going to come out of trance...

S: But I do know that you can come out of trance suddenly or gradually as I count by increments, 1, 2, 3...

C: ...or whether you'll be completely out just because you managed to open your eyes or maybe you'll be out of trance even before you open your eyes.

S: Four , a little more, 7, 8.

C: Ten, 12.

S: You might want to have yourself remove from trance slowly enough to let your arm come up again and demonstrate your ability to use an unconscious learning outside your own awareness even if it's not spoken about again.

C: Fourteen, 16, and just roll those ideas around and allow them to settle comfortably in a fabric of your own design, your own choosing.

S: Seventeen, 18.

C: Nineteen and 20.

In this standard reorientation by counting, we have again incorporated the paradox and counterintention. The first example occurs in the debate over which day to change. The fact that change will happen is again presupposed. Given the structure of the story that has preceded this reorientation, Frank can either be like the protagonist and succeed in life but break one rule and not feel remorse for his past mistakes, or rebel and not be like the protagonist. In the latter case, he will feel remorse and be following the rules.

We assumed that, in keeping with his personality style, Frank would decide to compete and outdo all possible rivals. In that case he would be changing. Our only question was how to be in charge of the change. The answer was simple: Give him a time and expect him to rebel against it. We mapped this out for him in the discussion of change happening on Tuesday or Wednesday. In the metaphor, the client "showed us" and changed on Monday. So we provided what seemed a way for the client to beat us. But paradoxically the client only apparently beat us, since from a larger frame of reference (a higher logical level) we have still defined that the client change. In order to distract Frank's conscious mind from examining this higher level and possibly reconciling the paradoxical bind, a final paradoxical intention was offered with the challenge, "But you don't know what rate you're going to come out of trance." Once again the client can seemingly defeat us or rebel against our suggestion at the level of apparent content; in so doing he must follow our suggestions at the higher logical level.

Finally, Frank was reoriented with the closing remark at the content level that he allow the thoughts to settle into "a fabric of your own design, your own choosing." Again he was given a paradoxical symptom prescription. Since he was bound to modify the thoughts from his personal need to compete, improve, find exception, contradict, or criticize, we simply made it explicit that he was to do just that. Frank must frame the entire session in the paradoxical bind that he either accept our suggestions and modify the thoughts that were stimulated or reject our suggestion that he modify his thoughts, in which case he would accept the thoughts that were stimulated, and those of course were also our suggestions!

After reorienting from trance, Frank reported that fifteen minutes had passed; in actuality an hour had elapsed. This severe time distortion is a rough indicator of his depth of trance. He also stated that he had in the past taken many psychedelic drugs such as LSD and STP. He stated that, to his astonishment, during (what he assumed must have been) the midportion of the trance, he had felt more disoriented than he had ever felt on the drugs. He took this as evidence that something powerful had happened to him. We considered the middle segment to be the portion in which he was experiencing his tender feelings and imagining a close relationship with a father. His degree of fear, which manifested itself in the trance as coughing and severe jerking of the abdominal muscles, indicated the strength of the treatment approach. It had served as a vehicle in which he effectivly confronted some of his dependency needs, tender feelings, and vulnerability. He had even been able, upon emerging from the trance, to explain to us that he had experienced a unique feeling state and that he was scared by it—but he had lived through it to brag about it. We took this to mean that the trance had become significant to him in the way his drug usage had been important. Identifying with it was a vehicle for discovering his own autonomy. He would use it to change.

Finally, Frank's amnesia about the events of the trance and his loss of content, evidenced by the severe time distortion, stood as a testimony to the value of using paradoxical Ericksonian interventions—including symptom prescription, binds, and paradoxical metaphors—to distract, overload, confuse, bypass, and utilize Frank's conscious mind and rebellious personality traits.

Although we do not intend to imply that effective treatment can always be accomplished with a single session, one session was all that was necessary with this client. In a follow-up five months after this session, Frank reported continued amnesia about the actual content of his trance. All he could surmise was that it involved "a series of things that related around a boy and his father." He also reported that shortly after the session he grew a beard, something he had hesitated to do for some time. The result of this symbolic action was that Frank changed his self-image in a way apparent to him each time he looked into a mirror. He stated that he "feels older and much more sexually mature" which seemed to us to be indication of changes in Frank's self-image and age appropriate intimacy. He summarized that others now seemed to perceive and respond to him as a man rather than a boy. Though he tended to attribute this change to the presence of his beard, we concluded that he actually evoked such differences in response by the use of different behaviors that were shaped with metaphoric detailing.

The act of growing a beard probably would *not* by itself have resulted in the feelings Frank reported; these were more likely the result of the metaphoric guidance he received in areas of affect. The beard did, as we mentioned, illustrate Frank's increased attention to the social characteristics of his self-image in a way that is consistent with the self-image thinking metaphor. And as a symbolic representation of trance learnings, his beard seemed to provide a daily stimulus for Frank to associate to all of those learnings and act in ways consistent and appropriate for someone who is "older," "more sexually mature" and no longer "a boy" even though he did so without conscious insight or awareness of this unconscious aspect of association.

We attributed Frank's amnesia and lack of resistance to change to the use of symptom prescription and the paradoxically confusing structure of his trance. More importantly, we observed evidence in his self-report of the impact created by the coordinated, simultaneous, and concurrent use of thoughtfuly planned metaphors which indirectly stimulated a controlled elaboration of his experiential resources.

Since our goal was to illustrate the planning and therapy with lesser used forms of paradoxical intervention, we used a transcript from a hypnosis session. We expect that readers will be able to recognize how many of these interventions can be applied in their own work even if that work is not done in hypnotic trance. We have offered an assessment and treatment planning format as a framework that will translate directly to the work of marital, family, group, or gestalt therapists who do not use hypnotherapy per se in treatment. In so doing, we hope to stimulate an increased understanding of how a variety of Ericksonian styles of paradoxical intervention can be beneficially employed—even in non-Ericksonian treatment approaches.

REFERENCES

Aristotle. *Rhetoric and poetics of Aristotle.* New York: Modern Library, 1954. (Originally published, 1459.)

Bateson, G. *Steps to ecology of mind.* New York: Random House, 1972.

Erickson, M. H. Personal communication. August 7, 1977.

Erickson, M. H. The application of hypnosis to psychiatry. In E. Rossi (Ed.), *The collected papers of Milton H. Erickson on hypnosis* (Vol. 4). New York: Irvington, 1980.

Erickson, M. H., & Rossi, E. L. *Hypnotherapy: An exploratory casebook.* New York: Irvington, 1979.

Erickson, M. H., & Rossi, E. L. *Experiencing hypnosis: Therapeutic approaches to altered states.* New York: Irvington, 1981.

Fisch, R. Personal communication. December 2, 1982.

Haley, J. *Strategies of psychotherapy.* New York: Grune & Stratton, 1963.

Jung, C. The relations between the ego and the unconscious. In V. DeLaszlo (Ed.), *The basic writings of C. G. Jung,* New York: Modern Library, 1959.

Lankton, S., & Lankton, C. *The answer within: A clinical framework of Ericksonian hypnotherapy.* New York: Brunner/Mazel, 1983.

Lankton, S., & Lankton, C. *Multiple embedded metaphor and generative change* (Audio tape # M323-37C). Phoenix: Milton H. Erickson Foundation, 1982.

Lao Tsu. *The tao te ching; The writings of Chuang-Tzu; The thai-shang.* (J. Legge, Ed. and trans.). Taipei: Ch'Eng-Wen, 1976.

Lustig, H. S. *The artistry of Milton H. Erickson, M.D.* (a videotape). Haverford, PA: Herbert S. Lustig, M.D., Ltd., 1975.

Perls, F., Hefferline, R., & Goodman, P. *Gestalt therapy: Excitement and growth in the human personality.* New York: Dell, 1951.

Weakland, J., Fisch, R., Watzlawick, P., & Bodin, A. Brief therapy: Focused problem resolution. *Family Process,* 1974, *13,* 141–168.

Webster, M. *Webster's third new international dictionary of the English language unabridged.* Chicago: Encyclopedia Britannica, 1976.

Yalom, I. *The theory and practice of group psychotherapy.* New York: Basic Books, 1970.

7

Paradox in Context*

by Howard Tennen, Ph.D.
Joseph B. Eron, Psy.D.
Michael Rohrbaugh, Ph.D.

Paradoxical interventions such as prescribing the symptom and encouraging resistance are in seeming opposition to the therapeutic goals they are designed to achieve. These intriguing techniques are receiving increased attention in the psychotherapy literature, as evidenced by the following examples:

1. A patient complaining of intense anxiety in public places is asked to have a panic attack deliberately as the first step in bringing the symptom under control (Weakland et al., 1974, pp. 141–168).
2. After reviewing a voluminous history of unsuccessful medical and psychological therapies, a psychiatrist tells a headache patient that her condition is probably irreversible and that therapy should concentrate on helping her live with the problem. Despite persistent pessimism by the doctor, the headaches improve (Watzlawick et al., 1967, pp. 246–247).
3. A depressed stroke victim, who would attend only an initial family interview, improves dramatically over six meetings in

*The authors wish to thank Laurie Pearlman, who reviewed earlier versions of the manuscript.

which a therapy team coaches his spouse and grown children to be ineffectual and helpless in his presence (Watzlawick & Coyne, 1980, pp. 13–18).

4. A therapist asks a symptomatic husband to *pretend* to be irresponsible and inadequate three times before the next session and instructs his wife to try to find out whether he is really feeling that way (Madanes, 1980, pp. 73–85).

5. A therapist asks an overinvolved grandmother to take full responsibility for a misbehaving child. Grandmother backs off to a supporting role, allowing mother to take charge, and the child begins to behave more appropriately (Haley, 1976, p. 132).

6. A psychiatrist tells a well-educated, depressed, young homemaker in the presence of her preoccupied, career-oriented husband that her true nature is to find happiness in serving others. She therefore should relieve her husband of all responsibilities at home so he can work undisturbed in his study. The husband becomes more involved in the household and the wife in activities outside the home, saying she is no longer depressed (Hoffman, 1981, p. 307).

7. A team of therapists gives a family a letter to read aloud at prescribed times before the next session. The letter praises the identified patient for acting crazy to protect his father, explaining that by occupying mother's time with fights and tantrums, he allows father more time for work and relaxation (Palazzoli, Boscolo, Cecchin, & Prata, 1978, pp. 127–128).

8. A team compliments a severely obsessional young woman and her parents for protecting each other from the sadness associated with the death of a family member several years earlier. The team prescribes that the family meet each night to discuss their loss, and instructs the patient to behave symptomatically whenever her parents appear distraught (Hoffman et al., 1981).

Presented in this way, paradoxical interventions appear to be simply new tricks or techniques which can be added to a clinician's armamentarium. We will argue, on the contrary, that these methods are most effectively (and responsibly) used, not as isolated techniques, but within the framework of a coherent theory of problem maintenance and problem resolution. The most useful framework is one in which paradoxical methods have been used most extensively: It combines a systemic or cybernetic understanding of clinical problems with a strategic orientation to change. Though paradoxical interventions can also be used and understood in other (e.g., psychoanalytic, behavioral, existential) frameworks, we will review them here in the context of a strategic approach (Hoffman, 1981; Rohrbaugh & Eron, 1982). As background, we will examine briefly other perspectives on paradox.

FROM PARADOXICAL INTENTION TO INTENTIONAL PARADOX

The use of paradox in resolving human problems is not new. References to it appear as early as the 18th century (Foucault, 1973). More recently, Dunlap (1930) applied the technique of "negative practice" to problems such as stammering and enuresis. Frankl (1960) used "paradoxical intention" to alter the meaning of symptoms for his patients, and Rosen's (1953) "direct psychoanalysis" stressed the benefits of encouraging psychotic patients to engage in symptomatic behaviors, particularly when relapse is an issue.

The most significant contributions to the literature on paradox come from Gregory Bateson's 1952–62 research project on communication (Bateson et al., 1956; Haley, 1976). Bateson, Jackson, Haley, Weakland, and others explored the role of "double bind" communications in resolving as well as creating problems. Watzlawick, Beavin, and Jackson (1967) summarize the ingredients of a therapeutic double bind: Within the context of an intense relationship, the psychotherapeutic situation provides that

> an injunction is given which is so structured that it (*a*) reinforces the behavior the patient expects to be changed, (*b*) implies that this reinforcement is the vehicle of change, and (*c*) thereby creates a paradox because the patient is told to change by remaining unchanged. (p. 241)

Haley, Weakland, Watzlawick, and colleagues, combining ideas from communications and systems theory with clinical methods inspired by master-hypnotist Milton Erickson (Haley, 1973) went on in the late 1960s and early 1970s to develop therapy models with paradox as a central feature.

Historically, applications of therapeutic paradox have been associated with particular theoretical frameworks or paradigms. Negative practice was understood in terms of learning theory, Frankl's paradoxical intention in terms of existentialism, direct psychoanalysis in terms of psychoanalytic psychotherapy, and therapeutic double binds in terms of cybernetics and systems theory. In recent applications, some of these methods have been removed from their original contexts. For example, Frankl's para-doxical intention technique, used originally to help patients gain perspective on their existential pain, was adopted by pragmatic behavior therapists who discarded the existential framework. Be-haviorists have demonstrated that such techniques can be useful with specific symptoms such as insomnia (Ascher & Turner, 1979), urinary retention (Ascher, 1979), blushing (Lamontagne, 1978), obsessional thought processes (Solyom et al., 1972), and school attendance (Kolko & Milan, 1983). But downplaying theory in a framework of technical eclecticism offers a limited and limit-ing vision, not only of paradox, but of possibilities for interven-tion generally. A similar trend can be seen in the family therapy literature, where paradoxical techniques are being described and/ or explained apart from the models in which they were originally developed (Fisher et al., 1981).

Taking paradoxical intention as a point of departure, we can begin to recontextualize paradox in the framework of a systemic theory of behavior and a strategic orientation to intervention and technique. Explanations of paradoxical intention in the behavior therapy literature suggest that the intervention works because it interrupts an "exacerbation cycle" through which a symptom is maintained and exaggerated. In cybernetic terms, an exacerbation cycle is a simple positive feedback loop cycling at the level of the individual (e.g., the more the person tries to go to sleep the more s/he stays awake). The circularity implicit in the idea of exacerba-tion cycle embodies the systemic view that the way a problem is maintained is more relevant to therapy than is the way it started (Weakland et al., 1974; Sluzki, 1981).

Still, localizing problem maintenance at the level of the individ-ual overlooks the possibility that similar feedback loops may be operating at the level of the patient's interaction with other peo-ple—family members, friends, or even therapists. This highlights a second important systems idea—that the social context of a problem is highly relevant to understanding and changing it. Thus in all but the first vignette at the beginning of this chapter, intervention was targeted at *relationships* as well as symptoms. When the conceptual problem unit is larger than an individual therapy must address people other than, or in addition to, the identified patient.

With respect to strategy or technique, paradoxical intention raises the question of whose intention is (or should be) paradoxi-cal—patient's or therapist's? As Frankl used paradoxical intention (and as most behaviorists use it), the "intention" referred to is clearly the patient's. That is, if the patient can adopt the paradoxical attitude of trying to bring on a symptom deliberately, s/he may lose it by attempting to keep it. The therapist's intention is not paradoxical: S/he wants the patient to do (or at least attempt to do) what s/he says. But in other paradoxical approaches (Examples, 2, 5-8), the therapist expects the patient (or family) to do the opposite of what is proposed, and in this sense it is the therapist's intention that is paradoxical.

The distinction between what the patient expects and what the therapist expects—between patient strategy and therapist strategy—is fundamental to the strategic orientation. The strategic therapist usually does not explain his/her strategy to the patient and, following Erickson's principle of accepting what the patient brings, attempts to use the patient's strategy (attempted solutions) as a fulcrum for therapeutic leverage. For greater impact, suggestions and directives may be framed in a manner consistent (or deliberately inconsistent) with a patient's own idiosyncratic "language" (Weakland et al., 1974; Watzlawick et al., 1974).

Strategic intervention (of which paradox is a subclass) is designed to provoke change irrespective of insight, awareness, or emotional release. The strategic therapist does not assume that change with awareness is more efficient or enduring. In fact, as Madanes (1980) states, "If a problem can be solved without the family knowing how or why, that is satisfactory" (p. 75). The strategic orientation introduces new possibilities for therapeutic intervention as well as the occasion for its adherents to view themselves as manipulators with potential ethical implications. As Watzlawick (1978) notes, the therapist becomes

> more a chameleon than a firm rock in a sea of trouble. And it is at this point that many therapists dig in behind the retort, "Anything but that," while for others the necessity of ever new adaptations to the world images of their clients is a fascinating task (p. 141).

The systemic and strategic themes converge in three interrelated models which together best define a context for paradoxical intervention. These are: (1) the brief, problem-focused therapy developed by Watzlawick, Weakland, Fisch, and others at Palo Alto's Mental Research Institute (MRI); (2) the strategic/structural approach of Haley and Madanes (Haley, 1976, 1980; Madanes, 1981) and Stanton (1981[b]); and (3) the systemic family therapy pioneered by Selvini-Palazzoli et al. in Milan, Italy (Palazzoli et al., 1978, 1980). Each assumes that problems are maintained in ongoing cycles of interaction and are inextricably interwoven with the social context. In each, the therapist (or team) intervenes deliberately, on the basis of a specific plan, to resolve the presenting problem as quickly and efficiently as possible.

THE STRATEGIC SYSTEMS THERAPIES

In the Palo Alto (MRI) brief therapy model, a fundamental premise is that problems would be self-limiting were it not for the problem-solving attempts of the people involved. For example, insomnia may be maintained by trying to go to sleep deliberately, or depression by well-intentioned reassurance and prodding. From this perspective, the attempted solution is the problem, and interdicting these problem-solving efforts paves the way for change (Watzlawick et al., 1974; Watzlawick & Coyne, 1980). In the structural approaches, on the other hand, circular sequences involve at least three people. These sequences are the basis for inferring organizational anomalies such as confused family hierarchy (Haley, 1980) or relationships in which people are too involved with one another or not involved enough (Madanes, 1980). The goal of intervention is to establish a workable relationship structure.

System descriptions in the Milan approach (Palazzoli et al., 1980) are more abstract and formulated as hypotheses about the "rules of the family game" in which homeostatic processes are responsive to "a family system in danger of change" (Palazzoli et al., 1980, p. 7). Here, the clinician's hypotheses specify both the nature of that danger (e.g., the threat of separation) and ways in which interlocking behaviors of family members protect against it. Strategic interventions attempt to change dysfunctional family rules, but not by pointing them out to family members. Rather, as in Examples 7 and 8 at the beginning of the chapter, the rules are challenged indirectly by positively connoting and prescribing the very sequences of interaction that define these rules.

Haley (1980) believes that the chief value of systems theory is that it teaches therapists to recognize repeating sequences and so make predictions. If there is a fundamental concept in the strategic systems therapies and their reliance on paradoxical interventions, it is the idea of sequence or problem cycle. Strategic interventions—paradoxical or straightforward—are designed to bring about change by interrupting recursive (cyclical) patterns of behavior. The breadth of context considered relevant to intervening in the cycle defines one's unique approach: For the MRI brief therapy approach, analysis is usually limited to one or two people, while the structuralists generally adopt a triadic view and the systemic (Milan-style) therapist looks for broad historically based patterns of interaction.

DIMENSIONS OF PROBLEM MAINTENANCE

Whatever the unit of interaction, problem cycles may be seen as governed by premises, beliefs, labels (epistemologies), and expectations (axiologies). Whether a premise is functional or dysfunctional depends on the context in which it is used. When premises are applied rigidly, they are more likely to become the impetus for problem-maintaining patterns of behavior. A few interrelated epistemological or axiological assumptions appear to be tied repeatedly to problem maintenance in one way or another. We will describe four such dimensions which govern problem cycles at both the individual and interactional level.

Perhaps the most pervasive premise involved in problem maintenance is the dimension of *perceived control*. Indeed, some therapies maintain strict adherence to certain premises concerning people's control and responsibility over their lives (e.g., Perls et al., 1951). These therapies also assert a correlated expectation about the way people *should* control their lives. Simply stated, their epistemological-axiological position can be summarized by the statements: "People are masters of their fate and they are responsible for their behavior. Furthermore, people *should* take responsibility for their own behavior." While there are some contents where premises of mastery and control are adaptive, there are many in which such premises are dysfunctional and problem maintaining.

One class of problems maintained by a premise of mastery and control is that in which a person tries to be spontaneous. Here a person *tries* to produce a state of affairs which, by its very nature, requires not trying. For example, an erection is something that, for most men, cannot be willed. It just seems to happen when the time is right (and, embarrassingly, sometimes when the time is wrong). For the man who is having difficulty maintaining an erection, it may seem reasonable to try to create an erection by willing one. The problem-maintaining premise of course is that there is a correlation between effort expenditure and intensity of erection. The harder he tries, the softer he becomes, which is interpreted as evidence that he is not trying hard enough, and so on.

Another example of a problem cycle maintained by trying to assert control in a situation requiring spontaneity is the student who cannot concentrate on his studies because he is distracted by more pleasant thoughts. He usually tries to force himself to concentrate, but without success. It has been found that improvement can be quickly achieved in these cases if the therapist can get the student to set himself a reasonable time limit for his studies, after which he can do anything *except* study. Here, leisure time is redefined as punishment and consequently loses its lure (Watzlawick, 1978). As in the case of trying to have an erection, trying to not be distracted seems to rest on the premise that pleasant distractions are within the realm of one's personal control. When the therapist redefines pleasant distractions as punishment, s/he interrupts the problem cycle of trying, distraction, more trying, and so on. Whether one is trying to make something happen (an erection) or trying to make something *not* happen (pleasant thoughts) it is the *trying* that represents what Watzlawick refers to as "more of the same."

A second set of premises often implicated in problem maintenance has been labeled utopian (Watzlawick et al., 1974; Watzlawick, 1977) and usually takes two forms, utopian expectations and utopian assertions. Utopian expectations are based on the notion that "All life events should be perfect, delightful, and just the way I want them; nothing less is acceptable." A large number of adolescents who come for consultation (more often than not, at the request of a parent) maintain utopian expectations.

Utopian assertions, on the other hand, imply that all is well, perfect, and delightful in situations where in fact others would contend that some action is needed. The father of a delinquent adolescent boy referred by the courts, may talk about his son as if, rather than having been picked up by the police, the boy had just been picked as class valedictorian. Utopian assertions are usually tied to underaction as a means of problem maintenance. The therapist might define his or her task as reframing the meaning of the boy's behavior so as to energize father into appropriate action. Just how to do this depends, among other things, on the father's "language," which we will discuss below as a parameter of technique.

A third class of problem-maintaining beliefs which is particularly important in governing complex patterns of family interaction concerns whether behavior is labeled *mad* or *bad*. A label of mad or bad may be clearly articulated or, like the premises already discussed, may remain covert. In either case, people will act in accordance with the way they label others' behavior. Those who are labeled mad are not treated in the same way as those labeled bad, the best example being our legal system's distinction between "guilty" and "not guilty by reason of insanity."

In the world of human relations, labels have distinct effects on those labeled (Berger & Luckmann, 1966). Whether mad-bad labels are clearly articulated, for example, "you are mentally ill" or merely implied, when these labels are part of a problem sequence, the therapist's task is to shift the meaning of that behavior so that new patterns of interaction emerge.

An elegant example of reframing mad-to-bad in the sevice of therapeutic change is provided in Lynn Hoffman's (1976) description of Jay Haley's training tape "Leaving Home." In this tape, Haley from the start reframes his work with a hospitalized 24-year-old as helping him leave home. For this man, who had been in and out of hospitals for eight years, the problem-maintaining cycle was a familiar one:

> After he came back home, he would become threatening and abusive; he would then be moved out to an apartment; after that he would get on drugs, and go out and cause trouble in the community. The police would find him, the parents would hospitalize him, and the whole cycle would start again. (Hoffman, p. 515)

The therapist's first intervention was to have the parents sign a paper in their son's presence, stating that the next time the young man got into trouble, they would have the police put him in jail. This intervention would prevent the parents from visiting their son as often as they would if he were in the hospital. More important is how, without confrontation, this intervention reframed the son's actions from mad (for which one goes to the mental hospital) to bad (for which one goes to jail).

Later in therapy, the identified patient threatened his mother with a knife and his sister with a bat. At the next family session, the therapist arrived with a bat and a knife. He pushed the young man so hard that he threatened the therapist with the bat. Finally, the father took the bat from him, and the parents and therapist agreed that using weapons was unacceptable (bad) and would not be tolerated. These interventions helped pave the way for other redefinitions of the family situation which culminated in the young man being on his own and out of the hospital.

In this example, undesirable behaviors were labeled as mad by family members, contributing to a long-term problem cycle. Just as often, however, the label *bad* governs a problem cycle. For example, for many alcoholics, the label badness or moral depravity is precisely what maintains the pattern of drinking → immorality

→ "swearing off" → drinking. In fact, Bateson (1972) attributes much of the success of Alcoholics Anonymous to their implicit redefinition of alcoholism as a sign of madness, evidenced by their dictum: "We admitted we were powerless over our lives— that our lives had become unmanageable."

The fourth and final premise to be discussed is the definition of who's up and who's down in a relationship—who takes are of whom. These hierarchical definitions, like mad and bad labels, secure roles for the principals of the scenario. Clinical symptoms may be seen as a way of defining relationships hierarchically. The command aspect (Bateson, 1972) of a symptom includes the injunction "care for me," which can play an important role in problem cycles. For example, a young man makes an appointment with a therapist for himself and his "frigid" wife. This young man is quite invested in his masculinity, and his obviously angry wife simply "cannot" enjoy sex with him. The therapist turns to the wife, and *in the husband's presence*, gently supports her efforts to make her husband look good by not enjoying sex. The systemic reframes of M. Palazzoli and the Milan Group (1978) provide elegant examples of changing relational structures by redefining up as down and down as up.

"LANGUAGE" AND PATIENT COMPLIANCE

The effectiveness of most intervention in therapy seems to depend in one way or another on the patient's accepting the therapist's definition of reality or complying with his or her suggestions or directions. Unfortunately, patients often don't listen, don't follow directives, and may even defy our attempts to redefine their reality.

An important contribution of the Palo Alto group is their emphasis on maximizing therapeutic influence by framing interventions in the client's own "language" or construct system. From a cognitive-behavioral perspective, Mahoney (1980) has discussed the importance of considering a patient's "paradigm" while Watzlawick (1978) chooses to refer to the person's "world view." Consistent with Erickson's principle of accepting and using what a patient offers (in a manner analogous to psychological judo), the assumption is that people are more likely to accept new definitions of reality if they represent extensions or variations of their own views. Consider the following examples:

To a client associating his problem with low self-esteem, we may consider that he is evidently in need of self-punishment and that this is an excellent way of fulfilling this need. To somebody involved in Eastern thought we may recall the seeming absurdity of Zen koans. . . . And to types like ourselves, we may even lecture in terms of Group Therapy, the Theory of Logical Types, first-order change and second-order change. (Watzlawick et al., 1974, p. 126)

In practice, a patient's "language" is inferred. The therapist might ask him- or herself, "How does this person want to be seen?" Clinically useful answers might be: "as unique and creative," "as always in control of myself," "as a sacrificing spouse and parent," or even "as discovering things on my own, not because someone else tells me" (Rohrbaugh et al., 1981). We might then conceive of language as a series of bipolar constructs (Kelly, 1955), for which each patient perceives a desirable and an undesirable pole. Examples are "carefree-dutiful," "tough-delicate," "in control-loose." This dialectical nature of language sets the stage for two distinct forms of intervention, which we will now discuss.

COMPLIANCE AND DEFIANCE

In 1981 (Rohrbaugh et al.) we differentiated two types of paradoxical intervention. In one, change follows from attempted compliance with a therapist's directive; in the other, change follows from defiance. The compliance-defiance distinction has been used by Papp (1980), Madanes (1981), and others (Rohrbaugh et al., 1982) in discussions of paradoxical and strategic intervention.

Compliance-based interventions, such as prescribing the symptom, work because complying with a therapeutic directive interrupts or short-circuits the process that maintains the symptom. This type of paradoxical symptom prescription can be effective with obsessions, anxiety, insomnia, and other problems that are maintained in part by attempts to stave them off. When the patient attempts to bring on such a symptom deliberately, s/he cannot continue in usual ways of trying to prevent it, and under these conditions, the symptom often dissolves.

Defiance-based interventions work because people change by rebelling. Haley (1976) cites the example of disengaging an overprotective mother from a symptomatic child. A therapist might ask the mother to hover even more, setting aside a full hour each night to warn the child about all of life's dangers. "If this approach is done well, the mother will react by rebelling against the therapist and hovering over the child less" (p. 71).

We suggested two assessment parameters, derived from J. W. Brehm's (1972) theory of psychological reactance (S. Brehm, 1976), which guide the use of compliance- and defiance-based paradox with individuals. One concerned the relational stance vis-à-vis the therapist of the person or persons to be influenced—specifically, whether the potential for reactance (rebellion) is high or low. The second parameter was whether the person to be influenced (not necessarily the identified patient) perceived the target behavior as "free," or under voluntary control.

We hypothesized that defiance-based intervention is indicated when reactance potential is high and the target behavior is perceived as free, whereas compliance-based paradox is appropriate when the target behavior is unfree (e.g., a symptom) and the probability of reactance is low. Since the overprotective mother in Haley's example would probably define her hovering as free, she may do it less if told to do it more. If the child's symptom were stuttering, it would probably be unfree and not a good target for defiance-based intervention. If the child were cooperative, however, s/he might be asked to practice stuttering deliberately, which might interrupt problem-maintaining attempts to avoid disfluency.

Brehm and Brehm (1981) assume that a good deal of patient behavior is "unfree," and according to them this seems to "vitiate the utility of the free versus unfree distinction. Moreover, . . . the 'freeness' of the symptom may not be as relevant to therapy as the 'freeness' of trying to cope with the symptom" (p. 318). Brehm and Brehm eliminate the free versus unfree distinction from our model and work only with the characteristics of the symptoms and the reactance potential of the patient.

While reactance theory has implications for *how* to intervene, we used the Palo Alto brief therapy model for guidelines about *where* to intervene. The basic premise of brief therapy is that irrespective of how problems originate, they are maintained by the well-intentioned but persistently misapplied solutions of the problem bearer and those with whom s/he interacts. The task of therapy, therefore, is to identify these "problem-maintaining solutions" (e.g., a parent's hovering, a spouse's reassurance, a patient's attempts to conceal his or her own nervousness), and interdict them as parsimoniously as possible. In this framework, compliance- and defiance-based interventions are used to help people do less of the same.

Although the compliance-defiance distinction is helpful in thinking about the general direction of intervention, the model itself has some disadvantages. In practice, concepts such as "reactance potential" and "freedom of target behavior" draw attention away from patterns of interaction to traits and behaviors of individuals. "Psychological reactance" is a hypothetical motive state aroused when a person's perceived freedom is threatened. The concept is therefore linear (*caused* by threats to freedom), individualistic (localized in one person), and not easily reconciled with the circular, cybernetic, epistemology of a systems approach. Although reactance theory and brief therapy each offer important perspectives on paradox, attempting to integrate them may only confuse further what we had hoped to clarify.

MODES OF STRATEGIC INTERVENTION

One way to describe the how of strategic therapy and its paradoxical components is in terms of three interrelated modes of intervention: *prescribing, reframing,* and *restraining. Prescribing* means telling people what to do (giving tasks, making suggestions, etc.) either directly or indirectly. The compliance-defiance model predicts that change may come about regardless of whether the patient follows the therapist's directive. *Reframing* involves redefining the meaning of behavior in a way that makes change possible. As we've already suggested, such redefinitions are designed to alter premises or labels which govern problem-maintaining patterns of interaction. Although reframing may resemble interpretation, its goal is to provoke change rather than provide insight and reality testing—and the accuracy of the redefinition is less important than its impact.

Many psychotherapies implicitly assume that the role of the therapist is to replace a patient's faulty world view with the correct (true, logical, rational) view. Therapy ends when the patient's world view parallels that of the therapist. The strategic therapist, in his/her use of paradox, contends that meaning depends on context. Adaptive functioning does not require being in touch with reality and having an accurate view of the world. Rather, *any* world view that interdicts problem sequences is considered in planning interventions. This position is nested not only in "functional theory," but in a growing empirical literature pointing to the healing effects of illusion (Lazarus, 1983; Taylor, 1983). Adaptive functioning has been associated with denial (Lazarus, 1983), the illusion of control (Alloy & Abramson, 1979; Tiger, 1979) and the *mis*perception of one's success and its causes (Greenwald, 1980; Muller & Ross, 1975). High self-esteem (Tennen & Herzberger, submitted for publication; Tennen et al., submitted for publication), lack of depression (Lewinsohn et al., 1980; Abramson & Alloy, 1981) and better adjustment to illness and injury (Bulman & Wortman, 1977; Taylor, 1983; Tennen et al., in press) have been associated with *non*veridical and illogical perceptions and beliefs. The shift from psyche to system and from reality testing to useful illusions may represent the most significant contributions of the strategic therapist in his/her use of paradox.

Restraining strategies discourage or caution against change in some way. The therapist's message is "you should not change as much as you want to," or "you shouldn't change in the way that you want to," or even, "perhaps you shouldn't change—*at all.*" This intervention alters the therapist's actual or potential role *inside* a problem-maintaining system. For example, when a patient has sought help repeatedly but failed to benefit, or therapy is stuck after straightforward approaches have failed, the therapist might reverse the cycle by being pessimistic or even advising against change.

In practice, the prescribing, reframing, and restraining modes are interwoven: Each may be implicit in any intervention, and each is an important element in therapeutic paradox. Before considering some examples of the use of these interventions in combination, we will discuss the use of therapeutic restraint in greater detail.

PROMOTING CHANGE BY DISCOURAGING IT: RESTRAINT AS A STRATEGIC (PARADOXICAL) INTERVENTION

Paradoxical restraining maneuvers are powerful interventions. They are also easily misused. Their potential for therapeutic influence is high—but their potential for therapist-induced deterioration effects is equally high. The various restraining interventions can be arranged along a compliance-defiance continuum (see Figure 1) based on whether the therapist desires attempted compliance or outright defiance and based on the therapist's creative use of "language."

Implicit restraints are compliance-based interventions. They work because the patient accepts what the therapist tells him/her. For problems maintained by trying too hard, implicit restraints can effectively interrupt problem cycles. Implicit restraints allow the patient to do less of the same. From the very start of therapy,

FIGURE 1

Varieties of Therapeutic Restraints

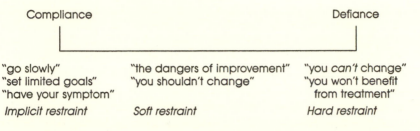

Compliance		Defiance
"go slowly"	"the dangers of improvement"	"you *can't* change"
"set limited goals"	"you shouldn't change"	"you won't benefit
"have your symptom"		from treatment"
Implicit restraint	*Soft restraint*	*Hard restraint*

setting minimum, concrete goals counteracts the problem-maintaining, utopian premise that change is an all-or-none affair. Simply convincing a patient that the best way to get going is to get a *slow* start can interrupt a problem cycle. Another variation of implicit restraint is the "no step is too small" principle—a notion well known to behavior therapists. Finally, having a patient voluntarily express his/her symptom can interrupt overaction in an attempt to ameliorate the problem. In cases of obsessions, certain sexual dysfunctions, and insomnia—to take a few examples—*symptom prescriptions* can be considered variants of implicit restraint because they interrupt trying too hard problem cycles.

Soft Restraint

In the class of interventions we call soft restraint, the therapist either suggests directly or implies that the patient *shouldn't change* the very behavior that s/he or others find troublesome. Often the therapist will worry about the dangers of improvement and express the possible unfavorable consequences of change.

The Milan Group (Palazzoli et al., 1978) describes the use of what appears to be soft restraint in their work with families. In one case, the identified patient is a six-year-old boy diagnosed as severely autistic. After assessment sessions, and after taking into consideration the material gathered from those sessions:

> We began by praising Lionel (the identified patient) for his great sensitivity. He had thought that his grandmother, generous as she was, needed to love only those who weren't loved. Since Uncle Nicola (grandmother's son) had gotten married six years ago and was therefore loved by his wife, and no longer needed his mother's

love, Granny was left with no one unloved to love. Thus, ever since he had been small, he had done everything he could to make himself unlovable. (pp. 63–64)

The implication of course is that perhaps the identified patient, in his ultimate wisdom, exhibits his "symptoms" because he is protecting his grandmother and that perhaps he shouldn't do otherwise. With regard to soft restraint, note that the therapist in the case just described implied that change might not be an altogether good idea and framed that comment in a way that enhanced defiance. Specifically, the family's world view was that Lionel, the identified patient, was weak and helpless. The therapist redefined his symptoms as helping his needy grandmother. To prove the therapist wrong, something would have to change.

Jay Haley (1976) offers another example of soft restraint with a problem child who will not go to school. The therapist, suggests Haley, can talk to the family about how perhaps the boy should not go to school. The therapist "can suggest that it might be better if the boy just stayed home and can offer various reasons for this, depending on the particular family. He might say that perhaps the family would get upset if the boy went to school like normal children and therefore it would be better if he stayed home" (pp. 68–69).

As Haley points out, soft restraint must be used carefully. The therapist is saying things to the family that can be interpreted as insulting. It is important that the therapist show benevolent concern (Haley, 1976) and clearly frame the problem behavior with a positive connotation (Palazzoli et al., 1978). The greatest danger of soft restraint is that the individual or family perceive the therapist as insulting, uncaring, or malevolent. Given what we've said about utilizing a patient's (family's) "language," the therapist's difficult task begins to crystallize. S/he must use the negative pole of the patient's language without appearing sarcastic or uncaring.

Worrying about whether change *should* occur or about the possible dangers of improvement early in therapy is a general strategy with many applications. First, it can be used as a strategy by itself. Sometimes an initial soft restraint can initiate changes and problem resolution. Consider the treatment of a five-year-old boy who had never been toilet trained and who several times a day had a bowel movement in his pants (Haley, 1976). The therapist decides that he would treat the family by doing only one thing—restraining the family from improving by being benevolently concerned about what would happen to the family if the child became normal. He raised the question of whether the mother could tolerate being a mother who successfully solved her child's problem. He ever so subtly implied that he thought she *could* tolerate success, but he wanted to be sure. The therapist also questioned the couple's capacity to deal with a free evening together if they did not have this problem to discuss. After three interviews, the symptom began to remit. One way of looking at this soft restraint is that the therapist makes an intolerable suggestion in a tolerable fashion.

Soft restraint can also facilitate other (compliance-based) interventions which the therapist—perhaps reluctantly—offers. For example, there may be a task which, if carried out, will initiate change. Within the context of a soft restraint, the patient can prove the therapist wrong by carrying out the task that the therapist thought s/he shouldn't jump into. The task itself need not be very fancy, it might be a very simple assignment or a graded task, like those often suggested by therapists. The purpose of the soft restraint is to increase the likelihood that the patient will carry out the task—usually to prove the therapist wrong.

An interesting use of soft restraint is to embed a paradoxical symptom prescription within the restraint. When carried out sensitively, this approach provides a potent "double-barreled" paradoxical strategy, especially when a patient seems unlikely to comply. For example, when a patient suffering from insomnia has failed to comply with several tasks suggested early in the treatment, such as charting his or her sleep schedule, the therapist might suggest several dangers of improvement, and then imply that staying awake all night for several nights could offer a better understanding of the problem (assuming, of course, "understanding" were a part of the patient's language), but again it might not be the best idea because of the potential dangers of losing the symptom. If the patient defies the therapist once more—by trying to stay up all night for several consecutive nights—his problem is likely to begin to resolve.

The creativity and subtlety necessary in framing these therapeutic restraints cannot be overemphasized. Very subtly, the therapist defines the implications of remaining the same in a manner that is inconsistent with the patient's view of himself and his world. The therapist should never be sarcastic or degrading. Instead, the implicit message should be "you shouldn't change for the following reasons, all of which are unacceptable to you."

Haley (1976) speaks of restraining as challenging people to be "normal." He suggests that these maneuvers work best with middle-class families. A challenge to be normal probably strikes a sensitive note with middle-class families because for many middle-class families, an important dimension of their world view is appropriate/normal—inappropriate/abnormal. Nonmiddle-class individuals and families, however, can be induced to change if the implications of remaining the same are defined in a manner subtly inconsistent with their world view.

Hard Restraint

Hard restraint is the most extreme of the restraining strategies. It requires, perhaps even more than implicit and soft restraints, a careful assessment of the patient's language and a sensitivity to his or her plight. Here, the therapist suggests that the patient probably can't change. The message about the improbability of change can be strongly assertive or mildly pessimistic; in either case, it is offered empathically.

Perhaps one of the most common mistakes of novice therapists applying paradoxical techniques is to confuse hard restraint with sarcasm or one upsmanship. They forget that if therapy is to help a person, that person has to remain in treatment long enough to be helped. Not many people will endure a sarcastic therapist.

In a milder form, hard restraint can focus on the patient's capacity to carry out a therapeutic task. Here the therapist predicts that the patient won't be able to do what is required to initiate change. Of course the therapist mentions exactly what the "it" is that the patient can't do, and supports his or her pessimistic outlook with the appropriate use of language—in this case the subtle utilization of the negative pole of the patient's language. Of course if the patient just happens to engage in the task (which may be a symptom prescription or behavioral task), s/he is likely to start the change process.

TOWARD A RECONTEXTUALIZATION OF PARADOX

We can not place the opening vignettes in context. The first is a simple symptom prescription aimed at an intraindividual exacerbation cycle. The second is a hard restraining maneuver that breaks a "help-rejecting-complainer" cycle in which therapists have repeatedly failed to cure the headaches. Examples 3 and 4 target cycles of family interaction. The frustrated relatives of the stroke victim had been vacillating between encouraging the patient and coercively attempting to motivate him—but he only became more depressed. The paradoxical prescription reversed this pattern even though the patient himself did not attend the sessions. The prescription in Example 4 interrupts another marital cycle by subtly reframing the symptom: Since the husband may only be "pretending," it is now difficult for the wife to continue in her usual ways of responding to him.

In Examples 5 and 6, paradox is used to change relationship structures. When asked to take all of the responsibility for her grandchild, the grandmother backs off, establishing clearer generational boundaries. When the psychiatrist exaggerates the problem-maintaining complementarity of the couple in Example 6, they reorganize in a more symmetrical way. Both of these interventions could be called defiance-based, but it would be a mistake to say they work because the people involved are "defiant." The systemic explanation is that paradox introduces an imbalance in the family (or in the balance of internal and external forces for change) such that the system recoils to a more workable pattern of organization (Hoffman, 1981).

Examples 7 and 8 illustrate Milan-style systemic paradox in which the entire pattern of problem-maintaining family interaction is positively reframed and prescribed (Palazzoli et al., 1978). These interventions simultaneously combine several modes of strategic intervention. The therapist *reframes* the identified patient's behavior as protective of his parents, thereby altering the hierarchical meaning of the symptom. Consistent with this reframing, the therapist *restrains* the family from precipitous change (an example of soft restraining). The implicit *prescription* is that no one change just yet since a shift might destabilize a delicately balanced family structure. The strategy is defiance-based in that change comes about by the family reorganizing against the therapist's cautionary directives. In this approach, the paradoxical stance is often maintained throughout the therapy and implemented by a team of therapists using a one-way mirror. The consultation team plans the strategy and provides outside support for the therapists who work with the family directly. The team is also a powerful source of therapeutic leverage in the form of high-impact, hard-to-disqualify messages from unseen experts. Papp (1980), in likening the consultation team to a Greek chorus, shows how some (outside) team members can take a position against change, so that others (inside) can encourage it more directly.

RESEARCH STRATEGIES

The strategic approach to treatment described in this chapter has now developed to the point where empirical research is both possible and necessary. There appear to be two major research tasks (Rohrbaugh & Eron, 1982). One is the documentation and clarification of the role of interactional-contextual factors in the development and maintenance of clinical problems. The work of Minuchin, Rosman, and Baker (1978), Wynne (1978), Coyne (1976), and Madanes, Dukes, and Harbin (1980) represent significant first attempts in this area.

The second research task is to demonstrate that the strategic therapies compare favorably to other well-established treatments (see Stanton, 1981[b]; Gurman & Kniskern, 1981). Brehm and Brehm (1981) note that many clinical problems described in our previous work as appropriate for compliance-based strategies would also seem to be appropriate for treatment by systemic desensitization (Wolpe, 1959). In view of the strong evidence for the effectiveness of systemic desensitization (e.g., Kazdin & Wilcoxon, 1976), Brehm and Brehm (1981) believe that it is the treatment of choice for anxiety reduction.

Defiance-based strategies have received few empirical tests; most supportive evidence derives from case studies. Studies by Ayllon, Allison, and Kandel (unpublished manuscript) and Kolko and Milan (1983) used multiple baseline designs. Unfortunately, these studies involved very small samples of children.

One reason for the dearth of empirical research in this field is that the notion of *patterns*, which underlies strategic therapies, presents serious methodological issues (Dell, 1980; Abeles, 1976). Therefore, research on clinical outcome may have to advance in the absence of "basic" research. The "effects" of the strategic therapies must be held up to the same scrutiny as competing therapeutic approaches. In a series of studies on procrastination and depression, Strong and associates (Beck et al., 1982; Feldman et al., 1982; Lopez & Wambach, 1982; Strong & Clayborn, 1982; Wright & Strong, 1982) test the effectiveness of positive connotation, symptom prescription, and defiance-based strategies.

These studies are commendable because they test directly the efficacy of certain paradoxical interventions. Unfortunately, each has some serious limitations. Each study uses a no-treatment control group rather than a placebo control. In each study, the therapists were graduate students and the dependent measure was self-report. Subjects received the same intervention without consideration of language in the service of compliance regulation. Finally, these studies used student subjects who received course credit for their participation. These factors limit the ecological validity of the investigations. Nonetheless, they represent the first systematic investigations of paradox in psychotherapy.

ETHICAL ISSUES

The question arises: To have a systems orientation is it necessary to be strategic and manipulative? Perhaps not, yet systems by definition are controlled. To a large extent, cybernetics is the study of reciprocal influence and control. In therapy, therefore, one cannot *not* influence, just as one cannot *not* communicate (Watzlawick et al., 1967). The question is not whether to influence, but how to do it most constructively. Needless to say, strategic methods raise important ethical questions, such as what is a reasonable degree of informed consent, and should or can it be obtained from all whose lives may be touched by an intervention?

Significantly, therapists such as Haley and Palazzoli who pioneered the use of paradoxical methods are now giving them less emphasis. Indeed, as paradoxical techniques become more popular, there is reason for concern about ways in which they can be misused. Encouraging a symptom or restraining people from changing can be disastrous if done sarcastically or from a sense of frustration ("There's the window—go ahead and jump!"). Nor should paradox be used for shock value or to give the therapist a sense of power (Weeks & L'Abate, 1979). Since strategic work presents the special risk of making patients objects for dehumanized treatment by therapists, it is most important that paradoxical methods be used in a systemic framework that views the therapist or team as part of the environment being modified.

The strategic-paradoxical approach to psychotherapy appears to raise ethical concerns among its practitioners as well as its critics. We have been warned against giving prepackaged directives and against making strategic interventions without linking them to the family system (Stanton, 1981[b]). We have also been reminded that paradoxical interventions may be manipulative with respect to concealing treatment goals, use of a controlling method, and absence of informed consent (Weeks & L'Abate, 1982).

Perhaps the most extensive discussion of the ethics of paradoxical interventions is found in the work of Haley (1976), who reminds us that all therapy is "manipulative." The psychoanalyst, for example, decides upon the proper timing and depth of an interpretation. Haley correctly points out that by considering issues of timing and depth, the analyst conceals many of his/her observations from the patient, until the patient is ready to make optimum use of the insights offered. Behavior therapists similarly reinforce their client's adaptive behaviors without always announcing their intent. Haley goes so far as to claim that when a therapist refrains from offering insight, s/he is simply being courteous.

A thornier and perhaps the most crucial ethical issue facing practitioners of strategic-paradoxical interventions is whether a therapist can ethically give a patient false information in an attempt to initiate change. Haley (1976) believes that it is generally unwise for a therapist to lie to a patient, but he cautiously endorses more "complicated lies" such as a therapist telling a phobic patient that the therapist wants the patient to be afraid in a particular situation.

When confronted with this ethical dilemma, we may be tempted to retreat to epistemological sanctuaries. For example, we might claim that it is naive to be concerned with truthtelling in therapy, since there is no such thing as objective reality. There is now considerable empirical support for the saying "the truth hurts." Depressed people appear to be more realistic about their ability to control their environment (Alloy & Abramson, 1979) and their effects on others (Lewinsohn et al., 1980) than are nondepressed people. When the depression lifts, these people join their nondepressed counterparts in maintaining an "illusory glow." Is a therapist bound to a code of ethics which forces him/her to reveal the depressing truth to a formerly depressed patient?

The epistemologically oriented therapist might also note that denial has many benefits (Lazarus, 1983; Taylor et al., unpublished manuscript). Acknowledging certain "truths" has been associated with poorer coping and mood disturbance (Affleck et al., 1982). Does a therapist have an obligation to point out these harmful truths, or is Haley (1976) correct in labeling this behavior "discourteous?"

Finally, one might note that false beliefs about blameworthiness have been associated with better coping and less personal distress in young diabetic patients (Tennen et al., in press), breast cancer patients (Timko & Janoff-Bulman, submitted for publication), and accident victims (Bulman & Wortman, 1977). Once again, should a therapist be required to tell "the whole truth," or is the withholding of certain truths acceptable?

These epistemological arguments can lead a therapist to ignore truthfulness as an ethical issue. In the treatment situation, however, epistemology cannot claim priority over ethics, and the moral domain of *intended* deception must be considered along with issues of truth and falsity (Bok, 1978).

The clinician who uses paradoxical interventions runs up against these and other complicated ethical issues, which might be minimized by the following four guidelines for not misusing paradoxical interventions:

1. *Define behavior positively.* Avoid attributing unseemly motives to people (like needing to "control," "resist," or "defeat" one another). When reframing, ascribe noble intentions not only to the symptom but to what other people are doing to support it (Hoffman et al., 1981; Papp, 1980; Stanton, 1981[b]). Be most careful with challenging or provocative interventions such as in Example 2 at the beginning of the chapter: it is better to suggest that change is not advisable (soft restraining) than to predict it will not be possible (hard restraining).

2. *Consider context.* Evaluate interactional as well as individual levels of problem maintenance. When both are present, give precedence to the former.

3. *Work with colleagues.* In paradoxical work with difficult cases, it is most helpful to have a consultation team and one-way mirror, or at the very least to discuss the case with a supervisor or colleagues. It is easy to lose one's moorings, and outside consultants provide valuable grounding and support.

4. *Have a theory.* The most important guideline for paradoxical (or any other) intervention is to have a coherent rationale for using it. This requires a clear formulation of how a symptom is being maintained and how a particular intervention will change the pattern of problem maintenance. If we are saying anything here, it is that theory and technique are (or should be) inseparable. Before telling patients not to change, a strategic systems therapist should give as much attention to problem cycles, confused hierarchies, and family rules as a psychoanalyst would give to intensity of transference, level of resistance, and the availability of a reasonable ego before offering an interpretation.

REFERENCES

Abeles, G. Researching the unresearchable: Experimentation on the double bind. In C. E. Sluzki & D. C. Ransom (Eds.), *Double bind*. New York: Grune & Stratton, 1976.

Abramson, L. Y., & Alloy, L. B. Depression, nondepression, and cognitive illusions: Reply to Schwartz. *Journal of Experimental Psychology: General*, 1981, *110*, 436–447.

Affleck, G., Allen, D., McGrade, B. J., & McQueeney, M. Maternal causal attributions at hospital discharge of high risk infants. *American Journal of Mental Deficiency*, 1982, *86*, 575–580.

Alloy, L. B., & Abramson, L. Y. Judgment of contingency in depressed and nondepressed students: Sadder but wiser? *Journal of Experimental Psychology: General*, 1979, *108*, 441–485.

Ascher, L. M. Paradoxical intention in the treatment of urinary retention. *Behaviour Research and Therapy*, 1979, *17*, 267–270.

Ascher, L. M., & Turner, R. M. Paradoxical intention and insomnia: An experimental investigation. *Behaviour Research and Therapy*, 1979, *17*, 408–411.

Ayllon, T., Allison, M. G., & Kandel, H. G. *Changing behavior through systematic verbal persuasion.* Unpublished manuscript, Georgia State University, 1980.

Bateson, G. *Steps to an ecology of mind.* New York: Random House, 1972.

Bateson, G., Jackson, D. D., Haley, J., & Weakland, J. H. Toward a theory of schizophrenia. *Behavioral Science*, 1956, *1*, 251–264.

Beck, J., & Strong, S. Stimulating therapeutic change with interpretations. A comparison of positive and negative connotations. *Journal of Counseling Psychology*, 1982, *29*, 551–559.

Berger, P. L., & Luckmann, T. *The social construction of reality.* Doubleday, 1966.

Bok, S. *Lying: Moral choice in public and private life.* New York: Random House, 1978.

Brehm, J. *Responses to loss of freedom: A theory of psychological reactance.* Morristown, N.J.: General Learning Press, 1972.

Brehm, S. *The application of social psychology to clinical practice.* Washington, D.C.: Hemisphere, 1976.

Brehm, S. S., & Brehm, J. W. *Psychological reactance: A theory of freedom and control.* New York: Academic Press, 1981.

Bulman, R. J., & Wortman, C. B. Attributions of blame and coping in the "real world": Severe accident victims react to their lot. *Journal of Personality and Social Psychology*, 1977, *35*, 351–363.

Coyne, J. C. Toward an interactional description of depression. *Psychiatry*, 1976, *39*, 28–40.

Dell, P. F. Researching the family theories of schizophrenia: An exercise in epistemological confusion. *Family Process*, 1980, *19*, 321–326.

Dunlap, K. Repetition in the breaking of habits. *Science Monthly*, 1930, *30*, 66–70.

Feldman, D. A., Strong, S. R., & Danser, D. B. A comparison of paradoxical and nonparadoxical interpretations and directives. *Journal of Counseling Psychology,* 1982, *29,* 572–579.

Fisher, L., Anderson, A., & Jones, J. E. Types of paradoxical intervention and indications/contraindications for use in clinical practice. *Family Process,* 1981, *20,* 25–36.

Foucalt, M. *Madness and civilization: A history of insanity in the age of reason.* New York: Random House, 1973.

Frankl, V. Paradoxical intention: A logotherapeutic technique. *American Journal of Psychotherapy.* 1960, *14,* 520–535.

Greenwald, A. G. The totalitarian ego: Fabrication and revision of personal history. *American Psychologist,* 1980, *35,* 603–618.

Gurman, A. S., & Kniskern, D. P. (Eds.). *Handbook of family therapy.* New York: Brunner/Mazel, 1981.

Haley, J. *Uncommon therapy: The psychiatric techniques of Milton H. Erickson, M.D.* New York: W. W. Norton, 1973.

Haley, J. Development of a theory of a research project. In C. Sluzki, D.C. Ransom (Eds.), *Double bind.* New York: Grune & Stratton, 1976.

Haley, J. *Problem-solving therapy.* San Francisco, Calif.: Jossey-Bass, 1976.

Haley, J. *Leaving home: The therapy of disturbed young people.* New York: McGraw-Hill, 1980.

Hoffman, L. Breaking the homeostatic cycle. In P. J. Guerin (Ed.), *Family therapy: Theory and practice.* New York: Gardner, 1976.

Hoffman, L. *Foundations of family therapy.* New York: Basic, 1981.

Hoffman, L. *Therapeutic paradoxes: A model for working with difficult families.* Conference presented by faculty of Ackerman Institute for Family Therapy, New York, 1981.

Kazdin, A. E., & Wilcoxon, L. A. Systematic desensitization and nonspecific treatment effects: A methodological evaluation. *Psychological Bulletin,* 1976, *83,* 729–758.

Kelly, G. A. *The psychology of personal constructs* (Vols. I and II). New York: Norton, 1955.

Kolko, D. J., & Milan, M. A. Reframing and paradoxical instruction to overcome "resistance" in the treatment of delinquent youths: A multiple baseline analysis. *Journal of Consulting and Clinical Psychology,* 1983, *51,* 655–660.

Lamontagne, Y. Treatment of erythrophobia by paradoxical intention. *Journal of Nervous and Mental Disease,* 1978, *166,* 304–307.

Lazarus, R. S. The costs and benefits of denial. In S. Breznitz (Ed.), *Denial of stress.* New York: International Universities Press, 1983.

Lewinsohn, P. M., Mischel, W., Chaplin, W., & Barton, R. Social competence and depression: The role of illusory self-perceptions. *Journal of Abnormal Psychology,* 1980, *89,* 203–212.

Lopez, F. G., & Wambach, C. A. Effects of paradoxical and self-control directives in counseling. *Journal of Counseling Psychology,* 1982, *29,* 115–124.

Madanes, C. Protection, paradox, and pretending. *Family Process,* 1980, *19,* 73–85.

Madanes, C. *Strategic family therapy.* San Francisco: Jossey-Bass, 1981.

Madanes, C., Dukes, J., & Harbin, H. Family ties of heroin addicts. *Archives of General Psychiatry,* 1980, *37,* 889–894.

Mahoney, M. J. Psychotherapy and the structure of personal revolutions. In M. J. Mahoney (Ed.), *Psychotherapy Process.* New York: Plenum, 1980.

Miller, D. T., & Ross, M. Self-serving biases in the attribution of causality: Fact or fiction? *Psychological Bulletin,* 1975, *82,* 213–225.

Minuchin, S., Rosman, B., & Baker, L. *Psychosomatic families.* Cambridge: Harvard University Press, 1978.

Palazzoli, M., Boscolo, L., Cecchin, G. F., & Prata, G. *Paradox and counterparadox.* New York: Jason Aronson, 1978.

Palazzoli, M., Boscolo, L., Cecchin, G. F., & Prata, G. Hypothesizing, circularity, neutrality: Three guidelines for the conductor of the session. *Family Process,* 1980, *19.*

Papp, P. The Greek chorus and other techniques of family therapy. *Family Process,* 1980, *19,* 45–58.

Perls, F., Hefferline, R. F., & Goodman, P. *Gestalt therapy.* New York: Dell, 1951.

Rohrbaugh, M., & Eron, J. The strategic systems therapies. In L. E. Abt, R. I. Stuart (Eds.), *The newer therapies: A workbook.* New York: Van Nostrand Reinhold, 1982.

Rohrbaugh, M., Tennen, H., & Eron, J. Paradoxical interventions. In J. H. Masserman (Ed.), *Current Psychiatric Therapies, 21.* New York: Grune & Stratton, 1982.

Rohrbaugh, M., Tennen, H., Press, S., & White, L. Compliance, defiance and therapeutic paradox: Guidelines for strategic use of paradoxical interventions. *American Journal of Orthopsychiatry,* 1981, *51,* 454–467.

Rosen, J. *Direct psychoanalysis.* New York: Grune & Stratton, 1953.

Sluzki, C. Process of symptom production and patterns of symptom maintenance. *Journal of Marriage and Family Therapy*, 1981, *7*, 273–280.

Solyom, L., Garza-Perez, J., Ledwidge, B. L., & Solyom, C. Paradoxical intention in the treatment of obsessive thoughts: A pilot study. *Comprehensive Psychiatry*, 1972, *13*, 291–297.

Stanton, M. D. An integrated structural/strategic approach to family therapy. *Journal of Marriage and Family Therapy*, 1981, *7*, 427–440. (a)

Stanton, M. D. Strategic approaches to family therapy. In A. S. Gurman, D. P. Kniskern (Eds.), *Handbook of family therapy*. New York: Brunner/Mazel, 1981. (b)

Strong, S. R., & Clayborn, C. D. *Change through interaction: Social psychological processes of counseling and psychotherapy*. New York: John Wiley, 1982.

Taylor, S. E. Adjustment to threatening events. *American Psychologist*, 1983, *38*, 1161–1173.

Taylor, S. E., Lichtman, R. R., & Wood, J. V. *Adjustment to breast cancer: Physical, socio-demographic, and psychological predictors*. Manuscript submitted for publication.

Tennen, H., Affleck, G., Allen, D. A., McGrade, B. J., & Ratzan, S. Causal attributions and coping with insulin-dependent diabetes. *Basic and Applied Social Psychology*, in press.

Tennen, H., & Herzberger, S. *Depression, self-esteem, and the absence of self-protective attributional biases*. Manuscript submitted for publication.

Tennen, H., Nussbaum, N., Sharp, J. P., & Baldya, B. *Depressive attributional style: The role of self esteem*. Manuscript submitted for publication.

Tiger, L. *Optimism: The biology of hope*. New York: Simon & Schuster, 1979.

Timko, C., & Janoff-Bulman, R. *An attributional model of coping with breast cancer*. Presented at the meetings of the American Psychological Association, August 1982.

Watzlawick, P. *How real is real? Confusion, disinformation, communication*. New York: Random House, 1976.

Watzlawick, P. *The language of change*. New York: Basic, 1978.

Watzlawick, P., Beavin, J., Jackson, D. D. *Pragmatics of human communication*. New York: W. W. Norton, 1967.

Watzlawick, P., & Coyne, J. C. Depression following stroke: Brief problem-focused treatment. *Family Process*, 1980, *19*, 13–18.

Watzlawick, P., Weakland, J. H., & Fisch, R. *Change: Principles of problem formation and problem resolution.* New York: W. W. Norton, 1974.

Weakland, J. H., Fisch, R., Watzlawick, P., & Bodin, A. Brief therapy: Focused problem resolution. *Family Process,* 1974, *13,* 141–168.

Weeks, G. R., & L'Abate, L. A complication of paradoxical methods. *American Journal of Family Therapy,* 1979, *7,* 61–76.

Weeks, G. R., & L'Abate, L. *Paradoxical psychotherapy: Theory and practice with individuals, couples, and families.* New York: Brunner/ Mazel, 1982.

Wright, R. M., & Strong, S. R. Stimulating therapeutic change with directives: An exploratory study. *Journal of Counseling Psychology,* 1982, *29,* 199–202.

Wynne, L. C. Knotted relationships, communication deviances, and metabinding. In M. E. Berger (Ed.), *Beyond the double bind.* New York: Brunner/Mazel, 1978.

Part Three

Research on Paradoxical
Techniques

8

An Introduction to Research on the Clinical Efficacy of Paradoxical Intention

by Ray S. Kim, MA
James Poling, MA
L. Michael Ascher, Ph.D.

In the first edition of this book, Ascher, Bowers, and Schotte (1985) reviewed the data of many of the studies incorporating control—or some semblance of control—procedures that were available at that time. Using their review as a point of departure, the present authors aim to discuss research that largely has been undertaken subsequently. Of course, science moves in a slow and deliberate fashion, and an updated review on this topic would ordinarily not have been warranted after the relatively brief interval since the appearance of Ascher, Bowers, and Schotte's earlier work (1985); the amount of additional data do not, on their own merit, require a progress report at this time. However, as opportunities do not always arise under optimal circumstances, the present authors agreed to revise the chapter of Ascher, Bowers, and Schotte (1985) as sufficient new material was available to permit at least one just noticeable difference between the former and the present chapters.

Attesting to their popularity, various forms of therapeutic paradoxical procedures appear in almost every approach to psychotherapy (e.g., Seltzer, 1986). It was therefore inevitable that behavior therapists would become interested in them as well. As each group of therapists applies these techniques in a manner that is roughly consistent with their own orientation, behavior therapists have approached therapeutic paradox in a characteristic fashion. In applying the procedures, behavior therapists have used the traditional manner of supporting conventional behavioral programs by enhancing cooperation (Ascher, 1989a). More unique has been the use of paradoxical intention as a central procedure in programs directed toward the amelioration of anxiety disorders and anxiety-based difficulties (Ascher, 1989b). Here, the attempt has been to demonstrate that paradoxical intention can serve as a central concept in organizing conventional behavioral programs. In close association with the clinical practice is a basic tenet of behavior therapy: the empirical validation of the efficacy of procedures employed. The emphasis in this updated chapter is on controlled studies in which subjects exhibit clinically significant levels of the target behavioral disorder.

RESEARCH IN PARADOXICAL TECHNIQUES

Insomnia

Insomnia, the chronic inability to fall asleep within a satisfactory period of time and/or to maintain a satisfactory level of sleep, has been estimated to affect 10 to 15 percent of the population in its milder forms and 10 to 15 percent in its more severe forms (Kales, Bixler, Lee, Healy, & Slye, 1974; Webb, 1975). Research on the use of paradoxical intention in the treatment of insomnia demonstrates the increasing experimental sophistication in the investigation of paradoxical techniques.

Early reports were based on uncontrolled case studies (e.g., Ascher, 1975), and later progressed to single case, experimental designs of varying degrees of sophistication (e.g., Ascher & Efran, 1978; Relinger & Bornstein, 1979; Relinger, Bornstein, & Mungas, 1978). Recent investigations have compared paradoxical intention to placebo and no-treatment control groups (e.g., Ascher & Turner, 1979a), as well as to other more established behavioral treatments (e.g., Lacks, Bertelson, Gans, & Kunkel, 1983; Espie, Lindsay, Brooks, Hood, & Turvey, 1989; Turner & Ascher, 1979, 1982).

The first, empirically based claim for the effectiveness of paradoxical intention as a treatment for sleep-onset insomnia was made by Ascher (1975). At the time, Ascher reported success in the treatment of a small number of clients who had sleep-onset insomnia that was refractory to a standard behavioral program. However, the omission of experimental controls with some clients precludes making causal inferences for a variety of reasons (Ascher & Schotte, 1983; Hersen & Barlow, 1976).

Building on this early success with the technique, Ascher and Efran (1978) applied paradoxical intention in the treatment of 5 individuals complaining of clinically significant levels of sleep-onset insomnia who had not benefitted from a standard behavioral treatment program. Client self-report data on a number of variables (e.g., mood when retiring, latency of sleep onset, time of retiring, number of awakenings, restfulness of sleep) were collected pre- and posttreatment. Paradoxical intention instructions were presented using either an assessment rationale or a veridical explanation, with the intention of having the client attempt to stay awake at bedtime. The assessment rationale subjects were asked to stay awake so that their therapists could gain detailed descriptions of their thoughts prior to falling asleep. The subjects receiving the veridical explanation were asked to lengthen the period of bedtime relaxation, even if this meant resisting the urge to fall asleep.

In response to the paradoxical intention instructions, clients often reported that they had been unable to comply with the directives because they had fallen asleep too quickly. Self-reported, sleep-onset latency decreased from a pretreatment mean of 48.6 minutes to less than 9.8 minutes during the second week of paradoxical therapy. A further test of this treatment was made by asking one subject to return to the initial behavioral treatment program for an additional 3 weeks. During this period, the self-reported, sleep-onset latency increased from 6.0 to 28.3 minutes. Subsequent readministration of paradoxical instructions once again resulted in a reduction in sleep-onset latency for this subject.

Bornstein and his associates conducted several investigations in an effort to replicate and extend the findings of Ascher and Efran (1978). In the most interesting of these, Relinger and Bornstein (1979) employed paradoxical intention to treat 5 clients complaining of severe, chronic sleep-onset insomnia. The design incorporated a multiple baseline across subjects. Randomly selected subjects were treated sequentially, each receiving one more week of baseline assessment than the previously assessed individual. Self-report data on multiple variables were collected following pre- and posttreatment intervals and at follow-up.

Paradoxical instructions were provided in association with an assessment rationale. This was supplemented by counterdemand instructions (Relinger, Bornstein, & Mungas, 1978) to control for the effects of subjects' expectancies and demand factors. Thus, subjects were informed not to anticipate any improvement until the end of treatment. Presumably, any effect occurring despite these instructions could be attributed more to the treatment than to experimental demands. While not as powerful as designs involving a return to the baseline phase, this approach lends more credence to claims of efficacy than do the AB and ABC designs used in previous studies.

Over the course of five treatment sessions, sleep-onset latency decreased by over 50 percent from a baseline average of 110 minutes to a posttreatment, sleep-onset latency of 47 minutes. By the end of the three-month follow-up period, clients reported an average sleep-onset latency of 20 minutes. Statistically significant improvements were also found for degree of restfulness, difficulty falling asleep, and number of awakenings, both at the end of treatment and at follow-up. In addition, results supported the efficacy of the counterdemand control procedure.

While these case studies support the treatment of sleep-onset insomnia with paradoxical intention, a series of case studies reported by Espie and Lindsay (1985) highlights the variability of client response to paradoxical intention. Six subjects reporting chronic sleep-onset insomnia received therapy utilizing paradoxical intention over an eight-week period. Although three subjects obtained a rapid decrease in sleep-onset latency, three evidenced significantly exacerbated insomnia. Eventually, 1 subject from the latter group did exhibit improvement following several weeks of additional sessions; the remaining two clients were unable to continue with paradoxical intention but experienced success with progressive relaxation.

For a variety of reasons, including factors inherent in the single-case designs of studies described to this point, it is impossible to dismiss, with confidence, the influence of nonspecific factors in the positive results obtained. Therefore, experiments incorporating appropriate controls and comparisons with other effective behavioral treatments are necessary to validate the qualifications of innovative behavioral techniques.

The first of these investigations was conducted by Turner and Ascher (1979). They compared paradoxical intention to behavioral techniques that were established as treatments of choice for sleep-onset insomnia. Individuals complaining of clinically significant levels of sleep-onset insomnia were randomly assigned to 1 of 5

groups: paradoxical intention, stimulus control, relaxation training, attention placebo, and no-treatment control. In addition to the
self-report outcome measures typically employed in such studies,
ratings of sleep behavior from spouses or roommates were
obtained. Paradoxical instructions were presented in a straightforward treatment rationale. Statistical analysis demonstrated the
superiority of the active behavioral treatments over the two control
conditions. In contrast, paradoxical intention did not differ from
the treatments of choice.

A major criticism of this study concerns the use of only 1
experienced therapist who was not blind to the hypothesis
being tested. The largely subjective nature of the dependent
measures was another problem. Although the results of a variety of control and evaluation procedures (e.g., counterdemand
instructions, subject ratings of treatment credibility and relevant
therapist characteristics) served to mitigate the criticism, the
concerns remain valid and limit the extent to which the results
are generalizable.

In a partial replication of their original study (Turner & Ascher,
1979), Ascher and Turner (1979a) randomly assigned 25 individuals (10 males, 15 females) with clinically significant levels of
sleep-onset insomnia to paradoxical intention, credible placebo (a
quasi-desensitization procedure), or no-treatment conditions. The
paradoxical intention subjects reduced their sleep-onset latency
by over 50 percent and showed statistically significant improvements on most self-report measures, as compared to subjects in
the placebo and no-treatment conditions. No difference in credibility was reported by subjects regarding the placebo and paradoxical treatments. Spouse-roommate checks again supported the
reliability of the sleep-onset data. This study and Turner and
Ascher's earlier study provide evidence for the effectiveness of
paradoxical intention as a treatment for sleep-onset insomnia.
However, the criticisms associated with Turner and Ascher (1979)
apply to this study as well.

To study the role of experience in the administration and outcome of paradoxical intention in Turner and Ascher (1979), Turner
and Ascher (1982) compared the data obtained in the 1979 study
with data collected using less experienced therapists. The results
were interesting, but inconclusive. For each of the treatment
groups, posttreatment, sleep-onset latencies were twice the length
of the sleep-onset latencies obtained by the experienced therapist.
This result is surprising since the literature generally indicates that
experimenter differences were not obtained for progressive relaxation or stimulus control. With regard to paradoxical intention, the

subjects seen by the inexperienced therapists failed to demonstrate significant posttreatment reductions in sleep-onset latency, as compared to the significant improvements obtained by the subjects of the experienced therapist.

Although a variety of factors might explain these differences, an important distinction concerns the subject pools. The baseline sleep-onset latency of the paradoxical intention group in the replication study was significantly shorter than that of any other group treated by either experienced or inexperienced therapists. This finding suggests that initial symptom severity may affect response to treatment, indicating the possible need to control for symptom severity before direct comparisons between studies can be made (cf., Lacks et al., 1983). Certainly, from a data analysis perspective the paradoxical intention groups in the two studies had disparate potentials for improvement.

Results similar to Turner and Ascher (1979), and Ascher and Turner (1979a) were obtained by Ladouceur and Gros-Louis (1986). In this study, 27 subjects were randomly assigned to one of four experimental conditions: paradoxical intention, stimulus control, an educational control condition, and a no-treatment condition. Procedural details were generally similar to those of Turner and Ascher's study (1979). Although both paradoxical intention and stimulus control produced results superior to control conditions, the two behavioral treatments were equally effective. Since the mean sleep-onset latency in this study was approximately 60 minutes, as it was in the Turner and Ascher (1979) and Ascher and Turner (1979a) studies, direct comparisons among the studies seem appropriate.

Ott, Levine, and Ascher (1983) compared the efficacy of paradoxical intention using both self-report information and, possibly, more objective information obtained from a sleep-monitoring unit. Fifty-five subjects with an average sleep-onset latency of 60 minutes were randomly assigned to one of the following conditions: paradoxical intention, feedback from a sleep-monitoring unit, feedback plus paradoxical intention, or no-treatment. Pretreatment analyses revealed no differences among groups regarding age, sex, problem duration, and MMPI scores. Posttreatment analyses found no group differences regarding adherence to instruction, correctness of sleep log, and constancy of medication intake. Counterdemand instructions and an assessment rationale were used in an attempt to offset demand characteristics.

Decreases in sleep-onset latency were found in subjects receiving paradoxical intention alone or feedback alone, while subjects receiving both treatments actually experienced increases in sleep-onset latency. In an attempt to explain this latter ostensibly anomalous finding, the authors suggest that the use of the recording device may have facilitated the subjects' literal adherence to the therapist's request to "remain awake as long as possible."

Among this study's shortcomings is the use of univariate analyses where a multivariate analysis was indicated. Due to the greater number of analyses being performed, the chances of obtaining spurious results are increased. In addition, only 1 therapist conducted all of the therapy sessions, which, of course, introduces the possibility of experimenter bias. A further problem is that the "objective" measure could be manipulated by the subject. Finally, the experimental design does not seem completely suitable for the stated objectives.

Lacks, Bertelson, Gans, and Kunkel (1983) studied the interaction between the level of severity of sleep-onset latency and various behavioral treatments associated with success in the treatment of insomnia. Sixty-four subjects were matched for self-reported, sleep-onset latency and were randomly assigned to one of the following conditions: paradoxical intention, progressive relaxation, stimulus control, or credible placebo. Counterdemand instructions were employed to compensate for demand characteristics.

The results revealed no interaction between the severity of sleep-onset latency and the type of treatment. However, unlike previous researchers, Lacks and associates (1983) found stimulus control to be significantly more effective than any other treatment procedure regardless of the level of severity. Paradoxical intention produced results that were not significantly different from the placebo condition. As was the case with Espie and Lindsay (1985), Lacks and colleagues (1983) noted that paradoxical intention sometimes increased sleep-onset latency.

In a replication of the studies of Turner and Ascher (1979) and Lacks, Bertelson, Gans, and Kunkel (1983), Espie, Lindsay, Brooks, Hood, and Turvey (1989) studied a sample of 84 physician-referred, chronic insomniacs (mean sleep-onset latency of 83 minutes). Subjects were assigned randomly to one of five conditions: progressive relaxation, stimulus control, paradoxical intention, placebo, or no-treatment. While one therapist conducted all of the sessions across treatments, ratings of nine randomly audiotaped sessions revealed no significant differences across patients and treatments. As an additional control, counterdemand instructions were used in the first four weeks of treatment, followed by four weeks under positive demand.

Subjects were evaluated on a variety of self-report variables including sleep-onset latency (mean and SD), total sleep duration (mean and SD), restedness, and sleep enjoyment. An important additional measure assessed night to night variability in sleep, a factor potentially as important in sleep distress as the mean sleep-onset latency. The validity of the self-report measures was assessed using the Sleep Assessment Device (SAD), which tape records responses to a fixed interval cue tone (Kelly & Lichstein, 1980). Twenty subjects were thus evaluated for a combined total of 110 nights. Comparisons of the self-report and objective measures produced highly significant correlations in measures of sleep-onset latency and total sleep time ($r = .85$ and $r = .87$, respectively). While subjects did overestimate sleep-onset latency by a 17 percent margin, the high correlations indicated that they did so consistently.

The results showed that only active treatments were associated with significant improvement, and that the nature of the improvements varied. Stimulus control very quickly reduced sleep-onset latency, whereas some subjects in the paradoxical intention condition experienced an exacerbation of sleep-onset latency. Stimulus control subjects who completed therapy experienced a reduced sleep-onset latency of 62 percent (around 32 minutes), as well as a more predictable pattern of sleep-onset latency. However, perceived quality of sleep did not increase during stimulus control treatment.

By the end of treatment, the paradoxical intention group achieved a final sleep-onset latency at levels similar to the stimulus control group, but the treatment progress was less straightforward. For example, five of the 15 subjects exposed to paradoxical intention instructions experienced increases in sleep-onset latency during the first week of treatment. On the other hand, night-to-night variability in sleep-onset latency was significantly reduced in the paradoxical intention group prior to reductions in sleep-onset latency. In other words, the paradoxical intention subjects experienced increased stability in sleep-onset latency prior to their average sleep-onset latency decreases. Corresponding to this finding are the subjects' reports of greater restedness after sleep following completion of the treatment program.

In contrast to stimulus control and paradoxical intention, relaxation achieved its primary results with significant improvements in the subjects' perception of sleep quality and daytime measures of concentration and general well-being. These improvements occurred in spite of relatively limited effects upon sleep-onset latency. Total sleep duration increased by about 40 minutes, as it did with the other treatments.

The authors concluded that stimulus control appears to be effective in habit restructuring, although patients will not necessarily be more contented with their sleep, and relaxation may be used when qualitative improvements are more important than quantitative. Paradoxical intention seems to reduce internight variability prior to decreasing latency. Thus, paradoxical intention may produce improvements in both sleep-onset latency and quality of sleep, although the authors caution that some patients seem to show temporary exacerbation of sleep problems.

In summary, the three previously discussed studies examining the most popular behavioral treatments for sleep-onset insomnia (paradoxical intention, progressive relaxation, and stimulus control) produced different results. Turner and Ascher (1979) found that these three treatments were equally effective and superior to no treatment or placebo treatment conditions. Lacks, Bertelson, Gans, and Kunkel (1983) demonstrated superior results for stimulus control regardless of severity, with paradoxical intention providing an outcome that was not significantly different from a placebo condition. Espie, Lindsay, Brooks, Hood, and Turvey (1989) found that stimulus control very quickly and effectively reduced sleep-onset latency, while paradoxical intention achieved comparable reductions in sleep-onset latency over a longer period of time.

A vast majority of experimental studies on the effectiveness of paradoxical intention has employed a counterdemand procedure to control for the effects of experimental demands (e.g., Espie & Lindsay, 1985; Espie et al., 1989; Lacks et al., 1983; Ladouceur & Gros-Louis, 1986; Ott, Levine, & Ascher, 1983; Relinger & Bornstein, 1979). However, the counterdemand instruction—not to expect any results in a specified time period—can be viewed as a paradoxical treatment in its own right. Viewed in this way, the treatment procedures employed by Lacks et al. (1983) and by Espie et al. (1989) may be more correctly termed: stimulus control plus paradoxical intention, progressive relaxation plus paradoxical intention, and paradoxical intention alone. This, in turn, may account for the relatively quick decrease in sleep-onset latency established in subjects assigned to the stimulus control groups, in contrast to the slower response of individuals in the paradoxical intention groups of the Lacks et al. (1983) and Espie et al. (1989) studies. It is, therefore, not surprising that stimulus control procedures used along with paradoxical instructions should yield better results than paradoxical intention instructions alone. The most obvious reason for this is that as sleep disturbances are multiply determined and morphologically varied, the greater is the diversity of treatment components and the higher is the probability of a successful outcome. This suggests that counterdemand instructions confound treatments in paradoxical intention studies. The continued use of this method of control in such studies should be accompanied by design modifications that would serve to rectify the confusion.

Despite the discrepancies found among these studies, the efficacy of paradoxical intention as a treatment method for primary sleep-onset insomnia appears to be reasonably well supported in both the single-case (Ascher & Efran, 1978; Relinger et al., 1978; Relinger & Bornstein, 1979) and group experimental design (Ascher & Turner, 1979a; Espie et al., 1989; Turner & Ascher, 1979, 1982). The studies further suggest that clinically significant improvements in sleep complaints can be produced with relatively minimal expenditures of therapists' time. The results of these initial reports (although flawed to some extent) are comparable to those obtained with other established behavioral techniques and indicate that paradoxical intention, progressive relaxation, and stimulus control are all useful procedures in the amelioration of sleep disturbances—all producing results superior to those of credible placebo and no treatment control conditions.

Noting that different paradoxical intention instructions have been utilized under a variety of circumstances, several investigators have evaluated diverse methods for presenting paradoxical instructions. In the first, "assessment" or traditional explanation, subjects are instructed to remain awake for as long as possible in order to become aware of cognitions to be used in an upcoming desensitization procedure. In this approach, individuals are kept blind to the true nature of the intervention to which they are being exposed. In the second approach, termed the "veridical" explanation, subjects are informed of the relationship between performance anxiety and insomnia and are provided with relatively straightforward paradoxical instructions aimed at neutralizing performance anxiety. In the "authoritarian" explanation (Fisher, Nietzel, & Lowery, 1985), the importance of following instructions in order to obtain the desired results is emphasized, but subjects are provided with no specific rationale.

Fisher, Nietzel, and Lowery (1985), in an analogue study, investigated the credibility of these explanations on the effectiveness of paradoxical intention with insomniacs. College students were presented with veridical, bogus, or authoritarian instructions and asked to rate their credibility. The authors also included a progressive relaxation rationale for insomnia treatment. Respondents found the explanations for paradoxical therapy to be equally credible. Overall, however, the students preferred the relaxation rationale (70 percent) to both the paradoxical explanations (30 percent) and the authoritative directions (0 percent); the latter finding is not surprising since the authoritative condition provides no rationale. The preference of the progressive relaxation rationale over that of paradoxical intention is in contrast to the previous investigations of Turner and Ascher (1979) and Ascher and Turner (1979a) in which rationales tended to be equally acceptable. Fisher, Nietzel, and Lowery (1985) attribute this difference to the commonsensical nature of progressive relaxation as a means of treating insomnia, in contrast to the paradoxical procedures which are counterintuitive in nature. Of course, the fact that the subjects of Turner and Ascher (1979) and Ascher and Turner (1979a) were treated in a clinical setting for severely disturbed sleep, in contrast to the use of college students in the analogue situation employed by Fisher, Nietzel, and Lowery (1985), might also account for some differences.

The authors also investigated the role of impulsivity as a personality trait when assigning preference to these rationales. The authoritarian rationale received its highest acceptance from subjects rated high on impulsivity, whom the authors speculated may have been willing to suspend judgment or may have been unconcerned about the lack of a logical explanation. Subjects high on control, however, preferred the assessment rationale over the veridical explanation. Fisher, Nietzel, and Lowery (1985) argued that to highly controlled subjects, a veridical instruction to relinquish control must seem alien. Such people are likely to assume that maintaining tight control is the best way to achieve their goals.

In another investigation of this issue, Ascher and Turner (1979b) compared the effectiveness of veridical explanations versus an "assessment" rationale. Forty subjects were randomly assigned to one of four groups: paradoxical intention with either veridical or "assessment" rationale, attention control, or a waiting list control. A variety of self-report outcome measures were employed.

In the veridical condition, subjects were asked to remain awake for as long as possible once in bed, and were informed of the hypothesized relationship between performance anxiety and sleeping difficulties (as in Ascher and Turner, 1979a). In the "assessment" condition, it was suggested that clients remain awake in order to become aware of anxiety-producing thoughts. Placebo subjects received quasi-desensitization by pairing 18 hierarchical bedtime scenes with neutral images. Subsequent to treatment, subjects completed a questionnaire designed to tap the credibility of the procedures and the quality of the therapeutic relationship.

Subjects exposed to the veridical procedure exhibited significantly greater improvement than those in the "assessment" group or in either of the control groups. Confounding factors such as differential treatment credibility, therapist differences, and statistical probability pyramiding were ruled out. However, other possible confounds do impact on these findings. Since the therapists were also the authors, a variety of sources of bias may have been incorporated. In addition, the "assessment" rationale instructions indicated that desensitization would begin after the disturbing thoughts were collected. Consequently, there is the possibility that these subjects assumed that "therapy" had not begun, thereby serving to dilute the potential effects of the "assessment" procedure. Of course, the most ethical method of administration is full disclosure of the nature and purpose of paradoxical procedures, which apparently also produces better outcomes.

Agoraphobia

It is possible that as much as 5.8 percent of the population of the United States could be classified as agoraphobic (Barlow, 1988). As a result of this prevalence, great effort has been expended in developing and testing treatment methods for this clinical population. Among these is paradoxical intention, the efficacy of which is supported by data from a variety of sources ranging from uncontrolled case studies (e.g., Frankl, 1955, 1975, 1985; Gerz, 1966) to controlled experiments.

Ascher (1981) evaluated the efficacy of paradoxical intention in alleviating the travel restriction experienced by agoraphobic individuals. Ten agoraphobic clients (nine females, one male) were randomly assigned to two treatment conditions. In the first, clients were given graded *in vivo* exposure for six sessions following a baseline phase, after which they received paradoxical intention instructions. In the second, clients were exposed to six sessions of paradoxical intention following the baseline phase. Statistical analysis indicated that individuals reduced travel restriction to a significantly greater extent in the context of paradoxical intention as compared with graded exposure.

In a subsequent study, Ascher (1983) hypothesized that agoraphobic clients might experience more rapid improvement for travel restrictions if paradoxical instructions were employed earlier in the course of therapy and if the procedure was to be complemented by supportive, ancillary techniques. Three procedures were compared: paradoxical intention, "enhanced" paradoxical intention, and the "enhancement" component alone (consisting of various behavioral and cognitive-behavioral techniques). Fifteen agoraphobic clients were randomly assigned to these three groups. The results revealed that both paradoxical intention groups significantly reduced travel restrictions more rapidly than the enhancement group alone. Also, individuals in the enhanced paradoxical group seemed to use the procedure earlier in the course of therapy. However, there were no other differences between these two groups.

These data are compromised by various aspects of the design, procedure, and method of subject selection. However, they provide the first tentative support for the efficacy of paradoxical intention in reducing travel restrictions in agoraphobic individuals and suggest a method by which this treatment procedure might be employed by clients earlier in the course of therapy.

Mavissakalian, Michelson, Greenwald, Kornblith, and Greenwald (1983) compared paradoxical intention to self-statement training in treating agoraphobics. Twenty-six clients were randomly assigned to one of the two procedures, each of which was conducted in groups of four to five over the course of 12 ninety-minute sessions. Subjects in the paradoxical intention group improved significantly more than did those who received self-statement training. However, at a six-month follow-up assessment, the self-statement training group exhibited a level of improvement equivalent to that of the paradoxical intention group.

In an interesting series of experiments, Michelson and his associates systematically investigated several popular strategies for the general treatment of agoraphobia. In the first of these, Michelson, Mavissakalian, and Marchione (1985) compared the relative efficacy of paradoxical intention (PI), graduated exposure (GE), and progressive relaxation training (RT). Thirty-nine severe and chronic agoraphobics with panic attacks were randomly assigned to one of these groups. Twelve weekly two-hour group sessions were conducted by experienced therapists. Analyses revealed that subjects in all conditions showed significant improvements on a variety of measures. However, GE and RT were associated with more rapid effects than PI. In fact, subjects who received PI actually experienced increases in physiological reactivity during treatment. Not until a three-month follow-up period were they equivalent in their physiological functioning. This finding suggests that PI may require greater time for subjects to effectively employ this strategy.

Using the same data set, Michelson, Mavissakalian, Marchione,

Dancu, and Greenwald (1986) investigated the role of self-directed *in vivo* exposure (SDE) practice in the treatments mentioned in the previous study. SDE involves a conscious decision by the client to engage in phobic encounters in order to cause therapeutic change. Overall, RT was the most effective strategy in enhancing practice time, while GE followed closely. PI was least effective in increasing SDE practice. These results suggest the importance of developing treatments that significantly affect SDE.

In a second reanalysis of these data, Michelson (1986) focused on the interaction between client and treatment variables. It was determined that those clients whose treatments were consonant with their symptom profiles showed higher rates of improvement than those whose treatments were dissonant. Thus, clients with a symptom profile that was dominated by cognitive factors did best with PI. Those with a symptom profile largely reflecting behavior difficulties exhibited greatest improvement with GE. Finally, clients whose profiles indicated that physiological symptoms were most salient benefitted most from RT. This study, then, underscored the importance of matching a subject's response profile with a consonant treatment modality.

In a final project, Michelson, Mavissakalian, and Marchione (1988) provided a more comprehensive outcome investigation on a large group of clients. In this study, 88 agoraphobics with panic attacks were randomly assigned to either PI, GE, or RT. Analyses showed significant improvement across all domains and treatments with few between-group differences. The three interventions were found to be equally effective at posttreatment and at a three-month follow-up. These authors concluded that in the treatment of agoraphobic clients, individual procedures might be more likely to produce incomplete results, whereas the appropriate combination of techniques would serve to provide a more satisfactory outcome.

Obsessive Disorders

Solyom, Garza-Perez, Ledwidge, and Solyom (1972) employed a quasi-experimental design in the treatment of 10 individuals with obsessional concerns. After a pretreatment assessment consisting of several questionnaires and a psychiatric interview, two obsessions were selected for each subject. One served as the control obsession, while the other served as the target obsession. Subjects were instructed in paradoxical intention and told to associate this procedure with the target obsession. The results of this study were mixed and, of course, without the necessary control procedures were difficult to assess. However, the fact that five of the 10 individuals reported some reduction in the target obsession supported the myriad of previous case studies reporting such a relationship.

Milan and Kolko (1982) evaluated the effect of paradoxical intention on the obsessional ruminations of a 33-year-old female client. The client sought treatment to help deal with anxiety regarding her perceived high incidence of malodorous flatulence. Previous medical evaluation had ruled out physical problems or dysfunctions, and she had had prior unsuccessful courses of pharmacotherapy, dietary management, and psychotherapy.

The authors used an ABC design and collected follow-up data. Throughout the baseline and treatment phases, the client monitored the frequency and intensity of her perceived flatulence on an hourly basis. The first phase of treatment involved the correction of misconceptions through the use of scientific evidence. The second phase involved the use of paradoxical intention. Here, the therapist "acknowledged the imprecision of modern science" and instructed the client to enhance flatulence during each episode in order to expel her flatus completely. The latter procedure produced an immediate reduction in the client's perceived frequency and intensity of flatulence episodes by approximately 75 percent. Data collected during two weeks of self-monitoring conducted one year after treatment revealed the client's further improvement, suggesting an overall reduction of nearly 95 percent.

Unfortunately, the design employed in this study incorporated several methodological shortcomings, including serial treatment effects and several threats to internal validity (Hersen & Barlow, 1976). In the absence of more powerful single-case experimental designs (e.g., those involving a return to baseline phase) or group research, causal inferences are speculative at best. Thus, the evidence for the efficacy of paradoxical intention in the treatment of obsessions is weak. The studies cited here, however, do suggest the possibility of the efficacy of paradoxical intention with this behavioral difficulty; further investigation, using more sophisticated designs and larger groups of subjects, seems warranted.

Disorders of Elimination

Both urination and defecation require a complex interaction between social control and autonomic nervous system activity. One reason for a disruption of this interplay may be one's continuous, zealous attempts to control. This effortful behavior and the associated performance anxiety might serve to inhibit the natural occurrence of the appropriate eliminative reflexes. That is, trying too hard can paradoxically hinder successful elimination behavior (Jacob & Moore, 1984).

Functional Urinary Frequency.   Timms (1985) treated a 13-year-old boy who complained of urinary frequency associated with school attendance. The discomfort occurred in the morning, just before leaving home for school. This problem became so profound that eventually the client did not bother to make an attempt to go to school. Paradoxical intention was the major procedure employed in the treatment program. Pretreatment recordings showed that the urinary frequency occurred on each school day. Posttreatment data indicated that the paradoxical instruction was carried out and complaints of urinary frequency rapidly extinguished. Follow-up at 6 months showed no recurrence of the frequency problem.

Functional Urinary Retention.   Functional urinary retention is the condition in which individuals cannot urinate in certain bathrooms but function normally in others. People with urinary retention have been treated behaviorally using a wide variety of behavioral techniques, yet because of the difficulty of the problem results are inconsistent. For this reason, additional strategies are of interest to clinicians who seek to increase probability of success by approaching such clients with expanded behavioral repertoires. Recently, paradoxical intention has been shown to be effective with some cases of psychogenic urinary retention.

Ascher (1979) conducted a study in which 5 clients were treated in the context of an ABC design consisting of a two-week baseline phase followed by an eight-week conventional behavior therapy program. Following this experience, these individuals were dissatisfied with their level of progress, and a series of sessions was instituted, during which paradoxical intention was employed. Clients were instructed to enter a discomforting bathroom and to engage in all the normal activities associated with urinating, but to actively inhibit the passage of urine. Then they were to conclude their visit and leave the bathroom. The rationale for this technique, involving the deleterious effects of performance anxiety, was presented to the clients. Subjective ratings of discomfort functioned as the dependent variable. Results indicated that greater improvement occurred following the institution of paradoxical intention as compared with the trial of the more conventional procedure.

Functional Encopresis.   Encopresis is characterized by inappropriate fecal soiling. A number of studies have been conducted to test the efficacy of paradoxical intention in treating this disorder (e.g., Margolies & Gilstein, 1983–1984; Propp, 1985). However, only that of Bornstein, Sturm, Retzlaff, Kirby, and Chong (1981) incorporated an acceptably controlled (ABAB) design.

In their investigation, Bornstein, Sturm, Retzlaff, Kirby, and Chong (1981) used paradoxical procedures in the treatment of a nine-year-old boy who suffered from infrequent bowel movements, daily soiling, and considerable anxiety related to toileting behavior. Parental records of appropriate bowel movements and soiling episodes functioned as the dependent measure. Following a three-week baseline period, the boy was required to enter the bathroom each hour and sit on the toilet for five minutes. He was to act as though he was going to have a bowel movement, although he was instructed not to have a bowel movement. This procedure was intended to decrease anxiety associated with toileting. Following 3 weeks of treatment, a return to baseline was instituted for two weeks. Subsequently, paradoxical procedures were reinstated and eventually faded.

The results supported the efficacy of paradoxical intention in the treatment of encopresis. During the initial baseline phase, the child had an average of 6.7 soiling incidents and 0.7 appropriate bowel movements per week. Paradoxical intention resulted in a decrease to 0.0 soiling incidents and an increase of 4.3 appropriate bowel movements per week. When treatment was withdrawn, the dependent measures returned to near-baseline levels (5.0 soiling incidents and 0.5 appropriate bowel movements per week). With the reinstatement of paradoxical procedures, soilings decreased to 0.0 and appropriate bowel movements increased to 4.8 per week. Treatment effects were maintained through a one-year follow-up.

Miscellaneous Clinical Complaints

In addition to the previously discussed behavioral complaints, paradoxical intention has been associated with a vast array of disorders and adjustment difficulties. These include, but are not restricted to, anorexia nervosa, erythrophobia, panic attacks, generalized anxiety, psychogenic nausea, social phobia, depression, and procrastination. Although the research in each of these areas is extremely limited, typically involving uncontrolled single cases, they do illustrate the clinical potential of paradoxical intention. In this section, studies of particular interest will be highlighted.

Hsu and Lieberman (1982) used a short-term (six sessions)

paradoxical intervention with eight chronic anorexic clients. These individuals had previously been unsuccessful in maintaining treatment-related weight gains. When rehospitalized, they were placed on a program that incorporated paradoxical intention. It was suggested that maintaining anorexia nervosa was, in ways specific to each client, better than attempting to defeat it, especially since previous attempts had resulted in only temporary remission. At two to four years after treatment, half of the clients reported normal weight (within 15 percent of average) and only one exhibited very low weight (75 percent of average); one remained in treatment at the time.

Lamontagne (1978) reported the results of paradoxical intention in the treatment of erythrophobia, the fear of blushing. The client was a 25-year-old male who had a 12-year history of the complaint. His social, educational, and occupational functioning were severely hindered by this concern. Baseline data, collected in the month prior to treatment, showed 28 severe episodes of blushing, each with an average duration of 13 minutes. During the month-long treatment program, it was suggested to the client that he stop fighting his symptoms and avoiding places where they tended to occur. Further, he was to attempt to blush as much as possible for three, 10-minute periods every day at home and in situations where he felt anxious. Results indicated that during treatment there were only three episodes of blushing. These treatment effects were maintained at the end of an eight-month follow-up interval in which the client typically reported fewer than two severe episodes of blushing per month.

In a related study, Boeringa (1983), employing a paradigm similar to that of Lamontagne (1978), also described the treatment of a single case of erythrophobia. The patient was a 27-year-old male for whom blushing had become a significant problem. The difficulty had started when he accepted a promotion to a position that involved interaction with many people each day. Blushing frequency and intensity increased to the extent that it began to disturb the client and became significantly noticeable to co-workers. Boeringa's paradoxical intervention resulted in significant improvement after seven sessions.

The use of paradoxical intention in the treatment of panic attacks was illustrated by Dattilio (1987). He provided a brief case example and discussion of the nature and use of the technique. Ingrid, a 32-year-old married woman, had experienced over 200 panic attacks within 18 months before being referred for psychological treatment. The first session involved a detailed behavioral analysis to gather information for treatment. A detailed hierarchy was developed in the next two sessions to indicate the anxiety-producing situations that were associated with her panic attacks. Ingrid was then instructed to expose herself to the least feared situations while allowing herself to become anxious without trying to interfere with it. When she tried to exaggerate her attacks, she was unable to do so. With this method, eventually her anxiety was greatly reduced through the other hierarchical levels.

The effects of paradoxical intention on generalized anxiety were investigated by Last, Barlow, and O'Brien (1983). This study utilized an alternating treatment design in which a single client was exposed to different treatment procedures on successive days. The two treatment procedures that were compared were paradoxical intention and Meichenbaum's (1977) self-statement training. The client was exposed to four sessions of each technique while participating in *in vivo* exposure. In addition, he was asked to employ a particular day's technique throughout the week. Although treatment was conducted in a group format with agoraphobic group members, the results focused only on the one client with generalized anxiety disorder. Results showed a marked decline in fear hierarchy measures, which was maintained throughout the one-year, follow-up period. Although there appeared to be no significant difference in efficacy between the two treatment procedures, the client reported that paradoxical intention caused her greater discomfort than the alternate strategy.

Analogue Research

Clinical analogue research presents a model representative of significant aspects of the actual clinical situation, in order to provide an empirical framework for testing process and outcome hypotheses. Analogue studies are popular because they require less cost, are generally more quickly and easily executed, and typically involve subjects who are more accessible and plentiful, when compared with actual clinical trials. The major disadvantage is that because they are only representative of real clinical conditions, the data of analogue studies are not entirely generalizable to the clinical setting and therefore often lack clinical utility. For example, many clinical analogue experiments use volunteer college students as subjects, who report some degree of concern regarding the advertised target symptom. The focal problem has a high probability of occurrence in a college setting and is less likely to have complicating clinical correlates (e.g., procrastination, test anxiety). Often these subjects receive remuneration in terms of course credit or a small fee. If this situation is compared to one in which an individual goes to a clinical psychologist, in a clinical setting, and pays a substantial fee for assistance with some significant behavioral problem, one can immediately imagine the difficulty of developing functional relationships based on the former analogue research that would be useful for the latter clinical situation.

Notwithstanding this note of caution, clinical analogue research can provide helpful direction in this preliminary stage in the investigation of the efficacy of therapeutic paradox. The following section is composed of a survey of the more notable contributions to this category of inquiry.

Several studies have evaluated the efficacy of paradoxical intention in the treatment of college students complaining of procrastination. For example, Wright and Strong (1982) contrasted paradoxical and choice directives. Thirty students were randomly assigned to one of three experimental conditions: a paradoxical condition in which the subjects were instructed to continue procrastinating exactly as they had been, a choice procedure in which they were instructed to choose to continue some of their procrastination behaviors, or a no-intervention control group. Both treatment groups achieved equal and marked reductions in procrastination compared to the control group, thus showing that directives to stay the same were as effective as directives to change. However, since both active treatments caused equivalent amounts of change the possibility remains that, in the analogue situation employed, any treatment procedure generates similar results. The effects of an attention placebo would serve as a response to this criticism. It is interesting that although both conditions could be characterized as paradoxical to some extent, subjects in the paradoxical condition attributed their change to spontaneous, nonvolitional causes, whereas subjects in the choice condition attributed their improvement to volitional causes.

Lopez and Wambach (1982) employed 32 students who complained of procrastination and randomly assigned them to a paradoxical, a self-control, or a no-interview control condition. Subjects in the paradoxical condition were provided with a "bogus" rationale—to deliberately bring about their procrastination for the purposes of observation and control. Subjects in the self-control condition were told that procrastination is a learned habit, alleviated by the development of new behaviors incompatible with procrastination. They were then provided with strategies compatible with this hypothesis. Both treatment groups were seen for two, 30-minute sessions spaced one week apart. As was the case with

Wright and Strong (1982), the results suggest that both active-treatment groups exhibited greater improvements on self-report measures of procrastination frequency and controllability when compared with the no-treatment control. However, the nature of these improvements varied greatly between treatments. In the paradoxical control condition, five of the 10 subjects experienced an exacerbation of their procrastination behaviors before showing sharp decreases in procrastination. Progress in the self-control condition was of a more even, steady nature, spread out over the four-week experimental period. With regards to controllability, subjects in the self-control situation reported viewing their procrastination as controllable by direct effort. Subjects in the paradoxical condition, despite reporting improvements in their procrastination, did not view their problem as significantly more controllable. The findings of Wright and Strong (1982) corroborate this relationship to some extent. Again, treatment gains due to therapists' attention cannot be ruled out due to the lack of an attention control.

Shoham-Salomon, Avner, and Neeman (1989) studied the role of "reactance" in change induced by paradoxical intention and self-control interventions. The authors defined reactance as "the state of mind aroused by a threat to one's perceived legitimate freedom, motivating the individual to restore the thwarted freedom" (p. 590). Their experimental design mirrors that of Lopez and Wambach (1982), whereby 58 undergraduates complaining of procrastination were randomly assigned to a paradoxical condition, a self-control condition, or a no-treatment control condition.

Reactance was experimentally manipulated by having each subject read two generic descriptions of treatments: an attractive description and a less attractive, but not appalling description. Both descriptions were appropriate for either treatment condition. Subjects were then requested to pick the treatment they would like based on these descriptions. Since everyone picked the more attractive description, high-reactance subjects were created by telling one-third of the subjects that they were being assigned to the less desired treatment, even though they were initially told that they would be able to choose their desired therapy. A no-reactance condition was also created by assigning clients to a treatment without indicating that a choice was possible.

Therapy consisted of two, 30-minute sessions spaced one week apart, with an advanced graduate student therapist. Data consisted of study logs completed at home and submitted at the beginning of each session and at one- and four-week follow-up intervals. During the follow-up session, subjects also filled out the

Perceived Self-Efficacy Scale (PSE)—a scale measuring how much clients think they are able to do.

The main results of this study were consistent with those of Wright and Strong (1982) and Lopez and Wambach (1982), showing that, on average, both treatment conditions increased students' self-rated, effective study time by the same amount. However, within each treatment condition, the nature of the results differed for high- and low-reactance subjects. In the paradoxical condition, high-reactance subjects showed significant improvement in effective study time, while low-reactance subjects showed little improvement. On the other hand, for the self-control condition, high- and low-reactance subjects showed similar, moderate improvement.

Regarding perceived self-efficacy, subjects in the high-reactance paradoxical condition showed minimal increases, whereas low-reactance subjects in the same condition showed much larger increases. Those in the self-control, high-reactance condition showed somewhat larger increases in perceived self-efficacy than did low-reactance subjects. The authors concluded that the paradoxical condition incorporated an"either/or" pattern not found in the self-control condition. That is, with the paradoxical intervention, individuals experienced more reactance and came to study more effectively, or experienced less reactance and showed increases in perceived self-efficacy in controlling their procrastination. Thus, in keeping with Watzlawick, Beavin, and Jackson's (1967) contention that "you are changed if you do and changed if you don't."

As with the previously mentioned procrastination studies, the investigation of Shoham-Salomon, Avner, and Neeman (1989) also fails to include, among other things, an attention placebo which limits interpretability. However, the study is important because of its focus on a significant, mediating factor implicated in the success of paradoxical intention. Again, the data are useful only for the formulation of hypotheses since the authors' manipulation of reactance occurs in the absence of any reliable, objective measure of this construct. Thus, there is no way to determine whether they were successful in generating and manipulating the reactance variable.

Depression among college students represents another area in which analogue research into paradoxical interventions is concentrated. For example, Beck and Strong (1982) compared two types of interpretations and a no-interview condition with moderately depressed, volunteer college students. In the first condition, students' depressive symptoms were interpreted as connoting negative and undesirable behaviors such as irrational thinking and attempts to manipulate others. In the second condition, the paradoxical approach, depressive symptoms were associated with positive and desirable personal characteristics, such as sensitivity or self-sacrifice. Although both groups had improved at posttesting, subjects who had received the negative interpretations relapsed quickly, whereas those in the paradoxical condition maintained their gains.

Feldman, Strong, and Danser (1982) also studied moderately depressed college students by administering consistent or inconsistent paradoxical or nonparadoxical interpretations and directives using a 2 × 2 design. There was also a no-interview control condition. Through the course of two interviews, six interpretations and two directives were given. Students in the interview conditions reduced their depression scores more than those who did not participate in the interviews. Those who received paradoxical interpretations or directives, regardless of their consistency, improved more than those who received nonparadoxical interpretations and directives. Consistency, however, resulted in more favorable impressions of the counselor.

Kraft, Claiborn, and Dowd (1985) employed 47 college students who reported "negative emotions." Using a 2 × 2 design, subjects randomly received (1) either paradoxical or nonparadoxical directives and (2) either positive reframing statements or no reframing statements. Each subject participated in two, 30-minute counseling sessions, focusing on the individual's negative emotions. Change was measured by pre/post differences on the Beck Depression Inventory and on a self-report mood scale. The study found that positive reframing produced greater reduction in negative emotions than no reframing, although negative emotions were reduced in all conditions. Neither of the two directive conditions (paradoxical and nonparadoxical) evidenced greater improvements than the other. These results suggest that while directives contribute to client improvement, it does not seem that paradoxical directives have any advantage over other directives. The findings are mitigated, however, by the authors' stated uncertainty as to the success of the paradoxical manipulation. Subjects in this condition were asked to schedule time each day to feel negative emotions "so that you will understand them more clearly." It is possible that, in some cases, this turned out simply to be a self-monitoring task. Thus, while this study would seem to indicate that positive reframing statements are an effective means of reducing "negative emotions," it is not possible to support conclusions regarding the paradoxical directives.

In another attempt to account for the mechanisms of success in the use of paradoxical therapy, Zodun, Gruszkos, and Strong (1985) evaluated the use of paradoxical therapy with moderately depressed college students. Specifically, they assessed the role of internal, nonvolitional attributions of change (e.g., developmental maturation, personal growth) and therapeutic double bind (e.g., diffusing the impact of the double bind in paradox through explicit identification of the paradoxical nature and intent of the treatment). The authors argue that if paradoxical techniques achieve their effects by instilling nonvolitional, internal change in the client, then students receiving this type of explanation should evidence greater treatment gains than those receiving a differing explanation. Conversely, if paradoxical treatments produce their gains through therapeutic double bind, as in preparation asserted by Haley (1976), then a clear explanation of the nature and intent of paradox should attenuate improvement (a veridical explanation).

The depressed students were randomly assigned to one of five treatment conditions: paradoxical interpretations and directives only, paradox plus developmental rationale, paradox plus veridical rationale, nonparadoxical interview, or a no-interview control. The results did not support either hypothesis. Students in the developmental rationale group improved very little. Similarly, provision of a veridical rationale did not seem to enhance treatment effects as those in this group did as well as those in the paradox-only group.

An analogue study of the effects of various rationales on symptom prescription was conducted by Boettcher and Dowd (1988). Fifty college undergraduates who reported performance anxiety and were identified as anxious by the State-Trait Anxiety Inventory (STAI; Spielberger, Gorsuch, & Lushene, 1970) participated in the study. The subjects were asked to increase their anxiety for 15 minutes, twice each day, under one of the four rationale conditions: (1) no rationale given; (2) positive reframing, which stressed the positive characteristics of the anxiety symptoms; (3) a description of the vicious cycle created when direct attempts are made to decrease anxiety; or (4) a double-bind condition, in which subjects were told that they may choose to defy the directive and that the counselor expected them to change whether they followed the directive or not. A no-attention condition was also included. The procedures involved four individual interviews designed to differ only in the nature of the rationale discussed.

The students were evaluated using the STAI and a Mood Perception Inventory, which assessed their beliefs about the nature, causes, and controllability of their anxiety. The data indicated that the treatment conditions did not significantly differ from the control condition. The authors interpreted these results as suggesting that therapeutic interventions that direct clients to increase unwanted symptoms are an effective means of reducing performance anxiety, regardless of the rationale given. Such a finding conflicts with those of Ascher and Turner (1980), who demonstrated that a rationale defining the directive as a vehicle for change (the "performance anxiety" rationale in both studies) was superior to a rationale that did not explicitly create this expectation (e.g., the "awareness" rationale in the Ascher and Turner study, and the "positive reframing" rationale in the Boettcher and Dowd study). This discrepancy is possibly attributable to the differences between analogue (Boettcher & Dowd, 1988) and clinical studies (Ascher & Turner, 1980) and to the different clinical diagnoses.

Robbins and Milburn (1990) have also attempted to account for the effects of paradoxical interventions. These researchers investigated reattribution, preparatory, reactance, and self-regulatory reorientation models of paradoxically induced change. A reattribution model states that replacing dysfunctional attributions with more adaptive ones (e.g., a reframing) results in problem relief as a result of decreased concern and worry. A preparatory model postulates that paradoxical procedures serve to prepare the recipients for arousal, thereby normalizing the anxiety. The reactance model has been discussed in relation to Shoham-Salomon, Avner, and Neeman (1989). In essence, it states that subjects resist paradoxical techniques in an attempt to assert behavioral freedom, thereby causing abandonment of the target behavior. The final model, self-regulatory reorientation, is said to act by disrupting the client's use of maladies arousal reduction strategies, thereby disrupting the performance anxiety cycle.

In the first of two experiments, the authors randomly assigned 122 subjects reporting high and low test anxiety to one of four experimental conditions in a 2×2 matrix: positive or neutral expectations with paradoxical or task-focusing instructions. The primary dependent measure was the number of correctly solved anagrams in an analogue testing situation. Analysis of the data indicated that of the subjects who originally reported high anxiety, those in the paradoxical condition reported lower levels of anxiety and evidenced better performance than those subjects in the task-focusing condition, regardless of their expectancy of success. An analysis of subjects' attributions did not support a reattribution explanation. The authors interpreted that these findings supported a self-regulatory reorientation model rather than a reattribution explanation.

In the second experiment, Robbins and Milburn (1990) investigated the role of preparatory and reactance models as explanations for paradoxical treatment success. The authors hypothesized that preparatory information would actually serve to direct students' attention to their arousal, thereby increasing anxiety and reducing performance. They further hypothesized that any reactance on the part of the subjects would cause them to give negative evaluations of the experimenters on several bipolar ratings. The results showed that for high, test-anxious subjects, preparatory information did not decrease their performance; however, low, test-anxious subjects did exhibit decrements under this condition. The authors also found that high, test-anxious subjects did not tend to rate the experimenter more negatively following paradoxical instructions, thereby failing to support the reactance model.

Overall, Robbins and Milburn (1990) report little evidence for preparatory, reactance, and attributional models of paradoxical intention. In contrast, Shoham-Salomon, Avner, and Neeman (1989) found reactance to be a significant mediator in the results obtained in paradoxical intention therapy. To some extent, the difference may be due to the relatively arbitrary manner in which this construct has been measured. A more reliable and objective method for assessing this construct would seem to be a prerequisite for additional investigation of this topic.

Paradoxical intention has also been investigated as a strategy for pain management. Gilligan, Ascher, Wolper, and Bochachevsky (1984) studied 32 subjects in a cold-pressor task. The subjects were randomly assigned to one of three treatment conditions (paradoxical intention, rational self-statements, or self-observation) or an expectancy control group. Paradoxical intention instructions proposed that fear and anxiety would be reduced by "going with" the discomfort rather than trying to fight it. Rational, self-statement instructions emphasized selection and focus on the positive aspects of the experience. Self-observation subjects were informed that detailed analysis of the sensory aspects of the procedure, excluding the discomfort (e.g., wetness, coldness, numbness), would decrease the discomfort and increase their tolerance. Finally, it was suggested to expectancy control subjects that the second, comparative, cold-pressor experience would be less painful than the first. Pain thresholds, tolerances, and discomfort ratings were gathered for each subject.

The data indicated that only the self-observation condition produced significantly higher pain tolerance scores than the expectancy control group. In line with Blitz and Dinnerstein (1971), the authors hypothesized that self-observation appears to be effective because it redirects the focus of attention away from the painful aspects of the experience toward more neutral components, thus providing an effective strategy for enhancing tolerance. From this perspective, the other conditions (paradoxical intention, rational self-statements) are less helpful as they served to direct attention toward painful aspects of the cold-pressor procedure.

Efran, Chorney, Ascher, and Lukens (1989) also studied the effectiveness of paradox and coping styles in a cold-pressor task. Ninety-two male undergraduate subjects were randomly assigned to one of four conditions: self-observation, exaggeration (paradoxical instructions), rational self-statements, or a control group. The authors also studied the effect of individual coping styles on the effectiveness of these conditions. "Monitors" (individuals who prefer having information about stressors) were compared with "blunters" (individuals who avoid cues associated with stressors). The results revealed each of the treatment conditions to be equally effective compared to the control condition. Paradoxical intention was no more effective than the other treatment strategies on cold-pressor task performance. Furthermore, subjects tended to do better when an instructional set of coping styles was consistent with their preferred coping style. These results are in line with those of Gilligan, Ascher, Wolper, and Bochachevsky (1984) who also failed to find any advantage in the use of paradoxical intention over other strategies in a cold-pressor task.

Concerns about the use of paradoxical interventions have been voiced by several researchers (Cottone, 1981; Feldman, Strong, & Danser, 1982; Greenberg & Pies, 1983). To evaluate possible negative effects associated with their use, Perrin and Dowd (1986) examined the effects of counselor self-disclosure and paradoxical homework directives on clients' perceptions of counselor social influence. Eight undergraduate students experiencing problems with test anxiety (as identified by the Test Anxiety Scale-Short Form; Sarason, 1978) were randomly assigned treatments in a $2 \times 2 \times 2$ factorial design under the following conditions: (a) a paradoxical intention directive for test anxiety or a nonparadoxical directive; (b) a moderate level of counselor self-disclosure or reflective statements only; or (c) a gender condition. Subjects were seen for four 30-minute videotaped interviews. These videotapes were then viewed by 89 test-anxious undergraduates, who rated them on the basis of perceived counselor willingness and ability to help, level of trickiness, manipulativeness, client anger toward therapist, and level of confusion created by the homework directive. The subjects also rated the counselor using the Counselor Rating Form-Short Version (CRF-S; Corrigan & Schmidt, 1983). This scale measures subjects' perceptions of the counselor's attractiveness, expertness, and trustworthiness.

The data indicated that subjects perceived the paradoxical directives to be more tricky and/or manipulative and confusing than nonparadoxical directives, but that this did not influence their perceptions of the counselor's willingness or ability to help or increase feelings of anger toward the therapist. No gender effects were found. As the authors point out, the subjects' perceptions of the paradoxical interventions as tricky and manipulative may be an objective perception of reality that is not necessarily value-laden. Furthermore, counselor self-disclosure does not necessarily enhance or limit positive perceptions of the counselor's social influence. These results point to the possibility that the use of paradoxical techniques does not serve to degrade the therapist-client relationship. In addition to problems typical of analogue studies, several difficulties specific to this investigation further limit the generalizability of its data. Significant among these is the fact that results were obtained from a group of subjects who were not themselves clients, but who observed sessions with a third person.

Notwithstanding the significant problems of internal and external validity inherent in clinical analogue studies, the results suggest that paradoxical directives are at least as effective for the complaints of the college samples studied as are nonparadoxical directives. In addition to outcome data, information regarding aspects of the process associated with the use of paradoxical directives was also obtained. For example, those who receive paradoxical treatments are likely to attribute change to internal, nonvolitional causes (Wright & Strong, 1982; Lopez & Wambach, 1982; Shoham-Salomon et al., 1989). However, it appears that attempting to maximize this attribution may be detrimental (Zodun et al., 1985). Furthermore, this research suggests that paradoxical interpretations (e.g., reframing) may produce more lasting change than interpretations that imply negative connotations of presenting symptoms (Beck & Strong, 1982).

Although paradoxical interpretations and directives need not be consistent to be effective, consistency is likely to increase the recipient's confidence in the provider (Feldman et al., 1982). Also, conscious awareness of the nature and intent of paradoxical techniques is not necessarily detrimental to the effectiveness of these procedures. These findings suggest that the mechanism for client change may involve more than simple, therapeutic double bind (Zodun et al., 1985). Also noteworthy, preliminary evidence of the use of paradoxical techniques and perceived counselor social influence indicates that the use of these techniques is not detrimental to the therapist-client relationship (Perrin & Dowd, 1986).

Finally, with certain methodological flaws which make it difficult to draw firm conclusions, these studies are generally well conceived and conducted. As such, analogue studies may be viewed as cost-effective pilots for the formulation and initial testing of process and outcome hypotheses. Those obtaining support at this preliminary level can then be exposed to forms of clinical research that require more extensive resources.

SUMMARY AND CONCLUSIONS

Since at least the 1950s, therapeutic paradoxical procedures have gained prominence within a variety of therapeutic orientations. However, despite numerous positive anecdotal claims extolling these procedures, until recently, there has been a paucity of controlled empirical data supporting the efficacy of this approach. Currently, there has been a growth of empirical research in the form of controlled case, analogue, and clinical outcome studies, evaluating the efficacy of paradoxical interventions.

Although clinical outcome data are available for a wide variety of disorders, most of these problems are the focus of few studies. Thus, the present review has emphasized insomnia and agoraphobia, as these behavioral difficulties are associated with the greatest depth of data. Based on the lack of available studies, a definitive statement on the efficacy of paradoxical techniques would be premature. The old joke about two women vacationing at a Catskill resort sums up the problem: One woman says to the other, "The food here is *terrible*." And, the other woman responds, "Yes, and such small portions." There are many criticisms that one can lodge against even the best controlled studies and there are not sufficient data, even in the case of insomnia and agoraphobia, to resolve conflicts and support useful conclusions.

Generally, results are encouraging with most studies, suggesting that paradoxical intention is at least as effective as—and sometimes more effective than—conventional behavioral procedures. This is the case with both clinical and analogue studies. Providing further corroboration are several meta-analyses. Both Shoham-Salomon and Rosenthal (1987) and Hill (1987) found paradoxical procedures to be as effective as conventional comparison treatment, and sometimes more effective than these treatments of choice, for a number of behavioral problems. Again, however, the conclusions of these meta-analyses share a significant flaw—they are based on insufficient numbers of experiments. Thus, as data from an increasing number of reasonably well-controlled studies accumulate, a reasonable conclusion is that paradoxical procedures seem to hold potential as effective therapeutic procedures, in some cases treatments of choice, and ancillary techniques in others. Effort expended in experimental demonstration of this efficacy might very well be rewarded.

REFERENCES

Agras, W. S., Syllvester, D., & Oliveau, D. The epidemiology of common fear and phobia. *Comprehensive Psychiatry,* 1969, *10,* 151–156.

Anderson, L. T. Desensitization in vivo for men unable to urinate in a public facility. *Journal of Behavior Therapy and Experimental Psychiatry,* 1977, *8,* 105–106.

Ascher, L. M. *Paradoxical intention as a component in the behavioral treatment of sleep onset insomnia: A case study.* Paper presented at the meeting of the Association for the Advancement of Behavior Therapy, December 1975, San Francisco, CA.

Ascher, L. M. Paradoxical intention in the treatment of urinary retention. *Behaviour Research and Therapy,* 1979, *17,* 267.

Ascher, L. M. Employing paradoxical intention in the treatment of agoraphobia. *Behaviour Research and Therapy,* 1981, *19,* 533–542.

Ascher, L. M. *Enhanced paradoxical intention and the self-recursive anxiety disorder.* Paper presented at the meeting of the Boston Behavior Therapy Interest Group, September 1983, Wheaton College.

Ascher, L. M. Therapeutic paradox: A primer. In L.M. Ascher (Ed.) *Therapeutic Paradox.* New York: Guilford Press, 1989a.

Ascher, L. M. Paradoxical intention and recursive anxiety. In L. M. Ascher (Ed.) *Therapeutic Paradox.* New York: Guilford Press, 1989b.

Ascher, L. M., Bowers, M. R., and Schotte, D. E. A review of data from controlled case studies and experiments evaluating the clinical efficacy of paradoxical intention. In G. R. Weeks (Ed.) *Promoting Change Through Paradoxical Therapy.* Homewood, Ill.: Dow Jones-Irwin, 1985.

Ascher, L. M., & Efran, J. The use of paradoxical intention in cases of delayed sleep onset insomnia. *Journal of Consulting and Clinical Psychology,* 1978, *8,* 547–550.

Ascher, L. M., & Schotte, D. E. The use of the single case design for research in paradoxical intention. In *Proceedings of the 3rd World Congress of Logotherapy, Anaelecta Frankliana III*, 1983.

Ascher, L. M., Schotte, D. E., & Grayson, J. B. Enhancing effectiveness of paradoxical intention in treating travel restriction in agoraphobia. *Behavior Therapy,* 1986, *17*, 124–130.

Ascher, L. M., & Turner, R. M. Paradoxical intention and insomnia: An experimental investigation. *Behavior Research and Therapy,* 1979a, *17*, 408–411.

Ascher, L. M., & Turner, R. M. A comparison of two methods for the administration of paradoxical intention. *Behaviour Research and Therapy,* 1979b, *18*, 121–126.

Ascher, L. M., & Turner, R. M. A comparison of two methods for the administration of paradoxical intention. *Behaviour Research and Therapy,* 1980, *18*, 121–126.

Barlow, D. H. *Anxiety and its disorders: The nature and treatment of anxiety and panic.* New York: Guilford, 1988.

Beck, J. T., & Strong, S. R. Stimulating therapeutic change with interpretations: A comparison of positive and negative connotation. *Journal of Counseling Psychology,* 1982, *29*, 551–559.

Blitz, B., & Dinnerstein, A. J. Role of attentional focus in pain perception: Manipulation of response to noxious stimulation by instruction. *Journal of Abnormal Psychology,* 1971, *77*, 42–45.

Boeringa, J. A. Blushing: A modified intervention using paradoxical intention. *Psychotherapy: Theory, Research and Practice*, 1983, *20*, 441–444.

Boettcher, L. L., & Dowd, E. T. Comparison of rationales in symptom prescription. *Journal of Cognitive Psychotherapy: An International Quarterly,* 1988.

Bornstein, P. H., Sturm, C. Z., Retzlaff, P. D., Kirby, K. L., & Chong, H. Paradoxical instruction in the treatment of encopresis and chronic constipation: An experimental analysis. *Journal of Behavior Therapy and Experimental Psychiatry,* 1981, *12*, 167–170.

Corrigan, J. D., & Schmidt, L. D. Development and validation of revision in the counselor rating form. *Journal of Counseling Psychology,* 1983, *30*, 64–75.

Cottone, R. R. Ethical issues related to use of paradoxical techniques in work adjustments. *Vocational and Work Adjustment Bulletin*, 1981, *14*, 167–170.

Dattilio. The use of paradoxical intention in the treatment of panic attacks. *Journal of Counseling and Development*, 1987, *66*, 102–103.

DeBord, J. B. Paradoxical interventions: A review of the recent literature. *Journal of Counseling and Development*, 1989, *67*, 394–398.

Efran, J. S., Chorney, R. L., Ascher, L. M., & Lukens, M. D. Coping styles, paradox, and the cold pressor task. *Journal of Behavioral Medicine*, 1989, *12*, 91–103.

Elliot, R. A case of inhibition of micturition: Unsystematic desensitization. *Psychological Record*, 1967, *17*, 525–530.

Espie, C. A., & Lindsay, W. R. Paradoxical intention in the treatment of chronic insomnia: Six case studies illustrating variability in therapeutic response. *Behavior Research and Therapy*, 1985, *14*, 21–33.

Espie, C. A., Lindsay, W. R., Brooks, D. N., Hood, E. M., & Turvey, T. A controlled comparative investigation of psychological treatments for chronic sleep-onset insomnia. *Behavior Research and Therapy*, 1989, *27*(1), 79–88.

Feldman, D. A., Strong, S. R., and Danser, D. B. A comparison of paradoxical and nonparadoxical interpretations and directives. *Journal of Counseling Psychology*, 1982, *29*, 572–579.

Fisher, S. G., Nietzel, M. T., & Lowery, C. R. *The credibility of rationales for paradoxical intention in the treatment of sleep-onset insomnia.* Unpublished manuscript, 1985.

Frankl, V. E. *The doctor and the soul: From psychotherapy to logotherapy.* New York: Knopf, 1955.

Frankl, V. E. Paradoxical intention and dereflection. *Psychotherapy: Theory, research and practice*, 1975, *12*, 226–237.

Frankl, V. E. Logos, paradox, and the search for meaning. In M. J. Mahoney & A. Freeman (Eds.) *Cognition and psychotherapy.* New York: Plenum, 1985.

Gerz, H. Experience with the logotherapeutic technique of paradoxical intention in the treatment of phobic and obsessive-compulsive patients. *American Journal of Psychiatry*, 1966, *123*, 548–553.

Gilligan, R. M., Ascher, L. M., Wolper, J., & Bochachevsky, C. Comparison of three cognitive strategies in altering pain behaviors on a cold pressor task. *Perceptual and Motor Skills*, 1984, *59*, 235–240.

Goldstein, A. J. Case conference: The treatment of a case of agoraphobia by a multifaceted treatment program. *Journal of Behavior Therapy and Experimental Psychiatry*, 1978, *9*, 45–51.

Greenberg, R. G., & Pies, R. Is paradoxical intention risk-free?: A review and case report. *Journal of Clinical Psychiatry*, 1983, *44*, 66–69.

Haley, J. *Problem solving therapy.* New York: Harper & Row, 1976.

Hersen, M., & Barlow, D. H. *Single case experimental designs: Strategies for studying behavior change.* New York: Pergamon, 1976.

Hill, K. A. Meta-analysis of paradoxical interventions. *Psychotherapy,* 1987, *24,* 266–270.

Hsu, G. L. K., & Lieberman, S. Paradoxical intention in the treatment of chronic anorexia nervosa. *American Journal of Psychiatry,* 1982, *139,* 650–653.

Jacob, R. G., & Moore, D. J. Paradoxical interventions in behavioral medicine. *Journal of Behavior Therapy and Experimental Psychiatry,* 1984, *15,* 205–213.

Kales, A., Bixler, E. O., Lee, I. A., Healy, S., & Slye, E. Incidence of insomnia in the Los Angeles metropolitan area. *Sleep Research,* 1974, *4,* 139.

Kelly, J. E., & Lichstein, K. L. (1980). A sleep assessment device. *Behavior Assessment,* 1980, *2,* 135–146.

Kraft, R. G., Claiborn, C. D., & Dowd, E. T. Effects of positive reframing and paradoxical directives in counseling for negative emotions. *Journal of Counseling Psychology,* 1985, *32,* 617–621.

Lacks, P., Bertelson, A. D., Gans, L., & Kunkel, J. The effectiveness of three behavioral treatments for different degrees of sleep onset insomnia. *Behavior Therapy,* 1983, *14,* 593–605.

Ladouceur, R., & Gros-Louis, Y. Paradoxical intention vs stimulus control in the treatment of severe insomnia. *Journal of Behavior Therapy and Experimental Psychiatry,* 1986, *17,* 267–269.

Lamontagne, Y. Treatment of erythrophobia by paradoxical intention: Single case study. *Journal of Nervous and Mental Disease,* 1978, *166,* 304–306.

Lamontagne, Y., & Marks, I. M. Psychogenic urinary retention: Treatment by prolonged exposure. *Behavior Therapy,* 1973, *4,* 581–585.

Last, C. G., Barlow, D. H., & O'Brien, G. T. A comparison of two cognitive strategies in a patient with generalized anxiety disorder. *Psychological Reports,* 1983, *53,* 19–26.

Lesage, A., & Lamontagne, Y. Paradoxical intention and exposure *in vivo* in the treatment of psychogenic nausea: Report of two cases. *Behavioural Psychotherapy,* 1985, *13,* 69–75.

Lopez, F. G., & Wambach, C. A. Effects of paradoxical and self-control directives in counseling. *Journal of Counseling Psychology,* 1982, *29,* 115–124.

Margolies, R., & Gilstein, K. W. A systems approach to the treatment of chronic encopresis. *International Journal of Psychiatry in Medicine,* 1983-84, *13,* 141–152.

Mavissakalian, M., Michelson, L., Greenwald, D., Kornblith, S., & Greenwald, M. Cognitive-behavioral treatment of agoraphobia:

Paradoxical intention vs. self-statement training. *Behaviour Research and Therapy,* 1983, *21,* 75–86.

Meichenbaum, D. *Cognitive-behavior modification: An integrative approach.* New York: Plenum Press, 1977.

Michelson, L. Treatment consonance and response profiles in agoraphobia: The role of individual differences in cognitive, behavioral, physiological treatments. *Behaviour Research and Therapy,* 1986, *24,* 263–275.

Michelson, L., Mavissakalian, M., & Marchione, K. Cognitive and behavioral treatments of agoraphobia: Clinical, behavioral, and psychophysiological outcomes. *Journal of Consulting and Clinical Psychology,* 1985, *53,* 913–925.

Michelson, L., Mavissakalian, M., & Marchione, K. Cognitive, behavioral, and psychophysiological treatments of agoraphobia: A comparative outcome investigation. *Behavior Therapy,* 1988, *19,* 97–120.

Michelson, L., Mavissakalian, M. Marchione, K., Dancu, C., & Greenwald, M. The role of self-directed *in vivo* exposure in cognitive, behavioral, and psychophysiological treatments of agoraphobia. *Behavior Therapy,* 1986, *17,* 91–108.

Milan, M. A., & Kolko, D. J. Paradoxical intention in the treatment of obsessional flatulence ruminations. *Journal of Behaviour Therapy and Experimental Psychiatry,* 1982, *13*(2), 167–172.

Mozdzierz, G. J. The use of hypnosis and paradox in the treatment of a case of chronic urinary retention/"bashful bladder." *American Journal of Clinical Hypnosis,* 1985, *28,* 43–47.

Ott, B. D., Levine, B. A., & Ascher, L. M. (1983). Manipulating the explicit demand of paradoxical intention instructions. *Behavioural Psychotherapy,* 1983, *11,* 25–35.

Perrin, D. K., & Dowd, E. T. Effect of paradoxical and nonparadoxical self-disclosure on counselor social influence. *Journal of Counseling Psychology,* 1986, *33,* 207–210.

Propp, L. A self-control treatment for encopresis combining self-charting with paradoxical instructions: Two case examples. *Journal of Child and Adolescent Psychotherapy,* 1985, *2,* 26–31.

Ray, I., & Murphy, J. Metronome conditioned urinary retention. *Psychosomatic Medicine,* 1975, *25,* 543–555.

Relinger, H., & Bornstein, P. H. Treatment of sleep onset insomnia by paradoxical instruction: A multiple baseline design. *Behavior Modification,* 1979, *3,* 203–222.

Relinger, H., Bornstein, P. H., & Mungas, D. M. Treatment of insomnia by paradoxical intention: A time series analysis. *Behavior Therapy,* 1978, *9,* 955–959.

Robbins, B. P., & Milburn, T. W. *The effect of paradoxical intervention on the performance of test anxious college students.* Unpublished manuscript, 1990.

Sarason, I. G. The test anxiety scale: Concept and research. In C. D. Spielberger & I. G. Sarason (Eds.), *Stress and anxiety* (Vol. 5). Washington, DC: Hemisphere, 1978.

Seltzer, L. F. *Paradoxical strategies in psychotherapy: A comprehensive overview and guidebook.* New York: John Wiley and Sons, 1986.

Shoham-Salomon, V., Avner, R., & Neeman, R. You're changed if you do and changed if you don't: Mechanisms underlying paradoxical interventions. *Journal of Consulting and Clinical Psychology,* 1989, *57,* 590–598.

Shoham-Salomon, V., & Rosenthal, R. Paradoxical interventions: A meta-analysis. *Journal of Consulting and Clinical Psychology,* 1987, *55,* 22–28.

Solyom, L., Garza-Perez, J., Ledwidge, B. L., & Solyom, C. Paradoxical intention in the treatment of obsessive thoughts: A pilot study. *Comprehensive Psychiatry,* 1972, *13,* 291–297.

Spielberger, C. D., Gorsuch, R. L., & Lushene, R. E. (1970). *STAI manual for the State-Trait Anxiety Inventory.* Palo Alto, CA: Consulting Psychologists Press, 1970.

Timms, M. W. The treatment of urinary frequency by paradoxical intention. *Behavioural Psychotherapy,* 1985, *13,* 76–82.

Turner, R. M., & Ascher, L. M. Controlled comparison of progressive relaxation, stimulus control, and paradoxical intention therapies for insomnia. *Journal of Consulting and Clinical Psychology,* 1979, *47,* 500–508.

Turner, R. M., & Ascher, L. M. Therapist factor in the treatment of insomnia. *Behavior Research and Therapy,* 1982, *20,* 33–40.

Watzlawick, P., Beavin, J., & Jackson, D. D. *Pragmatics of human communication: A study of interactional patterns, pathologies and paradoxes.* New York: Norton, 1967.

Webb, W. B. *Sleep: The gentle tyrant.* Englewood Cliffs, NJ: Prentice-Hall, 1975.

Wright, R. M., & Strong, S. R. Stimulating therapeutic change with directives: An exploratory study. *Journal of Counseling Psychology,* 1982, *29,* 199–202.

Zodun, H. I., Gruszkos, J. R., & Strong, S. R. *Attribution and the double bind in paradoxical interventions.* Unpublished manuscript, 1985.

Part Four

Future Directions

9

The Mysterious Affair of Paradoxes and Loops

by Steve de Shazer and Elam Nunnally

FOREWORD

The purpose of this chapter is to examine the puzzles of paradox and strange loops through the use of a double description of a case example. The results of this twin explication suggest that we use Occam's razor to cut through the complexity, and that a more simple explanation is available.

In the classic murder mystery, the sleuth is surrounded by a not so bright sidekick (the Watson figure) and not so bright police (the Lestrade figure). During the course of the story the police view the crime from a particular point of view which turns out to be false; they are continually led astray by following red herrings (clues which when followed too far lead an investigator in the wrong direction). The sidekick too is led astray by viewing events from the wrong perspective, although his comments sometimes help to illuminate the problem for the sleuth. After a while, the sleuth solves the puzzle by considering the same "facts" the police and the sidekick did, but from a different perspective—usually "upside-down."

The clues, red herrings, and use of the wrong perspective are all part of the writer's craft, designed to mystify and entertain the readers: The readers' game is to arrive at the proper solution before the sleuth does. If readers are too quick, they spoil their own pleasure. Therefore, the successful author needs to be very clever indeed in the use of clues.

If the field of "murder mystery" had commentators and conceptualizers similar to those in the field of family therapy, the story might be seen as follows: Each of the suspects and witnesses has a perspective (frame) that explains the meaning of their behavior and their perceptions, as do the police, sidekick, and sleuth. Each of the clues, and red herrings is intended to promote framing of the story in a "wrong way." At the end, the sleuth reframes all prior frames, gets a new understanding (or new perspective) of all the facts, and designs a counter red herring with this new point of view. In the classic final chapter, which includes a meeting of all the suspects, the detective uses his counter red herring to break the old frames that frequently causes the culprit to confess (some new behavior).

The sleuth then gives a post hoc explanation of how he arrived at the solution. Often this explanation is just a simple matter of redescribing the story from the point of view that inevitably led him to the real culprit. If a clue pointed the police in one direction, the sleuth saw it point in the exact opposite. Of course, during the development of the story, the sleuth too might have been led astry now and then, but by the three quarter point, he knows the proper frame to use to understand the problem.

Read in the spirit of murder mysteries, the history and development of family therapy seem littered with clues as to the nature and identity of the agent of change. Who or what is the real agent of change? For quite some time, many investigators followed the clue of "insight." (Some still pursue it.) Discouraged with their progress in pursuing that path, many investigators picked up on the clue of "awareness." Although awareness seemed more promising than insight for a time, it soon became apparent to investigators—especially the statistically minded—that awareness accounted for very little of the variance in observed change. This is not to say that the clues offered by insight and awareness added nothing to the search, for in figure/ground terms, the study of how insight and awareness related to change provided some detail for the ground portion of the picture.

Investigators were thus stimulated to seek a new clue to flesh out the shadowy figure and discern the true identity of the change agent. Soon this new clue was found—a clue so pervasive that investigators kept stumbling over it everywhere—paradox. In a murder mystery, such a pervasive clue usually alerts the reader to consider its possible falseness and wonder whether it is a red herring designed to lead him astray. If he then follows the clue to try to find out what paradox means, he finds it leading in many different and unrelated directions.

When a murder mystery reader is repeatedly confronted with red herrings, the reader begins to wonder if the "clues" mean anything at all. An apt analogy here is *The Floating Admiral*, the combined effort of various authors such as Christie, Sayers, and Chesterton (1980), each of whom contributed a chapter to the story. Not knowing what the previous author had in mind or what the clues meant to him or her, the author of each subsequent chapter tries to be more clever by half. At the end of *The Floating Admiral* each author submitted his or her solution (and some were too dumbfounded to figure it out at all). The reader may be reminded of Agatha Christie's *Murder on the Orient Express* in which all the various clues meant *nothing* because they contradicted each other and led to each of the various suspects in turn proving in the end that "everybody done it."

PARADOXES

The *Oxford English Dictionary* gives several definitions and examples of paradox. Among them are:

Paradox 1.   "A statement or tenet contrary to received opinion or belief, often with the implication that it is marvellous or incredible; sometimes with unfavourable connotation as being discordant with what is held to be established truth, and hense absurd or fantastic, sometimes with favourable connotation, as a correction of vulgar error."

Translation, Burgersducems' *Logic II*, 1697, *XV*, p. 65. "A Paradox is said to be a probleme true against the common Opinion...such as that viz, the Earth moves; which though it be true, yet it may be so against the common Opinion, and therefore a Paradox."

de Quincey Templars' *Dial*, 1854, Wks *IV*, p. 183. "A paradox you know is simply that which contradicts the popular opinion—which in too many cases is the false opinion."

Paradox 2.   "A statement or proposition which on the face of it seems self-contradictory, absurd or at variance with common sense, though on investigation or when explained, it may prove to be well founded (or according to some, though it is essentially true)."

J. Norden Surv., *Dial*, 1607, *IV*, p. 195. "I can tell you a pretie paradoxe...Boggy and spungy ground...though it owne nature it be too moist, yet if it be overflowed with water it will often settle and become firme" (Warner, 1982, pp. 3-4).

Historical Paradoxes

Zeno of Elea is well known for several paradoxes, among them "Achilles and the Tortoise" and "The Flying Arrow." The flying arrow conundrum goes like this: An object is at rest when it occupies a space equal to its own dimensions. An arrow in flight occupies, at any given moment, a space equal to its own dimensions. Therefore, an arrow in flight is at rest.

The logic here follows from the assumption that time is composed of discrete moments. If this assumption is not held, then Zeno's conclusion will not follow. Zeno's assumptions further included the idea that space is infinitely divisible and thus any finite distance contains an infinite number of points: It is impossible to reach the end of an infinite series in finite time. According to Nahm,

> Zeno's argument involves the assumption that the flying arow is at rest at any point in its trajectory. But this can be said of every point in the trajectory and what is at rest at every point does not move at all. The solution to the paradox is impossible for philosophy until mathematics, by the development of the differential calculus could deal with the general problem of velocity at a point. Once the mathematics is developed, the paradox of the flying arrow may be considered as one involving a definite velocity for the arrow at every point of its trajectory. (Nahm, 1964, p. 99)

The Achilles and the tortoise paradox follows: The tortoise, given a head start, will never be overtaken in a race by the swifter Achilles, for it is necessary that Achilles should first reach the point from which the tortoise started, so that necessarily the tortoise is always somewhat ahead. By the time Achilles reaches point two, the tortoise will be at point three and by the time Achilles reaches point three, the tortoise will have moved on again, and so on, ad infinitum.

According to Quine,

> When we try to make this argument more explicit, the fallacy that emerges is the mistaken notion that any infinite succession of intervals of time has to add up to all eternity. Actually when an infinite

succession of intervals of time is so chosen that the succeeding intervals become shorter and shorter, the whole succession may take either a finite or an infinite time. It is a question of a convergent series. (Quine, 1976, p. 3)

Since Zeno's time, various conceptual schemes have developed and shifted, each changing the understanding of this conundrum. Quine points to a fallacy:

the notion that an infinite succession of intervals must add up to an infinite interval. But surely this was part and parcel of the conceptual scheme of Zeno's day. Our recognition of convergent series, in which an infinite number of segments add up to a finite segment, is from Zeno's vantage point an artificiality. (Quine, 1976, p. 9)

Eastern Paradoxes

Paradoxes of various types have long fascinated man, Eastern as well as Western. While in the West paradoxes have been considered intellectual, philosophical, mathematical puzzles to be solved, the tradition in the East is different. Here paradoxes are part of the path to enlightenment, particularly in the Zen Buddhist tradition. The paradox or koan is accepted as is; the Buddhist is mainly interested in the consequences of getting beyond the conundrum. For instance, in the famous Zen illustration, a Buddhist monk stood holding a stout stick over the head of his student. He is reported to have said to his student: "If you say this is a stick, I will hit you with it. If you say this is not a stick, I will hit you with it. Speak: Is it a stick or is it not?"

Within the Zen tradition, the student is very dependent on the monk and their relationship is a highly valued one. Part of the way a student becomes enlightened is by solving these riddles posed by the monk. In a Western or any either/or context, it looks as if the student is sure to be hit but in the Zen context, the student might get beyond the monk's either/or koan by leaping up, grabbing the stick, and screaming nonsense.

Perhaps this fascination with paradox is based on the idea that people like to puzzle themselves (the murder mystery) and confuse themselves and each other, or that people like to make the world problematic. While conundrums can be frustrating, they can also be fun. Be that as it may, in the field of family therapy alone, paradox has been part of some of the best, most profound thinking, and part of some of the most obtuse and confusing thinking.

The Concept of Paradox in Family Therapy

In an effort to bring order out of confusion, one investigator consulted the oracles. In *A Delphi Study on Paradox in Therapy*, Christine Watson (1982)—no relation to Dr. John H. Watson—consulted a panel of expert therapists, pooling their opinions about therapeutic paradoxes and searching for common themes and the possibility of consensus. When asked "What elements are necessary for an intervention to be categorized as a paradoxical intervention?" responses from 18 oracles were distinguished as much by their variety as by any commonalities. Watson also invited the experts to suggest criteria for using paradox and for not using paradox in their interventions. As with the definition of paradoxical intervention, "The criteria for use seem to be very individual—each therapist using very different stylistic variables in deciding when paradox is appropriate" (Watson, 1982, p. 101).

A third feature of the study was a request for the experts to tell what they would consider doing as a strategic paradoxical intervention if involved with a case for which they were provided a short summary. Watson (1982) found that the 19 responses received were "as varied as the approaches to a definition" (p. 83). Watson makes the point, however, that "There exist an infinite number of possible paradoxical interventions which could jolt or surprise the client out of his/her current pattern" (p. 84). Furthermore, "Regarding which particular modus operandi to use in therapeutic communication, almost every expert appeared to use different conceptualizations" (p. 84). Commenting on the variety of responses to the case, Watson concludes that the results "warrant emphasizing the seeming looseness of the term 'paradoxical intervention.' It has come to mean 'all things to all therapists'" (p. 85). Nevertheless, Watson does not appear to be calling on therapists to set the term aside, for she adds that "The term's definition stands as a metaphor for itself—encouraging variety, creativity in problem solving, and a subtle sense of confusion about what is happening" (p. 85).

Although the terms paradox and paradoxical intervention were found to refer to slippery concepts, elusive of definition, a special case of paradox—the double bind—has a widely accepted definition. (Editor's Note: The double bind hypothesis was first proposed by Gregory Bateson, Don Jackson, Jay Haley, and John Weakland in a paper called "Toward a theory of schizophrenia." This hypothesis has been interpreted in different ways, as shown in Chapter 1.) Perhaps the double bind concept offers a useful clue to the identity of the change agent.

A DOUBLE BIND MAPPING

Watzlawick has described the double bind concept as follows:

1. Two or more persons are involved in an intense relationship that has a high degree of physical and/or psychological survival value for one, several, or all of them.
2. In such a context, a message is given which is so structured that (*a*) it asserts something, (*b*) it asserts something about its own assertion, and (*c*) these two assertions are mutually exclusive.
3. Finally, the recipient of the message is prevented from stepping outside the frame set by this message, either by commenting on it or withdrawing (Watzlawick et al., 1967, p. 212).

It is further assumed that these patterns are recurrent in the relationship, and that the complete set of ingredients is no longer necessary when the people concerned have learned to perceive the universe in double bind patterns.

It is important to recognize the distinction between contradictory and paradoxical injunctions. With a contradictory injunction, the recipient is faced with a choice: He can decide on one alternative, but then must suffer the consequences of not picking the other. With a paradoxical injunction, the choice is an illusion: No behavior is logical, and a self-perpetuating oscillation is set in motion. According to Wilden,

> If the double bind generates irresolvable oscillations between "yes" and "no," it can do so only within a digitalized context of either/or; the context of analytical logic. Such oscillations do not present a problem for dialectical logic, which is of a higher logical type than analytical logic and (paradoxically) subsumes it. In other words, double binds are irresolvable only when metacommunication—in logic or in life—is prevented through the way in which allowable communication is framed or punctuated by those with the power to do so. (Wilden, 1980, p. 123)

That is, if the either/or frame is not part of the context in which the "paradoxical message" is sent and received, then the oscillation or illusion of choice will not be "pathological."

Case Example

A couple was referred for therapy by a drug counselor who viewed their marital problems as precluding treatment for drug abuse.[1] (The couple was using cocaine three or more times per week; this had been their pattern for over two years.) The wife Jane (not her real name) described their situation to the team as one in which their joint drug use was messing up their marriage; therefore, she wanted to stop the drugs to save the marriage. The marital problems were, in her view, symptoms of their drug problem.

Ralph (not his real name) did not see their use of drugs as the real problem but rather their fights (some of which became physical) and their arguments (some about drugs) as the main concern. He thought the fights and arguments needed to stop to save their marriage.

Up to this point, their dilemma might be described as a simple contradiction, but their situation was not this either/or—even to them. Interestingly, they also shared the notion that using drugs prevented boredom (which neither of them handled well) and that stopping the drugs might lead to the breakup of the marriage they both valued highly because they would have less or maybe even nothing in common.

Plotting this couple's situation onto a double bind map, we see that this is a relationship in which

1. Use of drugs is messing up their marriage; fights and arguments—some about drugs—are increasing.
2. Their use of drugs prevents boredom; if they stop drugs, their marriage might break up.
3. Withdrawing from this bind might be accomplished by separating, but this is the very action they wish to avoid.
4. Increasing use of cocaine might provide a way to withdraw in a sense by soothing them through some of the conflicts, but then the arguments and fights would probably increase, because they are in conflict about their drug use, and the arguments and fights are breaking up their marriage.

Unless they could find some way to step outside the frame, the couple seemed destined to remain in a self-perpetuating oscillation, which could well become lethal.

The team developed the following intervention message, which was delivered by the therapist (or conductor) at the close of the session:

---

[1] The therapy described in this illustration was done by the team at the Brief Family Therapy Center (BFTC) which includes, in addition to the authors, Insoo Berg, Marilyn La Court, Eve Lipchik, and Alex Molnar.

You've got a problem.

It seems to us, Ralph, that your marital problems are being exacerbated by the drugs, or fogged over by the drugs, or perhaps even created by the drugs. Perhaps you need to stop the drugs, just to see what is going on. But, on the other hand, we agree with you, Jane, that if you two were to stop the drugs, then there might be nothing there. And, you might not have time to create anything before the marriage broke up. In short, we don't know what the f—— you are going to do.

I suggest you think about what I just said, and decide what actions you are going to take.

Mapped as a counter double bind, the intervention contains messages which state that the team views this as a relationship in which

Stopping the drugs may be necessary to save the marriage.

Not stopping the drugs may be necessary to save the marriage.

Either of the above may break up the marriage.

Any alternatives you have thought of pose great risks to your marriage.

You should take actions you have not thought of.

That is,

1. Within the context of therapy which has a high survival value for their marriage, a message is sent.
2. The message (*a*) asserts that stopping the drugs is necessary for saving the marriage, (*b*) asserts that this assertion is false—stopping the drugs might break up the marriage, and (*c*) these are mutually exclusive (either stop or not stop).
3. A nonspecific action is demanded (think about what you are going to do and do it) which is designed to promote their getting outside their either/or frame.

By the next session one week later, Jane and Ralph had cut their drug use by two-thirds, although their use followed the same schedule. Furthermore, without talking about it, they had initiated some new joint and separate activities. This time the main thrust of the intervention message centered around the team's worry about a relapse.

One week later, Jane and Ralph reported having eliminated the drugs: They were continuing new activities—both together and separately—and enjoying them, and arguing much less. In the intervention message, the team again worried about a relapse, specifically about how soon a relapse might occur.

Follow-up contact at six months and one year indicated that there had been no relapse (no drugs and only infrequent arguments). The couple also reported further improvements in their life, both together and separately.

Notwithstanding that Jane and Ralph's dilemma and the intervention can be plotted *retrospectively*[2] onto double bind maps, we have to ask ourselves: Is this particular kind of map useful in *generating* effective interventions, and could other kinds of maps do the job better? Putting the question in terms of our detective story metaphor: Are double binds and counter double binds clues to the nature of persistence and change or are they red herrings, distracting us from a better explanation? To help answer this question, we turn our attention to alternative ways of mapping.

A "STRANGE-LOOP" MAPPING

Cronen, Johnson, and Lannamann (1982) have developed a new theory of reflexivity in systems of social meaning and action. In their view, Russell's Theory of Types (and, therefore, the double bind) was based on an "inappropriate and largely outdated epistemology" (p. 91). Their theory considers reflexivity to be a natural and necessary feature of human systems of meaning and rejects the idea that reflexivity and paradox are coterminus. Behavior, content, episodes (interactions), relationships, life scripts, and cultural patterns are all seen hierarchically, mutually defining each other: Some loops are problematic and some are not (de Shazer, 1982[a]).

When the meaning of a situation cannot be determined by moving through the hierarchical levels, the situation can be described as a "strange-loop." According to Hofstadter, a strange loop can be mapped when, after moving through the hierarchical levels "We unexpectedly find ourselves right back where we started" (1979, p. 10). A "charmed-loop" can be distinguished from a strange-loop when the natural and normal reflexivity is not problematic. A mapping technique developed by Karl Tomm (1982) will be used to illustrate the application of the strange-loop description of the above case example.

If the couple's situation could be described as a charmed-loop, then the meaning of the situation could be picked from any of the

---

[2]The double bind and counter double bind map was not used for the actual design of this intervention. Over the past 6 or 7 years we at BFTC have found using this map in designing interventions to be cumbersome and time consuming, that is, it takes longer than the 10–12 minutes allotted for intervention design during the hour-long session.

following, perhaps by moving up to another level of the hierarchy: (1) stopping the drugs should lead to saving the marriage, or (2) not stopping the drugs should lead to breaking up the marriage, or (3) stopping the drugs should lead to breaking up the marriage, or (4) not stopping the drugs should lead to breaking up the marriage.

But the situation is not that simple, not that charmed. Both people (and the observers) think that stopping the drugs might either break up the marriage or save the marriage, *and* both people (and the observers) think that continuing the drugs might either break up the marriage or save it. The couple's situation is clearly a conundrum for the couple as well as the observers. Each individual's position, which seemingly should be distinct from the other's includes its opposite, which should be logically excluded—a strange-loop. Within the context of this marriage, neither stopping nor not stopping the drugs can determine staying or not staying together. The reflexivity of this couple's situation is such that meanings (and therefore actions) cannot be determined through the context in which the behaviors and episodes appear. The situation can be mapped by an observer in this way:

FIGURE 1

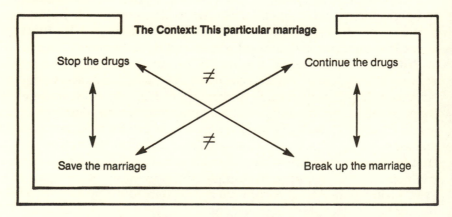

This map is an attempt to clarify the impasse and make understandable the pragmatic effects of a strange-loop. It is important to remember that strange-loops, charmed-loops, and double binds do not exist. They are simply part of the descriptive tools an observer brings to the observed situation, a way of organizing data. Loops are part of the map, not part of the territory. Like any mapping tool, they are either useful for the observer or they are not. (The description either *fits* the observation or it does not.) One reading of the map goes as follows: If one should want to break up the marriage, then one should continue the drugs—but that might save the marriage: Therefore, one should stop the drugs. But stopping the drugs might break up the marriage; therefore, one should continue the drugs to save the marriage. Here is another reading of the map: If one should want to save the marriage, then one should stop the drugs; but this might break up the marriage; therefore, one should continue the drugs to save the marriage.

The strange-loop map is a figure eight (on its side) which can be read by starting at any of the four elements and then following the arrows. Clearly this map *fits* the situation the couple described and points out that the meaning of their situation cannot be determined, thus preventing the couple from making any decisions and taking any actions since they are caught in confusion. There is no way to resolve this interactional situation.

This strange-loop description of the couple's situation needs to be placed within the context of therapy. This context includes the therapist, the team behind the screen, and the videotaping equipment (since the couple can see the camera and gave permission to tape). Furthermore, the description also needs to include the meanings given to that context since the couple system is now a subsystem within the therapeutic suprasystem (de Shazer, 1982 [a] & [b]). The wife came to therapy to stop the drugs in order to save the marriage. The husband thinks that therapy is nothing but talk and any advice will be useless. The therapist and the team by definition think that therapy *can* be useful, but they need to qualify and modify their views based on the couple's definitions and meanings. That is, for this couple, *effective* therapy needs to be more than just talk and needs to exclude useless advice.

The intervention message (repeated here for clarity) is an attempt to give new meanings to the couple's situation.

> You've got a problem.
> It seems to us, Ralph, that your marital problems are being exacerbated by the drugs, or fogged over by the drugs, or perhaps even created by the drugs. Perhaps you need to stop the drugs, just to see what is going on. But, on the other hand, we agree with you, Jane, that if you two were to stop the drugs, then there might be nothing there. And, you might not have time to create anything before the marriage broke up. In short, we don't know what the f--- you are going to do.

I suggest that you think about what I just said, and decide what actions you are going to take.

The team attempts to redefine the situation as one in which some unspecified action is necessary, but that action is not stopping the drugs or not stopping the drugs since neither can save the marriage. (The team does, however, imply the need to stop the drugs, but not because that action will save the marriage.)

The team attempts to define the situation as one in which the couple needs to "create something" in order to save the marriage; furthermore, they deliberately make the presupposition (in the last sentence) that the couple is going to take action. Clearly this intervention can be seen as an attempt to introduce new criteria about saving the marriage—taking action or doing something different rather than fighting about stopping or not stopping the drugs.

In short, the intervention can be seen as based on the same strange-loop map. The reframing attempts to change the meaning of the arrows, or to disconnect them to break the recursive cycle. There is some chance that the meaning is slippery enough to prompt a different response from either husband, wife, or both. The intervention introduced the possibility of some new behavior which might make a "different enough difference."

OCCAM'S RAZOR

William of Occam is best known for suggesting that we look for the simplest explanation that fits. This advice is extremely pertinent to therapists designing interventions. The strange-loop is no better than the counter double bind map when designing interventions, although both are useful *retrospectively*.[3] In the everyday world of doing therapy, there frequently is not enough time to use either map: The criteria are too complex and both are more suited to post hoc explanations.

Typically, when a client presents a complaint, some behavior (i.e., not sleeping) will be seen as a "symptom," and one facet of the context (i.e., being depressed) will be seen as a "problem." The context and the behavior are recursive and inseparable, each defining the other. Within the context of the particular marriage discussed in this chapter, stopping or not stopping the drugs, saving or not saving the marriage, are the problem. As O'Hanlon

---

[3]As is the case with the double bind map, the strange loop map is too cumbersome and time consuming. See Footnote 2 and below.

puts it: "If the loop generates itself again and again, we can speak of the pattern being maintained by the redundant sequence (really itself). At this point, as Bateson says, 'the pattern is the thing'" (1982, p. 27).

If, as Bateson maintains, the breaching of the Theory of Types is continual and inevitable in human communication (Bateson et al., 1956) and if, as Cronen (1982) maintains, this sort of reflexivity is normal and necessary, then we need Occam's razor to simplify the clinical situation in order that effective interventions can be designed within the usual clinical environment.

Implicit within the double bind and counter double bind explication and the strange loop explication, is the notion that the intervention needs to be a *mirror image of the problem*. The criteria for a therapeutic double bind is simply the mirror image of the criteria for a pathogenic double bind: Like cures like. The central premise implied by both the above explications is that therapeutic interventions can be built on the same description (map) as that used to describe the interaction.

It is the *fit* between the therapist's description of the pattern and the form or map of the intervention that seems central to the process of initiating therapeutic changing. That is, the couple describes the problematic pattern within a certain context/meaning/frame, and then the therapeutic intervention is based on the same pattern, but—importantly—with a difference. The pattern upon which the intervention is designed is a mirror image of the couple's pattern. A mirror reflects what is placed in front of it with one difference—the right-left reversal.

DOUBLE DESCRIPTION

Bateson referred to the double description (1979) of the same pattern or sequence as the source of "ideas." If two descriptions of the same sequence are not identical or are simply redundant, then the combined descriptions will include some news of difference. Two identical descriptions without any difference are useless because the combination includes no news of difference; therefore, no idea or bonus is possible. However, if two descriptions are not isomorphic to a high degree, the difference may be too great to prompt ideas—almost like two descriptions of two different sequences.

This descriptive process has been compared to the way our two eyes work together to develop depth perception (Maruyama, 1977; Bateson, 1979; de Shazer, 1982 [a] & [b]). Similarly, it is the difference between what each eye sees that leads to the bonus of depth perception, which is unavailable to *one* eye. If the individual eyes were set too far apart, the degree of isomorphism would be too low for the brain to compute the difference and there would be no depth perception bonus. However, if the views from each eye were too similar, or we were to use only one eye, there would be no news of difference and no depth perception.

The information from two descriptive processes with a high degree of isomorphism and yet some difference is of a different logical type than that included in one description or monocular vision. The bonus is only available through the information contained in the difference between the two descriptions. For instance, there is more and different information in two descriptions of two different chess games being played than in either description by itself. The comparison informs us of the difference between the two games and the play options. This helps us develop an idea of the "game of chess."

The double bind maps and strange loop maps of the case illustration presented here allow for the use of Occam's razor. Both descriptions involve mapping the same intervention pattern onto the map, or describe the problematic pattern. Both include many of the same elements: There is a high degree of isomorphism between double bind maps and strange-loop maps. A bonus (or idea) develops from this double description of the couple's situation and the therapy situation: The intervention, regardless of the principles behind its design, needs to fit with the client's pattern in such a way that it becomes a mirror image. This is the simpler explanation that follows from the use of Occam's razor.

Initiating Changing

Maruyama extends the metaphor of binocular vision to systems and suggests that systems use polyocular ways to know (1977). "The Japanese think in poly-ocular vision...and they do not even bother to find out 'objectivity,' because they can go much further with cross-subjectivity" (Maruyama, 1977, p. 84). That is, the way human systems know is based on the differences between the various views of the members of that system.

This line of thinking is at least implied in the various team approaches to family therapy. Team approaches can be described as using Bateson's double or multiple description (a polyocular view) to get at the idea of system and understand what is going on in the therapy room (Palazzoli et al., 1978; de Shazer, 1982[b]). The family presents (shows) their polyocular description and simultaneously each member of the team develops his or her own description, all of which are placed in a collective (polyocular) context during the consultation break in the therapy session.

Thus the team (a system) evolves systemic notions about the family's (a system) problem, and more than one interactional description is used to describe the interaction during the session. Then "ideas" about those patterns or sequences within a context start to evolve. When the team presents their mirror image back to the family in the form of a message, the family can receive a bonus, which results from the ability to map the team's intervention upon their own descriptions. Thus a difference can be noted. When this is a *different enough* difference, the intended bonus develops and changing is initiated.[4]

Since the couple (in the case example), like any human system, can be described as showing regularities or redundancies, changing or noticeable difference cannot be initiated unless there is some source of randomness that an intervention attempts to provide through the difference between the client's description and the therapist's. As Bateson put it,

> A sequence of events is said to be *random* if there is no way of predicting the next event of a given kind from the event or events that have preceded and if the system obeys the regularities of probability. Note that the events which we say are *random* are always members of some limited set. The fall of an honest coin is said to be *random*. At each throw, the probability of the next fall being heads or tails remains unchanged. But the randomness is within the limited set. It is heads or tails; no alternatives are to be considered. (Bateson, 1979, p. 230)

Between the intervention and the following session, the couple initiated some new, joint activities and some new, separate activities, and reduced their drug use. At the time of the intervention, neither the couple nor the team would have been able to predict these changes, particularly in light of the impasse. Further changes followed, including the elimination of the drug use and a drastic reduction in the frequency of arguments. These further changes frequently follow once changing is initiated, a process which Spiegel and Linn (1969) call the ripple effect.

---

[4]A team approach (and thus the polyocular view) is the ideal research setting for this type of comparative study. In addition to being useful for research tasks, a team approach is also valuable for training purposes. We have found the concept of *fit* (isomorphism, double description) to be more teachable and more readily usable for designing interventions when working than either the double bind map or the strange loop map because it is less time consuming and less cumbersome. See Footnotes 2 and 3.

CONCLUSION

The "solution" to the paradox puzzle suggested by the double description of the case example helps to clarify how changing is initiated. Rather than paradox being the agent of change, this view suggests instead that changing has something to do with the *fit* between the couple's pattern and the pattern of the intervention. The fit between the two is not exact, even though both descriptions can be mapped onto each other with a high degree of isomorphism. The difference between the two patterns can be seen to prompt a bonus, that is, the introduction of something new or random into the couple's system.

In no way do we mean to imply that the concepts of paradox, double bind, counter double bind, and strange/charmed-loops are somehow "wrong." Each is a good mapping tool, but it is important to remember the differences between maps and the territories represented. Paradoxes and loops are part of our descriptive tools and are useful only to the extent that they promote successful intervention. The difficulty arises when the concept becomes reified and paradox is seen as the change agent. This reification can prove to be a barrier that separates one subsystem from another in the therapy situation, thus obscuring the interactive, systemic nature of successful intervention.

We do suggest that the reified concept of paradox/paradoxical intervention is similar to a red herring in a murder mystery. Like the manner in which any witness gives a description, observations are grounded by "facts," and like any such story, observations are made from the observer's point of view—which includes biases. The paradox clue became a red herring as soon as it led therapists to think that the concept was somehow real and true (reification). Therefore, paradox was both the cause of human problems and the agent of change. This leads to applying paradoxes (as interventions) to problems which can be mapped more simply in other ways and therefore can use different interventions. This line of thinking can clear up the definitional muddle that Watson (1982) confirmed.

Unlike Sherlock Holmes or any sleuth in a murder mystery, we are not suggesting that our solution to the puzzle is "true" or the only one. Instead we suggest that the mirror image concept and the polyocular view are useful in designing effective interventions within the context of the usual therapeutic environment, and not just post hoc explanations. Over the past six years, we have found these concepts useful with a large number of clients with a wide range of presenting problems or complaints. During this time, we have found no need to describe what clients are doing or what we are doing as "paradoxical."

POSTSCRIPT

Because the couple in our case example reported such radically different behavior than that which they had demonstrated prior to our intervention and the follow-up session, we were struck by the similarity between the intervention and a Zen koan. This connection is not a new one (Watts, 1961). In terms of the so-called pragmatic effects of the intervention (the causal relationship probably is not this simple), the couple did not try to figure out the message in Western fashion. They responded more in an Eastern way, similar to the Zen student's new behavior of leaping up, grabbing the monk's stick, and screaming "nonsense." Our explanation is not very useful as it explains by using the unexplainable koan. But this is the Zen way of doing things!

REFERENCES

Bateson, G., Jackson, D. D., Haley, J., & Weakland, J. H. Toward a theory of schizophrenia. *Behavioral Science*, 1956, *1*, (4), 251–264.

Bateson, G. *Mind and nature: A necessary unity*. New York: Dutton, 1979.

Christie, A., Sayers, D., Chesterton, G. K., & Certain Other Members of the Detection Club. *The floating admiral*. New York: Charter, 1980.

Cronen, V., Johnson, K., & Lannamann, J. Paradoxes, double binds, and reflexive loops: An alternative theoretical perspective, *Family process*, 1982, *21*, (1).

de Shazer, S. Some conceptual distinctions are more useful than others. *Family Process*, 1982, *21*, (1), 71–84. (a)

de Shazer, S. *Patterns of brief family therapy*. New York: Guilford, 1982. (b)

Hofstadter, D. R. *Gödel, Escher, Bach: An eternal golden braid*. New York: Basic Books, 1979.

Maruyama, M. Heterogenistics: An epistemological restructuring of biological and social sciences, *Cybernetica*, 1977, *20*, 69–86.

Nahm, M. C. *Selections from early Greek philosophy*. New York: Appleton-Century-Crofts, 1964.

O'Hanlon, B. Strategic pattern intervention. *Journal of Strategic and Systemic Therapies*, 1982, *1*, (4), 26–33.

The Oxford English Dictionary, Vol. VII. Oxford: Clarendon Press, 1961, 450.

Quine, W. V. *The Ways of Paradox and Other Essays* (rev. ed.). Cambridge: Harvard, 1976.

Selvini-Palazzoli, M., Cecchin, G., Prata, G., & Boscolo, L. *Paradox and Counterparadox*. New York: Aronson, 1978.

Spiegel, H., & Linn, L. The "ripple effect" following adjunct hypnosis in analytic psychotherapy. *American Journal of Psychiatry*, 1969, *126*, 53–58.

Tomm, K. Clinical Applications of Strange Loop Theory, Paper presented at the *Brief Family Therapy Center's Distinguished Speakers' Program*, 1982.

Warner, J. Paradox and the eye of the beholder. *Underground Railroad*, 1982, *3*, (4).

Watson, C. *A Delphi study on paradox in therapy*, 1982, unpublished manuscript.

Watts, A. *Psychotherapy east & west*, New York: Pantheon, 1961.

Watzlawick, P., Beavin, J., & Jackson, D. D. *Pragmatics of human communication*. New York: Norton, 1967.

Wilden, A. *System and structure* (2nd ed.). London: Tavistock, 1980.

10

Contradiction and Its Resolution among the Psychotherapies: Results of a Preliminary Investigation*

by Michael J. Bopp, Ph.D.

INTRODUCTION

Psychotherapy has generated a vast array of sophisticated methods and constructs. Currently, much is known about the promotion of human change. Yet pervading the field, there persists a marked conceptual confusion. Amidst the motley assortment of ideas and methods, there has been little hope for unification. Despite the current popularity of "eclecticism," there are still dogmatic, insular claims by proponents of various theories that their own model is more "true" than the others. There is also the sense that what we do as psychotherapists is more an art than a science, and that we have not yet reached the status of "real doctors" (Berne, 1966).

This lack of coherence reflects the preparadigmatic phase of science, as evidenced by: (1) the presence of numerous competing perspectives; (2) the sense that the field, like that of physical optics before Newton, can be characterized as "something less than science" (Kuhn, 1970, p. 13); (3) the continued need to justify premises each time a new claim is made rather than take them for granted (Kuhn, 1970).

*The author wishes to thank Sam Kirschner, Dierdre Kramer, and Karyn Scher for suggestions and constructive criticisms.

Earlier in the development of psychology in general and psychotherapy in particular, efforts were made to fit facts to the Newtonian framework. Such attempts have met with quite limited success (Buss, 1975, 1979; Matson, 1964; Overton & Reese, 1973; Ratner, 1971; Reese & Overton, 1970; Rychlak, 1968, 1976). Subsequently, the general systems outlook became influential (e.g., Bertalanffy, 1968; Miller, 1975; Watzlawick et al., 1967; Watzlawick et al., 1974). At least partially an outgrowth of the influence of the systems approach, there has been a recent proliferation of philosophical activity, particularly within family therapy (e.g., Keeney, 1982; Keeney & Sprenkle, 1982; Liddle, 1982). With such work still in the divergent stage of concept generation, there is if anything less conceptual consolidation than before (Coyne, 1982).

A premise of this chapter is that while still far from consolidated, a paradigm is in fact emerging within social science. This paradigm is based on dialectical philosophy. It is not new, but dates back to ancient Greece. According to Rychlak (1968), an ongoing oscillation has existed between demonstrative (empirical, reductionistic, analytic) and dialectical (holistic, synthetic) world views over the course of Western scientific history. Particularly with the conceptual shifts of the 20th century, physics and the other physical sciences have been moving away from Newtonian demonstrative metaphors toward ones more closely affiliated with dialectical notions such as contextualism, holism, relativity, pluralism, and paradox (Koplowitz, 1978; Oppenheimer, 1956; Riegel, 1973; Schrodinger, 1967; Sinnott, 1981; Zukav, 1979).

In social science in general, numerous developments mark a similar progression (Buss, 1979; Riegel, 1973, 1979). Within the particular branch of social science called psychotherapy, a crucial development has been the increasingly active interest in phenomena that fall under the rubric of contradiction and paradox. Of course paradox is important in the context of this book for its technical relevance to the promotion of therapeutic change. Yet it has far-reaching consequences on a metatheoretical level.

Paradox implies a type of illogic, a contradiction. It pertains to two (or more) apparently opposed statements regarded as simultaneously true. Taken together the two statements seem absurd; what makes them a paradox is that they also seem true. A paradox is experienced as unsettling and provocative because it breaches a fundamental assumption of our understanding. This assumption is so deeply ingrained as to be taken for granted; it is a facet of "common sense."

To grasp why a paradox is so unsettling requires that one struggle to reveal just what assumption is being violated. That assumption is the Aristotelian premise of noncontradiction, namely that an assertion and its negation cannot both be true (Aristotle, 1952; Riegel, 1973). In Western culture this is a perceptual invariant: A desk is just that, a desk. Those who would view it otherwise we pronounce to have lapsed from "reality testing" and to merit the terms "delusional or hallucinatory" (Arieti, 1955).

Returning to metatheory, that which is so interesting about paradox in social science is that its pervasive relevance is forcing us to explore some conceptual unsettlements (anomalies, in Kuhn's terms). Indeed paradox has drawn us to reflect upon deeply embedded assumptions.

Outside the laboratory or therapy room we would regard the desk as just that. Our conceptual inclination in professional practice is to apply the same logic and think of an emotion, a stimulus, a behavior, or a thought as a singular, unipolar phenomenon. Yet the further the psychotherapeutic field develops in its understanding of such phenomena, the more it encounters bipolar or multipolar constructs and the less able it is to rely on implicit Aristotelian categories. Consequently, making sense of double binds, paradoxical injunctions, the contradictions of ambivalence, id-superego oppositions, hypnosis, and primary process thought generates the same unsettled feeling that would derive from viewing a desk as both itself and something else simultaneously. The more contradiction-laden concepts we reveal, the more pressure we feel to scrutinize our assumptions.

In a way, the psychotherapeutic field can be said to be becoming delusional, seeing double or multiple meanings where singularities had previously resided. Yet the current break with existing cognitive structures does not indicate a regression, but rather a step forward. In life-span developmental psychology, there is accumulating experimental evidence that the hypothetico-deductive, Aristotelian logic of formal operations is not, as presumed by Piaget (1967), the culmination of intellectual development. Instead there is much to support the existence of a more mature, "postformal operations" stage, central to which is the capacity to locate, appreciate, and integrate contradiction (Basseches, 1978, 1980; Clayton, 1975; Kegan, 1979; Koplowitz, 1978; Kramer, 1983; Riegel, 1973, 1976; Sinnott, 1981). Analogously, psychotherapy's current concern with paradox and contradiction suggests a reorganization to a higher stage of understanding.

That this reorganization is occurring is strengthened when we consider that paradoxical formulations have been appearing not just in one branch of psychotherapy, but across all of the major ones (Andolfi, 1974; Ascher, 1980; Ascher & Efran, 1978; Bopp, 1983; Esterson, 1970; Frankl, 1975; Haley, 1963; Mozdzierz et al., 1976; Raskin & Klein, 1976; Selvini-Palazzoli et al., 1978; Watzlawick et al., 1974; Weeks & L'Abate, 1979. See Weeks & L'Abate, 1982, for overview and integration). This reorganization is quite significant given the field's historical factionalism. Moreover, that such convergence culminates in a construct anomalous to conventional scientific logic suggests not only the possible emergence of a new order of understanding, but also that such a new order may have the potential to integrate diverse theoretical and practical perspectives. This claim gains additional support in light of the fact that the logic of contradiction, which a dialectical outlook applies to ontological problems, is also relevant to epistemological ones. That is, rather than trying to achieve a singular theoretical account, the dialectical approach attempts to synthesize contradictions among diverse perspectives at a higher level. Theoretical oppositions persist while a more integrative "truth" is forged.

Paradox is not the only concept signaling the increasing relevance of dialectical metatheory in psychotherapy. The following is an alignment of dialectical concepts with theoretical contributions in the literature that illustrate their application: (1) the premise of *bidirectional (interactive) or multiple causation* (e.g., Bandura, 1978; Bertalanffy, 1968; Jung, 1961; Koplowitz, 1978; Langs, 1976, 1978; Progoff, 1973; Riegel, 1973; Rogers, 1980[b]; Stanton, 1980); (2) the concern with *organization and related notions of system, context, and structure* (Boszormenyi-Nagy & Spark, 1973; Minuchin, 1974; Speck & Attneave, 1973; Stanton, 1980); (3) the premise of *the ontological primacy of directed (i.e., developmental) motion and change* (Boszormenyi-Nagy & Spark, 1973; Haley, 1973; Rogers, 1980[b]; Weeks & Wright, 1979; (4) the premise of *the ontological primacy of relations* (Boszormenyi-Nagy & Spark, 1973; Esterson, 1970; Langs, 1976; Rogers, 1980[b]); and (5) the attention to *the integration of change and stability,* coined in dialectical terms, *transformation or "movement through forms"* (Basseches, 1978, 1980; Watzlawick et al., 1974; Weeks & L'Abate, 1982).

The goal of this chapter, like that of the study (Bopp, 1983) from which it has been abstracted, is to attempt a metatheoretical clarification in psychotherapy. Its intention is to illustrate how the psychotherapies manifest a movement toward an overarching dialectical world view. The claim is not that this world view is fully formed, or that there is a perfect alignment between theory and underlying metatheory in psychotherapy. Rather, this is a preliminary effort to achieve some congruence between what we do as therapists and an appropriate, corresponding model of science.

While the Bopp study's concern was the presence of an overall dialectical metatheory among psychotherapies, the present chapter will focus only on those aspects of dialectical metatheory germane to paradox, the concern of this book. Thus we will exclude consideration of other central categories in the dialectic world view, such as motion and relationship. Instead, we will focus on contradiction, the metatheoretical underpinning of applied paradox (Esterson, 1970; Weeks & L'Abate, 1982).

METHOD

The data for this study included a lengthy interview (1 to 2½ hours) with a prominent psychotherapist/theorist from each of the following four schools: humanistic, cognitive-behavioral, family therapy, and psychoanalytic. The interviewees were Carl Rogers, Ph.D., Arnold Lazarus, Ph.D., Ivan Boszormenyi-Nagy, M.D., and Robert Langs, M.D., respectively.

The interview transcripts were coded using the Dialectical Schemata framework (Basseches, 1978, 1980; Bopp & Basseches, 1981). This framework consists of an inventory of moves in thought or conceptual strategies which characterize various aspects of dialectical thinking. It was compiled through a survey of the types of thinking employed by philosophers like Hegel and Marx, who are clearly associated with the dialectical framework. Like the experimental approach of Piaget (1967) and Kohlberg (1971), the procedure involved demonstrating the logical organization of the subjects' thinking. Like the transformational grammar method (Chomsky, 1968), its intention was to illuminate "deep structure" modes of understanding as they interact with an array of specific thought contents. It was also similar to the work of Bandler and Grinder (1975) as it involved generating a model that cuts across schools of psychotherapeutic practice despite marked differences at the level of theory. In short, this study constituted a preliminary exploratory effort to demonstrate the presence of a common style of understanding based on dialectics.

Each interview was semistructured and open ended insofar as it revolved around five core questions chosen to generate discussion rather than lead to definitive "answers." The questions were:

1. How do you explain how people change—in general, and by means of psychotherapy?
2. What would you say is the goal of psychotherapy? How do you establish that "cure" or "successful outcome" has taken place?
3. How would you explain psychopathology in nontheoretical, common sense terms? Similarly, how do you understand the etiology of psychopathology?

The following questions pertained to case material (either hypothetical or actual) which the subject had presented as indicative of successfully conducted therapy within his particular model:

4. What were the most important changes engendered in the client(s) over the course of therapy? What defined success in the treatment of this case?
5. What features of treatment were most responsible for its efficacy? How do you understand the cause of the successful results obtained?

The questions were sent to subjects prior to the meeting.

In addition, the interview was interactive. The interviewer was an active participant in dialogue in the form of posing questions, introducing alternative viewpoints, and pursuing digressions from the core topics that appeared useful for exploring implicit cognitive and philosphical underpinnings. Finally, the interviews were in depth in that the probing was thorough and comprehensive, intending to document not only the substantive content of the interviewee's thinking, but also the general forms of cognitive organization (Basseches, 1978).

As defined by Basseches (1978, p. 46), dialectic is "developmental transformation (i.e., developmental movement through forms) which occurs via constitutive and interactive relationships." To think dialectically is to approach the process of understanding from the vantage point of this definition. Basseches has generated 24 schemata representative of this approach. One such schema involves the location of contradictions, while another pertains to assertion of the existence of relations, the limits of separation, and the value of relatedness. The 24 schemata operate as an organized whole of understanding, a world view. In the following text, we will consider only those schemata relevant to contradiction, the central concern of this chapter. The reader should bear in mind that what follows represents only part of the type of thinking employed by dialectical thinkers. Elaboration is contained in Bopp (1983).

Definitions[1]

One approach to contradiction in dialectical metatheory is to *recognize and describe thesis-antithesis-synthesis (T-A-S) movement.* In these terms, a thesis can be an idea, element, or force and its antithesis is that which is opposite, excluded from, outside of, apart from, or contrary to the thesis. The synthesis is an integration of

---

[1]From Basseches, 1978; Bopp and Basseches, 1981.

thesis and antithesis. Synthesis is usually more complex than either of its predecessors because it includes both of them, brings them into relation, and binds them. T-A-S movement may be cyclical in that the synthesis becomes the thesis for a new antithesis. That is, to the extent that a synthesis is not all-inclusive, that which has been left out of it constitutes a second antithesis.

Relatedly, theses and antitheses can be regarded as correlative. Applying this mode of understanding, one *recognizes the correlativity of a thing and its other.* To view things as correlative, a thinker sees them as relative to each other. Each is in some sense dependent on the other. This leads to the *notion of the interdependence of opposites.* To assert that the concept of figure depends on that of ground, and vice versa, is to appeal to this idea. The *recognition of composition by interpenetrating opposites* is another corollary of the correlativity construct. To apply this strategy is to regard whatever can be seen as a synthesis in terms of the thesis and antithesis which compose it.

When the "things" under consideration are understood in formal terms (i.e., as structures or systems) then sources of contradiction can be found either within or outside the form. Such thinking is termed the *location (or description of the process of emergence) of contradictions or sources of disequilibrium within a system (form) or between a system (form) and external forces and elements antithetical to the system's (form's) structure.* In other words, through the application of this schema, one attends to forms and seeks to locate sources of disequilibrium either internal or external to them. The *understanding of the resolution of such contradictions* involves a *notion of transformation in developmental direction.* This transformation is a "metaformal" movement through forms, consistent with the definition of *dialectic* above.

The italicized phrases above are the names of Dialectical Schemata. They represent facets of dialectical thought. In the following section, we will consider how these schemata apply to thinking about psychotherapy.

RESULTS

The Humanistic Tradition: Carl Rogers

Earlier in his career, Rogers (e.g., 1959) tried to establish a conceptual foundation for his phenomenological orientation. At the time, the empiricist perspective held prominence in American psychology and there was not sufficient conceptual coherence to hold forth an alternative position supportive of phenomenology (Rogers, 1980[b]). As discussed in the interview (Bopp, 1983) and in Rogers (1980[b]), numerous developments have taken place recently, particularly in the natural sciences, that have given support to such an alternative position. In the interview, Rogers refers to findings from chemistry, biology, and physics implicative of dialectical concepts such as pervasive complexity, ontological interconnectedness, the interdependence of change and form, and the constructive role of consciousness in the shaping of scientific knowledge. As he states in the interview, Rogers experiences a sense of satisfaction now because he views these advances as facilitating the metatheoretical frame for which he had searched.

The following excerpt demonstrates the application of the contradiction metaconstruct, that is, it involves the *location of contradiction or sources of disequilibrium between a form and elements external to the form's structure.* Herein, psychopathology is described in terms of an external contradiction between the self-concept (the form) and organismic experience.

Rogers: I think that we *build* [defensiveness] *in*[2] socially, that the child ...gradually *builds a self-concept which is not matched by what the organism is experiencing.* And then, since they are trying to live by this self-concept, that means they *must defend themselves against some of their organic experiencing.* (pp. 9–10)[3]

Here, the self-concept is construed in terms of a structure that the individual "builds."[4] This internal form comes to be at odds with "organic experiencing." In other words, the self-concept can integrate only certain aspects of the person. These aspects therefore exist in contradiction to the self-system. The threat to the equilibrium of the self-concept implied by the organic experience is conveyed in the notion that there must be a defense against that experience. That is, the defense is an aspect of the self-concept's functioning whose purpose is to preserve the current level of structural organization in the self-concept.

Rogers expands this line of thinking subsequently:

---

[2]Italicized phrases in this and the following quoted passages represent clear manifestations of particular dialectical schemata.

[3]Page numbers for this and the following quoted passages (unless otherwise identified) refer to locations of the quote within the interview transcript (Bopp, 1983).

[4]The formal aspects of the self-concept had been discussed earlier in the interview and in published sources (Rogers, 1951, 1959, 1980[a]). When viewed from an external frame of reference, the self-concept is termed the *self-structure* (Rogers, 1959).

Rogers: I want to say in advance, I don't like the term "psychopathology," but I don't know of any other general area that covers it. Anyway, *disharmony within the self, maladjustment,* or *psychopathology,* is, in my estimation, a fairly extreme *discrepancy between the self-concept, on the one hand, and what is actually being experienced.*   (p. 10)

In this passage, psychopathology is being defined in terms of disequilibrium (disharmony, maladjustment). The source of this disequilibrium is the "discrepancy" between the self-concept and the experience which is antithetical to it.

The *understanding of the resolution of disequilibrium or contradiction in terms of developmental transformation* is a related facet of dialectical thinking. In effect, it provides the thinker with a way to grasp the resolution of a problem located by attention to contradiction. The following illustration of this metaconstruct pertains to the process of growth in psychotherapy.

Rogers: ...as one becomes *more integrated, more whole,* one also demands more of relationships, demands more of life, and so there are *new crises at a higher level of complexity.* ... *I've been very much fascinated by Prigogine's work—the Belgian scientist, chemist—and I think that his notion of the process of change is quite fitting to psychotherapy. That, in a chemical molecule or in an organism, as the perturbations increase, change is becoming necessary, it's forced.* And *that change is to a higher degree of complexity where such complex situations are the most liable to change,* ...change is more an expectation, ... It means that, yes, *you reach a new level of integration.* And so does that mean that you can stop growing? No, it means that the *new challenges will be of a different order and that you will in time produce new perturbations which will produce more change.*   (pp. 15–16)

This passage is an outgrowth of an earlier discussion about reconciling discrepant aspects of self. Rogers is stating here that the resolution of an earlier contradiction ("as one becomes more integrated, more whole") generates its own emergent contradictions ("new crises at a higher level of complexity"). In other words, the solution to one problem is the basis of a new one. This resolution process is synthetic. The discrepancies from earlier contradictions are not solved, in the sense of rejecting thesis in favor of antithesis (or vice versa), but are integrated within a new, higher level of organization. This movement to the next level is a movement through forms, or dialectical transformation. Moreover, in Rogers' view and consistent with dialectical formulations, this process is quite developmental, as suggested by these phrases: "more integrated," "more whole," "higher level of complexity," "new challenges of a different order." Particularly interesting in terms of this developmental aspect of dialectical thinking is the notion that the transformation process, while providing greater stability ("more integrated," "more whole"), paradoxically generates greater movement ("change is becoming necessary, it's forced").

Let us turn now to another aspect of dialectical thought relevant to the contradiction heuristic, namely *the assertion of the correlativity of a thing and its other.* Applied to the human condition, this metaconstruct has important implications. Rogers has consistently maintained the position that one's self becomes known as a function of other (Rogers, 1961, 1980[b]). This is the priority of empathy in human development. By being able to temporarily let go of one's self and experience the other's reality (i.e., the process of empathy), it becomes possible for each person to realize that that which at first appears "other," that is, not self, is also self. That is, it becomes possible to experience how one's self and another's self are the same.

This is one aspect of correlativity, namely, the notion of *interpenetrating opposites:* Though A and not-A from one perspective seem antithetical, from another A is not-A as not-A is A.

Rogers: . . . it depends on *empathy.* You could tell me about your reality. Unless I am willing to try to sort of *let myself go and understand it from inside,* your telling me about it may not produce much of any effect. It may have a little usefulness, but to *really experience a shared reality,* I have to try to understand yours from the inside and you have to understand mine from the inside. (p. 18)

* * * * *

. . . *it means letting myself go, knowing that I can come back to myself.*
(p. 19)

Interviewer: . . . So that to the extent that I can empathize with you, then I am you and I am yet myself.

Rogers: That's right, uh-hm. Buber's I-Thou relationship. (p. 20)

Starting from self, one becomes other ("to try to understand [your reality] from the inside") and vice versa, and returns to self with a clarified and enlarged reality. Self and other, in the context of empathy, become the same while retaining their respective uniquenesses ("knowing that I can come back to myself"). Further, self and other paradoxically become more defined as self and other by virtue of realizing their sameness. This is the notion of the *interdependence of opposites,* another aspect of correlativity. Referring to change in psychotherapy, Rogers states:

Rogers: . . . as I understand you from inside, you become more able to understand yourself. . . . (p. 22)

In other words, an outgrowth of empathic communication is a clearer delineation of self (which of course applies also to other). Self could not exist without other, nor other without self.

Pairs such as thing and its other, self and not-self, and self and other are instances of antithesis. Turning now to the conceptual strategy, the *recognition and description of thesis-antithesis-synthesis movement*, we can derive a clearer understanding of the *synthetic* nature of dialectical change. The following passage occurred in the context of the discussion from which the correlativity excerpts above were drawn:

> **Rogers:** Suppose *you hold some values* that are very *different from my own.* Our tendency is to say, "Well, you're bad then, or you're different," or something. *If I can let go of my values for a moment so as to really see what your values seem like inside,* then that will *enlarge my reality* and I can return also to the values that I hold. I probably will *return a little bit changed* from having seen someone else's values differently.... being willing to step out of myself for the moment out of knowing that I can return within that self. That's why it needs, ideally, it needs a fairly secure individual to do that, to let go of self and really see what it seems like from the other side. (p. 19)

In the opening line, Rogers establishes a thesis-antithesis relationship in terms of values: "Suppose you hold some values [antithesis] that are different from my own [thesis]." The relationship between the two sets of values is antithetical in the sense of an apparent mutual exclusivity.

Rogers then points to the tendency to invalidate the other's values, consistent with the logical formulation, A *or* not-A: "Our tendency is to say, 'Well, you're bad then, or you're different,' or something." His thinking then attends to the notion of correlativity ("see what your values seem like inside"), which leads to integration ("will enlarge my reality").

This resolution is not linear. It does not consist of an exclusion of one set of values as "bad" in favor of the other, presumed good; nor is it a compromise or alloy of the two values. The assertion that this process requires a "secure" individual implies that the empathizing person remains well defined unto himself, though nonetheless "changed." On the contrary, the resolution entails a synthetic integration at a higher level. The two sets of values remain polarized (rather than compromised), but now under the rubric of a more integrated and differentiated "enlarge[d]...reality." Apparently unrelated prior to synthesis, they are now brought into relation in terms of their correlativity. Note also the ongoing presence of contradiction in the resolution as if: I remain the same while yet I have changed. Finally, from the words *change* and *enlarge my reality,* we can also infer that the movement in this thesis-antithesis-synthesis process is developmental.

The Behavioral Tradition: Arnold Lazarus

The use of a logic of contradiction in the Lazarus interview was prominent in Lazarus's thinking about the case of Ms. A, a client whom he regarded as successfully treated by means of multimodal therapy. Before considering this material, an important caveat must be discussed. Made quite clear in Lazarus's recent writings (1981) and in the interview from which the following passages were extracted, the premise of technical pluralism is crucial in this model. That is, Lazarus does not advocate using the same psychotherapeutic approach with each client. Rather, based on a multimodal assessment across seven dimensions (behavior, affect, sensation, imagery, cognition, interpersonal functioning, biology), the therapist selects treatment methods specifically tailored to the needs of each client. Thus while his thinking and practice with Ms. A may be characterized as representing features of dialectic metatheory, he could proceed much differently with another client.

Let us turn now to the first passage.

Lazarus: ...she *couldn't tolerate ambiguity* was really one thing...so that there's much more of a *toleration-of-differences view.* We call it a kind of *relativity notion,* you see, that she has acquired *instead of an absolutistic idea* of *right/wrong, good/bad. The dichotomy has now become a continuum.* That's the major kind of *cognitive restructuring* that I would talk about. (pp. 47–48)

This passage illustrates that mode of dialectical thinking which follows along *thesis-antithesis-synthesis lines.* Lazarus describes the client as originally unable to "tolerate ambiguity." This absolutistic approach was based on thesis-antithesis "dichotom[ies]" such as right/wrong and good/bad. The implication is that Ms. A's inability to tolerate ambiguity was based on an either-or type of thinking through which antitheses (right/wrong and good/bad) were irreconcilable ("absolutistic").

Lazarus asserts that Ms. A made progress in therapy when she acquired a "toleration-of-differences view," such that she could integrate dichotomous perspectives within a synthetic whole. The idea of bringing into relation apparently mutually exclusive options (antitheses) is conveyed in the words: "The dichotomy has now become a continuum." That is, the fact that they can now coexist along a common dimension, a continuum, means that they have been brought into relation whereas previously they had been distinct. Such integration is also transformational. If we regard cognitive structure as a form and its "restructuring" in a positive direction as a movement through forms, then we have an instance of the metaformal aspect of dialectical thinking through which the thinker seeks to comprehend transformation.

The preceding excerpt demonstrated an attention to contradiction and its resolution in Lazarus's thinking about the client's cognitions. Turning now to the next excerpt, we can observe a similar mode of understanding applied to the therapeutic interaction. Continuing his discussion of the material cited above, Lazarus stated that "there was an all-or-none that just changed into a whole continuum of time and effort and meaning and value" (p. 49). In response to the interviewer's question of how he as Ms. A's therapist effectuated such progress, Lazarus states:

Lazarus: *Challenging* all the time, pointing out "Look what you are doing again and again and again. What can you do? Let's get the *options,* let's get the *alternatives. There is not one way of viewing it. It is not either right or wrong.* This idea of you are either for me or against me is ridiculous. There are *many, many possibilities.* Let's get you to look at them. What are they?" This was a very important part of the therapy, the *constructive alternativism,* if you will. (p. 49)

In this passage, Lazarus is employing the dialectical concern for interaction as a source of movement. The mode of exchange between himself and Ms. A entails a drawing to the client's attention of "options," "alternatives," and "possibilities." As the therapist, Lazarus establishes himself as an antithesis to Ms. A. In other words, he contradicts her contradictions or negates the negation (Engels, 1940). In contrast to her outlook of "one way of viewing it," and it's "either right or wrong," he is continuously challenging. That is, he repeatedly poses the antithetical position; for example, "There are many, many possibilities" "let's get the alternatives."

Whereas the first Lazarus passage cited above pertained particularly to the cognitive dimension, Lazarus subsequently asserts (p. 50) that this method of "constructive alternativism" also applied with regard to each dimension of human functioning listed above (behavior, affect, sensation, etc.).

The course of thinking described above is particularly interesting metatheoretically. It provides a clear demonstration of transformational dialectical ideas by a theorist whose roots are in the behaviorist tradition. This tradition has strong affiliations with reductionistic, demonstrative (Rychlak, 1968) and mechanistic (Overton &

Reese, 1981) assumptions. Lazarus's line of thinking indicates a shift from an exclusively linear, unidirectional, environmentalist outlook toward one which can accommodate, at least in part, organismic, interactive, and paradoxical features. Such a progression seems to correspond to the increasing theoretical appreciation among behaviorists of cognitive parameters in the regulation of behavior (e.g., Bandura, 1978; Mischel, 1973). That is, by attributing a measure of inner control to the organism, one establishes metatheoretically an interplay between person and environment where previously person had been regarded as passive and reactive and environment as unidirectionally causative.

Moreover, with the introduction of cognitive events as explanatory constructs, one is challenged to account for the numerous contradictions inherent in subjective phenomenology (ironically, these were among the conceptual problems that early behaviorism had tried to circumvent by its staunch objectivism). The sources of these developments are of course complex. For a fuller discussion, see Berman, 1978; Bandura, 1978; Mischel, 1973; Staats, 1981.

In any event, Lazarus's thinking in terms of Ms. A's therapeutic gains and his role in promoting them underscores the presence of attention to contradiction (and the broader transformational constructs of the dialectical world view) in at least one mode of cognitive behavior therapy. In particular, we have seen an effort to understand a particular client's "psychopathology" in terms of unresolved contradiction and an effort to promote therapeutic change through a playing out of interpersonal contradiction between client and therapist. A fuller account of Lazarus's use of this mode of understanding (Bopp, 1983) would illustrate his efforts to synthesize the contradictions among theories and therapeutic techniques which at the level of theory appear mutually exclusive (Lazarus, 1967, 1976, 1981).

The Family Therapy Tradition: Ivan Boszormenyi-Nagy

Family therapy, perhaps more than other schools of psychotherapy, has moved a considerable distance toward the articulation of an elaborated dialectical metatheory (Bopp & Weeks, 1984). In particular, Boszormenyi-Nagy has been quite explicit in his appeal to dialectical metaconstructs in the construction of his family model (Boszormenyi-Nagy, 1965[a], 1965[b]), giving rise to "dialectical intergenerational family therapy" (Boszormenyi-Nagy & Spark, 1973), a predecessor of the current "contextual family therapy" (Boszormenyi-Nagy & Ulrich, 1981). Thus the interpretation of the Boszormenyi-Nagy interview was unique insofar as less translation was required to get from theory to underlying metatheory: With Boszormenyi-Nagy the dialectical metatheory is quite explicit.

Leading into the following passage, the interviewer had asked Boszormenyi-Nagy to explain the logic he had used earlier in referring to an "internal contradiction."

Boszormenyi-Nagy: Well, *Hegel's dialectical thinking* is the most advanced model as far as I can think of for this and I try to make some connections there in one of the chapters of *Invisible Loyalties*. So then it's *inevitable that every thesis can be considered from its opposite, so the self from the side of the nonself or the other. And then it has to be placed in some kind of synthetic transcendence of the antithesis. That's the point. So there's nothing tragic about built-in antithesis and deal with it. How to transcend it, that's the problem. That's the way. That's the way. Not just the problem, but that's the way.* (pp. 11–12)

Here we have a clear instance of *attention to contradiction.* In the sentence, "So then, it's inevitable that every thesis can be considered from its opposite, so the self from the side of the nonself or the other," Boszormenyi-Nagy is pointing out that corollary of attention to contradiction termed the *correlativity of a thing and its other.* That is, he is explaining the constitution of a contradiction or antithetical relationship by asserting that a particular thesis can be understood from a consideration not just of itself but also of its opposite, the nonself or other.

This formulation is a central facet of the dialectical world view. Contrary to the Aristotelian premise of "identity," by which a thing is seen as having a singular, intrinsic nature, this formulation asserts that things are constituted as a function of their *relations* to other things. That is, self does not have an independent, monadic, ontological status, but becomes known as a function of its relation to not-self or other. When this metatheoretical assumption is applied on a theoretical level, it has major utility in the understanding of personality development.

Now one is led to understand psychic functioning not only on the basis of internal dynamics, but also in terms of how these dynamics are played out interpersonally. While this insight may appear obvious currently, it is useful to recall that the shift from an instinct-based personality theory to a more interpersonal outlook occurred only late in Freud's career and marked a conceptual advance in psychoanalytic theory when elaborated by members of the object relations school (e.g., Guntrip, 1956, 1971). Such thinking is also at the core of both Boszormenyi-Nagy's model of family therapy (as discussed presently) and Rogers's model of client-centered therapy (discussed earlier).

Returning to the interview passage above, we have just considered Boszormenyi-Nagy's establishment of the interdependence of a thesis and antithesis. Following this, his thinking attends to the process of movement toward resolution of antithesis. In other words, he applies an intellectual strategy called the *recognition and description of thesis-antithesis-synthesis movement*. This sequence of thoughts requires little interpretation as Boszormenyi-Nagy asserts the need for a "synthetic transcendence of the antithesis." Moreover, consistent with dialectical assumptions, the contradictoriness of an antithetical relationship is regarded as valuable, though problematic: "So there's nothing tragic about built-in antithesis. . . . How to transcend it, that's the problem. That's the way." Note the persisting contradictory complexity of the transcendence's being "Not just the problem, but. . .the way." While a resolution to the earlier antithesis, the "synthetic transcendence" still contains the problem; it is simultaneously a problem and a solution.

The mode of thinking has direct applicability to the process of contextual therapy. The following excerpt emanates from a discussion of the treatment of a delinquent. The author had asked Boszormenyi-Nagy to explain how in his model such a client would have "entitlement" while being blameworthy for destructive behavior.

Boszormenyi-Nagy: *That's the internal contradiction. Therefore,* the therapist, *the contextual therapist, has a dual approach to it. In one sense he certainly doesn't like destructive relating in the current behavior. On the other hand, he is willing to [trace]? partiality, which means empathy plus crediting, to where it belongs.* That means the past relationships of this person as a victimized child. And on that level there is a great deal of willingness to be partial without reservation from that point of view. Now that I have been partial to you on that basis, now I invite you to look at how you can be unjust to others, and *at that point, the person can hear me much better because I have been partial to his side.*   (p. 10)

This passage refers to the "revolving slate" notion (Boszormenyi-Nagy & Spark, 1973). That is, the individual's currently destructive behavior is an outgrowth of an injustice earlier inflicted on him. Prior to this passage, Boszormenyi-Nagy had criticized the traditional individual therapy model for focusing exclusively on the pathological, that is, negative aspects of the individual.

In contrast, the contextual model seeks to reveal the internal contradiction. While there is a need for the delinquent to be held accountable for misdeeds ("blameworthy"), there is also a need for partiality toward his side; that is, this individual is "entitled" to "empathy plus crediting." By thus addressing the original victimization, the submerged contradiction is drawn out, whereas in a traditional therapy model only one of its poles (the pathology) presumably would be addressed. Such a "dual approach" in contextual therapy rests explicitly on the heuristic category of contradiction.

A further implication of Boszormenyi-Nagy's thinking for the metaconstruct of contradiction pertains expressly to epistemology. Given that interpersonal systems are composed of two or more individuals, contradictions will be apparent in their construction of reality since the individual's perspectives will never be identical. With respect to the dyadic context, pressure is exerted on the theorist to devise a way to grasp a shared construction of "reality" despite contradiction between the two parties. This is demonstrated in Langs's concept of the "bipersonal field" (Langs, 1976) and Rogers's concept of empathy as "shared reality" (Rogers, 1980[b]).

When multiple parties comprise the social context, as in the case of a family, the conceptual demand is greater. An outgrowth of this problem is a recent proliferation of work in the family therapy literature to devise a sophisticated epistemological model (see 1982 editions of *Family Process*). Boszormenyi-Nagy addresses this issue in the form of a "multilaterality of fairness" (interview, Bopp, 1983, p. 25; Boszormenyi-Nagy & Ulrich, 1981, p. 25). Analogous to Rogers's effort to achieve a shared reality with the client, Boszormenyi-Nagy, through the application of this concept, strives to be "partial" to the perspective of each member of the social system involved. To the extent that each person has a unique and valid perspective, the family therapist encounters an array of epistemological contradictions. With the integration of each successive perspective into a broader multilateral understanding, there has been a resolution of contradiction and a corresponding epistemological transformation. This mode of understanding is far removed from unipolar, reductionistic epistemological premises.

The Psychoanalytic Tradition: Robert Langs

The presence of dialectical metatheory in psychoanalysis has been detailed in several sources (Fenichel, 1967; Rychlak, 1968, 1976; Stierlin, 1969). Yet the connections between the two intellectual traditions (psychoanalysis and dialectics) are uneasy, due at least partially to a confusion in psychoanalytic theory vis-à-vis goals of an ultimate reductionism (Rychlak, 1976). As touched on briefly above, however, it is in Freud's and his followers' work that invaluable contributions to the understanding of human contradictions were developed. Among such phenomena are interplays between: id and reality, unconscious and conscious, primary process and secondary process, eros and thanatos, reality and pleasure principles, and good and bad object representations. Through psychoanalysis, we have learned of bipolar crises of development (Erikson, 1963) and of the "synthetic" functions of the ego (Nunberg, 1960).

The metatheoretical strategy underlying such constructs is illustrated in the words of Freud:

> We find, then, that certain among the impulses to perversion occur regularly as pairs of opposites and this, . . . has a high theoretical significance.
>
> * * * * *
>
> An especially prominent part is played as factors in the formation of symptoms in psychoneuroses by the component instincts which emerge for the most part as pairs of opposites. . . .
>
> (Freud, 1962, pp. 50, 58)

Robert Langs has contributed a great deal toward clarifying and extending the Freudian mode of treatment. From his work in this area a number of constructs pertinent to the present discussion of contradiction in psychoanalysis can be brought to light. In particular, through discussion of the following excerpts, we will consider the applicability of the contradiction metaconstruct to: (1) the constitution of psychopathology as "madness" (Langs, in preparation); (2) the functioning of the psychotherapeutic frame; and (3) the nature of therapeutic communication.

The first instance of an *appeal to the notion of contradiction* is quite explicit. In the interview from which the following passages were extracted, Langs repeatedly associated his concept of madness with the term *contradiction*. When asked to elaborate he states:

Langs: *I think subjective madness is to experience contradiction, an unresolvable contradiction:* I'm alive but I'm gonna be dead, I was born but I was born to die, I'm thinking this thought but now I'm thinking another thought, I'm thinking an opposite thought, . . . *bearable contradictions lead to madness. . . . Unbearable contradictions create craziness and madness. Subjectively experienced unbearable contradiction is subjectively experienced madness. It really does drive you crazy when somebody gives you contradictory messages and then when you internalize them you begin to feel crazy.* (p. 55)

This is a particularly straightforward specification of contradiction. Langs states that bearable contradiction "leads to" madness while unbearable contradiction "creates" madness. He also gives examples of unresolvable contradictions such as, "I was born, but I was born to die." He further asserts that contradiction can occur interpersonally, as in the case of "somebody giv[ing] you contradictory messages" or intrapersonally, as when such messages become internalized, leading one to "begin to feel crazy."

A second instance of appeal to contradiction occurs in regard to Langs's concept of the therapeutic frame, defined as "a metaphor for the implicit and explicit ground rules of psychotherapy or psychoanalysis [through which to] create a basic hold for the therapeutic interaction" (Langs, 1982, p. 726). The management of the frame, in terms of set time, set place, set fee, confidentiality, relative anonymity of the therapist, and so on is considered indispensable to the proper conduct of effective psychotherapy (Langs, 1976, 1978, 1982).

In dialectical terms, the frame is a form construct that describes a set of physical and psychological boundaries and contains internal contradictions. When the frame is secure, it facilitates the experience of madness by both patient and therapist, defined above as internal contradictions such as being born to die. It is imperative in such a context that the therapist manage his own madness, that is, successfully tolerate contradictions so as not to impose them onto the therapeutic field. To the extent that this is accomplished, suitable conditions are thus provided for the therapist to interpret and synthesize and for the patient to achieve higher levels of integration.

The excerpt below illustrates the location of internal sources of disequilibrium within the frame.

Langs: What happens when you secure the frame is that they react now to the *meanings of the secure frame.* . . . What are the *problems of the secure frame?* That's what is so fascinating. This is where Freud's use of the couch came out so beautifully. The secure frame says you have to be here every time at the appointed hour. So the *secure frame entraps you.* The secure frame, which I believe includes the couch says, "You cannot look at me." So *there are interpersonal deprivation and separation issues.* The secure frame creates *depressive anxieties because you have an object loss in not being able to look at the therapist.* It creates *paranoid and phobic anxiety because you're entrapped and you are restricted and you're, again, with someone who is also capable of securing the frame.* Patients recognize that. It's a very powerful capacity, and it *makes you very threatening.* If you're that strong, you know, will you then turn against me? (p. 35)

This passage originated in the interviewer's asking whether there would still be issues for a patient to bring into the field if the frame were managed adequately; or, if there were no frame deviations evoking conflict in the therapeutic dyad. Langs's response is to specify the various internal contradictions within the secure frame. That is, with frame management issues out of the way, the patient is left to deal with sources of disequilibrium that are intrinsic to being within the frame. These include the experience of "entrapment," "interpersonal deprivation and separation issues," "paranoid and phobic anxiety," and the threat of the therapist's "powerful capacities."

Further, consider the paradoxical qualities of the frame. First, the frame simultaneously provides gratification (through encouraging symbiosis, self-reflection, interpersonal security) and frustration (e.g., "interpersonal deprivation and separation"). The tension between these two poles opens the interactive field for the patient and therapist to engage in the exchange of symbols requisite to insight, understanding, and growth. To shift too far in the direction of frustration would be to promote disillusionment in the patient (discussed elsewhere in the interview), while to shift too far toward gratification would impede the patient's toleration for ambiguity, conflict, and pain, without which growth could not occur.

A second, related paradox follows. While serving as the sine qua non of "cure," the secure frame also activates the patient's most frightening anxieties and experiences of madness. In this sense, a solution is simultaneously a problem. While the experience and expression of madness are the chief requirements for "cure," they contain the threat of severe disorganization.

Finally, consider Langs's concept (1978, 1982) of the me/not-me interface. Recall that according to the Aristotelian law of noncontradiction, a "thing" cannot be both itself and something else simultaneously. Recent advances in the physical sciences have repeatedly violated this tenet, as in accounts of physical phenomena that cannot be characterized in unipolar terms (e.g., as *either* matter *or* energy). In Freud's original work, this mode of understanding appeared clearly in the concept of overdetermination through which dreams and symptoms are viewed as a convergence of associations, meanings, and impulses. The significance of such a heuristic strategy lies in the fact that it transcends the quest for a monadic understanding of basic scientific phenomena in favor of a view of dual or multiple constitution.

The me/not-me interface construct illustrates this mode of thinking particularly well.

Langs: All I mean by that is that *when a patient is in therapy, every associa-tion, everything they do and say, every communication has some unconscious connection to a perception of the therapist, to an image of the therapist based on the therapist's intervention. That's the not-me part of the interface. On the other side, the same communications are also self-perceptions.* And often unconscious self-perception. I'm talking usually about encoded mes-sages. *The same communication will encode a perception of the therapist and of the patient.* Himself or herself. *So the me/not-me interface just simply meant that every communication faces both ways.* (pp. 8–9)

This is a particularly cogent example of the *interpenetration of oppo-sites* aspect of dialectical thinking. In this sense, Langs states that all of a patient's activity in therapy ("every association, everything they do and say," etc.) constitutes an intermixture of perceptions, of the therapist and of the patient. That is, the patient's activity represents a synthetic integration. Langs traces this out in his thinking. Encoded in "every communication" is a perception of the therapist, the not-me, and a self-perception, the me. Commu-nications therefore are certainly not simple and direct but rather quite complex, consistent with the definition of synthesis. Given this synthetic quality, therapeutic communications consist of in-terpenetrating opposites. Stated differently, the "whole" of the patient is represented in the singularity of the moment. Meta-theoretically, this mode of understanding illustrates an apprecia-tion of epistemological contradiction and of the dialectical concept "many-in-one" (Rychlak, 1976).

CONCLUSIONS AND DISCUSSION

The line of argument developed in this chapter is summarized concisely in the following passages from *Invisible Loyalties* (Boszor-menyi-Nagy & Spark, 1973).

We propose that the understanding of the structure of a relational world requires a dialectical rather than absolute or monothetical way of thinking. The essence of the dialectical approach is a libera-tion of the mind from absolute concepts which in themselves claim to explain phenomena as though the opposite point of view did not exist. According to dialectical thought, a positive concept is always viewed in contrast with its opposite, in the hope that their joint consideration will yield a resolution through a more thorough and productive understanding. The principles of relativity and indeter-minancy in physics and the concept of homeostatic regulations of living things are examples of increasingly dialectical orientation in natural sciences. (p. 18)

* * * * *

Psychology, psychotherapy and psychopathology have also been in a gradual transition toward a more dialectical viewpoint. (p. 19)

In this chapter, we have considered evidence of this position in the form of interview data with four prominent psychotherapists of diverse traditions. The most important observation was their common appeal to contradiction in expressing their comprehension of major psychotherapeutic issues. With Langs and Boszormenyi-Nagy, the reference to contradiction was explicit. In the Rogers and Lazarus transcripts, the metaconstruct appeared not at the level of theory, but in the form of their logic. The salient fact for each was that the contradiction category was applied with reference to both intra- and interpersonal features of psychotherapy. The intrapersonal contradictions were: the self-system and unassimilated experience (Rogers); dichotomous thinking, perception, and so on, leading to failure to tolerate ambiguity (Lazarus); the internal contradiction of blameworthiness and entitlement (Boszormenyi-Nagy); and the patient's experiences of madness (defined as contradiction) intrinsic to the secure analytic relationship (Langs).

Interpersonally there was: the correlativity of self and other in the process of empathy (Rogers); the contradicting of Ms. A's internal contradictions—the negating of negation—via the therapist-client interaction (Lazarus); the contextual therapist addressing not only the delinquent client's accountability for misdeeds but also his unmet entitlement to restitution for wrongdoings perpetuated on him, the second pole of contradiction (Boszormenyi-Nagy); and the analyst's curtailment of personal "madness" to promote synthesis of the patient's madness via the bipersonal field (Langs).

The concern with epistemological contradiction was also salient. With Rogers, particularly careful attention is given to the achievement of a "shared reality" with a client. He is strongly concerned with stepping outside of his own perspective to adopt that of his client, the purpose being to differentiate and further define each party's knowledge (defined in experiential terms) of self, other, and the bonds between the two. In the Lazarus material, the client's problem was construed in the explicitly epistemological terms of a propensity for "absolutistic" and "dichotom[ous]" ideas. Using his constructive alternativism method, which consisted of "challenging," and presenting "options...alternatives...possibilities," Lazarus strove to interrupt his client's usual mode of understanding and provoke growth to a more integrative level. In contrast to "absolutistic ideas," this new level entailed a "toleration of differences view."

Attention to epistemological contradiction and its resolution was evident in Boszormenyi-Nagy's concept, multilaterality of fairness, through which the contextual therapist endeavors to achieve partiality to the perspectives of each member of a family system. This process entails transcendence of the therapist's own biases and need-based predelictions in order to generate an inclusive, multifaceted, synthetic "truth." In Langs's work, this mode of thought was represented clearly in the me/not-me interface construct. That is, the analysand's activity at a given moment in treatment represents perceptions of not only the self but also the therapist. Included are contributions from a number of psychological sources such as associations, affects, thoughts, images, and so on, all culminating in the dynamic moment. Also relevant to epistemology in Langs's system is the analyst's effort to synthesize the numerous contradictions that comprise the patient's experience of "madness."

We noted in the Introduction that numerous psychotherapeutic concepts are provoking an exploration of underlying conceptual assumptions. With respect to the present discussion of epistemology, it is interesting to note how the utilization of an interactive or interpersonal approach to therapy leads to epistemological considerations.

In the early days of psychotherapy the therapist, presumed "cured" by a training analysis, was considered a blank screen for the patient's projections (Langs, 1976, 1978, 1982). In that context, linear, unipolar metaconstructs are apropos. With the adoption of an interpersonal model, however, the therapist enters the interactive field as another human being with conflicts and limitations. No longer an objective, mostly detached figure, the therapist has a construction of reality (though presumably more adaptive and managed constructively) which operates as an active epistemological force in the relationship. Now, rather than merely interpreting, the interpersonally oriented therapist must align his/her own reality with that of the patient in order to promote the latter's epistemological reconstructions.

With the development of the family therapy approaches, this alignment and reconstruction process becomes more challenging. Here it is no longer that one individual, the "identified patient," has lapsed from "reality testing"; rather, a social system has become dysfunctional, producing a scapegoat to embody the family's internal contradictions. Moreover, because the family therapist has refused to isolate one family member as "psychopathological," s/he now has the challenging philosophical tasks of (1) taking seriously the identified patient's perspective, loss of reality testing notwithstanding; (2) taking seriously the perspective of each family member and the family's aggregate understanding of the current crisis; (3) synthesizing an overall understanding that incorporates each family member's perspective, including that of the ostracized individual; and (4) performing the additional synthesis of integrating the previous synthesis with the theoretical constructs of the therapy model and the assumptions and biases of the therapist as human being in process. Such challenges, worthy of Socrates or Hegel, are an integral part of a therapist's day-to-day practice and provide insight into the currently prominent concern for epistemology, particularly among family therapists. Moreover, given how deeply ingrained assumptions of noncontradiction are, it is no surprise that so much of what therapists think and practice is termed *paradoxical*.

The study partially reported in this chapter was preliminary. Obviously it suffers from the problems inherent in the use of interview data and small sample size. Yet as an exploratory study, it is useful in illuminating connections between theory and metatheory in psychotherapy; further research and theory are clearly in order. In closing, we will turn to the implications that could follow from further empirical and conceptual support of this line of inquiry.

Implications for Psychotherapy

Metatheory. On a metatheoretical level, one implication of this work is the suggestion that psychotherapy may be moving toward an overarching integration. This impending integration derives from an examination and critique of philosophical presuppositions, especially the Aristotelian law of noncontradiction, and a corresponding shift to reliance upon the relevance of contradiction. The data in this study, in addition to conceptual arguments from various sources (Andolfi, 1974; Ascher, 1980; Berman, 1978; Boszormenyi-Nagy & Spark, 1973; Esterson, 1970; Fenichel, 1967; Koplowitz, 1978; Mozdzierz et al., 1976; Raskin & Klein, 1976; Rychlak, 1968; Staats, 1981; Stierlin, 1969; Weeks & L'Abate, 1982) have indicated that that which is vital in both the theory and practice of psychotherapy—across schools—is paradoxical. That such convergence centers on a construct anomalous to traditional scientific methods yet basic to dialectical ones suggests that the overarching integration is best accommodated through a dialectical approach.

Although much therapeutic work in the past utilized contradiction and paradox, efforts were made to force explanations to fit mechanistic, linear, and reductionistic terms. More recently, in the face of severe difficulties with such endeavors, a retreat from striving for conceptual coherence occurred by appealing to such notions as eclecticism.

With ongoing attention being given to paradoxical approaches and a corresponding articulation of dialectic metatheory, however, the methods and concepts of psychotherapy may be brought increasingly into phase. In other words, if psychotherapy has been largely based on paradoxical methods, and if the appropriate scientific framework for such methods is a dialectical one, then the upcoming era in psychotherapy may witness to a newfound conceptual order deriving from the field's current variegation. Such consolidation could in turn relieve the "anxiety" experienced by social scientists uncertain of the status of their fields relative to the natural sciences, which have been becoming considerably dialectical in outlook over the 20th century (e.g., Sinnott, 1981).

One way in which this reordering could happen would be to reframe the dogmatism and often contentious appeals to truth that have occurred within psychotherapy. Rather than perpetuating the view that only one theory can be correct, a dialectical outlook would promote the view that each theory is "true," that is, reflects a valid explanation ventured from a particular level of observation. Moreover, the contradictions among the theories would themselves be valued as they reveal the relative limitations of the individual theories as well as those of the theory construction process itself (a central problem being the historical failure to achieve an encompassing, internally consistent model). Intertheory contradictions also signal the potential for new understanding emerging from their syntheses.

Finally, this scientific approach would strive to multiply (rather than minimize) theoretical perspectives as a way to achieve an inclusive theoretical outlook (Basseches, 1978; Bopp & Basseches, 1981; Boszormenyi-Nagy & Ulrich, 1981). Viewed in this way, the development of psychotherapy as a whole, with all its variegation, represents the unfolding of a large-scale, conceptual enterprise. What has been lacking, however, has been a frame within which to consolidate this mosaic. The frame best suited to this end is a dialectical one.

Practice.   At the practice level, there are also important implications. First, emanating from the presupposition of contradiction as central is the view that effectively conducted psychotherapy would promote rather than obviate paradox within clients. The goal of psychotherapy would no longer be to achieve a state of unconflicted "health" or "cure." Instead, the therapy process would consist of efforts to locate and polarize contradictions beneath what might appear to be singularities. Further, such therapy would promote an ongoing state of dynamic tension formed precisely out of contradictory experience. An effort would be made not only to foster toleration but resilience and valuing of contradiction by the client (and certainly by the therapist as well). This notion has been advanced by Riegel (1976, 1979) as a criterion of successful human development.

A second implication for clinical practice is to broaden our view of paradox. In early work on this topic (e.g., Frankl, 1975) paradox was understood as a specific therapeutic technique. More recently, however, there has been a growing sense that many psychotherapeutic practices actually constitute expressions of implicit intra- and interpersonal paradoxes—despite the name a particular intervention has carried. In fact, the results of this study support this view through the finding of implicit or explicit reliance on contradiction metaconstructs in diverse areas of psychotherapy not associated with recent discussions of paradox. Extending this reasoning then, one might postulate that far from being a new technique, paradox has been in use all along. Further, there is a need for more explicit articulation of the paradoxes already occurring under different names throughout the psychotherapeutic field.

REFERENCES

Andolfi, M. Paradox in psychotherapy. *American Journal of Psychoanalysis*, 1974, 34, 221–228.

Arieti, S. *Interpretation of schizophrenia*. New York: Robert Brunner, 1955.

Aristotle. Metaphysics. In R. M. Hutchins (Ed.), *Great books of the western world*. Chicago: Encyclopedia Britannica, 1952.

Ascher, L. M. Paradoxical intention. In A. Goldstein & E. B. Foa (Eds.), *Handbook of behavioral interventions: A clinical guide*. New York: Wiley, 1980.

Ascher, L. M., & Efran, J. S. Use of paradoxical intention in a behavioral program for sleep onset insomnia. *Journal of Consulting and Clinical Psychology*, 1978, 46, 547–550.

Bandler, R., & Grinder, J. *The structure of magic I: A book about language and therapy*. Palo Alto: Science and Behavior Books, 1975.

Bandura, A. The self-system in reciprocal determinism. *American Psychologist*, 1978, *33*, 334–358.

Basseches, M. A. *Beyond closed-system problem-solving: A study of meta-systematic aspects of mature thought*. Unpublished doctoral dissertation, Harvard University, 1978. (University Microfilms International, 1979).

Basseches, M. A. Dialectical schemata: A framework for the empirical study of the development of dialectical thinking. *Human Development*, 1980, *23*, 400–421.

Berman, D. S. Cognitive-behaviorism as a dialectical contradiction: The unity of opposites. *Human Development*, 1978, *21*, 248–254.

Berne, E. *Principles of group treatment*. New York: Grover, 1966.

Bertalanffy, L. *General system theory*. New York: Braziller, 1968.

Bopp, M. J. *A study of dialectical metatheory in psychotherapy*. Unpublished doctoral dissertation, Temple University, 1983.

Bopp, M. J., & Basseches, M. *A coding manual for the dialectical schemata framework*. Unpublished manuscript, 1981.

Bopp, M. J., & Weeks, G. R. Dialectical metatheory in family therapy. *Family Process*, 1984, *23*, 49–62.

Boszormenyi-Nagy, I. A theory of relationships: Experience and transaction. In I. Boszormenyi-Nagy & J. L. Framo (Eds.), *Intensive family therapy*. New York: Harper & Row, 1965. (a)

Boszormenyi-Nagy, I. Intensive family therapy as process. In I. Boszormenyi-Nagy & J. L. Framo (Eds.), *Intensive family therapy*. New York: Harper & Row, 1965. (b)

Boszormenyi-Nagy, I., & Spark, G. M. *Invisible loyalties: Reciprocity in intergenerational family therapy*. Hagerstown, Md.: Harper & Row, 1973.

Boszormenyi-Nagy, I., & Ulrich, D. N. Contextual family therapy. In A. S. Gurman & D. P. Kniskern (Eds.), *Handbook of family therapy*. New York: Brunner/Mazel, 1981.

Buss, A. R. The emerging field of the sociology of psychology. *American psychologist*, 1975, *30*, 988–1002.

Buss, A. R. *A dialectical psychology*. New York: Irvington Publishers, 1979.

Chomsky, N. *Language and mind*. New York: Harcourt, Brace & World, 1968.

Clayton, V. Erikson's theory of human development as it applies to the aged: Wisdom as contradictive cognition. *Human Development*, 1975, *18*, 119–128.

Coyne, J. A brief introduction to epistobabble. *Family therapy networker*, 1982, *6*, 27–28.

Engels, F. *Dialectics of nature.* New York: International Publishers, 1940.

Erikson, E. H. *Childhood and society* (2nd ed.). New York: Norton, 1963.

Esterson, A. *The leaves of spring: A study in the dialectics of madness.* Middlesex, England: Penguin, 1970.

Fenichel, O. Psychoanalysis as the nucleus of a future dialectical-materialistic psychology. *American Imago,* 1967, *24,* 290–311.

Frankl, V. E. Paradoxical intention and dereflection. *Psychotherapy: Theory, Research and Practice,* 1975, *12,* 226–237.

Freud, S. *Three essays on the theory of sexuality.* New York: Avon Books, 1962.

Guntrip, H. Recent developments in psychoanalytical theory. *British Journal of Medical Psychology,* 1956, *29,* 82–99.

Guntrip, H. *Psychoanalytic theory, therapy and the self.* New York: Basic Books, 1971.

Haley, J. *Strategies of psychotherapy.* New York: Grune & Stratton, 1963.

Jung, C. G. *Memories, dreams, reflections.* New York: Vintage Books, 1961.

Kegan, R. G. The evolving self: A process conception for ego psychology. *The counseling psychologist,* 1979, *8,* 5–34.

Keeney, B. What is an epistemology of family therapy? *Family Process,* 1982, *21,* 153–168.

Keeney, B., & Sprenkle, D. Ecosystemic epistemology: Critical implications for the aesthetics and pragmatics of family therapy. *Family Process,* 1982, *21,* 1–20.

Kohlberg, L. From is to ought: How to commit the naturalistic fallacy and get away with it in the study of moral development. In T. Mischel (Ed.), *Cognitive development and epistemology.* New York: Academic Press, 1971.

Koplowitz, H. *Unitary thought: A projection beyond Piaget's formal operations stage.* Unpublished manuscript, 1978.

Kramer, D. A. Post-formal operations? A need for further conceptualization. *Human Development,* 1983, *26,* 91–105.

Kuhn, T. S. *The structure of scientific revolutions* (2nd Ed.). Chicago: University of Chicago Press, 1970. (Originally published 1962)

Langs, R. *The bipersonal field.* New York: Jason Aronson, 1976.

Langs, R. *The listening process.* New York: Jason Aronson, 1978.

Langs, R. *Psychotherapy: A basic text.* New York: Jason Aronson, 1982. (a)

Langs, R. *Cure through madness.* In preparation.

Lazarus, A. A. In support of technical eclecticism. *Psychological Reports,* 1967, *21,* 415–416.

Lazarus, A. A. (Ed.). *Multimodal behavioral therapy.* New York: Springer, 1976.

Lazarus, A. A. *The practice of multimodal therapy: Systematic, comprehensive and effective psychotherapy.* New York: McGraw-Hill, 1981.

Liddle, H. On the problem of eclecticism: A call for epistemological clarification and human-scale theories. *Family Process,* 1982, *21,* 243–250.

Matson, F. W. *The broken image: Man, science and society.* New York: Braziller, 1964.

Miller, J. G. General systems theory. In A. M. Freedman, H. I. Kaplan, & B. J. Sadock (Eds.), *Comprehensive textbook of psychiatry—II.* Baltimore: Williams & Wilkins, 1975.

Minuchin, S. *Families and family therapy.* Cambridge, Mass.: Harvard University Press, 1974.

Mischel, W. Toward a cognitive social learning reconceptualization of personality. *Psychological Review,* 1973, *80,* 252–283.

Mozdzierz, G., Macchitelli, F., & Lisieki, J. The paradox in psychotherapy: An Adlerian perspective. *Journal of Individual Psychology,* 1976, *32,* 169–184.

Nunberg, H. The synthetic function of the ego. *Practice and theory of psychoanalysis.* New York: International Universities Press, 1960.

Oppenheimer, R. Analogy in science. *American Psychologist,* 1956, *11,* 127–135.

Overton, W. F., & Reese, H. W. Models of development: Methodological implications. In J. R. Nesselroade & H. W. Reese (Eds.), *Life-span developmental psychology: Methodological issues.* New York: Academic Press, 1973.

Overton, W. F., & Reese, H. W. Conceptual prerequisites for an understanding of stability-change and continuity-discontinuity. *International Journal of Behavioral Development,* 1981, *4,* 99–123.

Piaget, J. *Six psychological studies.* New York: Random House, 1967.

Progoff, I. *Jung, synchronicity and human destiny: Non-causal dimensions of human experience.* New York: Julian Press, 1973.

Raskin, D. E., & Klein, Z. E. Losing a symptom through keeping it: A review of paradoxical treatment techniques and rationale. *Archives of general psychiatry,* 1976, *33,* 548–555.

Ratner, C. Principles of dialectical psychology. *Telos,* 1971, *9,* 83–109.

Reese, H. W., & Overton, W. F. Models of development and theories of development. In L. R. Goulet & P. B. Baltes (Eds.), *Life-span developmental psychology: Theory and research*. New York: Academic Press, 1970.

Riegel, K. F. Dialectical operations: The final period of cognitive development. *Human Development*, 1973, *16*, 346–370.

Riegel, K. F. The dialectics of human development. *American Psychologist*, 1976, *31*, 689–700.

Riegel, K. F. (Ed.). *Foundations of dialectical psychology*. New York: Academic Press, 1979.

Rogers, C. R. *Client-centered therapy: Its current practice, implications, and theory*. Boston: Houghton Mifflin, 1951.

Rogers, C. R. A theory of therapy, personality, and interpersonal relationships, as developed in the client-centered framework. In S. Koch (Ed.), *Psychology: A study of a science, 3. Formulations of the person and the social context*. New York: McGraw-Hill, 1959, 184–256.

Rogers, C. R. *On becoming a person: A therapist's view of psychotherapy*. Boston: Houghton Mifflin, 1961.

Rogers, C. R. Client-centered psychotherapy. In H. I. Kaplan, B. J. Sadock, & A. M. Freedman (Eds.), *The comprehensive textbook of psychiatry—III*. Baltimore: Williams & Wilkins, 1980. (a)

Rogers, C. R. *A way of being*. Boston: Houghton Mifflin, 1980. (b)

Rychlak, J. F. *A philosophy of science for personality theory*. Boston: Houghton Mifflin, 1968.

Rychlak, J. F. (Ed.). *Dialectics: Humanistic rationale for behavior and development*. Basel, Switzerland: Karger, 1976.

Schrodinger, E. *What is life? The physical aspects of the living cell*. Cambridge, Eng.: Cambridge University Press, 1967.

Selvini-Palazzoli, M., Boscolo, L., Cecchin, G., & Prata, G. *Paradox and counterparadox: A new model in the therapy of the family in schizophrenic transaction*. New York: Jason Aronson, 1978.

Sinnott, J. D. The theory of relativity: A metatheory for development? *Human Development*, 1981, *24*, 293–311.

Speck, R., & Attneave, C. *Family networks*. New York: Pantheon Books, 1973.

Stanton, M. D. Family therapy: Systems approaches. In G. P. Sholevar, R. M. Benson, & B. J. Blinda (Eds.), *Treatment of emotional disorders in children and adolescents*. Jamaica, N.Y.: Spectrum, 1980.

Staats, A. W. Paradigmatic behaviorism, unified theory, unified theory construction methods, and the Zeitgeist of separatism. *American psychologist*, 1981, *36*, 239–256.

Stierlin, H. *Conflict and reconciliation.* New York: Science House, 1969.

Watzlawick, P., Beavin, J., & Jackson, D. *Pragmatics of human communication.* New York: W. W. Norton, 1967.

Watzlawick, P., Weakland, J., & Fisch, R. *Change: Principles of problem formation and problem resolution.* New York: Norton, 1974.

Weeks, G. R., & L'Abate, L. A compilation of paradoxical methods. *American Journal of Family Therapy,* 1979, 7, 61–76.

Weeks, G. R., & L'Abate, L. *Paradoxical psychotherapy: Theory and practice with individuals, couples, and families.* New York: Brunner/ Mazel, 1982.

Weeks, G. R., & Wright, L. Dialectics of the family life cycle. *American Journal of Family Therapy,* 1979, 7, 85–91.

Zukav, G. *The dancing Wu Li masters: An overview of the new physics.* New York: Bantam, 1979.

11

A Metatheory of Paradox

by Gerald R. Weeks, Ph.D.

The purpose of this volume is to help define the term therapeutic paradox and to describe ways of working paradoxically. While all the contributors appear to work in a similar manner, their explanations or theories about how they work differ. The aim of this chapter is to create a theory of paradox that transcends any particular theory of paradox and any particular approach to psychotherapy. An attempt is made to develop a metatheory of paradox in psychotherapy.

PARADOX AS A UNIVERSAL ASPECT OF THERAPY

Weeks (1977) and Weeks and L'Abate (1982) proposed a dialectical theory of change for psychotherapy. This theory provided the foundation for the application of paradoxial strategies in therapy. As early as 1977, Weeks suggested that the common element of all psychotherapies was paradox. In their 1982 book, Weeks and L'Abate compared and analyzed the Adlerian, Behavioral, Gestalt, Logotherapeutic, Direct Analysis, Provocative, and Hypnotherapeutic schools to demonstrate the common element of paradox.

Seltzer (1986) has significantly extended Weeks and L'Abate's (1982) work in this area. He presents a thoroughgoing analysis of paradox in both Eastern and Western approaches to therapy. Seltzer gives us an idea of just how prevalent paradoxical thinking is in other schools of therapy by considering the labels used to describe paradoxical techniques within a few:

> From the psychoanalytic perspective, which includes the work of paradigmatic psychotherapists, we have inherited the descriptors "antisuggestion," "going with the resistance," "joining the resistance," "reflecting" (or "mirroring") the resistance," "siding with the resistance," "paradigmatic exaggeration," "supporting the defenses," "reductio ad adsurdum," "reenacting an aspect of the psychosis," "mirroring the patient's distortions," "participating in the patient's fantasies," "outcrazying the patient," and "the use of the patient as consultant." From the vantage point of behavior therapy, we may appreciate paradoxical elements in such procedures as "blowup," "implosion," "flooding," "instructed helplessness," "massed practice," "negative practice," "paradoxical intention," "stimulus satiation," and "symptom scheduling." In gestalt therapy, an approach where the term paradox is rarely employed, the attempt to foster change paradoxically may be recognized in the therapist's cruel-to-be-kind suggestions to "stay with the (negative) experience," or to "exaggerate the feeling" (sensation, experience, speech, movement, etc.). (p. 20)

Seltzer's (1986) theoretical analysis led him to develop a metatheory of paradox in psychotherapy. His metatheory can be further distilled to a theory based on social psychology developed by Strong and Claiborn (1982). Seltzer (1986) devotes considerable attention to the issue of how different schools of therapy are defined. He believed, like Weeks (1977), that the apparently sharp, theoretical differences among approaches begin to disappear when the clinician is viewed in the here-and-now context of seeing client(s). This idea is one that has been heard in clinical circles for many years. He argues that paradoxial strategies are present in all systems of therapy. These strategies share the common element of defying the clients' expectations and involve some form of reframing and/or symptom prescription.

A metatheory is required to bind together the various approaches. Omer (1981) was among the first theorists to proffer a unified concept of paradox. In an effort to arrive at the single common denominator of therapeutic efficacy, he proposed the concept of symptom decontextualization. This idea consists of the therapist modifying both the form and the context of the symptom. Form, in his definition, refers to the request to continue the symptom under different conditions (e.g., scheduling, exaggeration, different time or place). Context refers to the fact that what one had been trying to stop is now allowed expression. In Omer's view, the second change is one of meaning. The client must alter his or her attitude toward a behavior if it is allowed expression.

Omer's (1981) use of the term decontextualization is not as descriptive as Deissler's (1985) use of the term recontextualization. The meanings of these two terms are similar. Deissler states that in symptom decontextualization the symptom is changed by altering the "recursive context" (i.e., the number of people involved in the problem and/or the temporal and spatial contexts). It seems more descriptive to say that the symptom is recontextualized. When a client is able to change the context of the symptom, the meaning inevitably changes only because the client is able to demonstrate some control over the uncontrollable, some volition over the involitional, and some mindfulness over the spontaneous (mindless or automatic behavior).

What do all therapies have in common which is inherent in the paradoxial view of therapy?

Seltzer (1986) states, "*all* therapies can be perceived as endeavoring to assist clients in comprehending the voluntariness—and their controllability—of behaviors which have come to appear nonvolitional" (p. 164). Seltzer concludes that all paradoxical strategies decontextualize symptoms. In short, our metatheory is that paradoxical strategies change the meaning of the symptom from that which is uncontrollable to that which is controllable. This view is consistent with the core of Weeks and L'Abate's (1982) approach, which offers five principles for paradoxical intervention. These principles deal with both form and context. The third principle requires that the therapist change the direction of control of a symptom. In an individual, the symptom is placed under voluntary control, and for systems, the symptom is placed under the control of those who had allowed the symptom to heretofore control them.

This metatheory of paradox can now be used to examine the universal aspects of therapy. Seltzer (1986) discussed this problem from several different perspectives. First, the nature of the therapeutic relationship is such that the therapist must be in control. Establishing a therapeutic relationship is synonymous with taking control. However, the control the therapist takes is not to eliminate the problem, but to help *the client* eliminate the problem. The therapist is then taking charge by placing the client in charge. For example, in the client-centered school of Rogers, the client is placed in charge through the therapist's attitude of unconditional positive regard. A behaviorist would place the client in charge by being directive in using techniques and stating that these are only tools and the client must supply the rest. All therapy is built on the paradox of taking control by giving it away. It is only under this condition that the client can develop self-control.

Second, Seltzer (1986) argues that the therapist should maintain a positive view of symptoms. In other words, in all systems of therapy, the symptom is never directly attacked. The symptom is seen as serving some need of the client. It is important to understand, not attack, the symptom. This attitude is translated into action via a permissiveness toward symptoms. Even behaviorists give clients permission to have their symptoms during the baseline period. Weeks and L'Abate (1982) found that symptoms always represented something positive. Symptoms have been defined as allies, communications, existential statements, and vehicles of change. In fact, they found that the newer schools of therapy, especially the strategic school, started to define symptoms in more explicit, positive ways. Weeks and L'Abate (1982) and countless other therapists have proposed that symptoms be viewed as "friends" and not "the enemy" as many clients believe.

The third universal factor is the therapist's view of not only the symptom, but the person. The client enters therapy expecting to be changed and fearing the therapist may disapprove because of his or her symptomatic behavior. The client discovers that the therapist is attentive, supportive, empathetic, friendly, and receptive. The therapist maintains his or her attitude of acceptance, including acceptance of resistance; and the client's effort to resist not only fails, but is somehow redefined in a way that indirectly brings control back to the therapist.

The therapeutic relationship is marked by a number of characteristics that run counter to the client's expectations. It is a unique social relationship in several paradoxical ways. The therapist shows an attitude of detached concern or uninvolved involvement and takes control by giving it away. This process is accomplished by being indirectly direct (Seltzer, 1986). The goal is to help the client change spontaneously (Strong & Claiborn, 1982; Weeks & L'Abate, 1982). Change is not directly attributed to something the therapist did. Change is defined through the interaction between the therapist and client, with the client attributing change to him- or herself.

The fourth unifying theme is the paradoxical nature of the therapeutic process. Seltzer (1986) summarizes this idea in terms of the client(s) working *through*, rather than *around*. In every system of therapy, the client is encouraged to move toward the symptom rather than flee from it. Otherwise, the therapy would simply support the avoidant behavior of the client. In the psychodynamic literature, the term for this process is literally called working through (Singer, 1970).

Through some type of conditioning procedure, the behaviorist has the client focus attention on the symptom in order to reduce the anxiety associated with it. Gestalt therapists encourage the client to stay with the feeling. In fact, Beisser (1970) states the heart of Gestalt therapy is a paradoxical theory of change. He asserts that change occurs when one becomes what he is, not when he tries to become what he is not. In long-term analytic therapy, the therapist assumes that change will occur *very* slowly and only after a therapeutic relationship involving transference has occurred, precipitating greater insight. The underlying message to the client is "Don't change quickly and be who you are."

Seltzer's (1986) two final points deal with the paradox of how the therapist takes responsibility for the client taking responsibility for his or her problems. In short, the common denominator for different therapies is that the client learns to exercise self-control. The therapist must convince the client that she or he can learn to help him- or herself. This task may be accomplished directly or indirectly. The responsibility for change is always put back on the client. The therapist provides a framework for this task—not ready-made solutions.

When clients accept that they can do something to alleviate the symptomatic behavior, they are also forced to accept the fact that their symptoms must be under their control. By definition, a symptom is defined by the client as a behavior that is uncontrollable, involuntary, and spontaneous. Every system of therapy seeks to teach the client that symptoms are behaviors that are controllable, voluntary, and volitional. Every system of therapy recognizes and has techniques to deal with clients who deny, disqualify, and externalize responsibility for symptomatic behavior. On the contrary, every system has a set of rules which allows the therapist to deny, disqualify, and externalize any responsibility for the occurrence of change. This set of contradictory conditions forms a context in which the attribution for change must belong to the client.

Weeks and L'Abate (1982) fully recognize this framework. They note:

> The meta-level structuring of paradoxical therapy is not one of restriction. On the contrary, the intervention allows the client the fullest expression of freedom in developing a new frame of refer-

ence. From the outset of therapy, the meta-framework has been one of initiating changes. The fact that clients respond to paradox by attributing change to themselves serves as evidence of this view. (p. 246)

Seltzer (1986), Weeks and L'Abate (1982), and Stanton (1984) have shown how paradoxical strategies are deeply embedded in many systems of psychotherapy. Seltzer (1986) extends this work through his theoretical analysis to show that paradox is a unifying concept which is universal in the various systems of therapy. In spite of the fact that contents differ, the therapeutic process at the metatheoretical level remains constant. This metatheoretical understanding provides a new framework for integrating differential theories of therapy.

An attempt at defining a meta- or unified theory that incorporates both paradoxical and other methods of therapeutic change is the "geodynamic balance" theory of Stanton (1984). Stanton places symptoms within their *interpersonal* (e.g., familial) *context*, a context that both generates and maintains them, and also one that can be utilized by the therapist for symptom elimination. The symptom is seen as one element in an interpersonal sequence—a series of behavioral events among a group of people, such as a family. As each member of the group chimes in with his or her contribution to the symptom sequence, he or she is regarded as moving, at least symbolically in a kind of "orbit" *toward* some people and *away* from others; i.e., "in the service" of some, and not of others. The whole sequence thus takes on the image of a choreographed dance, in which the symptom is only one move in the dance. Such dances can be identified when one observes the symptom as it actually occurs in the real world, that is, within its normal interpersonal context.

In order to bring about change, the therapist has two general options. The "diversion" approach attempts to directly block or redirect the sequence, stopping it and perhaps offering an alternative, whereas the "compression" option (paradoxically) exaggerates a person's orbit by encouraging or pushing the person further in the direction he or she is already moving. An example would be to try to get the teenaged son in an enmeshed mother-son relationship to actually sit on the mother's lap, and also to have the mother accompany the son to school and hold his hand en route. Compression moves usually result in a rebound effect, in which the members counteract the intervention and stop doing what they were doing. In contrast, diversion, in order to be successful, usually requires energy that is equal to or greater than that of the behavior being blocked. Stanton (1984) notes eight therapeutic approaches that predominantly utilize diversion techniques and 15 therapies that emphasize compression (e.g., paradoxical) methods. In its delineation of a two-sided or opponent-process feature of therapy—going with the system or symptom versus counteracting it—good dynamic balance theory is consonant with both Taoist philosophy and Bopp and Weeks' (1984) formulations about the therapeutic dialectic. Perhaps, a distinctive feature of Stanton's theory is that it synthesizes almost all therapeutic techniques—both paradoxical and non-paradoxical—under one conceptual umbrella, making room for either approach depending on the nature, difficulty, and chronicity of the problem.

The bridge between the metatheoretical work of the authors reviewed thus far and the integration of differential therapies has been developed by Strong and Claiborn (1982). These theorists proposed a theory of change based on the principles and research of social psychology and psychotherapy.

The Paradox of Spontaneous Compliance

Strong and Claiborn (1982) identified two types of change processes. The first type is forced change or compliance. Forced compliance refers to a change in oneself that is attributed to another person. The experience of change is of *doing* something different, rather than *being* different. Every parent, spouse, and therapist who has ever tried to force another person to be (act) different knows this effort is futile. If compliance does occur, it is only under duress, and will persist only as long as is needed to placate the other person. This understanding prevents therapists from telling clients what to do or giving advice.

Therapeutic change is best defined as the therapist's ability to create the context for spontaneous compliance. The term itself is contradictory. How does the therapist get the client to do what the therapist wants, without getting the client to do what he or she wants? The therapist must take control without appearing to take control. Therapy is a paradox.

The idea of spontaneous compliance may seem unusual; however, it is a universal human experience. When we want someone to go to lunch with us, we do not say, "You will go to lunch with me at 12 o'clock." You might say, "Would you like to go to lunch with me at 12 o'clock?" In marriage, spouses do not give each other orders. If they do, they find themselves in an untenable situation. Spouses attempt to influence each other indirectly by making statements such as "I want to be with you," or "Would you like to talk?" When spouses attempt to control through forced compliance, dysfunctionality results. The therapist working with couples must help each member of the couple learn how to take control indirectly by taking control of the couple without appearing to take control.

The "affirmation" and "negation" paradoxes are used to create spontaneous compliance (Strong & Claiborn, 1982). The affirmation paradox (implicitly paradoxical) is made up of three elements:

1. The therapist presents the desired behavior and insists that the behavior be adopted as part of the definition of the relationship.
2. The therapist communicates that change is a result of processes internal to the client and is not in compliance with the therapist.
3. The therapist identifies an agent responsible for change that acts beyond the client's volitional control. (p. 145)

The therapist wants to create a context in which the client spontaneously complies by attributing change to self. The communications therapist may teach the couple new ways of talking. Such techniques are useless unless the clients want to learn to use them. Thus, the couple can attribute success to *their* wanting to work together in communicating more effectively.

The therapist using the negation paradox (explicitly paradoxical strategies) encourages the client to change by encouraging the client not to change. In fact, that behavior which is not to be changed has been defined as involuntary by the client. By encouraging the involuntary behavior, the therapist brings it under the control of the individual, which changes its meaning. In couples and families, the direction of control is changed by placing the person being controlled in charge. This task is done by reframing the behavior in such a way that it is good for the other person or it is perceived in such a way that the other has control over the symptom (Weeks & L'Abate, 1982). In both cases, the clients must change their behavior vis-à-vis the therapist in order to gain control.

The thesis of this chapter is that all psychotherapy has a paradoxical component. It has been shown that paradoxical strategies and techniques are embedded in many systems of therapy—a fact which has not been recognized or admitted because of practitioners' adherence to their own theoretical biases. The metatheoretical analysis of psychotherapy has shown how change is essentially facilitated in the same way across therapies. The therapist adopts a number of paradoxical stances vis-à-vis the client. This metatheoretical description has been reduced to an even more parsimonious description by showing that therapy is some combination of affirmation and negation paradoxes (Strong & Claiborn, 1982).

The goal of therapy is to enhance its paradoxical nature—to work toward creating conditions of spontaneous compliance. There are two basic therapeutic processes which help to achieve this end. These processes are reframing and prescriptions.

Reframing.   Reframing is the most common strategy used in the systems therapies as well as in psychotherapy in general. It is fundamental for psychotherapy because it helps the client change perspective in such a way that change is easier to make. Systems therapists have referred to this concept as: relabeling (Haley, 1973); reframing (Watzlawick et al., 1974); content reframing (Bandler & Grinder, 1982); redefinition (Andolfi, 1979); seeing the good (L'Abate, 1975); positive connotation (Palazzoli, et al. 1978); ascribing noble intentions (Stanton, Todd, & Associates, 1982); nonblaming (Alexander & Parsons, 1982); and context markers (Bateson, 1979; L'Abate, Ganahl, & Hansen, 1986; Viaro, 1980).

Watzlawick, Weakland, and Fisch (1984) were among the first to discuss the central role of reframing in therapy. They defined reframing as changing the conceptual and/or emotional meaning attributed to a situation. The behavior that is reframed is the behavior that has been defined or framed as being symptomatic by the client.

A reframing statement is quite different from an interpretation. An interpretation carries some truth value. The therapist actually believes the statement represents some aspect of reality. Reframing statements are not intended to have the same validity. The theory of truth which is used by the therapist is pragmatic. In the pragmatic theory of truth, that which works is considered true (James, 1907). The therapist attempts to construct a view of reality that is more conducive to change, rather than replace the client's faulty world view with one that is correct (Kelly, 1955). Tennen, Eron, and Rohrbaugh (1985) have stated:

> Adaptive functioning does not require being in touch with reality and having an accurate view of the world. Rather, *any* world view that interdicts problem sequences is considered in planning interventions. This position is nested not only in "functional theory," but in growing empirical literature pointing to the healing effects of illusion (Lazarus, 1983), the illusion of control (Alloy &

Abramson, 1979; Tiger, 1979) and the misperception of one's success and its causes (Greenwald, 1980; Muller & Ross, 1975). High self-esteem (Tennen & Herzberger, submitted for publication; Tennen et al., submitted for publication), lack of depression (Lewinsohn et al., 1980; Abramson & Alloy, 1981) and better adjustment to illness and injury (Bulman & Wortman, 1977; Taylor, 1983; Tennen et al., in press) have been associated with *non*veridical and illogical perceptions and beliefs. The shift from psyche to system and from reality testing to useful illusions may represent the most significant contributions of the strategic therapist in his/her use of paradox. (pp. 199–200)

The use of reframing in the literature usually has two meanings (Weeks & L'Abate, 1982). One is to change the way in which a symptom is defined in terms of some polarization (such as good versus bad and crazy versus sane). This use of reframing stems from the various models of psychotherapy, including medical, moral, psychological, statistical, and personal discomfort. A symptom defined in terms of the moral model is wrong, sinful, or bad. Individuals frequently attribute bad intent to behavior. This attribution leads to the moral perspective that they are okay and the behavior is bad. Reframing can be used to change the value attributed to the problem. For example, couples usually believe their fights are exclusively negative behaviors. The fights have been framed as destructive, negative, and so on and are seen as representing negative intent. In reframing the fighting behavior, the therapist wants to change the attributed meaning from bad to good. For instance, the therapist might say,

> The two of you must care a great deal about each other and yourself, because you invest so much of your energy in fighting. Couples who don't care or are indifferent don't fight. Your fighting shows there is something worth fighting for in spite of the fact that you may end up appearing to fight against each other.

The second use of reframing is to move the focus from the individual to the system. When couples or families present problems, there is usually a symptom bearer who is carrying the problem for the rest of the family. The other member(s) do not see the connection between their behavior and the behavior of the "sick" one. In couples, the "healthy" spouse externalizes and/or denies any responsibility for the problem. The attributional strategy in the couple is linear, not circular. One of the therapeutic tasks is to get them to see how the problem stems from their interaction. Reframing is the method whereby the therapist can move the couple from a linear attributional strategy to an interactional or circular attributional strategy.

The two uses of reframing described above are usually combined in a statement given to the client system. Palazzoli, Cecchin, Prata, and Boscolo (1978) call this technique positive connotation. The symptom is given a positive meaning and all the members of the system are linked together. Reframing as defined by Palazzoli and colleagues (1978) addresses all the factors comprising Strong and Claiborn's (1982) model. Reframing changes the definition of the relationship, changes the meaning of the behavior by altering or disrupting the interpretative framework, and disrupts one's ability to predict another's behavior. It also puts the participants on the same level so that one cannot take advantage of the other, thereby creating greater congruence.

One goal of the reframe is to prescribe a shared meaning in the relationship (e.g., fighting means you care). It also increases interdependence by suggesting that both want the same goal for the relationship. Finally, the most significant effects are to change the attributions from linear to circular and from negative to positive. If the reframe is successful and the couple believe they both deserve the same thing, then they must ask themselves if there aren't better ways to achieve it, rather than engaging in the same endless game. The result should be new efforts to change one spouse's impressions of the other by changing his or her behavior.

The use of reframing in psychotherapy and marital therapy deserves considerable attention. This discussion centers mostly on the theoretical aspects of reframing. Several recent reviews offer greater understanding: Weeks and L'Abate (1982); L'Abate, Hansen and Ganahl (1986); and Jones (1986).

In summary, reframing the symptoms has multiple effects. The most important effects in system therapy are to change the linear attributional strategy of the couple to a circular attributional strategy and to change the attribution of meaning given to the symptom to one which is positive. Positive actually refers to some aspect of the relationship which helps the couple bond. The positive dynamic (e.g., protection) helps to create greater congruence by defining something both desire. Once both partners see how they participate in the system, they are ready to work cooperatively rather than competitively. Additionally, by attributing positive intention(s), each partner is invited to try different strategies to manage the other, which means each partner must change.

Although reframing is an essential part of therapy, it is usually not sufficient to bring about change by itself. Weeks and L'Abate (1982) present cases in which reframing was enough to effect change, but these are the exceptions. Reframing sets the stage for the second phase of therapy, which is prescriptive in nature.

Prescriptions. The second major task of the therapist is to provide prescriptions for change. Reframing was used to create a context for change by altering the meaning of the problem. Reframing operates at the cognitive/perceptual level. The client is not asked to change behavior, although it's implied. The therapist must now proceed with a strategy designed to bring about change in the behavioral/affective areas. This task is accomplished through the use of "directives" (Haley, 1976) or "prescriptions" (L'Abate et al., 1986; Weeks & L'Abate, 1982). These two terms may be used interchangeably. The author has chosen to use the term prescription. A prescription is a set of instructions or injunctions the client is requested to follow. Unlike reframing, the prescription possesses some demand characteristics for change. The prescription may take a variety of forms and may be given in session or extrasession (homework).

It may seem too simplistic to reduce all the various approaches of therapy to reframing and prescriptions. However, by viewing psychotherapy as a coherent or systematic set of prescriptions, it is easier to break the bond of adherence to a particular theoretical system. Nichols (1984) recognizes the use of directives as one of the most widespread techniques in family therapy. He states:

> Experientialists use directives to promote affective experiences in therapy sessions; behaviorists use directives to teach parents new ways of disciplining their children; structural family therapists use directives in the form of tasks between sessions; Bowenian therapists use directives to advise patients how to improve relations with their parents; and strategic therapists use directives to outwit resistance and provoke change. (p. 87)

Prescriptions fall within the two categories of affirmation and negation paradoxes. In either case, all prescriptions are essentially paradoxical within the context of therapy because the therapeutic encounter is essentially paradoxical. Whatever prescriptions are used must be congruent with the paradoxical context of therapy (Seltzer, 1986). The reader will recall that Seltzer discusses (a) taking control by giving it away; (b) maintaining a positive view of the symptom and the person; (c) not attempting to force change; (d) allowing the client to have the symptom; (e) helping the client attribute change to self rather than outside forces; and (f) placing the client in charge of the symptom so that it is seen as controllable, voluntary, and volitional.

Ultimately, change results from the therapist's ability to change the direction of control in a relationship. A prescription is required which will change the control strategy used in the relationship without leading to one's supremacy or surrender. A sense of self-control *and* mutual control is the aim. Symptomatic behavior involves the denial of both self-control (I can't help my behavior) and mutual control (I am not trying to tell you how to behave). When more appropriate control strategies are found, there is no longer a need for symptomatic behavior.

REFERENCES

Alexander, J., & Parsons, B. *Functional family therapy.* Monterey, CA: Brooks, Cole, 1982.

Andolfi, M. Redefinition in family therapy. *American Journal of Family Therapy,* 1979, 7, 5–15.

Ascher, M., Bowers, M., & Schotte, D. A review of data from controlled case studies and experiments indicating the clinical offering of paradoxical intention. In G. Weeks (Ed.), *Promoting change through paradoxical therapy* (pp. 216–251). Homewood, IL: Dow Jones-Irwin, 1985.

Bandler, R., & Grinder, J. *Reframing: Neurolinguistic programming and the transformation of meaning.* Moab, UT: Real People Press, 1982.

Bateson, G. *Mind and nature: A necessary unity.* NY: Bantam Books, 1979.

Beisser, A. The paradoxical theory of change. In J. Fagan & R. Shepard (Eds.), *Gestalt therapy now* (pp. 77–80). NY: Harper & Row, 1970.

Bopp, M., & Weeks, G. Dialectic metatheory in family therapy. *Family Process,* 1984, 23, 49–61.

Deissler, K. Beyond paradox and counterparadox. In G. Weeks (Ed.), *Promoting change through paradoxical therapy* (pp. 60–99). Homewood, IL: Dow Jones-Irwin, 1985.

Haley, J. *Uncommon therapy: The psychiatric techniques of Milton H. Erickson.* New York: Ballantine, 1973.

Haley, J. *Problem-solving therapy.* San Francisco: Jossey-Bass, 1976.

James, W. *Pragmatism.* New York: World Publishing, 1907.

Jones, W. Frame cultivation: Helping new meaning take root in families. *American Journal of Family Therapy,* 1986, 14, 57–68.

Kelly, G. *The psychology of personal constructs, Vol. 1, A history of personality.* New York: W.W. Norton, 1955.

L'Abate, L. A positive approach to marital and family intervention. In L. Wolberg & M. Aronson (Eds.), *Group therapy 1975—an overview.* New York: Stratton Intercontinental Medical Books, 1975.

L'Abate, L., Ganahl, G., & Hansen, J. *Methods of family therapy.* Englewood Cliffs, NJ: Prentice Hall, 1986.

Nichols, M. *Family therapy: Concepts and methods.* New York: Gardner Press, 1984.

Omer, H. Paradoxical treatments: A unified concept. *Psychotherapy: Theory, Research, and Practice,* 1981, *18,* 320–324.

Palazzoli, M., Cecchin, M., Prata, G., & Boscolo, L. *Paradox and counterparadox.* New York: Jason Aronson, 1978.

Seltzer, L. *Paradoxical strategies in psychotherapy: A comprehensive overview and guidebook.* New York: Wiley, 1986.

Singer, E. *Key concepts in psychotherapy.* New York: Basic Books, 1970.

Stanton, M. Fusion, compression, diversion, and the workings of paradox: A theory of therapeutic/systemic change. *Family Process,* 1984, *23,* 135–167.

Stanton, M., Todd, T., & Associates. *The family therapy of drug addiction.* New York: Guilford, 1982.

Strong, S., & Claiborn, C. *Change through interaction. Social psychological processes of counseling and psychotherapy.* New York: John Wiley, 1982.

Tennen, H., Eron, J., & Rohrbaugh, M. Paradox in context. In G. Weeks (Ed.), *Promoting change through paradoxical therapy* (pp. 187–215). Homewood, IL: Dow Jones-Irwin, 1985.

Viaro, M. Case report: Smuggling family therapy through. *Family Process,* 1980, *19,* 253–271.

Watzlawick, P., Weakland, J., & Fisch, R. *Change: Principles of problem formation and problem resolution.* New York: W.W. Norton, 1974.

Weeks, G. Toward a dialectical approach to intervention. *Human Development,* 1977, *20,* 277–292.

Weeks, G., & L'Abate, L. *Paradoxical psychotherapy: Theory and practice with individuals, couples, and families.* New York: Brunner/Mazel, 1982.

Index